Other books by Bradley Booth:

Dare to Stand Alone
Plagues in the Palace
Prince of Dreams
The Prodigal
Shepherd Warrior
They Call Him the Miracle Man

To order, call
1-800-765-6955

Visit us at
www.reviewandherald.com
for information on other
Review and Herald® products.

Bible texts credited to Amplified are from *The Amplified Bible*. Copyright © 1965 by Zondervan Publishing House. Used by permission.
Scripture quotations identified CEV are from the Contemporary English Version. Copyright © American Bible Society 1991, 1995. Used by permission.
Scripture quotations credited to ESV are from *The Holy Bible*, English Standard Version, copyright © 2001 by Crossway Bibles, a division of Good News Publishers. Used by permission. All rights reserved.
Texts credited to Message are from *The Message*. Copyright © 1993, 1994, 1995, 1996, 2000, 2002. Used by permission of NavPress Publishing Group.
Scripture texts credited to NAB are from *The New American Bible*, coyright © 1970, by the Confraternity of Christian Doctrine, Washington, D.C., and are used by permission of copyright owner. All rights reserved.
Scripture quotations marked NASB are from the *New American Standard Bible*, © 1960, 1962, 1963, 1968, 1971, 1972, 1973, 1975, 1977, 1994 by The Lockman Foundation. Used by permission.
Scriptures credited to NCV are quoted from *The Holy Bible, New Century Version*, copyright © 1987, 1988, 1991 by Word Publishing, Dallas, Texas 75039. Used by permission.
Texts credited to NIV are from the *Holy Bible, New International Version*. Copyright © 1973, 1978, 1984, International Bible Society. Used by permission of Zondervan Bible Publishers.
Texts credited to NKJV are from the New King James Version. Copyright © 1979, 1980, 1982 by Thomas Nelson, Inc. Used by permission. All rights reserved.
Scripture quotations marked NLT are taken from the *Holy Bible*, New Living Translation, copyright © 1996. Used by permission of Tyndale House Publishers, Inc., Wheaton, Illinois 60189. All rights reserved.
Bible texts credited to RSV are from the Revised Standard Version of the Bible, copyright © 1946, 1952, 1971, by the Division of Christian Education of the National Council of the Churches of Christ in the U.S.A. Used by permission.
Verses marked TLB are taken from *The Living Bible*, copyright © 1971 by Tyndale House Publishers, Wheaton, Ill. Used by permission.

This book was
Edited by Steven Winn
Cover design by Ron J. Pride
Interior design by Heather Rogers
Typeset: Amasis

PRINTED IN U.S.A.

13 12 11 10 09   5 4 3 2 1

Library of Congress Cataloging-in-Publication Data
Booth, Bradley, 1957-   .
  Time warp : been there, done that? / Bradley Booth.
    p. cm.
  1. Seventh-day Adventist teenagers—Prayers and devotions. 2. History—Religious aspects—Christianity--Prayers and devotions. 3. Devotional calendars—Seventh-day Adventists. 4. Bible—Devotional literature. I. Title.
  BV4850.B6366 2009
  242'.63--dc22
                          2009026103

ISBN 978-0-8280-2495-2

DEVOTIONS FOR TEENS

TIME WARP

BEEN THERE, DONE THAT.

Bradley Booth

REVIEW AND HERALD® PUBLISHING ASSOCIATION
Since 1861 | www.reviewandherald.com

Midnight Messenger

He said: "I am the voice of one crying in the wilderness:
Make straight the way of the Lord," as the prophet Isaiah said.
John 1:23, NKJV.

A short but urgent whistle pokes through the blanket of darkness covering north Boston. A window slides open and a woman leans out, releasing a portion of her petticoat to the silent night air. It floats down to the waiting man outside. Grabbing it, he races back to the riverbank where he and his two friends rip it in shreds and wrap it around the oars. No longer afraid of being heard, they row silently, slicing across the river.

One of the men sprints to a nearby house where he is given the best horse in town, along with warnings that the enemy has been spotted along the dark roads. Slipping his foot into the stirrup, he swings onto the horse and immediately digs his spurs into its sides. The rhythmic pounding of hoofbeats shatters the silence of the country road.

"Halt!" Enemy soldiers. The rider lowers himself even more. Feeling the horse's mane flapping in his windblown face, he spurs the speeding beast again. On a fresh horse, the enemy gains on him. Seeing his only chance to escape, he steers off the road, feeling the slap of tree branches in his face. His pursuer's horse slips into a pond, and with a whinny and a snort, gives up the chase.

Back on the road, he gallops into the town of Medford and pounds on the door of a colonial captain. Between his short, exhausted breaths, he sputters, "The Regulars are out!" He mounts his steed once again, and galloping through several towns, he begins shouting his warning: "The British are coming! The British are coming!"

The midnight messenger begins the final leg of his desperate mission—to reach Concord and warn of the impending British attack. Suddenly, four mounted British soldiers race up and surround him. A British major shoves a pistol to his head, demanding to know who he is and what he's doing. Looking him in the eye, Paul Revere boldly tells him.

This fearless midnight messenger was born on this day in 1735. It's midnight and there are enemy troops along the dark roads. But you've been given the finest horse and the most urgent message. Are you willing to do whatever it takes to complete your mission?

Dead Men Can Tell Tales

For to this end Christ died and rose and lived again,
that He might be Lord of both the dead and the living.
Romans 14:9, NKJV.

Darkness embraces you. But not just any darkness—a rich, black, inky darkness that encircles you. A waft of cool, damp air joins hands with the darkness to wrap you in an icy hug. You consider turning back, but you feel you must go on, farther, deeper, colder, darker.

A small circle of yellow light illumines the cold, gray walls as you switch on your lamp. As you inch along, constantly searching for solid footing, your light sweeping around the cold, craggy indentions, you are startled by the presence of a grinning skeleton! Your hand instinctively covers your mouth, muffling your scream. Way too close for comfort, you step back, trip on a loose rock, lose your balance, and your lamp puts on a random light show as you fall to the ground.

On January 2, 1971, a team of Israeli archaeologists in Jerusalem announced that they had found something unusual in an ancient cave—a skeleton of a man crucified some 2,000 years ago. The skeleton was unique because it was the first of its kind to be found with a metal spike still lodged in one of its feet. The spike was bent as though it had hit a knot while being pounded into the wood, possibly the reason the soldiers left it right where it was.

Just outside the gates of the same city, Jesus Christ died in the same manner—crucified on a cross, spikes through His wrists and feet, left to bleed and die, and buried in a dark cave after He had finally breathed His last. Was the skeleton found by the archaeologists the remnants of Jesus? No way. Why not? Because Jesus, though His wrists and feet were scarred, stepped out of that cold, dark, damp cave into the blossoming morning under a sky streaked with purple and pink, just as the Bible says. Far from being the remains of Jesus, the rare discovery of the man with the spike in his foot serves only to convince us of the Bible's accurate portrayal of His victory over death.

You will never find the body of Jesus in a cold, dark cave. He shrugged off the cold, dark embrace of darkness. He broke free from the icy hug of death. And because He lives, you don't ever have to spend eternity in a cold, dark, cave.

Seward's Folly

The Lord does not look at the things man looks at. Man looks at the outward appearance, but the Lord looks at the heart.
1 Samuel 16:7, NIV.

Did you know that Alaska once had the nickname, "Seward's Folly?" William Seward was the United States Secretary of State who arranged to buy Alaska as a territory from Russia in 1867. The details of how the United States acquired the territory are truly amazing. In those days most people thought Alaska wasn't worth the money we paid for it, even though Seward dished out only about two cents an acre. Journalists of the day called the territory, "Icebergia," "Polaria," and "Seward's Icebox." And for decades that's the way most people felt about it.

On January 3, 1959, Alaska entered the Union as the 49th state, and now we know how incredibly lucky we were to get it. With nearly 600,000 total square miles and over 100,000 acres of wilderness set aside as federal and state parks, Alaska is our largest state and has given us billions and billions of dollars worth of gold, oil, fishing, and lumber. Turns out Seward knew what he was doing!

The prophet Samuel faced a big decision. Follow him down the dusty road to Bethlehem to select a new king of Israel. God had told him that a man named Jesse had a son who would be the next to enjoy the plush cushion of the nation's throne. Sounds easy enough, right? As Samuel approached Jesse's country property to invite his family to the selection ceremony, he must have snickered at God's sense of humor as Jesse presented not one son, but a whole line of them! *Very funny, Lord*, I can imagine Samuel thinking.

Inspecting the line of young men, Samuel thought for sure each one was the one. They were tall, strong, and looked extremely intelligent. But the Lord kept telling Samuel, No, this isn't the one I want. Finally, Samuel asked if there were any others. Jesse cleared his throat and mumbled, There's David—to a chorus of laughter from the brothers. When Samuel chose this awkward teenager, I wouldn't be surprised if people referred to him as "Samuel's Folly."

As we know now, David became Israel's most popular and productive king. Turns out God knew what He was doing.

Nice Wheels!

As I looked at these beings, I saw four wheels touching
the ground beside them, one wheel belonging to each,
(and) the spirit of the living beings was in the wheels.
Ezekiel 1:15, 21, NLT.

It's 1743. The Revolutionary War is more than 30 years in the future, and you're sitting at a theater play in London. Just as you are dozing off and that trickle of drool starts down your lower lip, your head snaps upright from the thundering sound of an actor rolling across the stage on wooden wheels! What was *that*? It was a pair of roller skates—well . . . kind of. We don't know who came up with these primitive wheels, but the idea sure caught on.

A few years later, Joseph Merlin had the bright idea of using square metal wheels. Great job, Joseph—except for the fact that the only direction you could go was straight ahead!

On January 4, 1863, the first roller skates resembling the ones we use today were invented. James Plimpton of New York patented these beauties with a double set of wheels, front and back, calling them quad skates. Now it was easier and safer for people to actually turn.

The skates were a huge success and led to the opening of the first skating rink three years later in Newport, Rhode Island. Plimpton's quad skate went on to dominate the skating industry for the next 100 years and led to other, more exciting inventions like skateboards, inline skates, and wheeled shoes. So the next time that kid zips in front of you on his wheeled shoes at the department store, tell him to thank James Plimpton—and to please stop running over your toes.

The prophet Ezekiel saw something that made his eyes even wider than those of the folks watching the actor wobble across that London stage on roller skates. The Bible says, "The heavens were opened and I saw visions of God" (Ezekiel 1:1). In this vision of God, he saw four living creatures, with a wheel beside each one. "The appearance of their workings [was], as it were, a wheel in the middle of a wheel" (verse 16). The wheels were part of a glorious machine that moved with four magnificent heavenly beings around the throne of God. The beings glowed like coals of fire, and the wheels spun so fast that streams of lightning streaked back and forth between them around the throne of God! Wow! What an awesome sight that must have been!

Whatever humans can invent, God can blow it away with something far superior!

One Trillion Dollar Budget

Render therefore to Caesar the things that are Caesar's,
and to God the things that are God's.
Matthew 22:21, NKJV.

How much is a trillion dollars?
Let's say a relative gave you a trillion one-dollar bills for your birthday. (Better than socks, huh?) To store it, you'd need a warehouse 125 feet high and covering nine square city blocks. If you sat down to count it all, you'd be counting 24/7 for 15,000 years! Hope you don't have anything else planned for a while.

Another way to imagine a trillion dollars is to think of a stack of $100 bills on its side lying next to the freeway. You'd have to drive 631 miles to reach the end of it!

On January 5, 1987, the United States annual federal budget reached one trillion dollars—money it gets from its citizens in taxes each year. What does our government pay for with 631 miles of $100 bills every year? It pays the salaries of presidents, congressmen and women, and senators. It pays Supreme Court justices in Washington, federal marshals, FBI agents, and ambassadors to foreign embassies. And, of course, that trillion dollars also pays for the people who work for them: accountants, secretaries, secret service men, speech writers, chauffeurs, and pilots. There's also the military that protects us worldwide, Army, Navy, Air Force, and Marines, meaning we need to pay for military bases, tanks, battleships, fighter jets, missiles, and spy satellites orbiting our planet. But we need to pay for things here at home, too, such as our national parks, bioengineering labs to grow better crops, AIDS relief, and schools. And that's just the beginning of the ways our government serves us. Although sometimes greed and corruption ripples through the ranks of our national leaders, our government serves us in many ways.

Just think of all the ways God has blessed you today. If you place your finger on your wrist or throat, you will feel your pulse—evidence of your beating heart. With every breath, every ray of sunshine, every nourishing bite of food, God keeps you alive. The federal government needs a trillion dollars (more now) every year to serve you. God, on the other hand, doesn't need any of your money to serve you. He serves you because He wants to, because He loves you. And one way to return that love is to return some of His own money to Him.

Mountain Man

Be strong and of good courage, do not fear nor be afraid…
for the Lord your God, He is the One who goes with you.
He will not leave you nor forsake you.
Deuteronomy 31:6, NKJV.

On this day in 1798, one of the most daring explorers in early American history was born. Jedediah Smith was a trapper, explorer, and mountain man second to none. During his short life span, he explored a huge area of the Far West. He fought hostile natives, braved impossible blizzards, and grunted his way over steep mountain precipices, losing an ear, and repeatedly nearly losing his life. A Black Hills grizzly bear once caught sight of him and lunged at him, its huge paws slicing into his body. By the time Jedediah was 30, he had lived through dozens of narrow escapes on his trips back and forth throughout the west.

But Jedediah did more than just survive the incredible risks of his extreme life. Between the new Americans and the western coast of their continent stood the purple mountain majesty of the Rocky Mountains. Towering above the settlers seeking gold, homes, and adventure, its rugged, seemingly impassable snow-capped peaks pierced the blue dome arching over the young continent. Overcoming the tense relations between settlers and native Americans, he secured a map of these towering peaks made of deerskin and sand from the Crow Indians. Using the map and the help of his new friends, he discovered the South Pass, an opening through the Rockies that became a nineteenth century superhighway for settlers leading to their final frontier.

In 1830 Jedediah finally decided to retire from his dangerous trade, and went into business for himself selling dry goods and other merchandise. But his new life proved more dangerous than his risky one as an explorer. While leading a caravan of traders along the Santa Fe Trail in 1831, he was killed by Comanche Indians. He was only 32 years old.

While God's mission for you may not include stomping through blizzards or being attacked by grizzly bears, the opportunity for adventure rises before you, like the Rocky Mountains rose before Jedediah Smith. Your mission may be in a third world country, or it may be right here in North America's mission field. The important thing is not the location, but the heart. So grab that musket, strap on those snowshoes, and step out into the blizzard. You'll find the Creator of those Rocky Mountains at your side to help you.

Transatlantic Cable

He will call upon me, and I will answer him.
Psalm 91:15, NIV.

No cell phones. I don't mean you need to switch it to vibrate mode. I mean they just don't exist. The telephone has recently been invented, but each one comes with strings attached—electric strings. Phone companies are stringing wires up on telephone poles all over town. Welcome to the 1920s.

If every phone requires an electric wire, what do you do if you want to talk to someone in Europe? Ask the phone company man and he will stroke his handlebar mustache, furrow his eyebrows, look around nervously, and clear his throat. Will it ever be possible to call someone on another continent? You couldn't put up a row of telephone poles across the ocean or lay a cable in the water—or could you?

Actually, that's exactly what that telephone man ended up doing. But it was a real chore. The cable was over 3,500 miles long and had to be several inches thick because the deep water kept breaking it. On this day in 1927 the first successful transatlantic cable was opened for commercial business as a telephone service between New York City and London. Thirty-one calls were made that first day with a charge of $75 for a three-minute conversation. That was a lot of money in those days—about $1,500 in today's economy.

Good-bye 1920s. We live in a world breaking free from wires. Cell phones vibrate and play ring tones from our favorite TV shows as we furiously text our friends. Wireless internet connects us to a worldwide superhighway of information. In just seconds we can do research for a midterm from our living rooms in our PJs, watch movies on our iPods, and call our friends—with not a wire in sight.

The 1920s style of wire-encumbered communication has almost disappeared in our modern world, and we may think we live on the sharp edge of communication technology. But if we look heavenward, we see a God who has invented a system of communication far more efficient than wireless, the speed of light, or even the fastest angel. He has promised us a way to call Someone in Heaven using the speed of thought! Ask the telephone company man if he can do that, and he will twitch his handlebar mustache, furrow his eyebrows . . .

Jim Elliot Martyred

But God demonstrates his own love for us in this:
While we were still sinners, Christ died for us.
Romans 5:8, NIV.

One of the saddest tales ever told is the story of five Christian American missionaries who were killed in the jungles of Ecuador. The names of these young men were Jim Elliot, Peter Fleming, Edward McCully, Nate Saint, and Roger Youderian. They were trying to bring the gospel to a primitive tribe called the Auca Indians. Unfortunately, the plan backfired when the Indians attacked from the jungle, killing all five men with poison arrows. This catastrophe happened on January 8, 1956, and will probably go down in the Christian history books as one of the most tragic cases of martyrdom.

The five men all knew the situation was risky because other men from American rubber companies had died at the hands of the Auca Indians. However, they all decided to take the chance anyway. They felt that if they could introduce these tribes to Jesus, it would be worth the sacrifice. When Jim and his friends considered the options, even death was not too great a sacrifice. To reach remote areas like the one where the Auca Indians lived, they decided to use a small airplane. Traveling by airplane was one of the newer modes of travel and would cut down on time. What would have been a trip of several days into the jungle could now be done in about 15 minutes.

Of course, the Auca Indians knew nothing about these Christian men who were giving their time and energy as missionaries for Jesus. Instead of guessing that the missionaries might be bringing friendship and the good news of salvation, the Indians assumed the men were an enemy invading their home. It wasn't until much later when some members of the Auca tribes were converted to Christianity that they realized how dreadfully wrong they had been.

How tragic! The missionaries who had come to bring them the good news of eternal life were the very ones they plotted to kill. But it's not much different than what we did to Jesus. He came to this world to bring friendship and eternal life from the Father, but we killed Him! What a tragedy! Like the Auca Indians, all we can do now is tell Jesus how sorry we are and give our hearts to Him! Why not do that today and every day?

United States Civil War Begins

When you go into battle in your own land against an enemy who is oppressing you, sound a blast on the trumpets. Then you will be remembered by the Lord your God and rescued from your enemies. Numbers 10:9, NIV.

It all started when a detachment of Confederate soldiers on an island off the coast of South Carolina, fired on a merchant steamship. The ship was bringing supplies to the U.S. military outpost at Fort Sumter, near Charleston. An attack on the fort could mean only one thing—that the southern Confederate states were ready for a break from the Union—and that's exactly what they got. The date was January 9, 1861, and with that firing shot, the American Civil War officially began. Carolina was the first state to secede from the United States of America, and within a few months 12 other states followed its example.

The Civil War was a terrible war lasting over four years. It turned families and whole communities against one another. In the end everyone paid a price. Roads and railroads were destroyed, ships were not allowed to deliver or pick up their shipments, and crops rotted in the fields. The South seemed to have the better generals, but the North had more men and the federal government on its side. During the first years of the war, the South seemed to win all the important battles, but lack of money and military fatigue began to take its toll. As three years turned into four, it became increasingly evident that the war was stalling for lack of inspiration. Slavery was probably the most serious issue at stake, but neither side had really used this as its reason for going to war. Some have attributed the war dragging on and on to a lack of leaders with clear moral goals who would stand up for the right.

Does it ever feel like you are in the middle of a war—standing unarmed in an open field with bullets whizzing by your head? Maybe you feel that your conscience is shooting at you for your past sins. Maybe the future seems like hostile enemy territory and impossible to navigate safely. Worst of all, maybe you feel that God is the One firing at you.

Let me assure you that, far from attacking you, God is right beside you, taking bullets for you that you don't even know about. But to be rescued, you must shout out to Him with all your heart. If you make this leap of faith and truly rely upon Him, your victory is guaranteed.

Church and State

Then I saw another beast, coming out of the earth. . . .
He was given power to give breath to the image of the first beast.
Revelation 13:11-15, NIV.

The Vatican is a city-state that is also a country—the smallest of its kind in the world. It's a mere 110 acres in size and has approximately 800 inhabitants, including the Pope, 58 cardinals, about 250 priests, and over 100 members of the palace guard. It has no airports or highways. However, a train brings tourists to its doors, and the city has a heliport for VIPs. The Vatican boasts some of the more famous religious sights on earth, such as the Sistine Chapel with its famous "Last Supper" painting, and St. Peter's Cathedral, the second biggest Catholic church in the world.

On this day in 1984 the United States once again established full diplomatic relations with Vatican City. The new alliance came after 117 years of no political relationship at all between the two powers. President Ronald Reagan was considered to be a pivotal player in this political achievement. Many religious leaders now believe that this relationship is the beginning of something that will become a threat to the freedoms we hold so dear in this country. For centuries the Roman Catholic system persecuted those who did not recognize its religious and political authority, until in 1798 the Pope was taken captive and forced into religious exile until the Vatican became his official residence in 1929.

In 1984 the United States signaled a new era in religious worship by pledging its support for the Vatican and its high leader. Eventually, according to the book of Revelation, the Pope will again claim full religious power in the world. Once a captive taken by Napoleon of France, he will burst upon the world stage with unbridled influence. It will seem that all the seething masses of the world will fall in behind him, shouting in agreement to his every word. This will signal the great doors of this planet to creak shut, and the end will be upon us.

But not everyone will be in that massive human throng, slavishly obeying every deceptive statement, bowing at the feet of lies. There will be another group, a much smaller group, of wide-eyed believers who refuse to be led by the ear. Chased and abused, threatened and mocked, yet they will cling to the promises of their high Leader, faithful promises of eternal safety and reward.

First Insulin Treatment

Don't you know that you yourselves are
God's temple and that God's Spirit lives in you?
1 Corinthians 3:16, NIV.

Imagine feeling terrible pain in one of your toes. You can't sleep and find it difficult to concentrate on anything because of the stabbing pain pulsing up your foot. Then your toe loses its color and fades to black. Your doctor announces that you have contracted diabetes, and within a short time your family is dressed in black, gathered around your casket.

Diabetes has plagued humans for a long time. One of the first doctors in history to mention the disease was a physician in Egypt named Hesy-Ra. Aretaeus, a Greek doctor, described the disease as one that melts down human flesh, and his definition seems to be right on. Through the millennia stretching from ancient Greece until the 1920s, diabetes meant death for the patient.

And then came January 11, 1922, when insulin was first used successfully to treat diabetes. The patient was Leonard Thompson at Toronto General Hospital in Canada. Although no longer fatal, during the last 20 years America has seen a large increase in the number of people who contract diabetes. Some say it is a genetic abnormality, but others think it is largely due to our diet.

Here's how it works. When you eat a lot of sugar, your body must race to lower the level of sugar in your blood. Too much sugar can damage your cells and make your body's metabolic processes go haywire. Large amounts of sugar can even kill your cells, including the cells in your pancreas, which produces the insulin you need to digest sugar. Because of this cell damage your pancreas must work overtime to make enough insulin to neutralize the effects of the sugar. If enough cells in the pancreas die, your pancreas shuts down and stops producing the insulin you need. This can send your body into shock, just as if you had swallowed a bottle of poison.

God wants you to be healthy and happy, and the path to health and happiness is through honoring the health laws He has given us. In His mercy, He has inspired humans to develop methods of treatment for some fatal diseases, such as diabetes. But the family car works the best and lasts the longest when it is maintained with consistent care for its engine. Why should the body be any different?

Forward Football Pass

Do not let this Book of the Law depart from your mouth; meditate on it day and night. . . . Then you will be prosperous and successful. Joshua 1:8, NIV.

Can you imagine football being played without a pass play? That can be the most exciting part of the game to watch! But it wasn't always that way. In the old days football players either ran with the ball or kicked it. You could run forward with the ball, but you couldn't throw it forward. If a player was being tackled he could pitch the ball backward to a teammate in order to keep the play alive. Those ideas probably came from the game of rugby that had been played for decades before football ever arrived on the scene. In rugby, that's what you do—run with the ball. It wasn't until rugby came to America that passing became part of the game. That's when football became a unique sport with rules of its own. On this day in January of 1905, an official football rules committee legalized forward passing in football games. That was over 100 years ago, and throwing forward passes has been part of the game ever since.

Close to half of the plays in any given game are ones in which the quarterback throws a pass. Pass plays have become so important to the sport that if your team doesn't have a passing game, you probably can't win the big games. To make things even more exciting, the football rule makers decided that you can't touch a receiver downfield until he has caught the ball. If you do, you may get flagged for pass interference. That usually creates higher scoring games, something the fans always like. Other rules have been made protecting the quarterback. Once the other team's quarterback has released the ball, if one of your players hits him, you could lose up to 15 yards on the penalty. But quarterbacks have rules to follow, too. Your team is penalized if your quarterback strays too far from where he was first given the ball to start the play and throws a pass. Without the rules, football players might have a very short life span!

The rules of football have been made so that the game will be fair and safe for the players, and more exciting for the fans. That's the way it is with God's law. Some would like to minimize the importance of God's law today, but the Bible tells us that His rules are fair and make our lives safer and happier! If we use His rules to get to know Him and how much He really loves us, we will get much more out of life. That sounds like a winning game plan!

Frisbee Invented

Believe on the Lord Jesus Christ, and you will be saved.
Acts 16:31, NKJV.

One of the simplest, and yet most ingenious toys ever invented was the Frisbee. Walter Morrison designed and manufactured it, and sold it to the Wham-O company in California. The Frisbee Flying Saucer, as Morrison called it, was inspired by the UFO craze sweeping the nation at that time.

The first Frisbees were lightweight metal throwing disks that looked like flying saucers. Wham-O's president, Richard Knerr, got the idea for the new toy's name when he saw college kids tossing pie tins around with the name "Frisbie" embossed on them, which was the name of a pie company at that time. He changed the spelling to "Frisbee" and began selling them on January 13, 1957.

The "flying saucers" went like hotcakes and soon were going by the millions. Who would have thought that such a simple toy would become so popular in the half century that followed? Probably no toy has ever enjoyed such fame or brought as much money to its manufacturer. The secret of its success wasn't in its complex parts—it had none.

Today it still consists of one single piece of plastic. And it's not expensive—the cheap, simple ones can be the most fun. Anyone, at any age, can toss a Frisbee. Kids love them, teenagers take it to the beach, and many old folks play Frisbee golf. And there aren't a lot of complicated rules. You can have throwing contests for distance, see who can make the fanciest catch, or toss it to your dog.

Like the Frisbee, salvation is a pretty simple concept. Today's verse of Scripture reminds us that God wants to keep it that way—simple. "Believe on the Lord Jesus Christ, and you will be saved." Can't get much simpler than that! Paul's words of advice to the early Christians in Philippi are the same ones we need today. You don't have to climb the highest mountain on your knees, chanting prayers all the way up. Hey, you don't even have to climb the mountain standing up! You don't have to wash in the Jordan seven times, go show yourself to the priest, or sacrifice a lamb. Your salvation is not based on your behavior at all, but on how sincerely you believe in *His* behavior for *you.*

Cesarean Operation

For we know that all creation has been groaning
as in the pains of childbirth right up to the present time.
Romans 8:22, NLT.

No one knows for sure how the term Cesarean section, for the surgical removal of a baby from its mother's womb, originated, but several theories exist. One is that ancient Rome mandated the removal of a woman's fetus if she died in childbirth. Another is that one of Julius Caesar's ancestors was born this way. Still another is that the term simply comes from the word caedere, meaning to cut.

In all of Europe only 79 such operations had been successful during the previous 300 years, and in most of those cases the mother had lost her life. The first successful Cesarean operation in the United States was performed in a frontier log cabin in Edom, Virginia, by Dr. Jessee Bennett on January 14, 1794. Dr. Bennett had asked another local doctor, Alexander Humphrey, to assist him, but Dr. Humphrey declined. He was afraid the operation posed too great a risk and would not be a success. After all, a cesarean had never been done before in the United States. And who was the patient? Dr. Bennett's wife, Elizabeth Hog Bennett. What a dilemma! The medical view of the day considered such an operation impossible both surgically and ethically. Doctors were advised to leave such predicaments in God's hand.

But Dr. Bennett knew the odds were stacked against him and his wife. If he didn't operate and she died, her death would be considered an act of God. On the other hand, if he did operate and she died, he would be considered a murderer. Either way he couldn't win—unless of course the operation was a success. With the assistance of two slaves Dr. Bennett did indeed perform the operation, on a crude table made with two wooden planks set on two wooden barrels. The two assistants held the patient while the doctor gave Elizabeth a dose of opium, a pain killer commonly used at that time. And wonder of wonders, both mother and baby did survive! Quite marvelous for the day!

Today our world is in trouble. Pregnant with sin and suffering, all creation cries out to be delivered, and only God can perform the necessary operation. He is the Creator of all things and the Great Physician. He has promised to deliver us and remove us from this wicked old world, and we can depend on Him to be successful.

First Super Bowl

I press on to reach the end of the race and receive the heavenly prize for which God, through Christ Jesus, is calling us.
Philippians 3:14, NLT.

The most popular single game in the history of sports is without doubt the Super Bowl. For several decades, this capstone of the football season has taken gigantic proportions. More than just a game, it features a star-studded halftime show and is the forum for the newest and potentially best TV commercials, costing advertisers over a million dollars per 30 seconds.

It all started on January 15, 1967. The first Super Bowl was held in the Memorial Coliseum in Los Angeles, California. The two teams playing were the Green Bay Packers and the Kansas City Chiefs, with the Packers winning 35 to 10. Each of the Packers received $15,000, and the Chiefs each received $7,500.

The game was created to be a world championship bout between the National Football League and the American Football League. Four years later the two football leagues were renamed the National Football Conference (NFC) and the American Football Conference (AFC). Including that first game there have been 43 Super Bowls with 17 different teams winning the Super Bowl trophy. The teams to win the most Super Bowls are the Pittsburgh Steelers at six, and the San Francisco 49ers and Dallas Cowboys each winning five. This most coveted prize is indeed an amazing achievement, as sports events go! For three to four grueling hours some of the best athletes in the world compete ferociously, never giving up. As the game winds down those who have the lead try to hold on. Those who are behind try to pull out one of those come-from-behind victories. For the winners it is truly the thrill of victory, but for the losers—the agony of defeat.

Paul compared winning eternal life to sports events like the Super Bowl. Sometimes you feel like you're ahead, and other times you are certain all you're doing is punting the ball to the other team. Sometimes you feel powerful, and other times you keep getting tackled before the play even gets started. Of course, reaching heaven will be infinitely greater than winning a mere Super Bowl. And no matter if you feel like you're progressing down the field or not, you have a Coach who loves you and has promised you the biggest win of your life.

Superman Born

But when the time had fully come, God sent his Son, born of a woman, born under law.
Galatians 4:4, NIV.

In 1939 the comic strip "Superman" began. This imaginary hero helped launch seven decades of animated comic books, cartoons, and movies for the Man of Steel. The plot of this saga has Superman coming to earth as an alien baby in a specially designed spaceship. The boy is adopted by an elderly couple and lives a simple life as he grows up on a farm in rural Kansas.

At a very early age he begins to realize that he is not an ordinary boy. He is gifted with superpowers. He is stronger than anyone he knows, and he is unbelievably fast. As his parents watch him develop, they finally tell him the truth about where he came from, and that he must have come to earth for a special reason. For years the hero disguises his bizarre powers in the life of an ordinary boy who works hard on the farm and blends into the small community where he attends school. He knows he is different, and sometimes it is especially hard to not use his unusual powers.

Eventually, though, he leaves home to become the man he was destined to be. His mission? To do good. To save people from danger. To fight the forces of evil and crime. He's faster than a speeding bullet, more powerful than a locomotive, able to leap tall buildings in a single bound. But criminal masterminds around Superman exploit his compassion for others, forcing him into situations that only the Man of Steel can solve. And though he is dedicated to this mission, people everywhere still misunderstand him, expecting more from him than he can give. People know what he stands for, but the appreciation goes only as far as his latest rescue. Not surprisingly his friends are few, and in the end he is forced to live a lonely life of sacrifice.

Now doesn't that sound familiar? Once upon a time there was another superhero from beyond the galaxies who came to live among men. He too came as a baby, was raised under ordinary circumstances, and eventually went public with a mission of mercy. He came to seek and to save, and deliver this world from evil. Religious leaders hoped to ride his coat tails, but when he refused to become a part of their plans, they turned against Him. That superhero was more than a Superman. He was Jesus, Creator of heaven and earth, Savior of the world, our High Priest and soon coming King. Now that's a real Superman, don't you think?

Operation Desert Storm

And there was war in heaven. Michael and his angels
fought against the dragon, and the dragon and his
angels fought back. But he (the dragon) was not strong enough.
Revelation 12:7, NIV.

On August 2, 1990, Iraqi Republican Guard tanks roared across the border into Kuwait, and the Iraqis quickly seized complete control of the tiny country. Almost as quickly, the United States initiated Operation Desert Shield in protest, assuring the impossibility of Iraq penetrating the oil-rich country next door, Saudi Arabia. The United Nations called for Iraq to immediately withdraw its soldiers, with the hearty approval of the United States and 27 other countries. Then commenced one of the fastest wars in United States history, Operation Desert Storm. In just four days the United States military liberated Kuwait, drove the Iraqi army back into Iraq, and forced hundreds of thousands of soldiers to surrender. That was on January 17, 1991.

Since 1979, Saddam Hussein, Iraq's ruthless dictator, had been considered one of the most vicious leaders of the modern era. When his military leaders displeased him, he would sometimes have them executed. If athletes on his national soccer team came home defeated, Saddam would often torture them mercilessly. Even worse, Saddam waged a civil war against opposing political tribes, such as the Kurds and Shiites, killing hundreds of thousands of them in what we call ethnic cleansing. When Saddam invaded Kuwait, the United States and its allies had had enough and gave him an ultimatum—get out of Iraq or suffer the consequences. Like any war, Operation Desert Storm was horribly destructive. In just 43 days of fighting, half again as many guided missiles were launched on Iraq as the total number of missiles in eight years of the Vietnam War. And yet, in spite of the violent destruction of that Desert Storm, there was almost no loss of American life.

Once upon a time there was another war, but one of much greater consequence. Satan, who would become the universe's original ruthless dictator, rebelled against God in Heaven, and not surprisingly, he was thrown out. He continued the fight here on earth, executing the faithful and torturing and killing millions. But the God of Heaven protested this treatment of His children and Jesus' resurrection from the dead spelled Satan's final defeat. In this storm in our desert, the war has been decided. All that remains is for you and me to decide whether or not we will accept our liberation.

Secret Bible Manuscripts

Thy word is a lamp unto my feet, and a light unto my path.
Psalm 119:105.

The Bible is the oldest book in the world, written by different kinds of people over a span of 1,500 years. Farmers, fishermen, shepherds, generals, preachers, and even a heathen king contributed. Unfortunately, as time passed the original copies wore out or were lost. During the Dark Ages most people in Europe couldn't read or write, so biblical knowledge almost came to a standstill. It was a time of castles and moats and Knights of the Round Table, a time of poverty and disease when men were so poor they could be bought and sold with the land they farmed. It was a time of great ignorance and superstition, and it seemed the whole world had fallen asleep spiritually.

But God wasn't asleep, and He kept a close watch over the copies of His sacred writings. He raised up special people down through the years who would go in search of the oldest copies of the Bible. On January 18, 1815, just such a man was born—Constantin von Tischendorf. He became a biblical scholar and traveled the world as an archaeologist trying to prove that the Bible was still the Word of God. Tischendorf is best known for his discovery of one of the oldest known manuscripts of the Greek Bible. Tischendorf made his big find while digging in a trash pile at a monastery near the legendary Mount Sinai. The manuscript was 44 pages of the New Testament, called the Sinaiticus, and was written in the fourth century. It's now considered one of the most valuable biblical manuscripts anywhere in the world.

In the early 1800s, a new age of science and enlightenment arrived. The world was in the heart of the Industrial Revolution, a period of powerful change in how people lived, worked, and were governed. Inventions began sprouting up everywhere that allowed people to do more work in less time. It was a time of tremendous human empowerment and people were feeling pretty good about themselves. Many began to wonder, Do I need the Bible anymore? Is it still accurate? Is it even the same book as it was in the days of the early Christian Church? Tischendorf's discovery of those ancient copies answered all those questions with a resounding, Yes! He found those ancient lines to be almost identical to the ones sitting on your shelf right now. Aren't you glad that God has been watching over the Bible all these years? The Word of God is as reliable today as it's always been.

Antarctica Discovered

Is there anything of which one can say, "Look! This is something new?" It was here already, long ago; it was here before our time. Ecclesiastes 1:10, NIV.

Antarctica is the coldest place on earth, with a glacier of ice over a mile thick in some places. It's no small piece of real estate either, at 15.5 million square miles big. Did you know that Antarctica is the fifth largest continent on earth with ice shelves as big as the state of California?

On this day in history, 1840, Captain Charles Wilkes completed an ocean voyage that encircled Antarctica and the South Pole. He claimed the icy continent for the United States, and for years after, it was known as Wilkes Land. In actuality, he wasn't the first explorer to see Antarctica, and neither were the other European and American explorers who saw it earlier in the nineteenth century.

Ancient legends among the natives off the coast of South America told of a large, uncharted continent in the far south. They indicated that the continent was free of ice, with a coastline of red cliffs. If these legends were true, then at one time Antarctica must have had a warmer climate. How long ago? Certainly after Noah's worldwide flood, and sometime before the glaciers of the ice ages began to cover the poles and coldest regions of our earth.

It doesn't really matter who first laid a claim to Antarctica, or who thinks he saw it first. It's been around a lot longer than any of us! Solomon says it well: "Is there anything of which one can say, 'Look! This is something new?' It was here already, long ago; it was here before our time." The explorers were excited to see Antarctica as if they were the first to lay eyes on it, but it's the same continent it's always been. Just a lot of ice to dress it up now, and enough cold to keep it uninhabitable. Like a lot of things in our lives, it just has a new design. It's been repackaged.

God is like that. He's been around a lot longer than we can imagine, and He'll go right on ruling the universe 10 million billion light years into the future. It doesn't really matter whether arguing scientists and philosophers admit that He exists or not. He exists because He is God, and that's all that matters.

Transatlantic Rowboat

Whatever work you do, do your best.
Ecclesiastes 9:10, NCV.

Would you consider taking a boat trip across the Atlantic Ocean? John Fairfax did it in a 22-foot rowboat. A rowboat! Wow! Can you imagine that? It must have taken a lot of determination and a ton of energy! People have made the trip across the Atlantic by plane, some even solo, and that's amazing since anything can go wrong when you're flying over seemingly endless water with no landing strips. Some have made the trip in a sailboat, and that would be a real challenge with nothing but the wind to keep your boat going in the right direction. But a rowboat! That would be tough, and John did it all by himself, using only his own two arms!

On January 20, 1969, John left the Canary Islands near Morocco, off the coast of West Africa. From there he rowed to the Cape Verde Islands, and then across the Atlantic Ocean, finally landing in Hollywood, Florida. Amazingly, the trip took him only 180 days. That's an average of about 22 miles a day, since the total distance was over 4,000 miles. Now there's not much to do while you're at sea in a rowboat. John had to eat, and he could do that while he was rowing, but he had to take time out to sleep, too. All things considered, he would have had to row about 14 to 16 hours a day.

The wisest man on earth, King Solomon, said that we should do our best in everything. "No matter what you do, work at it with all your might." Why not apply that to everything? Do your best in school. Do your best in the part time job you're trying to manage on afternoons and weekends. Do your best on the basketball team, football team, or volleyball team. Do your best to help out around the house. Do your best to make your parents proud. Do your best as a youth leader in your church. Do your best practicing the piano or fixing up that old car that's sitting in the driveway.

Life is like rowing across the Atlantic, and the only way to be successful is to attack it with all your might. When your arm muscles are aching, keep rowing with all your might. When the merciless sun beats down on you, scorching your shoulders, keep rowing with all your might. When you don't seem to be making any progress, keep rowing with all your might. Solomon says we should tackle our tasks with all the energy we have and that we should do them all for the glory of God.

Jenner's Smallpox Vaccination

You will not be afraid of diseases that come in the dark or sickness that strikes at noon.
Psalm 91:6, NCV.

What's the worst disease you can imagine? AIDS? Leprosy? Malaria? In the old days everyone was afraid of smallpox. On January 21, 1799, Edward Jenner came up with a vaccination to eradicate the dreaded and often fatal disease that had killed millions throughout history. Here's how his vaccination worked. Jenner took dead smallpox cells from an infected person and injected them into a healthy person in hopes that the resulting milder form of the disease would create immunity. And—wonder of wonders—it worked! Jenner was criticized for his methods, but the jeers soon turned to cheers, and his technique soon became common practice. By 1800 about 100,000 people all over the world had been vaccinated. The last outbreak of smallpox in the United States occurred in Texas in 1949, but only one person died. Most western nations were free of the disease by that time, but India and some countries in Africa still suffered from frequent epidemics.

In 1967 the World Health Organization began a worldwide campaign to eradicate smallpox. Amazingly, it took only 10 years to accomplish this, and the last recorded case occurred in Somalia in 1977. On May 8, 1980, the World Health Assembly announced that the world was free of smallpox. However, not everyone believes that the human race is safe from the legendary disease. New forms may soon crop up due to strains of the disease that act like the AIDS virus. Furthermore, bioterrorism could loom large on the horizon if terrorists figure out a way to infect large populations with smallpox germs.

Smallpox is only one of a plethora of diseases that plague this planet. While humans have developed vaccinations for some, others remain unsolved threats to humanity. These diseases can be contracted by everyone—even Christians. Choosing to follow God doesn't mean you're immune from all disease. What it means is that, like David, you don't have to live in fear that a deadly disease may invade your body. You can rest peacefully in the knowledge that God is with you, suffering when you suffer, every day of your life on this planet infected by the worst disease of all—sin.

Roe vs. Wade

Jesus said to him, "I am the way, the truth, and the life."
John 14:6, NKJV.

Human babies are some of the most precious creatures in all of God's creation. They are born under great pain, are totally helpless, cause us incredibly busy days and many sleepless nights—and yet we love them with the tenderness that God puts within our hearts. The tiny eyes staring at us while they eat, the smell of baby-soft skin, the pitiful cries when they are scared or hungry or lonely—each reminds us of the fragile creature we call a baby.

Unfortunately, the lives that God gives so miraculously are often snuffed out before their time. We call the procedure abortion, and it must cause our heavenly Father immeasurable grief.

On this day in 1973 the Supreme Court of the United States made a decision that it was legal for unborn babies to be aborted. What a horrible tragedy! Since that time, it is estimated that doctors in our country have performed nearly 50 million abortions in this country. That's about 1.4 million per year, or approximately 3,700 per day. Mothers who are unmarried have about 64 percent of those abortions, and 20 percent are performed on teenagers. Women who make less than $15,000 per year have about 30 percent of the abortions. In many cases they probably can't afford regular visits to a doctor to help them care for their unborn baby. But one of the saddest statistics is that over 90 percent of all abortions happen for social reasons— a baby will look bad for the family, the baby will require too much time, or the young woman doesn't want to give up her career.

In a land where we value life so much, it's amazing that we can allow this to go on and not stand up for the unborn babies. In days gone by, childhood deaths were a common occurrence. As recently as 1900, one in four babies died due to complications at birth, or from infection during or just after the birth. And before the age of 10, an additional child in four died from other fatal diseases.

Today those numbers are much, much lower. Now only one baby in 100 dies at birth. Here we are, a prosperous, medically-developed nation that has brought the death rate down from 25 babies in 100, to 1 in 100, and yet death by abortion is more common than ever.

Jesus said, "I am the way, the truth, and the life." He is our only source of hope and peace in this sinful world. Why not commit yourself to protecting the sacredness of human life today?

The Old and the New

*Great is the Lord, and greatly to be praised in the city of
our God, in the mountain of his holiness. Beautiful for
situation, the joy of the whole earth, is mount Zion,
on the sides of the north, the city of the great King.
Psalm 48:1, 2.*

Jerusalem has a history that is both glorious and tragic. It has been destroyed twice, besieged 23 times, attacked 52 times, and captured and recaptured 44 times. Over 4,000 years ago Abraham visited the city of Jerusalem and its king, Melchizedek. The name of the city at that time was Salem. Then, about a thousand years later David conquered the same city, but by this time its name had been changed to Jebus. David thought it would be a great place to set up his capital for the nation of Judah, and he did just that when he became king.

Four hundred years had rolled by when the capital city was destroyed by King Nebuchadnezzar of Babylon. When the Jews returned from Babylonian captivity a few years later, it was rebuilt and was the same city in which Jesus walked and talked. By the year 70, tensions between the Jews and Romans had peaked, causing the full wrath of the Caesars to descend upon the tortured confines. Roman General Titus and his army leveled Jerusalem, scattering even the stones of the temple, fulfilling Jesus' prediction.

The city was rebuilt again within the next 60 years and from time to time became the home of Jews, Romans, and Christians. Medieval times brought the crusades, and for 150 years Christian warriors came from all over Europe to try to reclaim the holy city from the Muslim hordes.

In the early 1900s the British took over Israel as a colony, but in 1948 Israel regained its independence. From that day to this, beleaguered Jerusalem has been a constant battlefield between Jews and Arabs.

Jerusalem will never again be the home of God's official church, but there is a day coming when the New Jerusalem will be our home. When Jesus, with His angelic army, returns to liberate His followers, He will take them to live with Him in that city of mansions, where gates of pearl open to streets of gold, and the river of life flows out from the throne of God. Why not make your reservation today?

Gold in Them There Hills

But lay up for yourselves treasures in heaven, where neither moth nor rust destroys, and where thieves do not break in and steal. Matthew 6:20, NKJV.

On January 24, 1848, gold was discovered in Coloma, California. A lot of it. The place was called Sutter's Mill, and the discovery took its place in the history books as one of the extraordinary events in American history—extraordinary not just because gold was found but because of the numbers of people who traveled the world to get there.

News of the find spread like wildfire. Men, women, and children from all over America headed across the wild continent in covered wagons. Others from the east coast, Europe, and even as far away as Australia came by sailboats at sea, often facing unbelievable hardships. By 1849, tens of thousands of "49ers" had arrived to stake their land claims and pan for the yellow metal among the rocks of streams and riverbeds. Before the whole adventure was over an estimated 300,000 folks had tried their luck at mining the gold. Billions of dollars worth of gold was found. A few got exceedingly rich, but most people did not fare so well. Though they invested everything they had, sacrificing their time and the safety of their families, most finally gave up. Some stayed on to farm or make a living in the towns that had sprung up around Sutter's Mill. Others returned home with little more than disappointment jingling in their pockets.

It was the gold rush that brought people to the west coast and helped California become a state. Today California is the largest state in population and the third largest state in area. It is known for its money-making ability today, too. From farming to the computer industry to tourism, it boasts more income than any other of the 50 states. If California were a country of its own, it would have the tenth largest gross domestic product in the world.

Would you have given up everything you had for the promise of gold at Sutter's Mill? How about if your investment were guaranteed? There's good news for anyone hoping for such a bonanza. God has promised that if we set out on a journey to know Him, a fabulous reward beyond imagination will be ours. Streets of pure gold, uninterrupted joy, but even better, eternity in the company of the God who would rather miss out on the treasure Himself, than for you to.

First Hand Transplant

Whatever your hand finds to do, do it with all your might.
Ecclesiastes 9:10, NIV.

Can you imagine living without your hands? Think of all the things that would be difficult to do without them—tying your shoes, pouring yourself a bowl of cereal, clapping after a musical performance. And if you lost your hands, what would you be willing to do to get new ones?

Matthew Scott of Absecon, New Jersey, knows all about that. Due to a firecracker accident in 1995, Matthew lost the use of his hand, and for four years he had to wear a prosthetic arm. Then, on January 25, 1999, the world's first successful hand transplant was done for him by Dr. Warren Breidenback and a team of surgeons in Louisville, Kentucky. Using a donor hand, wrist, and portion of a forearm, the doctors attached them to the bone in David's arm with metal plates and connected nerves and arteries with tiny stitches. The operation lasted an exhausting 15 hours, but now—miracle of miracles—Matthew has a hand again! Amazing!

The human hand is one of the most incredible tools in all of God's creation. Made of bone, muscle, and skin, it's a marvel indeed. A hand can draw circles in the sand, trace constellations in the night sky, and direct traffic. It can point accusingly at an enemy or beckon a friend. The hand can thread a needle, crack an egg, turn the pages of this book, and bend nails. Skilled hands can play a concert piano, paint a masterpiece, or perform surgery like Dr. Breidenback and his team of surgeons. Hands can cool a fevered brow or take a life. They can caress a baby, make a sculpture, catch a football, type a research paper, sign a name, and pray.

Cain used his hands to kill his brother. Abraham used his hands to welcome strangers who turned out to be angels. Moses used his hands to beckon the Israelites out of slavery in Egypt. King Saul used his hands to throw a spear at David in demonic rage. David used his hands to caress the face of another man's wife. Daniel used his hands to pray, even on pain of death. Jonah used his hands to wipe gooey whale blubber off his face. Mary used her hands to rock her Baby boy to sleep. And Jesus . . .

Jesus used His hands to heal a blind man, heal a leperous man, heal an ashamed prostitute, heal a dead man, and heal a world by allowing us to nail those very hands to a cross. How will you use your hands today?

Babysitter's Insurance

If we confess our sins, he is faithful and just to forgive us
our sins, and to cleanse us from all unrighteousness.
1 John 1:9.

On January 26, 1950, the first babysitter's insurance policy on record was sold in St. Louis, Missouri. Can you believe it! To take out such a policy today might make sense with all the lawsuits being run through our courts, but in 1950! In those days babysitters were normally a dime a dozen and parents worried more about convicts at the county jail than whether or not their babysitter was a criminal. This policy was made available by the American Associated Insurance Company, with sitters being bonded up to $2,500 for fraud and dishonesty. Wow! There must have been either some pretty shady sitters—or some pretty paranoid parents—in those parts. Evidently there were parents who felt they needed protection against a babysitter who was masquerading as a thief or con artist, at best.

Today you can buy insurance for your car. You can buy insurance for your house, your motorcycle, and even for your pets. You can buy dental insurance, insurance for your crops, your business, the parts you buy for your car, your phone, your credit cards, and even your body parts. Quarterbacks insure their arms, pop singers insure their faces and their figures, and sitters probably can't afford to practice their trade anymore without insurance, either.

Jesus came to this earth without an insurance policy of any kind. He was born into a poor family in an obscure, crime-ridden town. He worked in a very physical occupation, an occupation in which many have lost fingers or suffered other damage. He traveled treacherous terrain daily, giving His life in service while expecting nothing in return. He was accused of crimes he didn't commit, was crucified by His own countrymen, and His body was buried in a borrowed grave. He took real risks coming here and asked for no guarantees from those He came to redeem. In dying for us, He offered us insurance against the ultimate calamity—eternal separation from Him in a permanent grave. If we sign our name to this policy, He has promised to help us incorporate the cleansing forgiveness He already purchased for us. What does this policy cost? Everything. But He's already covered that cost, and all you have to do is sign on the dotted line.

Giant Locomotive

"Not by might nor by power, but by my Spirit," says the Lord Almighty. Zechariah 4:6, NIV.

Can you imagine a train engine that is 150 feet long? Wow! That's half the length of a football field! Why would anyone need a locomotive of that size? On January 27, 1948, the General Electric Company of Erie, Pennsylvania, built the world's largest locomotive ever to run on a railroad track. It weighed one billion pounds, had 16 driving axels, and boasted 6,800-horsepower electric engines. The mammoth locomotive first went to work for the Virginia Railway Company, pulling trainloads of coal over the mountains of West Virginia. The climb over the mountains was a long, hard one, so the railroad felt it needed all the help it could get.

Locomotives used to power our transportation system, for both products and passengers. From the earliest days locomotives were used to haul cattle to markets in Kansas City, coal to factories along the Great Lakes, and passengers across the Great Divide. There were steam engines, electric locomotives, and train engines powered by diesel. Today, diesel engines are still among some of the most efficient machines on earth. For the fuel they use they can haul more weight for greater distances at lower cost than almost any other means of transportation. Unfortunately, today's trains have been sidelined in much of America, sitting idle and quiet in railyards. Trucks do a large share of the heavy work anymore, and jets whisk people back and forth across our continent in just hours. Trains are still cheaper by a long shot, but trucks and jets give more people work.

In this life, there are many mountains to traverse, and sometimes it is a long, hard climb. Sometimes everyday is a long, hard climb. As you gaze up the rocky slope of the mountain you're facing, you may shake your head and think it's impossible to scale it. Maybe you're bummed about a math test coming up and feel that you just don't have it in you to get a passing grade. Maybe your younger brother is driving you up the wall. Maybe it seems your parents just don't understand you. Where can you get the power to conquer these slopes? Good news! Look up—not at the mountain in front of you, but beyond that. If you look sincerely, you will find power from the God who has more power than any locomotive. Keep asking Him to give you His power and you *will* find yourself at the peak of your mountain.

Space Shuttle Disaster

When I consider your heavens, the work of your fingers,
the moon and the stars, which you have set in place,
what is man that you are mindful of him?
Psalm 8:3, 4, NIV.

On this day in 1986 the space shuttle *Challenger* exploded just 74 seconds after liftoff and went down in flames off the coast of Florida. It was the worst space disaster in history. Six astronauts on board were killed—Michael Smith, Ronald McNair, Francis Scobee, Ellison Onizuka, Gregory Jarvis, and Judith Resnik. Christa McAuliffe, a teacher from New Hampshire, was also on board, because she had won a contest to become the first ordinary citizen to fly in space. The morning of the launch had been a cold one, so cold that the o-ring seals on the shuttle's solid fuel boosters cracked, allowing exploding gases to escape.

What a tragedy for the flight crew and their families, and what a tragedy for the space program. It's difficult enough to raise the money needed to fund space research and exploration, but a disaster like this could have been enough to cripple and even shut things down permanently. Some people thought the tragedy was the result of ignoring the obvious: we are meant to live on earth and not in outer space. Pushing the limits of space exploration, they say, can only bring more disasters like the one in 1986. Minds disagreeing with this view prevailed, and after a time of mourning, the United States space program got back on track. Most of us came to believe that the lives of those dear people were not sacrificed in vain. Since that time NASA has launched a total of 116 successful space shuttle missions.

God loved each and every one of those astronauts. He was mindful of them, as David said, and He is mindful of us, no matter how many bad things might happen to us. One day soon He will take us all on a journey through space, past brilliant stars and ringed planets, to our heavenly home. As space debris, moondust, and comets streak past us, we won't have to worry one bit about cracked o-rings, loose bolts, or faulty wiring. We won't even need spacesuits with an oxygen supply. We will be flying with the Creator of the universe, the Initiator of life! The same Creator who will lead us through the constellations is mindful of you this very day, this very moment. He's thinking about you! Although you can't see it now, a big smile rises on His face as He realizes that you are thinking about Him, too.

January 29

Beginnings of Baseball

*For what will it profit a man if he gains the
whole world, and loses his own soul?*
Mark 8:36, NKJV.

Baseball has traditionally been called America's favorite pastime, especially for the older generation. Maybe that's because it's been around for a long time. On this day in 1900, the American Baseball League was organized in Philadelphia. In the old days the league had only eight teams, but over 100 years has helped it expand into 30 major league teams. Some of the original teams that still exist today are the Detroit Tigers, Chicago White Sox, and Baltimore Orioles. Many baseball players have achieved stardom as they've run around those bases, players such as Babe Ruth, Lou Gehrig, Ted Williams, Pete Rose, Reggie Jackson, Jackie Robinson, Ken Griffey, Jr., Barry Bonds, Hank Aaron, and Joe DiMaggio.

It's a very complicated game—some say it has more rules than any other sport in America today. That may be, but it's basically still a kid's game. In the sport two teams of nine players each play against each other. One player throws a ball and another hits it with a stick. Then the person who hit the ball runs in a circle while other players try to catch the ball and tag the runner out. Sounds rather silly when we put it that way, doesn't it? Today many baseball players get paid millions of dollars to do nothing more than play the game. The highest paid contract to date is $27,000,000 per year, and some would claim the player got where he is by taking steroids.

Most baseball players play the game with honesty and integrity, but baseball, like other sports, is extremely competitive and the difference between winning and losing can be in just a slightly stronger swing, a more explosive jump on stealing a base, or a speedier fastball. This creates a choice for these uniformed heroes. Should they stay focused on their goal of being the absolute best they can honestly be, or take the "easier" route fraught with hidden, destructive drawbacks? Most choose the noble route, but others have chosen to cheat, injecting themselves with performance-enhancing steroids, compromising their integrity, their health, and their immediate and distant futures, while giving themselves and the game a bad name. Nothing is more pitiful than a fallen hero.

The Holocaust Begins

In this world you will have trouble.
But take heart! I have overcome the world.
John 16:33, NIV.

On this day in 1933, a time of terrible persecution began in Europe, known as the Holocaust. When Adolf Hitler came to power as the new chancellor of Germany, he brought a narrow agenda, an unpredictable behavior, and a dark philosophy with him. Within a few months he took full control of the government and became a dictator. Believing that his race was superior to every other race on earth, he initiated such surprisingly evil actions that even those closest to him didn't believe he would actually carry them out. The special target of his nefarious schemes was the Jewish race.

One of the first things he did was to enact a law proclaiming the inferiority of Jews, saying that they didn't deserve to be a part of Nazi Germany. This law did not affect just a few Jews, but masses of human beings all over the country. Hitler's secret police burst into Jewish restaurants, shops, and homes, barking their orders to get out. Many Jews were shoved into fenced-in sections of the city, called ghettos, where coughing children wearing only rags shivered in the night air. Other Jews were forced into slave labor in factories. Still others were herded into trains like cattle, destined for the places that became the grotesque face of the holocaust—concentration camps. Separated from family members, mere scraps of food to eat, plagued with infuriating insects, many Jews felt their bodies being slowly eaten away by starvation, others by disease. Then, the worst. Hitler ordered that Jewish people, one after another, be executed by firing squad or in gas chambers. During World War II, it is estimated that as many as 6,000,000 Jews died because of the holocaust.

Someday you and I may be faced with suffering for Jesus simply because we are Christians. Even now, in many parts of the world people suffer because they are followers of Him. The enemy carries a dark philosophy with him and desperately despises humans—the objects of God's love. But be of good courage. Jesus has overcome the world's malicious dictators, disease-ridden ghettos, slave labor, starvation, and gas chambers. When all precious humans of all races see their predicament and choose to be rescued, the war, and this holocaust, will be over. Forever.

Commander in Chief of the South

There is a way that seems right to a man, but its end is the way of death.
Proverbs 14:12, NKJV.

General Robert E. Lee is considered one of the greatest army generals in American history. On this day in 1865 he became the commander in chief of the Confederate army during the American Civil War. He fought in battles like Gettysburg and the Battle of Bull Run, which, with others, will live on in history because of the horrific numbers of men who died there. More American soldiers were killed in the Civil War than in any other war in our history. But it was not only the loss of life that made this war so tragic. It was also the painful division it brought to the nation—and to its families. It was not uncommon for loyalties to be split among family members, some favoring the North, some the South. Sometimes, one brother donned a blue uniform, the other a gray. "It is well that war is so terrible, or we should grow too fond of it," Lee said at the Battle of Fredericksburg. Just a few months after being named commander in chief, he surrendered his command on April 9, 1865, as the conflict was fading.

Although Lee fought in many terrible battles of the Civil War and is said to have sacrificed many lives with his particular strategy of war, he had a nobler side to him, too. When asked to choose his side in the war, he made a firm, unwavering decision. It must have taken much resolve to stick with this choice, because he knew it meant he would lose his home to the hands of the enemy. And he did. His house became the Union Army headquarters and a hospital and cemetery for soldiers.

Lee felt he was doing the right thing by fighting to divide the nation. Today we see clearly the true meaning and consequences of the Civil War, issues that were likely not so obvious to Lee and every soldier embroiled in the struggle. He and soldiers on both sides fought bravely for what they thought was right, their version of truth. When the last musket had fired and the last bloodied sword was plunged into another soldier's chest, over 600,000 hearts had stopped beating because of the difference of opinion over what was right. And over the silent battlefields strewn with lifeless bodies came the fulfillment of Scripture: "There is a way that seems right to a man, but its end is the way of death."

Two-hundred-inch Telescope

Then God made two great lights: the greater light to rule the day, and the lesser light to rule the night. He made the stars also.
Genesis 1:16, NKJV.

Can you imagine a telescope that is over 16 feet wide? The biggest telescope most people might have in their home would be four to six inches in diameter, and things can appear pretty big when we peer through a lens of that size. Now multiply a six-inch telescope by 32, and you have an idea of how big a telescope that would actually be.

On this day in 1949, a telescope that big became a reality at the Mount Palomar Observatory in San Diego, California. It had a convex lens 200 inches in diameter that weighed 20 tons. That's 40,000 pounds of solid glass. The lens took 11 months to cool from its liquid molten state, and then another 11 years to grind and polish. It took 22 years to produce this mammoth telescope! When it was finally finished, I'll bet a lot of people were relieved. All that work paid off, because now humans could see heavenly objects six sextillion miles away. Now that's a long, long way! It's difficult to wrap our minds around that kind of distance, but the experts tell us it's equal to six billion trillion miles. That's a six with 21 zeros behind it. The light from the stars this telescope can see began speeding toward earth over 100,000,000 years ago, and that light was traveling at 186,000 miles per second.

It boggles the mind to think that God has stars out there that are that far away. And that's just a drop in the bucket. We know that God has no birthday, because He has always *been*. And we know that He enjoyed creating our earth because when He was done He pronounced it to be very good. So, it seems reasonable to assume that our planet was not His first project, that He was engaged in His hobby of creating things as long as He's been around, fashioning suns, molding planets, arranging solar systems, and testing prototype galaxies. How truly amazing and infinite He is to design and accomplish all these masterpieces! It's even more amazing that we can observe His projects that boggle our minds and inspire our praise. But it's most amazing that He gives us the chance to be His sons and daughters and to inherit the vast universe we see through telescopes like the one on Mount Palomar. All it takes to become a daughter, a son, of the great Designer, is to invite Him into your heart.

First Lie Detector

Lying lips are an abomination to the Lord,
but those who deal truthfully are His delight.
Proverbs 12:22, NKJV.

Have you ever told a lie and thought no one would find out? Lots of people have done that, especially criminals, and Leonarde Keeler thought he had a pretty good idea on how to catch them in the act. While he was working in the scientific laboratories of Northwestern University School of Law, he built a machine called a polygraph, otherwise known as a lie detector. On February 2, 1935, the lie detector was first used in a court case where two men were accused of assault. With the help of the lie detector they both finally admitted to their guilt.

People on trial who are asked to take lie detector tests sometimes get so nervous that they fail the tests, even though they aren't actually guilty. On the other hand, there are some people who have learned to trick the machine by being absolutely calm. This is why lie detector tests can no longer be legally used in courts of law—they are too unreliable.

Being honest is always the best policy. A person's character is measured by what she does when no one is looking. The Bible is brimming with stories with plots revealing that honesty is the best policy—the one thing that brought God's blessings.

On a trip to Egypt, Abraham lied to Pharaoh, saying that Sarah was his sister, when actually she was his wife. He was fortunate that it didn't cost him his wife and his life. David lied to the high priest, telling Ahimelech that he was on the king's business when he was actually a fugitive fleeing for his life. The price? Eighty-five priests were executed by King Saul, because Ahimelech unwisely gave David food and a weapon. Peter lied when asked if he was a disciple of Jesus, and he regretted it for the rest of his life. Ananias and Sapphira offered to donate all the money from the sale of some property to the early church. However, while pretending to give the entire amount, they secretly kept some of the proceeds for themselves, and they died for their dishonesty.

Even worse than lying is the selfishness behind it. Our God is a holy God, and lying for selfish gain goes against His giving character. He loves us and wants us to enjoy the rewards of being honest and truthful.

First Paper Money in the New World

Do not lay up for yourselves treasures on earth, where moth and rust destroy and where thieves break in and steal.
Matthew 6:19, NKJV.

Have you ever heard the expression, "It's not worth the paper it's printed on?" That's because paper's not worth much. Duh! So why print paper money if it's not worth anything? Good question. Evidently people have faith that real gold is in some bank somewhere backing up the paper money they're making.

The first paper money in the New World was printed in the colony of Massachusetts on February 3, 1690. A war was in progress with Quebec to the north, and the colony needed money to pay the soldiers who were fighting. The Massachusetts colony started its own bank, printing only two bills: a two-shilling note and a five-pound note. Of course, this was British money, since the American colonies were still part of the British Empire at the time.

We've come a long way since that first paper money came off the Massachusetts presses. Until the late 1800s, paper money was still not being printed much because banks were using gold and silver coins to conduct most business transactions. But now the U.S. Treasury in Washington, D.C., prints millions of dollars in paper money each day, and most of it doesn't even have gold to back it up. For sure, "it's not worth the paper it's printed on." The most common denominations are $1, $5, $10, $20, $50, and $100. However, in the past there have been bills worth $500, $1,000, $5,000, $10,000, and $100,000. The largest denomination of a paper bill was $1,000,000, but it was made only as a gimmick.

Did you know that you don't really own the money sitting in your wallet right now, the dollars in your savings account, even the coins under your couch cushions? As hard as you may have worked to earn them, they are all a gift from God, a gift for you to manage for Him. Trusting these temporary objects that can rust, burn, be stolen, or evaporate in the stock market, is not a wise financial management strategy. It is saying that you trust man's wobbly financial markets more than the rock solid economy of Heaven. God has promised to pour out innumerable blessings on you for trusting Him as the real Owner, and His promises are worth even more than the paper they're printed on.

First U.S. President

*The Lord gave this command to Joshua son of Nun: "Be strong
and courageous, for you will bring the Israelites into the land
I promised them on oath, and I myself will be with you."
Deuteronomy 31:23, NIV.*

George Washington was quite a man! Some people think that he wasn't
much different than you or me, and that because he was our first president, we've somehow immortalized him and made him a legend. Actually, he
was a legend in his own time and remains one even today. He was active in
the Indian wars and the Revolutionary War. When he had proven himself to
be a capable general, he was asked to be commander of the Continental
Army and helped the Colonies become independent from England as the
new United States of America.

After the war was over some suggested that Washington set up a military dictatorship to help the country get back on its feet. But Washington
would have none of it, and after the Continental Congress ended, he retired
to run his Mount Vernon estate in Virginia.

However, several more times he was called on to work on the nation's
business. The U.S. Constitution needed to be written, and our leaders decided it needed to have a Bill of Rights added to it. At both these conventions
Washington showed unusual leadership skills once again, and some began
suggesting that he should be chosen as president of our new country.

To his surprise, on February 4, 1789, Washington was unanimously
elected as the first president of the United States. But he should have guessed
such a thing might happen. If the country was looking for a leader, in many
ways he was the ideal one for the job. As commander in chief during the
Revolutionary War, he had led his inexperienced and poorly equipped
Continental Army to victory over one of the world's superpowers.

Washington served in the office of president for two terms and would
have been elected to a third, but he declined and finally retired to his home
in Mount Vernon. Today his face is on our money, in our government buildings, and on the carved stone of Mount Rushmore. We continue to ask ourselves what it was that made Washington such a great man, and it must be
that he was a humble man, used by God, "First in war, first in peace, and first
in the hearts of his countrymen."

Pioneer of Religious Freedom

You will know the truth, and the truth will set you free.
John 8:32, NIV.

Religious freedom is a treasured right of Americans, but it wasn't always so. There are many stories that tell of famous Americans who sacrificed everything to gain that freedom. Here's one of them.

On February 5, 1631, a man by the name of Roger Williams arrived in Boston from England. Beginning as a teacher and then pastor in the Massachusetts Bay Colony, it soon became obvious that he strongly disagreed with how the Puritan colonial leadership treated the colonists and Native Americans. In those days, disagreement with leadership could lead to severe punishment—even death. To Roger, with his respect for individual liberty, this policy was unthinkable to him, and his schism with the Puritan leadership crescendoed into his banishment from the colony. With no other place to go, he trudged through the snow for several days to reach a village of the Narragansett Indian tribe. When he finally dragged himself into the friendly confines, he burned with fever and barely escaped an early grave. He did recover and eventually settled in what is now the state of Rhode Island.

Roger believed that everyone should be able to live in peace and worship God as he or she saw fit. Because of this freedom doctrine, he made people feel welcome, and all kinds of folks began moving to his settlement from everywhere. Jews and Quakers were some of the first religious settlers to be welcomed. As a result of the influx, Roger started his own colony, calling it Providence. He also started the first Baptist church in America, and he wrote the first dictionary in a Native American language. Wherever Roger went he brought peace and contentment with him. Today we consider him to be one of America's first real pioneers of religious freedom.

In the Palestine of Jesus' day, the people were enslaved by innumerable religious rules imposed upon them by the church leadership. Whatever poor peasant disagreed could be banished from the church. This policy was unthinkable to Jesus, so He spent His days restoring the truth about God—that He desperately wants our friendship, a friendship based on true freedom.

Pioneer Missionaries

*"Therefore go and make disciples of all nations, baptizing them
in the name of the Father and of the Son and of the Holy Spirit,
and teaching them to obey everything I have commanded you.
And surely I am with you always, to the very end of the age"
Matthew 28:19, 20, NIV.*

Adoniram Judson was one of the first successful missionaries of the modern era. From the moment he decided to be a missionary for God, his life was marked with hardship and sacrifice until the day he died. God could not have had a more faithful worker than Adoniram.

The day after he and his fiancée, Ann, were married, they were ordained as missionaries in Salem, Massachusetts. That was on February 6, 1812. His honeymoon ended up being a trip to the mission field of Burma where he spent the remaining 40 years of his life.

When he and his wife finally reached their destination in Burma, they were told by the Baptists there that evangelism would be impossible in a Buddhist country. But Judson set out to prove them wrong. He already knew Latin, Greek, and Hebrew, and now set out to learn Burmese. He hired a tutor to work with him for 12 hours a day, but even so, it took him over three years to successfully learn the language.

In 1819 he baptized his first Burmese convert. The most difficult task Adoniram had was convincing Buddhists that there is only one living God, and because of this, he had very few conversions during those first few years. It took him 12 years to make 18 converts.

During a war between England and Burma, Adoniram was imprisoned for 17 months at the famous "death prison" in Ava. While he was gone, his wife, Ann, worked tirelessly to get him released from prison, and she managed to have their third child in her spare time. However, when Adoniram finally returned, she died, worn out from the long months of disease and stress apart from him.

When Adoniram had first arrived in Burma, his goal was to translate the Bible into Myanmar and raise up a church with 100 members. By the time he died in 1850, he left a complete translation of the Bible, 100 churches, and over 8,000 believers. To this day his Bible translation remains the most popular version in the Myanmar language. His work had been overwhelming, but he always felt no sacrifice was too great for God. After all, Jesus had already done that and much more.

Space Walk

The heavens declare the glory of God;
the skies proclaim the work of his hands.
Psalm 19:1, NIV.

Have you ever wished you could be an astronaut? That's something little kids often say they want to be when they grow up, but honestly have no clue what it's all about. In spite of all the hard work and dedication it would take to train for such missions, would you go if you were asked to do it? Very few people have ever gotten a chance to do something like this.

What would it be like to fly like a bird in outer space—without the help of a spaceship? Without a cable hooking you to the mother ship? Without a space suit? OK, maybe that's stretching it a bit, but on this day in 1984, Navy Captain Bruce McCandless became the first man ever to fly in space without the help of a spaceship, or even a connecting cable. He was the first to walk outside of our planet without anything but a jet pack.

What glorious sights he must have seen, such as the earth, like a giant marble of blue suspended in space as though it too were motionless. To be able to move effortlessly above this oversized classroom globe must have been exciting! Dangerous, but exhilarating. Inside Captain McCandless' space suit was a climate prepared for the human body down to the last detail. The proper air pressure was maintained so that the vacuum of space outside the suit didn't cause his body to explode. The temperature was constantly adjusted to keep his body cool when the sun was shining directly on him during his space walk, and to keep him from freezing to death in the frigid temperatures of 200 degrees below zero and colder. Everyone hoped that there were no mini-asteroids in the area to pierce his space suit and cause leaks in the internal ecosystem. And of course, the suit was accessorized with all kinds of equipment, including a jet pack to propel him and safety devices should he become separated from the mother ship.

Have you ever wondered what it would be like to be an angel, flying at the speed of thought through the star-speckled heavens? Do these angels ever think about what it would be like to be a human being, chained to this disease-ridden planet, having to constantly fight to keep their eyes on their Creator for the desire and strength to keep trusting Him no matter what? I'm convinced that they watch humans closely, to see how they react when their friends ignore them, when their parents are unfair, when they suffer. They wonder, Will they keep trusting?

Boy Scouts

*"And you shall love the LORD your God with all your heart,
with all your soul, with all your mind, and with all your strength."
This is the first commandment. And the second, like it, is this:
"You shall love your neighbor as yourself."
Mark 12:30, 31, NKJV.*

Most boys love to go camping, play war games, and share stories about famous explorers and warriors from long ago. Good thing, because that's what *Boy Scouts* are all about. They learn about marching, Native American lore, how to give first aid, how to handle an ax and hunting knife, how to cook over an open fire, and how to tell which way is north on a cloudy day. They earn merit badges and awards for community service. And there are levels through which the boys can advance to prove their skill, bravery, and responsibility as young men.

Today there are over 110 million Boy Scouts worldwide, but once upon a time the organization was just a fledgling group of boys out to learn and have some fun. On February 8, 1910, the Boys Scouts of America became an official youth organization in our nation's capital, Washington, D.C. The group was designed for boys 7 years old and up, and was started by Daniel Beard, who got the idea from the Boy Scouts movement that began in England. The first boy recorded to become an Eagle Scout and receive merit recognition was Arthur Eldrid who lived in Oceanside, New York.

The Boy Scouts oath says: *On my honor I will do my best to do my duty to God and my country and to obey the Scout Law; to help other people at all times; to keep myself physically strong, mentally awake, and morally straight.*

And the Scout Law? *A Scout is trustworthy, loyal, helpful, friendly, courteous, kind, obedient, cheerful, thrifty, brave, clean and reverent.*

The Boy Scouts handshake is unique—a Scout extends his left hand to greet someone. What does this mean? No one knows for sure, but one explanation borrowed from medieval times says that a warrior carries a shield in his left hand. To shake with the left hand, he must drop his shield, indicating trust that the other man will not attack him while his guard is down.

Jesus said that we should love God with everything we have, and that we should love our neighbors as we love ourselves. These are the two basic components of God's character, and it looks like the Boy Scouts have that much figured out.

First Intercollegiate Basketball Game

For the earth bringeth forth fruit of herself; first the blade,
then the ear, after that the full corn in the ear.
Mark 4:28, KJV.

On this day in 1895 the very first intercollegiate basketball game was played in Minnesota. The Minnesota School of Agriculture defeated Hamline College 9 to 3. That score sounds more like a baseball score than a basketball score! Today third and fourth graders can score more points than that! In the first basketball games ever played, players aimed the ball at a peach basket fastened up on the wall. When the janitor got tired of bringing a ladder to retrieve the ball, someone got the bright idea of cutting a hole in the basket. It wasn't until sometime later that they replaced the peach basket with a basketball net.

Today there are nearly 350 colleges and universities that play in the 32 Division One basketball conferences. And that's just college teams in the United States, to say nothing of all the teams that play in Canada, Europe, Russia, China, and South America.

Athletics is an important part of college life. Some colleges put too much emphasis on sports, which places extreme pressure on players and coaching staffs to win. In some colleges coaches get paid as much as the coaches on the professional level. A sports team gives a college identity and TV ratings, which in turn bring in better, higher-profile athletes who will increase the college's prestige.

But it wasn't always that way. When college basketball was just getting started, the teams were small, not well-coached, and definitely lacking in skill, or maybe even in natural talent. Check out that 9 to 3 score between the Minnesota School of Agriculture and Hamline College. That's got to be embarrassing!

College sports has grown like the verse of Scripture says: "First the blade, then the ear, after that the full corn in the ear." We can't have it all overnight. At the start, college sports programs were insignificant and probably not so very important to the college programs. But over the years, those programs and rivalries matured, and now they bring in success for their schools. We've got to begin somewhere, and faith is the ticket that can help give us that extra little push toward success and spiritual growth.

February 10

Chess Computer

Let not the wise man glory in his wisdom,… But let him who glories glory in this, that he understands and knows Me, that I am the Lord, exercising lovingkindness, judgment, and righteousness in the earth. Jeremiah 9:23, 24, NKJV.

Are you good with computers? Are you a tech geek? Can you make the computer do what you want it to, or does it tell you what to do?

Computers are pretty dumb. They can do only what we program them to do, right? Nothing more, nothing less. They're machines and they have to obey us. Well, some computers are getting pretty smart—so smart that it seems they are almost beginning to think for themselves.

On February 10, 1996, in Philadelphia, Pennsylvania, a computer beat a world chess champion at his own game. The computer's name was *Deep Blue*, and its opponent was a Russian named Gary Kasparov, the world's best-ranked grandmaster of chess. It was the first time a computer had beaten a top human player under championship conditions. Chess fans the world over were surprised because Kasparov was said to be one of the strongest chess players in history. He had never lost a multi-game match to anyone, ever—man or machine. What had happened? Was he losing his edge?

After the initial loss, Kasparov did go on to win the six-game match, but in a rematch a year later, Deep Blue won fair and square. Deep Blue was developed by a team of IBM researchers in Yorktown Heights, New York. Able to evaluate 200 million chess moves per second, it could anticipate every possible move within 10 to 15 moves. Now that's a computer!

How smart are you? Smart enough to think for yourself? Smart enough to trust in yourself? According to Jeremiah, we can never count on our own smarts. Far better to depend on God's wisdom, because He who created the deep blue of our planet's sky and sea is infinitely wise. He is able to anticipate every possible move within zero moves. That's right, with God there is absolutely no margin of error! That's not a computer—now that's God!

It is not enough to know and believe that God is 100 percent accurate. God wants you to believe that He is 100 percent accurate and trustworthy in *your* life. When you come to God with the things that you can't understand, that's when you become truly smart!

First Women's College

Study to shew thyself approved unto God, a workman that needeth not to be ashamed, rightly dividing the word of truth. 2 Timothy 2:15.

On this day in history, 1836, the first women's college in the United States opened its doors in South Hadley, Massachusetts. The majority of the classwork at Mount Holyoke Female Seminary consisted, not of English, nursing, engineering, or medicine, but of what was called "cooperative household tasks." Sounds like plain old housework to me. During its first semester, 80 students filed in and out of the classrooms, and the total cost of tuition and board for the year was $64. Can you imagine that? Only $64!

Of course, that was a long time ago, and things have changed a lot since then. Today, over 4,300 colleges dot America's educational landscape, from liberal arts universities to colleges specializing in everything from business to medical assisting. If the collar you'd like to wear is more blue than white, there are colleges for plumbers, hair stylists, entrepreneurs, and more. Chances are, whatever career you'd like, there's a college for it. Looks like we now have more choices than just cooking and cleaning!

A student will pay around $150 to $200 per credit hour, per semester in a local community college. At an average of 16 credit hours per semester, the cheapest tuition a student would pay today for a full year of schooling is about $4,800. That's an increase of 7,500 percent from 1836! But that is nothing compared to the cost of tuition at a state, private, and especially an Ivy League college. Boston College charges about $49,000 per year, George Washington University will set you back $50,000, and Sarah Lawrence College is the granddaddy of them all, costing a whopping $53,000 per year. Of course, it's reasonable to have to pay for a respectable education, and with all the grants, loans, and special tuition packages available today, there really is no excuse for anyone to avoid opening those grand doors of higher education.

Going on to college increases your chance for success in any workplace, as well as for a bigger paycheck. God wants you to be successful, and your success is His success. So go ahead and open those great doors of higher education and walk with Him into a brighter future, a more fulfilling life, and true success.

New York to Paris

I can do all things through Christ who strengthens me.
Philippians 4:13, NKJV.

In 1908, on February 12, six automobiles started a race that ran from New York to Paris. Sound impossible? Well, maybe. The race began in Times Square, New York City, with over 250,000 people cheering the start of a race to circle the globe! It became the longest automobile competition in history.

The world-class event included six teams from France, Italy, Germany, and the United States. The torturous route went through Albany, Chicago, San Francisco, Seattle, Valdez, Alaska, across the frozen ice of the Bering Strait to Japan, then across Asia through the Russian cities of Vladivostok, Omsk, Moscow, St. Petersburg, Berlin, and on to Paris. The race was driven under terrible conditions, often on impassable roads, or no roads at all. It was begun during a bitterly cold winter, and included a stretch across the frozen Bering Straits in the dead of winter. And all this at a time when horses were thought to be more reliable than automobiles.

The race crossed three continents, 22,000 miles of roads, railroads, fields, and ice flows. It took 170 days, with 88 days of actual driving time. The average daily run was only 152 miles, and the longest run was 420 miles. With no roads, the drivers often had to ride the railroad tracks. It was forbidden to ride the rails, so the car straddled the rails bumping along from tie to tie for hundreds of miles. When there were no railroad tracks they had to go cross country, long before the days of four-wheel drive. Sometimes they had to pull themselves out of the snow and mud with horses.

The American team, George Schuster and his two mechanics, George Miller and Montague Roberts, ultimately won the race with a car provided by the Thomas Motor Company out of Buffalo, NY. The Thomas Flyer cost $4,000 and weighed 5,000 pounds loaded, and could speed along at 60 mph, pretty amazing for a car in those days. The feat has never been equaled. George and his buddies, now long gone, still hold the world record over 100 years later!

Sometimes we feel like God has asked too much of us. Our friends ask us to do things we know we shouldn't do. The sports we want to join are played on Friday nights. The people we love end up in the hospital or die after suffering much pain. But we should be courageous. Whatever He asks of us, we can do with His power.

First Recorded Living Quintuplets

Thank you for making me so wonderfully complex!
Your workmanship is marvelous.
Psalm 139:14, NLT.

Have you ever stood at the window of a hospital nursery and watched all those newborns in their cribs? Now imagine all those wriggling, hand-waving, crying, red-faced babies belonging to the same mother! Babies are cute, but that would be too much, you may say. On February 13, 1875, quintuplets were born to Mrs. Edna Beecham Kanouse of Watertown, Wisconsin. Quintuplets? That's five babies, and they were all boys. Can you imagine having to care for five baby boys—all the same age? One boy can be a handful, but five? Other stories of quintuplets in the United States date back to 1776 and 1800, but, unfortunately, all those precious infants lost their little lives shortly after they began. Mrs. Kanouse's babies were the first recorded quintuplets to live at least two weeks.

The odds of having multiple births decrease with every baby that's added to the set. The likelihood of naturally born twins for a couple is about 1 in 90. The odds of identical twins is 1 in 250. The likelihood of naturally born triplets is 1 in 8,100. When you're talking about quadruplets, it's 1 in 729,000, and the chance of having naturally born quintuplets is about 1 in 55,000,000. These are some seriously mind-boggling numbers! How about a mom having two sets of identical twins? The chance of having naturally born quadruplets made up of two sets of identical twins is thought to be as high as 1 in 36 million. Can we even comprehend this complexity?

But probably the most amazing statistics of all come from a California family giving birth to four identical boys in 1997, and two families, one in California and another in Washington, producing four identical girls in 2002. Impossible, you say? Just about. The chance of having naturally born identical quadruplets is thought to be about 1 in 600 million.

Wow! There's nothing left to say except that we are fearfully and wonderfully made. The human body is already intricately complex, and the miracle of birth propels that complexity into the stratosphere! The incredible event of having identical sets of creatures, made in God's image, is truly awesome and inspiring. We can only stand in the presence of God, wondering what He will do next!

First Electronic Computer

O Lord, what are human beings that you should notice them,
mere mortals that you should think about them?
Psalm 144:3, NLT.

What would we do without computers? We use them as word processors to type our research papers. We use them to chat with our friends, do our banking, play our music, and watch our movies. Some cars have them built right into the ignition so we can start them up with the push of a finger on an electronic car key. Computers run our home security systems, launch our rockets, operate our TVs, and locate our lost dogs, all with the touch of a button that communicates with computer chips in hundreds of gizmos all around us. How did all this start?

On February 14, 1946, the first electronic computer was demonstrated. Models of computers had been around for a very long time, but this was the first one to successfully make use of electronic components. It was built by the Moore School of Engineering at the University of Pennsylvania in Philadelphia and was officially called the Electronic Numerical Integrator and Computer. Off the record, it was dubbed The Giant Brain. It was so big that it required a room 30 by 50 feet. It contained approximately 18,000 vacuum tubes and required 130 kilowatts of electricity per hour to operate. The cost? Almost $500,000, or about 9.5 million in today's dollars. Amazing! The Giant Brain took 5,000 times more electricity than a laptop does today, and its memory was about 500,000 times smaller. Our laptops today run at speeds 4,000,000 times faster than The Giant Brain. Not surprisingly, the monster was 30 tons heavier.

But all of this pales in significance when we discover what the human brain can do.

Weighing in at about three pounds, this seemingly simple mass of gray tissue has a total of 100 billion brain cells. Each of those cells communicates electrically with at least 1,000 similar cells, firing about 200 times per second. A little number crunching tells us that 100 billion cells passing information to 1,000 other cells at 200 times per second tells us that the human brain processes around 20 million billion calculations per second.

Even more amazing than its capacity to calculate, is the brain's ability to choose who it's going to serve. Will your brain choose the enemy, who wants desperately to destroy you, or the God who created you and can't help but smile when He thinks about you?

First Teddy Bear in the United States

Then God said, "Let Us make man in Our image, according to Our likeness." Genesis 1:26, NKJV.

On this day in history, a toy store owner and inventor named Morris Michtom put two stuffed bears in his shop window, calling them "Teddy" bears. Michtom had received permission from President Theodore Roosevelt to use his nickname, "Teddy." The president went along with the gimmick and, before long, other toy companies began making the stuffed bears. Not surprisingly, the little bears soon became the favorite of children everywhere. The year was 1903.

In spite of the image a cute little bear brings to the average American mind, we should remember that President Roosevelt was a sportsman and a hunter. It was one of his favorite pastimes, causing him to take several safari expeditions into the interior of Africa to hunt wildlife. Wholesale slaughter of wildlife was not uncommon during his hunting trips. On one particular trip his hunting party killed more than 6,000 animals for sport and trophies.

However, it was another incident on one of his hunting trips in the United States that seems to have brought on the inspiration for making the little, stuffed toy bears. The story goes that Roosevelt was hunting in Mississippi in 1902, when he discovered his hunting guides had tied an old, injured black bear to a tree. While some reports claim Roosevelt shot the bear out of pity for its suffering, others insist he set the bear free. Political cartoonists later portrayed that under Roosevelt's tough, outdoorsy, macho image lay a much softer, more sensitive man.

You were made in the image of Someone, too, but it wasn't the image of a man who loved to kill. You were made in the image of a Man who was killed for love. God is love, and God is three Persons because by definition, love has to be shared. This three-in-one God has been basking in the joy of unselfish love from eternity past, each Member trying to outdo the others with acts of love. They made you in Their own image, meaning you were created for the same experience. You are not merely a trophy for Their mantel, but a carefully-crafted teddy bear for Them to love. And as you truly see the love that pounds in Their heart for you, you will want to share that love with all the other teddy bears in the toy shop.

First College for the Deaf in the United States

People were overwhelmed with amazement. "He has done everything well," they said. "He even makes the deaf hear."
Mark 7:37, NIV.

Can you imagine not being able to hear? When you turn on the TV, you see only a changing picture. When you walk toward a busy intersection, you hear no honking car horns, no roar of an accelerating motorcycle, no bass pumping in the lowered vehicle beside you. Not being able to hear your teachers or your friends, you'd still have to go to school. Today in 1857, over 150 years ago, the very first college for the deaf in the United States was inaugurated in Washington, D.C., and they called it the National Deaf Mute College. Currently, the United States offers at least 100 such schools for the deaf, with special libraries and a variety of other services to help them communicate.

Some people are born with the factors causing deafness. Others lose their hearing due to accidents, illness, or old age. Much is being done today to help deaf people hear again. Surgery is an option in many cases, and complete or at least partial restoration is sometimes possible with an inner ear implant. Efforts are being made to research the area of nerve regeneration to help people's hearing be completely restored. And of course, there's always the routine hearing aid—the ones being made now are hardly noticeable.

It's pretty amazing what we can do nowadays to communicate with the hearing impaired. Television offers closed-captioning for the deaf—transcripts of what is said onscreen, and sports events and concerts will often offer the service, too. But the development of numerous forms of sign language has been perhaps the greatest asset to people with hearing impairment. Just about every country has a form of sign language that hearing impaired people can use. Africa has at least 25 different ones. American Sign Language is the most popular form of sign language used in the United States today. Sign language not only helps the hearing impaired to communicate in daily life, but also is a beautifully expressive form of communication that can unite word and body in praise to God in worship services.

When Jesus was on earth he healed deaf people in a miraculous display of divine power. When He returns to our planet, He will open the ears of all those who now hear only silence.

First Submarine
Used in War

As for man, his days are like grass, he flourishes like
a flower of the field; the wind blows over it and
it is gone, and its place remembers it no more.
Psalm 103:15, 16, NIV.

The Civil War had been raging for four years. Both the North and the South were looking for decisive victories by land or sea, and success finally came for the North in a most unusual way. The first submarine attack on an enemy ship in history happened in the dead of night on February 17, 1864, and not until World War I—half a century later—would it be repeated. This attack was made by a submarine dubbed the *Hunley*, commanded by an officer named Lieutenant Dixon. The craft was tiny compared with typical submarines in use today—only four feet wide, five feet high, and 40 feet long. With no means of propulsion except its hand-operated propeller requiring the efforts of eight men, its maximum speed was only four knots (not quite five miles per hour). Amazingly, no provision was made for storage of air on board.

The fateful attack was made against a ship called the *U.S.S. Housatonic* where it rested just off the shore of Charleston, South Carolina. The *Hunley* managed to sink the confederate enemy ship by exploding a torpedo under its hull, killing 32 men in the process. Quite unexpectedly, the submarine also sank because of the open forward hatch. The explosion swamped the little sub, filling it with water and drowning the entire crew. For over 130 years, no one knew what had happened to the *Hunley*. Searchers swept the Charleston harbor for decades until they finally bumped into its long, narrow body in 1995.

War is a tragedy that has been around for a very long time. Like the men on the *Hunley* and the *U.S.S. Housatonic*, as well as the men and women on the horses, chariots, battering rams, submarines, fighter jets, and aircraft carriers in every war of history, people are sacrificed at an outrageous cost, their lives seeming to fade away like common, withering grass and flowers. But the flag-draped coffins are not the end for those who have chosen to live for God. This temporary, war-filled life is not all there is, but is merely a training ground where we find good and evil, happiness and pain, meaning and chance. Whatever may happen to us on this earth, we can smile, knowing that there is another, much better life to come. What an encouragement to know that the best is just around the corner!

February 18

Know-nothing Party

For we were born only yesterday and know nothing,
and our days on earth are but a shadow.
Job 8:9, NIV.

The Know-nothing Party. Can you imagine a political party with a name like that? On February 18, 1856, the Know-nothing Party nominated its first candidate for president of the United States—Millard Fillmore. Not surprisingly, Mr. Fillmore received only eight votes in the election of 1856. What could we expect from a political party with such a name?

Every political organization has a purpose, a reason for existing. Some join political parties, such as the Republican Party or the Democratic Party, to secure leadership positions in the government. Others are more interested in specific issues that are important to them, and join organizations such as Green Peace or Save the Whales. Sometimes people don't know a lot about the organization who made the banner they're holding; they just move with the crowd because it's exciting or because it seems like the best thing to do at the time. Others may join a popular organization, not to support that organization, but to use its influence to promote another agenda. It is a unique privilege to be active politically, and those who have the option to vote have an unparalleled opportunity to change the world for the better, whatever organization's banner they hold. Voting rights should be taken seriously. Even the Know-nothings have the right to speak their minds.

To make the most of the opportunity to change our world for the better, we should know more about the crowd we belong to than the name Know-nothing Party implies. But in this complicated and confusing world, sometimes we have to admit that we actually know very little. Like Job we say, "We were born only yesterday and know nothing, and our days on earth are but a shadow." Sometimes greatness is admitting that there is much we don't know. Confessing that we don't know much opens the door for us to express our trust in God, who truly does know everything. When we come clean about our lack of knowledge, like Job, we can then stand in awe at God's eternal knowledge. Even if we know very little about anything, we can know that He loves us more than anything. He has given us ample evidence of His love for us, and marching under His banner of love is better than joining any political organization in the world!

Phonograph Invented

But you, Daniel, close up and seal the words of the scroll until the time of the end. Many will go here and there to increase knowledge. Daniel 12:4, NIV.

On February 19, 1878, Thomas Edison took out a patent for a new invention called the "speaking machine." Maybe you've seen this machine in old movies or heard the scratchy sound of this primitive music player. "Phonograph" is the most recent name for the contraption, and although it caused quite a stir in the late 19th century, its popularity has become as faint as the sound it makes.

The first phonograph was made of a cylinder wrapped in tinfoil, was operated by a hand crank, and actually used two needles to make sound. Can you guess what the first song was that made people's eyes widen at the emanating melody? It was "Mary Had a Little Lamb." It wasn't until 10 years later that record albums were made, but, nothing like the record albums that lined your parents' shelves in the 1960s and 70s, they were made out of wax, not vinyl or plastic.

Since that time newer and better kinds of machines have been invented to do the same thing the phonograph was invented to do: play music. After the phonograph came reel-to-reel machines—you know, the monsters resembling movie projectors. Then came eight-track players, followed by cassette players. The Walkman was quite the rage when it appeared on store shelves in the mid-80s. Today we use CD players, MP3 players, iPods, laptops, and even cell phones to play music. And if you wait a year or two, they'll have something else ready for you to buy.

Knowledge is increasing at dramatic rates, and our ability to do even more amazing things will only increase as Jesus' coming approaches. Scientists are now telling us that the total volume of knowledge doubles every four years. Wow! Who knows what kinds of things we'll be inventing next? And yet, how much do we really know? We have lots of gadgets, and some of us know a lot about how they work and what they can do, but if we spend all of our time running here and there trying to get the latest gadget, will we ever really be satisfied? After we buy the latest technology and the electronics store cashier hands us our receipt, can we then breathe a sigh of relief and say, "Finally—I'm content?" Let's enjoy our increases in technology but be sure to make Jesus the focus of our lives. Besides, our latest technology is but a "speaking machine" to Him.

Airplane Car

We will all be transformed! It will happen in a moment, in the blink of an eye. . . . Our mortal bodies must be transformed into immortal bodies.
1 Corinthians 15:51-53, NLT.

How well do you multitask? Can you play basketball and eat cake at the same time? Can you take a math exam while you're sleeping? Can you drive a car one minute and fly it the next? On February 20, 1937, the Arrowbile, designed to be half plane and half car, rolled out of the shop of Waldo Waterman, ready for testing. Waldo was an airplane engineer in Santa Monica, California, with a flair for creative design. He figured most people couldn't afford both an airplane and a car, and since cars were becoming more and more of a necessity, why not build a car that could fly? What he came up with was the Arrowbile, a small car-plane with wings that could be removed in just a few minutes. The Arrowbile was made with standard car parts. It had a normal Studebaker engine to power the wheels in car mode, and a propeller in flight mode. The average car didn't move very fast in those days, but the Arrowbile could travel at speeds up to 120 miles per hour on land or in the air. Can you imagine that! A car that can drive along the road and then take off into flight! That's kind of like the aqua car that was built to go by land or sea. And there are planes that can fly or glide on water using pontoons. And, of course, the movies show us cars that can go underwater like submarines. No doubt, someplace, somewhere there's a plane being designed that can work like a sub.

When Jesus comes we'll be given all kinds of capabilities. On resurrection morning we'll be equipped to multitask and do all kinds of things we can't do now, like fly over shimmering lakes and leap over lofty mountains in a single bound. Those are just two possibilities, but the Bible says we can't even imagine the list of things we'll be able to do. When that day comes, God will truly change us physically and spiritually. The bodies we have now, riddled with disease and limited in strength, will be changed to supernatural, glorious machines—the way God originally intended. And, unlike Waldo Waterman and his Arrowbile, it won't take Him months to plan, design, build, and test us, scratching His head and puzzling over how to overcome snags in the blueprints. He'll complete the project in less than a second—in the blink of an eye. That's the wisdom and power of our God!

Phone Directory

Look, I've written your names on the backs of my hands.
Isaiah 49:16, Message.

Hardly anyone uses phone books anymore. Most people use their cell phones or computers to get addresses and phone numbers, but it wasn't always that way. On February 21, 1878, the very first telephone book was compiled and published in New Haven, Connecticut. It had a whopping 50 names in its directory.

Some telephone directories today are four to six inches thick, with separate government pages, white pages, yellow pages, etc. Large cities like Chicago, New York City, and Los Angeles have lots of phone books. They need books for the north side of town, the metropolitan area, and all the suburbs. Libraries used to have stacks of directories from all the important cities in America, but those books will probably just collect dust from now on. Very soon it's just not going to be feasible to print on paper anymore, when the internet is so much faster. Today telephone numbers can be accessed online or digitally through direct telephone satellite connections.

God has said, "Don't be afraid, I've redeemed you. I've called your name. You're mine." On a planet with billions of people, it's easy to feel left out, unimportant, lost. During these times, it is a refreshing relief to hear someone call your name. Anyone who has seen a child who has lost her mother in a large department store standing there frozen with fear and crying her lungs out knows the truth that when her mother calls her name and scoops her up in her arms, the crying stops. And it is comforting to realize that God knows us all by name. David assures us that God knew us before we were even born—before we were conceived, for that matter. Even if you're a twin or triplet, He can spot you from across the galaxy, and He will never call you "so-and-so's sister" or "what's his name's son." He has known you and everything that makes you smile, makes you angry, makes you scared—all the details of your life since before He started this planet spinning on its axis. How can you be sure of that? Because He made you. Let's be reasonable. If He can create all the billions of galaxies, with their hundreds of millions of solar systems, and every planet in space, then it is quite reasonable that He can remember the names of a few billion people on earth. Absolutely, positively, without a shadow of a doubt—yes. And you can bet that He doesn't need a dusty old telephone directory to do it.

Five-cent Store

If you had faith even as small as a mustard seed,
. . . nothing would be impossible.
Matthew 17:20, NLT.

One of the first wildly successful chain stores in America was the five-cent store. What on earth is a five-cent store, you ask? First seen in the late 1800s, a five-cent store was a new idea for a store where everything was on sale for just five cents—similar to dollar stores of today. Now, it may seem surprising to you that anything could be bought for five cents, except maybe candy. But you've got to remember that in those days five cents could buy all kinds of things. It could buy chocolate, children's toys, or even food staples. Four cents in those days would be about $1.00 today.

On February 22, 1879, Frank Woolworth opened his first five-cent store in Utica, New York. Unfortunately, Mr. Woolworth's idea didn't work out too well that first year. The store was a great disappointment. After the first few weeks, sales were as low as $2.50 a day. Woolworth finally moved his store to Lancaster, Pennsylvania, where it proved to be a real success.

Now maybe you've never even heard of Woolworth's. It was the forerunner of all the successful stores that got their start on street corners of local towns. Walgreens is a good example, or maybe CVS Pharmacies. Mr. Woolworth went on to set up a whole chain of stores known as Woolworth's, much like today's Walmart.

Mr. Woolworth started very small and things were very shaky for awhile. As day after day dragged by with that little bell on the door hanging silent for hours, maybe his friends finally advised him to start packing it up. Maybe his family tried to encourage him to get into another line of business. Maybe he went home discouraged every evening, wondering if it was worth the effort. But thoughts of success encouraged him to keep his faith in the idea, and finally, his once-faltering business grew into a mammoth, successful enterprise, eventually bringing him staggering amounts of money. Today, Jesus invites you to put your faith in Him. Maybe you feel like you don't have much faith and the faith you have is very shaky. But remember His promise that even a tiny bit no larger than a mustard seed, one of the world's smallest seeds, is big enough for Him to transform into a large, successful enterprise. Don't give up!

Animal Rights

For God will bring every deed into judgment, including
every hidden thing, whether it is good or evil.
Ecclesiastes 12:14, NIV.

On February 23, 1883, the American Anti-Vivisection Society was organized by Caroline White in Philadelphia, Pennsylvania. The AAVC? you
say. What's that? It's an organization something like the SPCA (Society for
the Prevention of Cruelty to Animals). The AAVC is the oldest non-profit animal advocacy organization in the United States, and its members are interested in stopping experimental research where live animals are cut open or
operated on without proper anesthetic. Today the organization also cam-
paigns against research labs that experiment on animals for the purpose of
manufacturing cosmetics, hair products, cleaners, and drugs of many kinds.

Caroline was very active in the organization and her husband, who was
a lawyer, helped her get government support for her programs. She also
worked very hard against captive bird shoots. A bird shoot is a sport in which
birds, such as pigeons, are released at shooting tournaments so the sports-
men can shoot them for target practice. Caroline worked to create animal
shelters for homeless dogs and cats, too, and worked to improve the conditions under which cattle were transported from place to place. In those days,
animals on the way to markets had to travel in open cattle cars or trucks,
even in bitterly cold weather. They were often crammed into dirty pens for
days at a time, in spaces much too small for normal comfort.

Having to kill an animal for one reason or another is one thing, but being
cruel to that animal and unnecessarily killing it or making it miserable is quite
another. Killing and producing misery are foreign concepts to God. In Old
Testament days, in harmony with the culture of the day, He did take credit
for sometimes killing groups of people, but that was because those groups
were threatening the very existence of His special people, the people He
promised to protect and prosper. He created animals to be a blessing to the
humans who would have dominion over them, and in the faces and behavior
of animals we see the wisdom and provision of a loving God. We see His
grace and agility in the flight of the bald eagle, His faithfulness in the family
dog, and His humor in the antics of tree monkeys. We can see a little bit of
God in every animal.

President Impeached

*So any person who knows what is right to do
but does not do it, to him it is sin.
James 4:17, Amplified.*

On February 4, the United States House of Representatives voted to impeach the President of the United States. In what year? 1868. Which president? Andrew Johnson. Why? Because he fired one of his cabinet officers, Edwin Stanton, Secretary of War. Evidently Stanton was a very popular man. Other charges brought against him included illegal use of federal law, corrupt use of his veto power, and interfering with government elections. The Senate then held its impeachment trial on the Senate floor with 54 senators serving as jurors. When the vote was tallied, it was 35 to 19 against President Johnson. However, the Senate needed a two-thirds vote to impeach him—this was one vote shy of the number required. And so, the first and only effort to impeach a president failed. Over 100 years later, President Richard Nixon came very close to being impeached because of the Watergate scandal, but he resigned.

The United States has a very good system of checks and balances built into its Constitution: Congress, the Supreme Court, and the President. Not everyone always likes what is going on at the top levels of our government, and although there is probably a good deal of corruption in every branch, we can still say that the United States of America has the best form of government in the world today.

Now, whether President Johnson was really guilty of all the things of which he was accused, we'll probably never know. But one thing's for sure. When you enter the world of politics, people will throw tomatoes at you if they think you are guilty—facts or no facts. To be successful, you have to get used to it, but more importantly, you should follow James' advice when he says, "any person who knows what is right to do but doesn't do it, to him it is sin."

Daniel was an excellent example of a politician who always did what was right. He had godly parents who taught him how to be faithful to God, a top-notch education, and plenty of real-time experience working in the top echelon of a world superpower. But the real secret of his success, as we see over and over in the pages of the Bible book dedicated to him, was that he made God relevant in his daily life. He clamped onto God's promises and direction and held on tight—even when he came eye-to-eye with those hungry lions. He did what was right. Always.

Temporary Insanity

Control your temper, for anger labels you a fool.
Ecclesiastes 7:9, NLT.

Have you heard of defendants in court basing their defense on grounds of insanity? It's done fairly frequently. Daniel Sickles, a congressman from New York, was the first accused person in United States history to cite insanity as his defense in a criminal case. That was on February 25, 1859. In a jealous rage over an issue concerning his wife, Daniel had shot and killed a man named Philip Key. (Interestingly, the man he shot was the son of Francis Scott Key, the author of The Star Spangled Banner.) Based on the circumstances, the defense lawyer on the case decided to use the plea of "temporary insanity," or, "not guilty by reason of insanity." Quite surprisingly, Mr. Sickles was acquitted, paving the way for similar acquittals in the future.

Hundreds of defendants have used the insanity plea since that time, but it was used most effectively during the 1940s and 1950s. About one percent of all cases tried use the insanity defense, and in 90 percent of the successful cases, the one pleading insanity was considered mentally ill. Many states, including Idaho and Utah, now prohibit this defense.

The question is, can a woman really lose all control of herself as the plea of insanity suggests? Can a man really go temporarily insane when he experiences a serious trauma or tragedy in his life? Many psychologists nod their heads in agreement, but how do we know who is truly insane and who is not, even if it is temporary? That is the million dollar question, isn't it? One thing is sure: if we are foolish enough to allow ourselves to become angry to the point of losing all control, we risk important things in our lives. We risk not only being locked up for a long time, but also our careers and our futures.

Life can throw all kinds of junk at us. People can mistreat us and accuse us of things we didn't do. They can steal from us or even cause us physical harm. The important thing lies not in what happens to us, but how we handle it. Consider Jesus, who was beaten, spit upon, and nailed to a cross in repayment for spending His life encouraging, healing, and giving life. If we spend time consistently and sincerely studying how God handled the injustices thrown at Him, we will gain the insight and capacity to respond similarly—successfully. And a plea for God's help beats a plea of insanity any day.

Trade Center Bombed

Anyone who hates his brother is a murderer, and you know that no murderer has eternal life in him. 1 John 3:15, NIV.

At 12:18 p.m. on February 26, 1993, a bomb exploded in the New York City World Trade Center, creating a blast crater 200 feet wide, killing six people, and injuring several hundred. Fifty-thousand people were safely evacuated in a rescue operation costing millions of dollars through the disruption of the city's business and transportation systems. It was a desperately fearful time for everyone trapped in the towers. Some had to flee down as many as 110 stories to escape the building. Many learned lessons that would save their lives eight years later when the towers would be attacked again, this time killing many times more people. An all-out manhunt was spearheaded by the FBI which eventually led to the capture of Omar Abdel Rahman in July of that same year. The radical Middle Eastern Islamic leader was found just outside a mosque in Brooklyn, New York City.

This desperately hateful crime was not the product of a moment of hate. For two months prior to the bombing, the terrorists, motivated by the hate destroying their hearts, worked persistently to gather the materials and assemble them for the maximum possible effect. They lived in New Jersey and rented storage space where they could work on the bomb before loading it into a Ryder rental van. Driving the 1,500-pound urea-nitrate bomb into the basement parking area of the World Trade Center, they set the timer, and fled. When it detonated, the explosion rocked the World Trade Center, bringing the dark dawn of a new age in terrorism.

John reminds us that those who love to hate, who allow that dark emotion to fester in our hearts, have no chance of eternal life. Hate always leads down the road of eternal death. Some who have allowed the black flower of hate to blossom into destruction have felt that they were forced down that road. It is simply not true. As humans we have complete freedom to choose between hate and love, between death and life. We may think that we would never detonate a bomb that would take lives, but if we choose to buy the materials, rent the truck, and spend our days assembling the components, we are abiding hate in our hearts. And it is the hate that will keep us from eternal life. Why not ask God right now to fill you so full of His love that there will be no room for hate in your heart?

Sugar Substitute

The law of the Lord is perfect, converting the soul . . . More to be desired are they than gold, yea, than much fine gold: sweeter also than honey and the honeycomb. Psalm 19:7-10.

Today we have all kinds of substitute sugar sweeteners like Sweet & Low, Sucrose, and Aspartame. Saccharin predated them all by at least 100 years. On this day in 1879, saccharin was invented. Now that's a very surprising fact! When we think about sugar substitutes, we don't usually think of them as having been discovered 130 years ago. After all, in the 1800s plain old sugar was just beginning to build up a head of steam itself as a sweetener in North American food companies, and on dinner tables everywhere.

Saccharin was discovered by Constantine Fahlberg at Johns Hopkins University in Baltimore, Maryland. He referred to it as toluenesulphochloride. (Say that five times fast!) Saccharin is a sweetening chemical that has some very interesting properties. It's 550 times sweeter than table sugar, has no calories, but is not able to be absorbed by the human body. It does not tend to promote dental cavities, has a rather long shelf life, but has a slightly bitter aftertaste. In the 1970s, laboratory studies suggested that saccharin could cause stomach cancer in rats. However, these findings were later reversed when it was discovered that the rats had dined on crazy amounts of the saccharin. Despite its attractive quality of having zero calories, even saccharin can cause health problems.

Our bodies are the temple of God and we need to keep them healthy for Him. David said that God's laws are perfect and designed to make us wise. His laws are not only the ten commandments but also include His health laws. God presented these health laws to us in the Garden of Eden with Adam and Eve, shared them in the wilderness with the children of Israel, and elaborated on them in great detail through the ministry of Ellen White. God did not arbitrarily make up these laws to rob our taste buds of temporary pleasure or to give us a guilt trip for not eating right. They are His gifts. He wants us to experience the lasting pleasure that comes from keeping our bodies in top condition. We will find that as we commit to eating healthy, natural foods, our taste buds will begin to like the change! His laws are more valuable than fine gold and even sweeter than honey. Why not help yourself to some today?

DNA Mapping

God saw all that he had made, and it was very good.
Genesis 1:31, NIV.

Today in 1953, scientists at Cambridge University announced that they had determined the shape and design of the human DNA molecule. The two scientists who made the discovery were James Watson and Frances Crick. Over 80 years before, in 1869, scientists had described it as deoxyribonucleic acid, or DNA, for short. However, it wasn't until 1953 that it was decided the DNA molecule was a double-helix, made up of chains of protein molecules strung together in the shape of a double spiral.

Now in case you missed something, here's what we're talking about. For the first time, scientists were thinking that they could possibly create life. In their minds, man would now be able to put together the basic building blocks of biology. A leaf, a worm, a human finger would not be beyond the realm of possibility now. Or so they thought.

When Watson went home that night, he stopped to have dinner with his friends and exclaimed, "We have found the secret of life." The truth wasn't that far off, actually. Now they understood better how genetic traits of hair color, eye color, and intelligence could be passed on from generation to generation. This concept changed the way scientists look at genetics completely. Now they realized that by looking inside DNA, they could tell if a baby was likely to have a genetic disease. They could now alter the way foods grow, help identify criminals, and find cures for diseases like AIDS.

But did any dangers come with this discovery? Only God can truly understand how DNA works, and if we tinker with it, not fully comprehending what we are doing, we may create bigger problems than we already have. The delicate balance within the human body depends on many things—hormones, energy levels, immunity to disease . . . the list goes on and on.

We are not God, and we need to remember that. Only God can create life. Even if man could learn to put all the pieces of a human body together, molecule by molecule, cell by cell, tissue by tissue, and organ by organ, how would we make them all work in harmony? Even more importantly, how would we give them the spark of life? Genetics is an amazing field, but knowing the Creator of the genetic DNA code is even more exciting. He's our all-compassionate God, our all-faithful Friend, and our all-wise Maker.

Yellowstone National Park

Then the Lord God took the man and put him
in the garden of Eden to tend and keep it.
Genesis 2:15, NKJV.

Have you ever been to Yellowstone National Park? Although the park has come to be known as one of America's favorite camping spots, in the early days it wasn't a very safe place to take your family. There were no ranger stations, fire towers, or constructed campsites, and poachers roamed the park freely.

On March 1, 1872, President Ulysses Grant set aside over 2,000,000 acres of land in Wyoming to be used as a national park for public use. But the park had a long way to go before it would be ready for the average camper. In the 1880s the army was sent in to run the poachers out so the park would be safe for animals and tourists alike. And then laws were passed that protected many of the animals, including the North American bison population that was nearing extinction. Tourism has always been a big part of Yellowstone National Park. By the early 1900s trains were taking visitors there by the carloads. Today it is estimated that on average, over 2,000,000 people visit the park each year. And the numbers of animals in the park have multiplied too, making the park one of the most popular places to visit for family vacations. Bison, elk, cougars, pronghorn antelope, wolves, black bears, and grizzly bears are just some of the wildlife you can see at the park. Unfortunately, down through the years the park has had trouble in the way it practices conservation and fire prevention. In 1988 a series of forest fires overran the park, burning over 1.4 million acres of forest and grasslands. Today the park rangers and administration run a more balanced program of forest conservation.

It tells us a lot about our God and how He feels about us that He didn't create a vast planet of only dirt. Or only rocks. Or only grass. He sculpted majestic mountain peaks, spread out meadows clothed with wildflowers, carved out places where sparkling water could tumble over cliffs, filled this varied landscape with all kinds of colorful birds and animals, and then handed it all to us to enjoy and explore with Him through places like the Garden of Eden and Yellowstone National Park. What a pleasure to thank Him for His beautiful creation by taking care of these glimpses of paradise!

Message to the Stars

By faith we understand that the universe was formed at God's command.
Hebrews 11:3, NIV.

On this day in 1972, a spacecraft was sent to outer space carrying a message intended to be read by living beings elsewhere in the universe. Pioneer 10 was the name of the planetary probe launched from Cape Canaveral, Florida, by NASA. Bolted to the outside of the spaceship was a gold plate, six by nine inches, that included several illustrations, including a human man and woman, a star map marked with the location of our sun, and a second map that showed the flight path of Pioneer 10. The message was designed by an astronomer named Carl Sagan.

Carl Sagan was a staunch atheist and believer in the theory of evolution. Someday, somewhere out there, he and other astronomers hoped they would find intelligent life. "Are we an exceptionally unlikely accident or is the universe brimming over with intelligence?" he used to say. "The significance of a finding that there are other beings who share this universe with us would be absolutely phenomenal. It would be an incredible event in human history." All his life Mr. Sagan lived with that dream, but when he finally died in 1996, mankind had still not made contact with alien life from other planets. Disappointed, he went to his grave, sadly misinformed about the theory of evolution and the real source of life.

By faith we understand that the universe sprang from the creative finger of God. And He created not only our planet and everything in it, but also other planets near and far, constellations, galaxies, and complex patterns of movement that man is still trying to understand. How sad it is to think that some believe that it all just appeared one day, that it sprang arbitrarily from the lifeless finger of chance. Believing that is like believing that when you toss a paper bag jingling with loose watch parts up into the air, that it will come down with a ticking watch inside! God's colorful creative ability is presented plainly and simply on the black-and-white pages of His Word. Unfortunately, that fact was too simple for Mr. Sagan and his fellow astronomers to believe—or too complex. They missed out on the delightful experience of trusting a God who can create a planet out of nothing. The astronomers sent Pioneer 10 to get information about intelligent life somewhere, and all the time God's Word was sitting right there, just waiting to tell them that He has a whole universe of intelligent life to see and visit when Jesus comes again.

Kids at Work

Jesus said, "Let the little children come to me, and do not hinder them, for the kingdom of heaven belongs to such as these."
Matthew 19:14, NIV.

Have you ever had to work when you would have rather played? Did you ever say to your parents, I wish there was a law that says children shouldn't be allowed to work? Well, get this! On this day in 1842 the first recorded child labor law was passed by Massachusetts Governor John Davis. In this new law the state said that children under 12 years of age were prohibited from working more than 10 hours a day. Ten hours? Wow! Now, that's a lot of time for children to have to work! And you think you have it bad?

The use of child labor in factories and mines was a common thing in those days. The children sometimes had to work as many as 12 to 18 hours, six days a week, to earn as little as a dollar. Some were as young as seven, hauling heavy loads, tending machines in spinning mills, or shoveling coal. The factories were often damp, dark, and dirty. Sickness was a big problem, and the number of children who went blind or died was high. By 1810, about 2,000,000 school-age children were working from 50 to 70 hours per week. There was little time for play or school, and poor folks sometimes gave their kids up to a mill or factory owner. One glass factory in Massachusetts was surrounded by a barbwire fence to "keep the young imps inside." Those "young imps" had to work all night carrying loads of hot glass for as little as 40 cents per shift. But labor groups, teachers, and church members were outraged by such cruelty and began to push for new laws. By 1900, 28 states had passed laws against child labor, and today every state has laws regulating it.

Jesus showed us how we should treat children. He held out His arms for the young ones and they scampered onto His lap, begging for another story. He answered questions from the older ones and amazed them with cool facts about the universe. When His disciples tried to send a group of children away, He strongly rebuked them and motioned for the kids to gather around Him anyway. Jesus made it obvious that He values children just as much as adults, and He gave dire warnings to anyone who mistreats them. Don't ever let someone look down on you or mistreat you because of your age. According to Jesus, Heaven was made for you just as much as it was made for adults.

Transcontinental Footrace

Let us lay aside every weight, and the sin which so easily ensnares us, and let us run with endurance the race that is set before us.
Hebrews 12:1, NKJV.

Do you like to run? Do you like watching other people run marathons? One of the first transcontinental footraces to be recorded in the United States began on March 4, 1928. It was a coast-to-coast contest that stretched from Los Angeles, California, to Madison Square Garden in New York City. A group of 275 runners began the race, but only 55 finished it. The route led the runners beside rivers and over mountains, through deserts and forests, was 3,422 miles long, and lasted 84 days. First prize went to a Cherokee Indian from Oklahoma by the name of Andrew Payne. He completed the race in just over 573 hours, and collected a $25,000 prize. That's a lot of money today, let alone in 1928. Today that same amount of money would be worth about half a million dollars!

Wow! A race that stretched all the way across the United States! If you were to run a race like that, you would have to run an average of almost seven hours each day. I'd like to think I could run in such a race, but I'd probably never make it.

There is another race we all can run. It's a race that requires endurance. And before we begin the race we must be willing to lay aside everything that would slow us down. The race I'm talking about is our race to Heaven. We don't have to get there before everyone else—we just need to get there. Everyone can come in a winner, but it is a race against time. Satan knows there's not much time left, and he wants as many of us as possible to get fatigued, discouraged, and distracted, and to drop out of the race. He will carry out whatever nefarious scheme he can think up—trip us, lead us off the race route, whisper temptations to quit in our ears. Jesus, on the other hand, wants us all to win the race. He stands with us at the starting line, at each rest station, as well as at the end. Most of all, if you sincerely look for Him, you'll see Him running with you. You'll hear Him whispering encouragement in your ear, and you'll also see Him up ahead, motioning for you to follow in His steps. He desperately wants you to cross that finish line. The prize that awaits you is an everlasting, face-to-face friendship with Him who would never think of leaving you to run alone.

Away in a Manger

Give to Caesar what is Caesar's, and to God what is God's.
Matthew 22:21, NIV.

For many, Christmas is the best time of the year, with its twinkling lights around snow-covered windows, decorated storefronts, and a noticeably more congenial attitude between strangers. For Christians, the most meaningful aspect of Christmas is the celebration we share about the coming of Jesus to earth as a baby. Though we now know Jesus was probably not born on December 25, many still consider Him the reason for the season. However, not all Americans see it that way, which brings us to today's story.

On March 5, 1984, the United States Supreme Court ruled that a city or town may use a manger scene as part of a Christmas display. Come again? The Supreme Court, the highest court in the land, needs to tell American citizens that? For centuries now we've been putting up manger scenes to illustrate the story of the baby Jesus in Bethlehem, and the coming of the shepherds and wise men on Christmas Eve. Why would a court feel it needed to make a ruling about such a thing? That's a good question.

Some people in this free nation do not believe in Jesus or His incarnation to this world. They are uncomfortable with anything that reminds them that God exists and that He loves them enough to be born among them. And so they try to pass laws that keep God out of public places. If putting up a manger scene were against the law of the land, because the majority of us didn't want it, then we would just have to obey the law and go on with our lives. If our "Caesars" today could wield that kind of power, we would have to learn to live with it. As Jesus said, "Give to Caesar the things that are Caesar's and to God the things that are God's." But this manger thing is not Caesar's thing at all. It's a personal thing. Someone somewhere feels more comfortable if we don't set out a traditional display of the manger scene in a public place. We should all be for freedom of speech, but the rights of the many should rarely, if ever, be controlled by the wishes of the few.

God uses government to maintain order and stability in our public lives and to regulate our relation to others in society, and the Bible is clear that we should obey our government officials. But when they come up with laws that directly contradict biblical principles, we should always obey God rather than man.

March 6

Remember the Alamo!

Fight the good fight of the faith. Take hold of the eternal life to which you were called. 1 Timothy 6:12, NIV.

You've no doubt heard the famous line, Remember the Alamo! It has a nice ring to it, doesn't it? Well, as stories go, it doesn't have a very happy ending, but when you're fighting for a cause, sometimes the end result is more important than the actual event. Here's the story.

On March 6, 1836, a ruthless Mexican dictator named General Santa Anna attacked the Alamo, a small fort in San Antonio, Texas. As the general and his army of 3,000 soldiers stormed the fortress, a small band of 188 Texans fought bravely to defend it, desperately wanting to help the Texas territory gain its independence from Mexico. For 13 days the Texans managed to keep Santa Anna out of Fort Alamo, which had once been a Catholic mission. However, in the dead of night on March 6, the superior Mexican army finally scaled the walls and broke through its gates. All of the Alamo's defenders were either killed during the fight or executed when the battle was over. Some of the famous men who died while defending the Alamo included Colonel James Bowie, famous for a knife he designed, and Davy Crocket, a well-known frontiersman and congressman. However, just a few days later General Sam Houston led another army of Texans to defeat General Santa Anna. As you can imagine, General Houston's battle cry was "Remember the Alamo!"

Through the years of this planet's tattered history, Satan has waged war against God's people. The battle crescendoed to a deafening pitch on a small hill called Calvary. There, the enemy finally scaled the walls and appeared to have won the ultimate victory as the Son of God, covered with blood and nailed to a cross, bowed His head and died. Did the enemy general have the last say? No! A short time later, God's Son rose from the dead, soundly defeating Satan and his forces. Someday, some of us may have to give up our plans, our reputations, or even our lives for Jesus because we choose to stand and fight with Him. But we fight a battle that has already been won by our brave Hero. He fights with us, and in the end He will place a crown of victory on our heads. Good will win out. Today, with God's people everywhere, let's shout the victory cry, Remember Calvary!

Bell's Telephone Patented

Hear, you deaf; And look, you blind, that you may see. Isaiah 42:18.

Today in 1876, at the young age of 29, Alexander Graham Bell received a patent for his new invention called the telephone. That's a pretty young age to have come up with one of the most revolutionary inventions in the last 200 years! Did you know that Bell's interest in the phone was greatly influenced by the fact that his own wife was deaf, and he wanted to develop the technology that might help her hear? Bell worked as a teacher of speech for deaf students at the Pemberton Avenue School for the Deaf. Bell considered the telephone a cross between a telegraph and a record player because it allowed individuals to speak to each other at the same time from a distance. The very first words spoken over a telephone weren't very inspiring. Only a simple, "Mr. Watson, come here, I need you."

Bell Telephone went on to become part of American Telephone and Telegraph (AT&T), and the telephone continues to revolutionize the world of communications. Cell phones have all but taken over our social lives and even the workplace. It's become common to see people sitting in a restaurant together at a table, but carrying on completely separate conversations with the people on the other ends of their lines. And now phones can be used to do much more than just talk to people. They can be used to send text messages, check football scores, watch movies, play games, download favorite tunes, and schedule appointments. In the future they may be used to unlock our cars, set home security systems, buy and sell stocks, and control our entertainment centers.

But we still use our phones to talk more than anything else. That's why they were invented. Everything else is just a marketing gimmick to sell more phones—voice mail, text messaging, photo options, and internet. When Jesus calls us He wants us to set aside all the interference that would distract us so we can hear His still, small voice. Today, will you give Jesus' call a chance to get through? Will you set aside all the gimmicks that are distracting you from a meaningful conversation with Him? Like Alexander's wife, we are deaf—spiritually deaf, but if we don't send Jesus' call to voice mail, we *will* find a fulfilling friendship with Him.

Babe Ruth's Salary

Whatever your hand finds to do, do it with all your might.
Ecclesiastes 9:10, NIV.

When the name Babe Ruth is mentioned, you probably think of baseball (or candy bars). Widely considered the best all-around player in baseball history, he set records in almost every aspect of the game. And he broke records when it came to salary, too. On this day in 1930, Babe Ruth signed a two-year contract with the New York Yankees worth a whopping $160,000, and that was during the Great Depression, when the economy had never been worse! Babe Ruth's manager made the ridiculous prediction that no one would ever be paid more than "the Babe."

Ruth was a superstar even by today's standards. He was the first player to hit 30, 40, 50, and 60 home runs in a season, and he was the home run leader a record 12 times. His record of being walked 2,056 times in his career still hasn't been beaten. He is best known for his hitting ability, but most people don't know that he was also a legendary pitcher. While playing for the *Boston Red Sox*, he pitched 29 consecutive scoreless innings in *World Series* play, a record that stood for 42 years. He pitched 24 shutouts in 1917 with a 1.75 earned run average. His batting average in that same year was .325, making him indeed the most valuable player of that era in both hitting and pitching. No one has matched the slugging average of .847 he had in 1920, nor his career average of .690. Not surprisingly, he appeared in 10 World Series showdowns. Yankee Stadium, where he really became famous, is known as "The House that Ruth Built."

But there is one more record he set that few people know about. He was the strikeout king of his day. How can this be? Well, he either hit home runs or he struck out. Clearly, he wasn't afraid to swing! He did everything with all his might so he could be the best. In the game of life, we stand in the batter's box every day. Fastballs, breakingballs, and curveballs come streaking toward us. Our General Manager signals for us to swing for the fences with the talents He's given us every time we step to the plate. We will be tempted to take half-swings or to get discouraged when we strike out, thinking the game is lost. But if we keep swinging with all our might, we will make contact and hear our General Manager, batting coaches, and a stadium of heavenly angels cheering as the ball disappears over the fence. We may never become the king of baseball like "the Babe," but we will always be blessed for giving it our all.

Amistad Mutiny

You will know the truth, and the truth will set you free.
John 8:32, NLT.

On this day in 1841, the United States Supreme Court freed a load of slaves on a ship that had been illegally captured in Africa and diverted to Cuba. Now that's an unusual story from the pages of American history.

It all started two years earlier, aboard a slave ship called the *Amistad* that was sailing west toward a sugar plantation in the Caribbean. During the short trip from one port in Cuba to another, one of the slaves, an African named Cinque, freed himself and the other slaves from their chains, and then planned a mutiny. On July 2, during a storm at sea, the Africans rose up against their captors with sugarcane knives they found in the ship's hold. They killed the captain of the vessel and several crewmembers, and put the two Cuban slave traders on board in chains. Cinque ordered the Cubans to sail the *Amistad* east back to Africa, but at night the Cubans turned the vessel north toward U.S. waters. The boat wandered back and forth at sea for nearly two months, until a U.S. Navy ship seized the *Amistad* off the coast of Long Island and escorted it to Connecticut. The slave traders were freed, but the Africans were imprisoned as they waited for a court hearing abut the revolt. The story of the *Amistad* mutiny got a lot of publicity in the newspapers of the day. Cinque, who was taught English by his new American friends, even testified on his own behalf. Finally, the abolitionists, led by John Quincy Adams, a former president of the United States, succeeded in convincing the Supreme Court that the slaves deserved their freedom.

We've all been captured by Satan and chained to lives of sin, and sometimes it seems that the odds of graining our freedom are against us. We may desire to do right, but our human nature is weak and we are constantly reminded of the chains gripping our hands and feet. The devil not only tempts us to sin, but accuses us before the Father in heaven, claiming that we don't deserve to be free. We tremble, thinking that maybe the enemy is right, that we don't deserve freedom. But Jesus points to His own hands and feet that were chained to that blood-soaked cross. The enemy has to flee at the sight of the symbols of the freedom that Jesus has already won for us. His imprisonment and escape truly sets us free.

Hospital for Mentally Ill

The Spirit of the Lord is on me, because . . . He has sent me
to proclaim freedom for the prisoners and recovery of
sight for the blind, to release the oppressed.
Luke 4:18, NIV.

Do you have any idea what it was like to live in an insane asylum in the old days? Asylums were more like prisons than hospitals because of the way people were treated. In those days, an asylum was for the insane, or "lunatics . . . who are furiously mad" as one source puts it. But patients with all kinds of other problems ended up there, too, such as the deaf, developmentally disabled, those afflicted with Down syndrome, and even the blind. Blind people? you may exclaim. Why would they put blind people in with the insane? The answer is simple. There were very few places you could take impaired people where they would be treated like human beings.

On this day in 1830, a hospital in Worcester, Massachusetts, was established for the purpose of giving "the insane" a safe place to live. Of course, today we refer to these folks as mentally ill, or patients with one of a myriad of psychotic disorders. The state legislature provided $30,000 to build and supervise the asylum that would hold 120 patients. The main promoter of the hospital was a man named Horace Mann, also known for his work in opening many public schools. Most of the patients who filled the rooms of this hospital had previously been kept in prisons.

Laws in the United States today have greatly improved the treatment of those suffering from mental illness and other debilitating diseases, and there is a facility for each category of need. This does not change the fact that this world is still loaded with suffering people. Depression, bipolar disorder, HIV, hunger, diabetes, influenza, to merely scratch the surface, threatens to strangle our race. The enemy of humanity works overtime to keep humans mired in awful pits of physical and emotional misery. The only thing he loves more than seeing you suffer is blaming it on God. The truth is that God is never the source of suffering—no, not even to bring about a higher good. He desires only your happiness, but He must give everyone sufficient time and freedom to make his own decision of who he will follow. He can't wait for the day when He opens Heaven's Hospital and wipes all the tears from our eyes.

Nuclear Bomb Accidently Dropped

You shall not be afraid of the terror by night, . . .
nor of the destruction that lays waste at noonday.
Psalm 91:5, 6, NKJV.

How would you feel if you were sitting out in your yard one day, and suddenly a bomb dropped out of the sky and detonated in your small town? How would you feel if you suddenly realized it was a nuclear bomb? The story sounds for all the world like one of the war zones you've read about in your history book—places like Russia, North Korea, or Japan during World War II. But it's actually much closer to home.

In 1953, on March 11, an American B-47 plane accidentally dropped a nuclear bomb on South Carolina. Fortunately, the bomb didn't go off due to six safety catches that failed to release. That must have been very embarrassing for our government and the people who almost made it happen, to say nothing of it being just plain scary. Accidently dropping a nuclear bomb on your own country—that wouldn't appear very high on a list of intelligent things to do, but then, we humans are known for sometimes doing dumb things.

Nuclear bombs are unique in that they cannot be detonated by dropping them. They must be set off. In the old days, that's the way most bombs were made, but not anymore. Now, bombs are made with delayed counters, digital timers, and remote controlled detonators that can even be set off by making a telephone call containing a secret number code.

Accidents like what happened over South Carolina probably happen more often than we think. The government surely doesn't enjoy reporting these kinds of slips, and it will probably hide whatever it can. More than that, it is staggering to think how close our planet has come to being completely destroyed, from the flood in Noah's day to the Cuban Missile Crisis, when the United States found itself a hair's breadth away from nuclear war with the former Soviet Union. Fortunately, God in His mercy keeps the forces of evil and destruction in check. As the book of Revelation says, the angels of the four winds are keeping trouble under control, and they certainly have had a big job! But someday—one glorious day—God will tell them that their work on earth is finished, that they can relax their muscles and get some rest! And we can trust this God because He has never, ever done anything accidentally.

Girl Scouts

Many daughters have done well, but you excel them all.
Proverbs 31:29, NKJV.

It seems that girls historically have not been given as many opportunities for adventure as boys. In the days of the Wild West, Annie Oakley thought so, too. At the early age of 9, she learned to hunt wild game to provide food for her brothers and sisters. When her father died suddenly, her mother sent her to a poor farm, which was a government facility for needy youth. Annie learned to be independent, and because of her skills as an ace markswoman, she went on to perform as a sharpshooter in one of the Wild West shows of her day. She even performed for U.S. presidents and royalty in Europe. People weren't used to seeing a woman performing like that in public, and for this reason it seems newspapers of the day tried to slander her name with shady stories about her background. But Annie was actually a woman of good standing and fought to keep a good reputation.

If the Girl Scouts had been around then, Annie probably would have joined them. On this day in history, that organization got its start—March 12, 1912. Juliette Gordon Low from Savannah, Georgia, was the founder of the organization that has inspired nearly 50,000,000 girls, age 11 to 17 years. The original name was The Girl Guides but was changed to Girl Scouts in 1913. Today, Girl Scouts are known for many things, especially all those good Girl Scout cookies. However, the organization's real purpose is to offer girls opportunities for adventure and learning and to raise them to be model citizens.

Today, like Annie Oakley, girls want to do just about everything boys do. They play rugby and drive race cars, start careers in law and engineering, and even get chances to run for president of the United States. Organizations like the Girl Scouts facilitate these adventures for girls. And Christian girls can make an even bigger impact. They have opportunities to change their world, not only through careers in any field they choose, but even more through faithful service in helping needy children, as well as adults, to live more meaningful lives. Like Jesus when He was on this earth, who treasured every single person He met, girls can encourage people they meet to experience the best adventure of all—a friendship with the God who created adventure. And Solomon will be speaking of them when he said, "Many daughters have done well, but you excel them all."

Planet Discovery

By the word of the Lord were the heavens made,
their starry host by the breath of his mouth.
Psalm 33:6, NIV.

How many planets are there in our solar system? Nine? Or maybe eight, depending on which astronomers you ask. (Pluto has been redefined by some as being only an ice ball and not really a planet at all.) Which planet is the seventh from the sun? If you said Uranus, you're right. On this day in 1871, Sir William Herschel of England announced its discovery after observing the planet through his own homemade telescope. At first he thought it might be a comet, but after careful calculations and charting its progress across the sky each night, he decided it must be a planet. Herschel named it Uranus, after the ancient Greek deity of the sky.

Today, we know it is the third-largest planet in our solar system and one of the five classical planets that can be seen without the help of a telescope. Astronomers in ancient times never really thought of it as a planet because of its dimness and slow orbit. Uranus is much like Neptune, and both planets are quite different from the larger gas giants, Jupiter and Saturn. Astronomers sometimes place Uranus and Neptune in a separate category, calling them the "ice giants." Uranus' atmosphere, like those of Jupiter and Saturn, is made of hydrogen and helium, but it has more water on it. Its wind speeds can reach up to 560 mph, and it has the coldest atmosphere of all of earth's neighbors, with a minimum temperature of −224°C. Brrrrr! Like the bigger planets, Uranus has a system of rings and several moons. Uranus revolves around the sun once every 84 earth years, has a rotational period of about 17 hours, and is almost 2 billion miles from the sun.

God must have had plans for all these amazing planets in our solar system, some of them hundreds of times bigger than our earth. It is amazing to consider that our solar system, with all nine (or eight) of its planets that seem so huge to us, is only a mere speck in the spectacular labyrinth of His creative works! If He cared enough to go to the effort of giving each planet, microscopic as it is to Him, distinctive and beautiful elements that distinguish it from the planet next door, how much more does He care about you, having gone to the effort of creating you with distinctive and beautiful elements that distinguish you from other people?

A Genius Born

Great men are not always wise. Job 32:9, NKJV.

Do you have trouble in school sometimes? Do you have a hard time getting your assignments done on time? Well, don't worry. One of the smartest people in history, born on this day in 1879, had trouble in school, too. He couldn't focus on his studies, and he asked too many questions. His teachers thought he would be a failure in life. His mother insisted that he take violin lessons, but his real hobby was building models and mechanical gadgets. And that was where his genius had its beginning.

Although he was a simple man at heart, Albert Einstein went on to master the greatest challenges in the fields of mathematics and physics. In 1921, his work with the properties of light won him the Nobel Prize in physics. And he was among the first to suggest the existence of black holes in space. His theory said that the forces of gravity were so great in these black holes that even light could not escape their gravitational forces. But Einstein is perhaps most famous for his energy formula ($E=mc^2$). His theory of relativity suggested that if one could travel fast enough, time would slow down.

When Hitler rose to power in Germany, Einstein left the country to eventually settle in the United States where he began teaching at the Institute for Advanced Study in Princeton, New Jersey. It was during this time that he helped developed the concept of the atomic bomb. He had hoped that atomic energy would help balance the forces of military power in the world, but he later realized that "the bomb" had only pushed us toward the possible annihilation of the human race. He regretted the part he had played in developing such a weapon and later became a leader in the race for peace.

Without doubt, Albert Einstein was one of the most creative minds in human history when it came to the physical level of human existence. But this world consists of more than just the physical level. When Jesus lived in our physical world, He desperately desired for people to explore the spiritual level of life, where God could communicate with and bless them the most. Even if you are a genius on the physical level, there remains a greater level to master. God reminds us in the book of Job that "Great men are not always wise."

First Blood Bank

He has delivered us from the power of darkness and conveyed us into the kingdom . . . of His love, in whom we have redemption through His blood, the forgiveness of sins. Colossians 1:13, 14, NKJV.

Blood has always been an important part of medical care, especially during times of war, natural disaster, and various accidents. On March 15, 1937, the concept of a blood bank was born at the Cook County Hospital in Chicago, Illinois—a brand new concept in the United States. Today a person can donate blood so that in times of emergency there is a supply to help victims who need it. And remember, the life you save though your donation may be your own!

Blood is perhaps the most precious commodity of the human body. It is used to bring life to every tissue, every cell. Every passing minute, more than 10 pints of blood make a complete circuit in the body via the heart. About 634 pints travel that distance in an hour, 15,216 in a day, and about 5,553,840 million in a year. Amazingly, the amount of blood pumped per day is about 100 times the weight of the body. The blood acts as a conveyor belt for the good nutrients our bodies need and for the rubbish that our bodies need to expel. The arteries, capillaries, and veins bring the life blood to every corner of the human body, such as to the intestines to absorb the food we eat and to the lungs to pick up oxygen and deposit carbon dioxide. The blood also passes through the liver and kidneys to expel the toxic wastes that act like poison to the body.

When you look down and see your hands covered with blood, you know that something is wrong. We humans like to keep our blood inside of us. Normally, God doesn't need blood to live. But when He became a Man and lived in our world as a human being, He needed blood to bring life to every tissue of His body, to absorb the food He ate, and to expel the toxins from His body. He needed blood to do all the things for His body that it does for ours. He was just like us. But there was a problem. Humans were on the road to eternal separation from Him because of Adam and Eve's choice of sin over obedience. Because He couldn't accept us dying forever, He chose to die, to lose all of His blood, in our place. He lost all His blood on our behalf to purchase the forgiveness of our sins and to expel these poisonous toxins. To lose a pint of blood for someone else is a sacrificial gift. But to lose all your blood for someone else is real love!

Natives' Revenge

If your enemy is hungry, feed him; If he is thirsty, give him a drink; . . .
Do not be overcome by evil, but overcome evil with good.
Romans 12:20, 21, NKJV.

On this day in history Samoset, an Abnaki Indian, befriended the Pilgrim settlers in Plymouth, Massachusetts. "Welcome, Englishmen!" were his first words. That was on March 16, 1621. Why was this historical event so significant? Because Samoset had suffered greatly at the hands of the English and the diseases the Europeans brought with them. The majority of his village had died of smallpox. Not long after this he introduced the Pilgrims to an Indian friend named Squanto, who later helped the pilgrims survive by teaching them how to grow crops in the poor New England soil. This is an even more remarkable gesture of friendship, because Squanto had previously been captured by the English and sent to Europe where he was a slave for a while. Eventually Squanto escaped and came back to New England as a translator aboard an English ship. A third Indian named Massasoit also befriended the Pilgrims and joined with them in a thanksgiving celebration in the fall of that year.

If it hadn't been for these three Indian men who befriended the Pilgrims, the history of Massachusetts, and the United States, might have been much different. Perhaps Samoset and his friends realized that in spite of the tragedies that had destroyed the families of the Indians and the Europeans, they all needed to find a way to work and live together if they wanted to survive. In the end, the Pilgrims did help Samoset, Squanto, and Massasoit in their fight against a warring tribe of Narragansett Indians. Samoset wasn't a Christian and didn't know about Jesus' advice to do good to his enemies. Squanto didn't know that Paul said a kindness to an enemy might make a friend out of him, but it worked.

Life can be extremely unfair. It is not fun to be misused, and it can give you a sour outlook on life. How could Jesus, who was betrayed, denied, and left all alone by His friends in His time of greatest need, and perjured, beaten, spit upon, and crucified by His enemies, have shown such pure and consistent love for people who treated Him so badly? Knowing that retaliation wouldn't accomplish anything, He valued the communication of love more than the preservation of self. He used these insults as opportunities to tell people how much God loved them. The greater the unfairness and severity of the insult, the more clearly true love showed up.

Chicken Pox Vaccine

Jesus went through all the towns and villages, teaching in their synagogues, preaching the good news of the kingdom and healing every disease and sickness.
Matthew 9:35, NIV.

Have you ever had chicken pox? Many kids these days haven't contracted the disease because of a recent breakthrough in the field of medical immunizations. On March 17, 1995, the chicken pox vaccine was approved for public use by the United States government. The vaccine was first sold in New Jersey and was found to be 70 to 90 percent effective. Chicken pox has never been as dangerous as smallpox used to be. The sores and symptoms can look similar at the beginning, but the end results are drastically different. Smallpox, now believed to be effectively eliminated, often ended in death.

During medieval times, the word "pox" meant "curse." This led many people to believe that chicken pox was a disease brought on children due to the use of black magic. Chicken pox is thought to have been first discovered and described by Giovanni Filippo during the 1500s in Italy. Richard Morton, an English doctor in the 1600s, called it chicken pox because he thought it was a milder form of smallpox.

Chicken pox is a highly contagious illness, and its open sores can cause itching all over the body. Chicken pox incubates over a 10- to 21-day period, and can be spread through coughs or sneezes, or through direct contact with an infected person. Chicken pox has rarely been found to be fatal, although it is usually more severe in adults than in children. It can be a pretty uncomfortable disease, but the good news is, once you've had it, you'll never get it again.

Chicken pox, along with a host of other diseases, is very uncomfortable. You can't focus on anything because your arm itches, then your leg, then your back. It is difficult to lie down or even sit. Most diseases are marked by varying degrees of discomfort. But there is one disease that can be quite comfortable—for a while. That disease is sin. When Jesus was on earth, He loved to heal people who were plagued with discomfort from various diseases. And He especially loved to heal people who were plagued with comfortable sin. Comfortable sin is extremely dangerous because we are not naturally inclined to dread it. Knowing that comfortable sin can lead us to permanent death, Jesus stretches out His healing hand to all those who are uncomfortable—and comfortable.

Tornado Disasters

You have been a refuge for the poor, a refuge for
the needy in his distress, a shelter from the storm.
Isaiah 25:4, NIV.

One of the worst tornado disasters in United States history took place on March 18, 1925. Sweeping across five states simultaneously, tornadoes struck Illinois, Indiana, Kentucky, and Tennessee, leaving horrendous damage in their wake. Over a span of three hours, 689 people died, 13,000 were injured, and more than $18 million of damage resulted.

Tornadoes are among the most powerful forces in nature. They can do more damage than perhaps any other natural disaster, except maybe earthquakes. Tornadoes form when cold air currents meet warm air currents. The funnel cloud that develops creates a vacuum tunnel that cuts swaths through forests and towns, exploding buildings, and sucking up everything in its path. Tornado wind speeds have been clocked at 450 miles per hour. The biggest tornado ever recorded was a funnel cloud that was two and a half miles wide. The costliest tornado touched down in Topeka, Kansas, in 1966. Tallied at today's figures it ran the state about $1.6 billion. May 2003 reported the most tornadoes, the total reaching 543.

And yet tornadoes are strange. They've been known to pick up houses, spin them around, and set them down again on the original foundation without so much as a scratch. Some tornadoes have picked up people and taken them miles away before setting them down safely. People have witnessed tornados that traveled down one side of a busy street, hopped across the street, and then traveled back up the other side, taking out businesses on that side of the street, too.

Do you ever feel like you're living in a tornado? Maybe the tornado of divorce has hit your family. Maybe the tornado of someone close dying has touched down in your life. Or maybe someone special has dumped you for someone else, and it feels like your heart has been picked up, turned around, and smashed to the ground. You are not left alone to deal with the destruction you feel in and around you. Jesus knows how to deal with storms. He can calm the storm, but more importantly, He can calm your heart. He is your refuge in the storm because He promises to weather it with you. Through all the worst days of your life, Jesus is your shelter in the time of storm.

Las Vegas Gambling

No one can serve two masters. . . .
You cannot serve both God and Money.
Matthew 6:24, NIV.

The early 1930s were a very hard time for Americans because of the Great Depression. Everyone was hurting financially. Like everyone else, the state of Nevada needed money and legislators were trying to come up with a plan to help raise taxes. And what was their solution? On March 19, 1931, they legalized gambling by setting up casinos. Can you imagine that! The United States was facing its worst economic crisis in history, and the state of Nevada made a plan to swindle people out of their hard-earned money!

Today, gambling takes many forms. People bet on football games, horse races, and boxing. They buy lottery tickets, play cards, challenge roulette wheels, and try their luck at the slot machines. Online gambling is the latest vice that's come to plague our country (and most of it is illegal). In spite of the federal restrictions against it, gambling has become the leading industry in the U.S. Its total income is greater than the combined wealth of the 100 largest companies in America, such as U.S. Steel, General Electric, Metropolitan Life, and others. Today, about 90 million adults are gambling away $500 billion annually, with almost $450 billion of it wagered illegally.

Gambling, like alcoholism, is a sickness and is destructive for any society. It encourages people to take chances on luck and sit around expecting something for nothing, instead of working hard to make real things happen in their lives. Worst of all, there are always people in every society who will continue to gamble away everything they've got, even when they have nothing at all.

Jesus lovingly advised us that we can't serve God and money at the same time. We'll either focus on God, or we'll focus on money. Focusing on God allows us to build a relationship with Someone who has risked everything to be with us and to provide us with a happy, meaningful life. Focusing on money allows us to buy more things that push us deeper and deeper into an increasingly narrow, shallow, and meaningless existence. Since those are the only choices, I'm betting—no, praying—that you choose the first option.

Drug for AIDS

If you listen carefully to the voice of the Lord your God . . .
I will not bring on you any of the diseases I brought
on the Egyptians, for I am the Lord, who heals you.
Exodus 15:26, NIV.

AIDS is possibly the most frightening disease of our time. When it was first discovered, panic set in because there was no known cure, and it became a serious threat to the health of our planet—and it still is.

But on this day in 1987 the United States government approved a drug for use in the fight against AIDS. The manufacture of the drug azidothymidine (AZT) was seen as a real breakthrough in the battle. Unfortunately, the initial cost per patient turned out to be more than $10,000 a year. In the early days of AIDS awareness, everyone was told that the disease could be transmitted only through homosexual relationships or through the use of dirty needles. Then we discovered that it could also be passed on through unprotected sex and through the blood from a mother to her unborn baby.

The number of people living with AIDS or HIV (Human Immunodeficiency Virus) has risen from around 8 million in 1990 to 33 million today. More than 25 million people have died of AIDS since 1981, and Africa has 11.6 million AIDS orphans. By 2007, 50 percent of HIV cases worldwide were found in women, and today young people make up half of all new HIV infections. In developing countries nearly 10 million people need immediate life-saving AIDS drugs, but only about 3 million are receiving them.

No one knows what will become of the AIDS epidemic. Scientists worldwide are working on solutions to help eradicate the disease, but new forms of AIDS are looming on the horizon. One of the latest concerns is the possibility that past fatal diseases like tuberculosis or smallpox will take on the characteristics of the AIDS virus.

God wants us to be free of disease, and listening to His advice to pursue faithful relationships according to His original plan goes a long way in protecting us. However, we live on a planet that has been infiltrated by an enemy, an enemy who brings disease on anyone he possibly can. But the day will come when this enemy will be seen for the nefarious being he is, and God will then be free to fulfill what He really wants to do—heal us completely and permanently.

One Hundred Five Games of Chess at Once

For we wrestle not against flesh and blood, but against principalities, against powers, against the rulers of the darkness of this world, against spiritual wickedness in high places. Ephesians 6:12.

The game of chess goes back a long way—as far back as 600 A.D. in what is now northern India or Afghanistan. Interest in chess seems to have followed the old trade routes through China and maybe even to the island of Japan. By 1000 A.D. Iranians were using it, and Europeans by 1200. By 1400 the chess rules we use today were incorporated.

Chess is a real mind game requiring strategies of multiple dimensions. A total of 16 chess pieces must be moved from place to place on the board to outwit the opponent and to eventually capture his king. The trick of the game is to not only strategize what you will do to win the match, but also to predict what your opponent will do. Unfortunately, some opponents are so gifted that they can calculate every possible move, for every chess piece, several plays in advance.

Since 1927, the majority of highly skilled chess players have been citizens of the former Soviet Union, and Gary Kasparov was one of the most talented ever to play the game. He could play multiple games simultaneously, and it's claimed that he never lost one of these matches. The youngest American ever to become a world chess champion was Bobby Fisher, age 14, and some consider him one of the top three players of all time. On March 21, 1916, a man by the name of Frank Marshall of New York City did an almost impossible thing. He played 105 games of chess simultaneously. One hundred five local players showed up at the National Press Club in Washington, D.C., to challenge this man. Amazingly, Frank won 82 of the games, lost eight, and drew or tied 15.

Chess is just a game, but the great controversy between good and evil is not a game. It's a real war being fought between Jesus and Satan, and we are the players. The strategy was set long ago before the world was created, and the match was won at Calvary. All that remains is a few decisive battles to be played out in the waning years of earth's history. In Jesus we are all promised victory. Do you want to be part of the victory celebration to come? Then turn your life over to Jesus today and join the winning team.

FDR Ends Prohibition

Wine is a mocker, strong drink is a brawler,
and whoever is led astray by it is not wise.
Proverbs 20:1, NKJV.

What's so wonderful about alcohol? The way people glamorize drinking today, you'd think it was the fountain of youth. But then—we might as well admit it—it's all about the money. On this day in history, 1933, President Franklin D. Roosevelt signed the Beer and Wine Revenue Act, legalizing the consumption of alcohol in the United States. Why would he need to do that? Hadn't people always drunk beer and wine in our country?

The 1920s were a time when the United States government had outlawed the manufacture, sale, and transportation of alcohol to anyone anywhere, including restaurants, dance clubs, and bars. But when 1933 came along, all that ended. Gone were the days of FBI agents chasing booze smugglers through streets, shooting them in back alleys of tenement housing, and exposing innocent citizens to flying bullets.

We're a long way from the 1920s and 1930s. Today, TV advertisers make alcohol look pretty good, but here are some sobering statistics telling the real truth about the smelly stuff:

- Alcohol-related car crashes kill someone every 31 minutes and injure someone every two minutes.
- In the United States drunk driving is the leading criminal cause of death. More than 17,000 people are victims of drunk driving accidents every year, with 13,000 of them losing their lives.

Fortunately, these numbers are down from two decades ago. Much is being done to educate people about the dangers of drinking and driving, but even one death is too many when it comes to people driving under the influence.

Please—don't drink and drive. Better yet, don't drink. The list of advantages of abstaining from alcohol is almost endless. We sometimes are deceived into thinking that people will look down on us if we make it known that we don't drink. However, the truth is that people generally respect those who make a stand and stick to it. When you make the decision to avoid alcohol, you will be respected and also save lives.

Free Fallers

For he will order his angels to protect you wherever
you go. They will hold you up with their hands
so you won't even hurt your foot on a stone.
Psalms 91:11, 12, NLT.

Have you ever fallen off your bike, or out of a tree, or off the roof of your house? Not much fun, is it? Think of what it would be like to fall from a plane, from thousands of feet up—three miles up, to be exact. That's what happened to Nicholas Alkemade, on March 23, 1944. On a bombing mission during World War II, Nicholas had to bail out of his plane and fell 18,000 feet without a parachute—and lived. That's right, no parachute. How's that possible? Only with the help of God's angels, you can be sure.

Nicholas was the tail gunner in a British bomber on a night mission to Berlin when his plane was shot down by German fighters. When the captain ordered the crew to bail out, Nicholas discovered that his parachute was in flames. Rather than be burned to death in an out of control plane, he chose to jump without a parachute. He landed in trees and drifted snow with only a twisted knee and some cuts. No broken bones!

Nicholas Alkemade was not alone in his miraculous fall, but was only one of a group of "free fallers." Lieutenant Chisov, a Russian airman, fell nearly 22,000 feet over Germany, hitting the edge of a snow-covered ravine, and surviving. In France, Alan Magee fell 20,000 feet and crashed onto the skylight of a train station. He recovered. Olen Bryant fell 10,000 feet into the mountains of Italy. Landing in deep snow, he suffered injuries to his neck, back, pelvis, and face, but survived. The only logical explanation for the survival of these free fallers is in the existence and work of angels.

God's promise to order His angels to protect you applies when you've fallen from a plane and are hurdling wide-eyed toward the earth with your hair in your face and no parachute on your back. It also applies when you want to follow God but keep falling to temptation, or when you feel like you've fallen too far for Him to save you. Let me assure you that you have never, ever fallen too many times or too far from Him for His angels to bear you up on their wings. You may not feel a parachute stopping your fall, or see the bright, silvery wings of His angelic agents, but His promise is *always* true, and it's always true *for you.*

Fanny Crosby Born

Sing to the Lord a new song, and His praise from the ends of the earth. Isaiah 42:10, NKJV.

Who's the most famous songwriter you know? How many of his or her songs have made it to the top of the charts?

On March 24, 1820, a well-known songwriter of a past generation was born. Fanny Crosby is still famous among Christian songwriters. She didn't begin writing hymns until her 40s, but she lived to be 95, producing over 8,000 hymns. Fifty of her songs are still sung as favorites in churches all across the country, including "To God Be the Glory," "Blessed Assurance," and "Redeemed, How I Love to Proclaim It!"

It's said that she composed the lyrics and music to her songs entirely in her mind before dictating them to someone else. Sometimes she composed as many as 12 hymns in that way before having her secretary copy them down.

She became one of the most famous women in the United States during her lifetime, rubbing shoulders with famous people, visiting presidents, generals, and other dignitaries. She was often invited to the White House, where she played her hymn "Safe in the Arms of Jesus" at President Ulysses Grant's funeral.

That Fanny could become such a prolific songwriter is amazing. It is even more amazing that she accomplished it in spite of being blind! She became blind at just six weeks of age, when the infection from a cold spread to her eyes. Crosby was never bitter about being blind. When she was only eight years old she wrote these verses about her condition:

"Oh what a happy soul I am,
Although I cannot see;
I am resolved that in this world,
Contented I will be.
How many blessings I enjoy,
That other people don't;
To weep and sigh because I'm blind, I cannot, and I won't."

She once said, "When I get to heaven, the first face that shall ever gladden my sight will be that of my Savior!" Wow! Now that's inspiring!

Billy Sunday Converted

*And what do you benefit if you gain the whole world, but
lose your own soul? Is anything worth more than your soul?
Matthew 16:26, NLT.*

Billy Sunday, a famous professional baseball player, grew up in hardship and poverty. When he was 12 he and his older brother were sent to live at Soldier's Orphanage in Glenwood, Iowa. But Bill hated the orphanage and ran away to work as a stable boy tending Shetland ponies.

When he finally got a chance to go to school, he learned how to play baseball. He wasn't much of a hitter in those days, but he could run like lightning, which made his base stealing fun to watch. Then a professional scout saw Billy play and signed him on with the Chicago White Stockings (now called the Chicago Cubs). Billy was so fast that he was declared to be the champion sprinter of the National League. He played eight years for three professional teams: the Chicago White Stockings, the Pittsburgh Alleghenys, and the Philadelphia Phillies.

In 1887, after a night of drinking with his teammates, Billy attended a service at the Pacific Garden Mission in Chicago, Illinois. Not long after that he accepted Jesus as his Savior and became a "born again" Christian. On March 25, 1890, he gave up his career in baseball and soon became even more famous as an evangelist.

Billy was one of the first big-time preachers to speak on a new invention called the "radio." He used his baseball background, slangy language, and outgoing personality to become the most popular evangelist of his time. It is estimated that he preached his "fire-and-brimstone" message to millions in his circus tent revivals, converting more than 300,000 souls.

You don't have to be an official evangelist to enjoy the exciting and fulfilling purpose of our existence—helping people see God. He doesn't want a planet full of evangelists. He wants professional athletes, college professors, administrative assistants, politicians, custodians, and programmers who will show sincere interest in the welfare of the people around them. If you allow Him, He can use you to encourage these precious souls and point them to Jesus. Like Billy Sunday, God has big plans for you and will lead you by His word, by impression, and by circumstances into the career in which you can make the biggest impact for Him.

Beethoven Dies

And my soul shall be joyful in the Lord; it shall rejoice in His salvation.
Psalm 35:9, NKJV.

Ludwig van Beethoven, one of the most famous composers in history, was born into a family of musicians at the royal court of Cologne, Austria. At an early age he showed rare talent as a musician, and by the time he was 8, his father, Johann, began making serious plans for him. Unfortunately, Johann was overbearing and harsh in his efforts to transform his son into a musical genius. He was still only 8 years old when Johann forced Ludwig to hold a solo concert.

By the time Ludwig was 10 he was composing music, and with the help of gifted teachers, he rose to fame rather quickly. He began to travel Europe and perform at concerts with other famous musicians. He was strongly influenced by Bach, Mozart, and Haydn. By now Ludwig was composing symphonies and concertos, and he was spending time with members of the Austrian royal court in Vienna.

Unfortunately, in his mid-20s Beethoven's hearing began to deteriorate until he went totally deaf at about age 34. No one really knows why. Some doctors thought it was because of lead poisoning, typhus, or even his habit of immersing his head in cold water to stay awake. Even though deafness silenced his hearing completely, it did not silence him. Beethoven continued composing, conducting, and performing. To help him hear the tones, he used a special rod attached to the soundboard of his piano. He would bite the rod so he could feel the vibrations transfer from the piano to his jaw, thus increasing his perception of the sound.

Sadly, Beethoven died prematurely on March 26, 1827, but his music lives on. He is not known for writing Christian hymns, but he did compose the music for Joyful, Joyful, We Adore Thee.

You may not be a great musician as Beethoven was, able to compose amazing music without the ability to hear sounds. You may think that you don't have any musical talents—or any talents at all. God does not call us to be talented, to be famous, or even to be able to carry a tune. He simply calls us to be faithful with what we do have—a sincere desire to praise Him. And one consistently content, smiling Christian in a gloomy world can make more of an impact than all its geniuses put together.

First Mormon Temple Built

To the law and to the testimony! If they do not speak
according to this word, it is because there is no light in them.
Isaiah 8:20, NKJV.

Joseph Smith, the self-proclaimed prophet of the Church of Jesus Christ of Latter Day Saints (sometimes called the Mormon church), had moved from New York with about 50 families and was trying to establish a religious community. His group built its first temple in Kirkland, Ohio, and dedicated it on March 27, 1837, a structure 59 feet long, 79 feet wide, 50 feet tall, and topped with a tower 110 feet tall.

Unfortunately, Smith and his "saints" had some strange beliefs that didn't sit well with the local folks, the foremost being polygamy. Mobs formed daily, threatening to vandalize the temple. Finally, the persecution drove Smith and his followers out of town.

The temple didn't fare too well in the months that followed their departure. People in the community herded cattle, sheep, and pigs into the basement. They used the upper floors for meetings, plays, dances, games, and shows. In later years, the place was converted into a school where James A. Garfield, future United States president, was educated. Regrettably, the historic temple was destroyed by an arson fire in 1848.

Meanwhile, the Mormons had moved to Illinois, before moving on to Missouri, Kansas, and, finally, Utah, where they settled in the Great Salt Lake Valley. This 1,300-mile trek west eventually led 70,000 Mormon pioneers to their new home. It was in Utah that the Latter Day Saints church got its real start and established itself as one of the United States' major religions, today with a membership of about 12 million.

Sadly though, the Mormon Church cannot be considered a true Christian church because of its teaching that any new messages given by prophets, such as Joseph Smith, supersede the old truths already established in the Bible. These old truths are identified by the Bible as the law and the testimony. Simply put, the law is God's character. When we read the law, we are looking at His personality traits of sincerity, respect, and love. The testimony refers to what the biblical prophets reported, or testified, about God's character. Any unbiblical teaching, especially one claiming to supersede God's own character and what was said about it, does not have any light in it.

March 28

First Ambulance

*They ran throughout that whole region and
carried the sick on mats to wherever they heard he was.
Mark 6:55, NIV.*

The first ambulance to be used at a hospital in the United States was in Cincinnati, Ohio. Its first day of service was on March 28, 1866. The ambulance, a covered, horse-drawn wagon, looked much like the paddy wagons used for transporting prisoners. One horse was usually enough to do the job. The first man to drive that ambulance was James Jackson, who was paid a salary of $360 a year.

During the years following the Civil War many hospitals in bigger cities began using the horse-drawn ambulance services for their patients. Nurses and doctors had learned a few things during the Civil War: lives can be saved if you act fast enough, and bringing patients to the hospital can keep doctors from having to run all over the countryside tending to the sick. The duties of these lone ambulance drivers included getting doctors out of bed at night for emergencies and picking up patients who were not contagious.

But times changed. By the 1920s horse-drawn ambulances were working alongside newer models that were engine driven, and soon they were replaced entirely by steam, electric, and, eventually, ambulances with gasoline driven engines. Today ambulances are a thousand times more sophisticated. And they also cost a thousand times more. Some trucks, with all their systems of hydraulic ladders, water pumps, and safety equipment, can cost more than $225,000.

In Jesus' days on earth, sickness was everywhere you looked. There were people who were unable to see, hear, or speak, people who had internal bleeding, and, likely the saddest cases, people plagued with leprosy. With no effective medical industry, imagine the helplessness and discouragement these poor patients suffered! Those who heard about Jesus brightened a bit at the thought of someone who had the ability to heal them, but they still had to get to Him! How? Of course! They called the ambulance! Far from a speeding truck with flashing lights, their ambulances were their friends who picked them up, bed and all, and carried them to Jesus. It was always a one-way trip, for Jesus was glad to heal them. You might be the only ambulance available for someone you know.

First United States Superhighway

The highway of the upright avoids evil;
he who guards his way guards his life.
Proverbs 16:17, NIV.

Do you like to travel? Have you ever thought about what it would be like to travel without good roads? Today roads go everywhere in the United States—across plains, over rivers and mountains, and through deserts. There are about 46,000 miles of interstate highways, 400,000 miles of major state roads, 800,000 miles of toll roads, and approximately 2.6 million miles of local roads. That's about 4 million miles of roads.

On March 29, 1806, Congress set aside $30,000 (about $6 million in today's dollars) from the national treasury to begin building the country's first road that ran from Cumberland, Maryland, to Vandalia, Illinois. This money was only the first installment of what the federal government would need to spend, but it got the project started.

They called it the Great National Pike, or the Cumberland Road. It was to be a superhighway, a forerunner of the interstate highways that would one day crisscross our great nation. Over the years, from 1806 to 1838, the road continued to be built, costing the government nearly $7 million (about $1.5 billion today). In 1856 the road was turned over to the individual states through which the road ran. From then on it would be each state's responsibility to maintain the road within its borders.

When you plan a road trip, you have two options: take the freeway or take the back roads. Flying down the freeway will get you there fast. There are plenty of rest areas and restaurants, making the trip as comfortable as it gets. Taking the back roads will get you there more slowly. There are usually fewer restrooms (at least man-made ones), but you will most likely enjoy better scenery, and the possiblity of memorable adventure increases on the back roads. Like road trips, life is full of choices. Most choices have a little good and a little bad in them, which can be frustrating. How do you know which road to take, which friends to have, which college to attend, which career to pursue? The good news is that you don't have to stress about always choosing the right road in life. All God wants is for you to desire Him in your life and to avoid evil. Then, even if you take the wrong exit, it is up to Him to lead you back to the best road for you. And, trust me, He will do it.

March 30

Pencil and Attached Eraser

And these words which I command you today shall be in your heart . . . You shall write them on the doorposts of your house and on your gates. Deuteronomy 6:6-9, NKJV.

Who came up with the idea of a pencil with an attached eraser? Hyman Lipman of Philadelphia, Pennsylvania. On this day in 1858, he invented and patented the nifty little tool. The pencil was unique because it had a groove at one end where a piece of rubber was glued. Now that's a breakthrough, and classrooms have never been the same since.

Clear back in the days of the Romans lead rods were used by scribes to write on papyrus, but graphite wasn't widely used until about 1600. To make pencil lead today, graphite and clay are crushed together into a fine powder. Water is added to the mixture to form a soft paste. The paste is pushed through metal tubes to form thin rods, and then heated in an oven at 1,800°F to make them smooth and hard. The pencils are finally made by gluing two grooved slats of wood together like a sandwich with a graphite rod fastened inside. Individual pencils are sanded, smoothed, and then painted with five to eight coats of paint. A metal ring and eraser are attached, and—presto! The pencil and eraser are one.

Here are some interesting facts about pencils:
- Laid end to end, the number of pencils made annually in the United States would encircle earth about 15 times.
- Most pencils made in the U.S. have erasers, but those in Europe do not.
- A pencil lead, or a line drawn by a pencil, will conduct electricity.
- Colored pencils are made from chalk, clay, or wax.
- About 75 percent of the 2.8 billion U.S. pencils are still painted yellow.

It is the words of His law that God wants to write in our hearts. What does this really mean? Your heart is the nerve center of what you truly want in life, of what is most important to you. (No doubt you've heard love songs with lyrics such as, I want you from the bottom of my heart.) His law represents His character of amazing, selfless love. So, when God says He wants to write His law of love in your heart, He means that He wants your most intense desire to be to bask in and reflect His amazing, selfless character. And rather than crushed graphite and clay, which can be easily erased, He writes with His blood.

Daylight Saving Time

There shall be no night there. They need no lamp,
nor light of the sun, for the Lord God gives them light.
Revelation 22:5, NKJV.

The daylight saving time program is now a part of just about every state in our country. With this plan, all clocks across the nation are set one hour ahead so that people can have one more hour of daylight in the evening. Most states still use it today by putting it into effect in early spring and then switching back to regular time in the fall. Of course, the sun comes up an hour later in the morning too, but most people don't notice that, since we all get up later today than our great-grandparents did in the old days. Farmers probably appreciate daylight saving time the most. In the morning, they can't get out to work in their fields very early because of the dew. The evening is the time they usually need more light to get jobs done. That all became possible on March 31, 1918, when the plan was put into operation.

There are a few stories in the Bible that mention daylight saving time. One can be found in the book of Joshua where he and the Hebrew army were fighting a battle. The contest far from over, the sun was dipping perilously close to the horizon. In those days of fighting battles without night-vision goggles, clashing swords in the darkness of night was one step away from insanity. How would you know if you were slicing off the head of the enemy or of your buddy fighting beside you? So Joshua asked God to freeze the sun in place, and amazingly, God granted him the favor! Thanks to God's daylight saving time, the Hebrews won the battle.

Another story tells of Hezekiah's unhappiness when he found out that he was going to die. He begged God for more years of life, and surprisingly, God complied, giving him 15 more years. As a sign that God would make good on His promise, He caused the sundial to move back about 10 degrees. According to our best estimates, that was about 45 minutes of daylight saving time that assuring Hezekiah of 15 years of lifesaving time!

The last story is not about an ancient Hebrew general or an ancient Hebrew king. It is about you! When you walk through those pearly gates and God Himself greets you with a huge hug, how will you react to the sun never going down? If you're like me, there have been times when you have had so much fun that you never wanted the day to end. Thanks to the light of God's continuous presence, in Heaven your day of endless delight will last forever!

Internal Combustion Engine

*But you will receive power when the Holy Spirit comes
on you; and you will be my witnesses in Jerusalem,
and in all Judea and Samaria, and to the ends of the earth.
Acts 1:8, NIV.*

The internal combustion engine is one of the most ingenious inventions of the modern era. Every time you climb into the family car, you're making use of this amazing assemblage of interworking parts. From cars to lawnmowers to go-carts, we've come to trust this invention to provide the power to get us to school, work, and grandma's house, to maintain the landscaping of our homes, and even to have fun in weekend recreation. It has permanently changed our civilization.

On April 1, 1826, Captain Samuel Morey of Oxford, New Hampshire, received a patent for the first successful internal combustion engine. "A gas or vapor engine" is what he called it. The engine had two cylinders, a crankshaft, valves, a carburetor, an electric spark, a flywheel, and a water cooling system. The only fuel he used for the engine was, not gasoline, but air and turpentine.

Captain Morey introduced his internal combustion engine 60 or so years before cars rolled onto the scene. In the 1830s, steam was the most common form of energy used to run machinery. Steam provided a tremendous amount of power, but it was also very dangerous. In some ways, steam provided too much power for what the machines were required to do. The internal combustion engine was superior to steam power in some ways, but it also had its dangers, the greatest of which was explosions. Incredible pressure would build and if the seals had cracks or the valves in the engine were a bit loose the whole engine could blow, and that was sometimes fatal. Improvements to the internal combustion engine have virtually eliminated this risk by balancing the weight-to-power ratio. Most car engines today are extremely lightweight but still get all the power they need for what they need to do. A small car engine can be easily lifted by an auto mechanic without a lift or jack.

There have been some political leaders in this world who have acquired so much power that it exploded in their faces. Some committed suicide, some were torn from their perch by scandal, and some were destroyed by their own people. Through God's Holy Spirit, we can trust that He will give us just the right weight-to-power ratio for a successful life.

The Fountain of Youth

And he showed me a pure river of water of life, clear as crystal, proceeding from the throne of God and of the Lamb. Revelation 22:1, NKJV.

On April 2, 1513, Juan Ponce de León waded ashore on a Florida beach and claimed the territory for the country of Spain. He knew he had found a new land, he just didn't know how big a find it was. And what he really came looking for is the best part of the story.

Ponce de León was one of the sailors who sailed with Christopher Columbus on his second voyage to the New World, and this voyage would change his life. When Columbus returned to Europe, Ponce de León decided to stay in Hispaniola. He became very popular and was named governor of Puerto Rico in 1508. While there, he heard many stories from sailors and Native Americans about a magical water source in the area that is now Florida. People called it the Fountain of Youth and said that drinking its water would keep you young. Ponce de León decided that he had to find this water source.

Asking permission from Spain's King Charles V to go in search of the legendary waters, the king agreed but directed that Ponce de León must pay for the ships and crew himself. Told that the magical water source could be found on an island called Bimini, he set sail in March of 1513. Instead of finding the island, however, he and his men landed on the coast of Florida, some of the first Europeans to do so. He led several expeditions inland to find the Fountain of Youth, but never managed to find it. In 1521, he returned to Florida in an effort to establish a Spanish colony on the island. However, hostile Native Americans attacked his expedition soon after landing, and the party retreated to Cuba, where Ponce de León died from a mortal wound suffered during the battle.

Even before Ponce de León, people have been looking for the Fountain of Youth. But instead of a Florida island, one of the places they search for it is at the local drugstore. Advertisers tout the qualities of age-defying makeup, products that are supposed to give you younger looking skin, and hair solutions to eliminate the gray. These may temporarily cover the evidence of growing older, but the only way to truly stop the aging process is to drink from the water of life, clear as crystal, that God holds out to you right now.

Pony Express

Some trust in chariots, and some in horses: but we will remember the name of the Lord our God.
Psalm 20:7.

Have you ever ridden a horse on the open prairie and felt the wind whipping through your hair? Have you gazed upon golden fields of waving wheat, seen the deep blue sky, and heard the meadowlarks calling to each other? If you had lived 150 years ago, you'd probably have experienced this and much more—rain storms and blizzards, wild wolves and bears, and unfriendly, renegade natives, especially if you were one of the Pony Express riders.

On April 3, 1860, the first Pony Express mail rider left St. Joseph, Missouri, and headed west. The riders rode 10 to 15 miles at top speeds to reach the next checkpoint, then got a fresh mount and headed out again. One hundred fifty relay stations peppered the pioneer trail across the present-day states of Missouri, Kansas, Nebraska, Wyoming, Colorado, Utah, Nevada, and California. The riders were paid $25 a week, and only orphans or men with no families were allowed to ride, since the job was such a dangerous one. Among the riders was the legendary frontiersman Buffalo Bill Cody who signed on with the Pony Express at age 14. Men like Buffalo Bill rode over prairies, forded rivers, and crossed mountains to deliver the mail. You've probably heard the old expression, "Neither rain nor snow, nor sleet nor dark of night shall stay these couriers from the swift completion of their appointed rounds." No doubt these words were inspired by the Pony Express.

And how long did it typically take for a rider to reach the west coast destination of Sacramento? Well, you're not going to believe this, but those riders and their mail packets arrived in Sacramento after 1,800 miles and just 10 days on the road. The Pony Express captivated America's imagination, but unfortunately lasted only a few short months, replaced by the telegraph soon after.

While we can gain inspiration from the courage and dedication of the Pony Express riders, David reminds us that we cannot trust in horses. There's always something that can stop a horse, but there is absolutely nothing that can stop God's name—love. Nothing can keep God from loving you. It's the only thing you can really trust.

Heart Transplant

I will give you a new heart and put a new spirit within you; I will take the heart of stone out of your flesh and give you a heart of flesh. Ezekiel 36:26, NKJV.

Can you imagine having a mechanical heart inside your chest? Instead of a beating heart of flesh you would have a robot heart made of silicone, titanium, and steel. Believe it or not, it's been done.

On the morning of April 4, 1969, Drs. Domingo Liotta and Denton Cooley replaced a dying man's heart with a mechanical heart at a hospital in Houston, Texas. The patient did well and recovered quickly. After 64 hours the mechanical heart was removed and replaced by a donor heart. Unfortunately, that proved to be a bad decision because 32 hours later the patient died. The second surgery was evidently done too soon after the first surgery, and an infection set in, soon spreading to the lungs.

Today, some 40 years later, open-heart surgery is quite common, with donors providing the needed hearts for about 3,500 transplants each year. In these procedures the patient's heart is sometimes removed and sometimes left inside the body to help support the donor heart. Wow! Walking around out there are some patients with two hearts beating inside their chest cavities! Even babies have been given transplanted hearts and have gone on to live healthy lives.

Sadly, there are about 800,000 people who need new hearts but can't get them because of a shortage of donors. This has caused an increased effort to use mechanical hearts and donor hearts from other species, such as baboons.

Our text for today gives us a quite different scenario. God is offering to take out our old hearts that have become encrusted with sin and give us new ones beating with the pulse of Heaven's goodness. Instead of trying to replace our diseased hearts with mechanical ones, God is offering to give us new ones now, fresh from the hand of the Creator. But one thing is sure. In this world the sins we cherish most must be surrendered to God. He's the Great Physician, so we can't be going into surgery telling Him how to operate. And once we experience His expert care, we won't want sin-encrusted hearts ever again. He can heal us now and give us that transplant. And one day soon when Jesus comes, He will give us new physical hearts—immortal hearts that will beat in perfect rhythm with Heaven forever.

Pocahontas

Therefore he is able to save completely those who come to God through him, because he always lives to intercede for them.
Hebrews 7:25, NIV.

Pocahontas is one of the most famous Native American maidens in American lore. Born in the New World, she entered the picture when she saved the life of John Smith, who later became governor of the Jamestown settlement. That was some 400 years ago, and this is how it all happened.

In 1607, 100 colonists arrived in Virginia to build the first permanent English settlement. Unfortunately, things didn't go too well for the new colony. Famine, disease, and native attacks plagued the settlers, and their numbers began to dwindle. On one of his exploring trips up the Chickahominy River, Smith and two other colonists were captured by Powhatan warriors. John's two friends were killed but Smith was spared and finally released because a young native girl named Pocahontas begged her father, Powhatan, not to kill John. The kindness she showed to John would save his life—and change hers forever.

Pocahontas often came to the Jamestown settlement, befriended the settlers, and learned English customs. Eventually, she met and married John Rolfe, a successful tobacco farmer of Jamestown. The timely marriage guaranteed peace for several years between the Jamestown settlers and the Powhatan tribe. Pocahontas and John were blessed with a baby daughter a year later, after which Pocahontas and her husband sailed to England for a visit. Tragically, she fell victim to smallpox, losing her life the day before her ship set sail for the New World.

Pocahontas was a kind young girl and demonstrated traits of mercy even though she most likely knew nothing about Jesus. It is probable that her efforts to save John Smith saved the entire colony, since he was the natural leader of the settlement. Jesus' act of kindness of dying on a cruel cross saved you—and your entire world. Jesus didn't have to convince God to save our lives, however, because God wanted us to live just as much as Jesus did. It was God Himself who died in our place and is now interceding for us in the heavenly courts. He loves us so much that He didn't just save our lives once, but is saving us day in and day out through His constant intercession.

First Modern Olympic Games

Don't you realize that in a race everyone runs, but only one person gets the prize? They do it to win a prize that will fade away, but we do it for an eternal prize. 1 Corinthians 9:23-25, NLT.

The Olympic Games have a long history. The first recorded Olympics were held in Greece in 776 B.C., but most historians believe that the Olympics were at least 500 years old by that time. The ancient Olympics, held every four years, occurred during a religious festival honoring the Greek god Zeus. Olympic competition was originally limited to footraces, but it wasn't long before wrestling, boxing, and chariot racing were added. The pentathlon event came even later and required five skills: footracing, long jumping, discus and javelin throwing, and wrestling. Unfortunately, the Olympics games faded away with the rise of Rome.

It wasn't until the late 1800s that Europeans began to show interest in reviving the games. The French were the ones to bring a proposal to the table, suggesting that the Olympics be an international competition that would occur every four years. On April 6, 1896, the Olympic Games were officially reborn in Athens. Two hundred eighty athletes from 13 nations competed in 43 contests, including track-and-field events, swimming, gymnastics, cycling, wrestling, weightlifting, fencing, shooting, and tennis. The track-and-field events were held at the Panathenaic Stadium, which was originally built in 330 B.C. and was restored for the 1896 Games.

Today, an average of 10,000 athletes from 200 countries compete in the Olympics every four years. Thirty-one sports are featured, including archery, baseball, basketball, canoeing, horse riding, cycling, gymnastics, judo, sailing, swimming, tennis, volleyball, weightlifting, and wrestling. In addition, many track-and-field events are popular, including relay races, shot put, and the grand-daddy of them all—the decathlon, a 10-skill event performed by one person in competition with others.

Trophies for top performances in the Olympics are given out as gold, silver, and bronze metals, but these trophies are just earthly ones. The course of life we run is a hard one on the straight and narrow track toward our heavenly home. The prize we seek as sons and daughters of God is not a temporary medal, but a face-to-face friendship with our loving God.

Rwanda Genocide

*Yea, though I walk through the valley of the shadow
of death, I will fear no evil; For You are with me.
Psalm 23:4, NKJV.*

On the morning of Thursday, April 7, 1994, those still asleep at the Adventist University of Rwanda in Africa awoke to the sound of the insistent ringing of telephones all over campus. The jingling was an alert to the missionary teachers and students that trouble would soon spread its dark cloak over the campus. Late the previous evening, Juvenal Habyarimana, president of Rwanda and member of the Hutu tribe, was returning from a peace conference when his presidential plane was shot down as it made its final approach to the airport in the capital city of Kigali. Although there were conflicting reports as to who was responsible for the death of the president, many Hutus wanted to believe that it was their longtime enemies, the Tutsis.

For hundreds of years the Hutu and Tutsi cultures had been at odds. As the president's plane lay in a crumpled heap, a massive cloud of suspicion blanketed the country as angry Hutus began seeking out every suspected Tutsi. Afraid that if they did not turn on the accused, they would become the accused, confusion and fear rained down on the people. The rain continued while a flood of genocide rose, swamping much of the country. On the Adventist campus, a tense but fearful peace hung on, with many Tutsis seeking refuge there, even as huts were being burned nearby.

An estimated 75 percent of the Tutsis living in Rwanda lost their lives during this conflict. By the time it was over, more than 900,000 people had died. Thousands of families had lost sons, daughters, mothers, fathers, aunts, and uncles in the genocide. Amid the rolling sea of death, however, surfaced islands of love, with some Hutus saving the lives of Tutsis at great personal risk to their own. Many people witnessed God's presence with them in the valley of the shadow of death.

Why did God allow this wave of death to crash over so many people who were guilty of nothing but belonging to a particular tribe? Did He allow it for some higher reason? Although God can use tragedies for our good, the Rwandan genocide was *not* His will, but another's. Will you serve the one who causes the shadow of death, or the One who walks with us through it?

Buddha Born

*Salvation is found in no one else, for there is no other name
under heaven given to men by which we must be saved.
Acts 4:12, NIV.*

Since the creation of the world, religion has always been an important part of life. It seems that everyone needs a higher power to worship and serve. The Muslims have Allah. The Chinese have Confucius. The Christians have Jesus. Some, like atheists, claim they worship nothing, but they too have a god. It is man himself, or possibly, the idea of what man can accomplish.

On this day every year, Buddhists celebrate the birth of Gautama Buddha, the founder of Buddhism. He lived in India from 563 to 483 B.C. Before becoming the Buddha, he was born as Prince Siddhartha among the Sakya people of present-day Nepal and India. On the day he was born, holy men predicted that he would either become a great king or a Buddha, which is a very enlightened teacher. Siddhartha was brought up in great luxury, and at age 29, he left the palace to become a wandering monk.

He studied meditation under the great teachers, fasted, and finally became a Buddha. For the rest of his life, Buddha gathered disciples. He died at age 80, but today his religion has spread to India, Southeast Asia, China, Korea, Japan, and the United States. There are an estimated 350 million people in 100 nations who adhere to Buddhist beliefs and practices.

Most people who worship Buddha have a small idol or picture of him in their houses. Christians, in contrast, do not worship pictures, objects, or people. Why not? Because God has said that His people won't worship any gods, or pictures of those gods, but Him. Christians know this as the first and second of His ten commandments of Exodus 20, but have you ever considered the first verse of this famous chapter? God began these commandments by identifying Himself as the Savior of His people, leading them out of bondage in Egypt. By beginning His law this way, it's like He's saying, "When you see Me as the true, real, powerful, loving God who has put His money where His mouth is and has saved you from the slavery that gripped you, you won't *want* to have any other gods before Me, and you won't want to worship pictures of them!" Christians worship God and God alone because He is the only God who first loved them and did whatever it took to save them.

First Astronauts Introduced

*Then I saw another Angel flying in the midst of heaven, having
the everlasting gospel to preach to those who dwell on the earth.
Revelation 14:6, NKJV.*

When World War II was over, the world was a very shaky place. Millions
had died, and countries that had once existed, were no longer even on
the map. Everyone had thought that since the War was over, life would return to normal again. But it didn't. The fear that inspired nations to fight
against one another was still alive. One of the worst things to come out of
World War II was the race for nuclear weapons. Today we remember it as
the Cold War, because although the United States and the Soviet Union had
been allies during World War II, they now became bitter enemies. The
United States had developed the first nuclear bomb, and the U.S.S.R. wasn't
far behind. And then this competition for power with weapons spread to the
race for space.

In 1957 the Russians announced that they had launched a satellite into
space. This news sparked fear again in the heart of everyone in America.
Would the Communists become so powerful that they would eventually take
over the world? Would we soon have to fight them as we had the Nazis and
Japanese, only this time with nuclear missiles? The U.S. government now put
every spare dollar it could into the space program, and on April 9, 1959,
NASA announced that it was going to send the first astronauts into space.
The first team to go were all trained military pilots: Scott Carpenter, Gordon
Cooper, John Glenn, Gus Grissom, Walter Schirra, Alan Shepard, and Donald
Slayton.

Today, the Cold War between The U.S. and the U.S.S.R. is pretty much
over, but as long as Satan is around, the war between good and evil persists.
Satan would love nothing more than to see nations go right on fighting. But
God has commissioned us to take a very special message to the world and it
involves more flight into space. It's the three angels' message of Revelation,
a message of hope and peace to the world. God won the Cold War between
Christ and Satan when Jesus died on Calvary, and today it is our job to take
that message to the world. Jesus is coming soon, and when He does, those
of us who have shared the three angel's message will take another ride into
space, only this time we won't have to go in a rocket or wear spacesuits.
We'll fly like the three angels themselves.

A Simple Little Gadget

Andrew, Simon Peter's brother, said to Him, "There is a lad here who has five barley loaves and two small fish, but what are they among so many?" John 6:8, 9, NKJV.

Have you ever wondered how a clever thing like the safety pin came to be? It really is quite a simple gimmick, and the story about how it was invented is almost as simple. On April 10, 1849, a man by the name of Walter Hunt from New York City came up with the concept. Within the space of just three hours, he thought of the idea, made a sample safety pin, and sold the idea to a manufacturer for $100. That doesn't sound like a lot of money, and it wasn't for such an innovative contraption. Even so, today that money would be worth about $1,500.

Can you imagine that! One hundred dollars for such a simple idea and for such little effort. And billions and billions of safety pins worth millions and millions of dollars have probably been made since it was first invented. We use safety pins for many things—to repair a dress or pair of pants missing a button, to hold up curtains that are falling down, or to pin something on someone, like a flower or ribbon. And, of course, we used them a lot more when there was no such thing as disposable diapers. Who would ever think that a safety pin could be so valuable? It's a very small gadget—yet very clever. Walter Hunt of New York City probably didn't realize how important it was going to become in our American culture.

The Bible is full of examples of little things that ended up being very important. As Jesus stood sharing the golden truths of Heaven on the hillside that day, the crowds of people pressed as close as they could. His messages were so relevant and fascinating that they didn't realize they had gone all day without eating. The disciples' eyes grew wide as they realized they had no food to give to the multitudes of men, women, and children. They thought about running to town to pick something up, but then, of course, realized they couldn't possibly afford it. Then Jesus suggested they give the people what they had. Looking around a bit, they found a little boy who had a little lunch of five small loaves of bread and two fishes. Jesus took this tiny lunch and did the impossible—something no one dreamed He could do—and fed the hungry masses. Jesus expected nothing from His followers but to give Him the very little they had. You're surrounded by hungry people. Jesus is asking you what you have, but don't worry that it's not much. The important thing is not how much you have, but that you give it all to Him.

Napoleon Exiled

As you saw the iron mixed with baked clay, so the people will be a mixture and will not remain united, anymore than iron mixes with clay. Daniel 2:43, NIV.

Napoleon was an interesting character. Historians agree that he was one of the greatest military leaders in history. Unfortunately, he developed a reputation for being power-hungry and insecure, which obviously gave him a complex. Psychologists say that when people feel insecure they try to compensate by appearing important in other ways, like getting a big car or truck, securing a high-powered executive job, or having lots of friends and lots of money. Napoleon tried to compensate by ruling the world. Now that's a pretty hefty way to compensate! As a military genius he set out to rule Europe, but he missed one very important detail—God and His Word.

But Napoleon tried anyway. After fighting in the French Revolution, he became a military dictator in 1799. In 1804 he became the emperor of France and by 1810 ruled most of Europe. For years he fought against the English, the Germans, and the Russians. When he began to lose battles, the tide turned against him, and he finally had to admit defeat. As a result Napoleon had to give up his throne. As punishment for his war crimes, Napoleon's enemies forced him into exile on the Mediterranean island of Elba. A year later he escaped from the island and managed to fight at least one more decisive battle at Waterloo. This time, when he lost, he was exiled again, and died just six years later at the age of 52.

Napoleon's dream of world domination was doomed to fail because he hadn't taken God into consideration. In the biblical books of prophecy God had said that after Rome there would be no more world empires. Modern nations would mix but would never completely fuse together into a one-world empire any more than iron can mix with clay. Adolf Hitler tried it with his Nazi government in the 1930s and 40s. And the Soviet Union had such ambitions in the 1950s, 60s, and 70s. Today it appears that the United Nations would like to set up a one-world government to regulate industry, run banks, and be a watchdog for the environment. But God reminds us in the words of Daniel that the nations of our world will never again be united under one government. That's God speaking, and He has never been proven wrong!

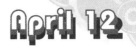

Astronomer Condemned

He shall speak pompous words against the Most High, shall persecute the saints of the Most High, and shall intend to change times and law. Daniel 7:25, NKJV.

Galileo was the most famous renegade astronomer of his day. His ideas about the solar system and our universe were a cut above what was being taught at the time, and they got him into a lot of trouble. The mid-1600s was a time of renaissance ideas in religion, world exploration, and science. Unfortunately, people sometimes don't like change, and neither did the church leaders of the day, who gripped the reins of society's power. Medieval times have been called the Dark Ages because the few people in power made sure that the light of general public knowledge glowed dim. The masses were discouraged from reading and writing and medical knowledge was almost nonexistent. The people and the leaders were also quite ignorant about the natural laws of science—except our hero.

When Galileo proposed that the earth was not the center of the solar system, he caused quite a stir, especially among church leaders. That such news could shake the religious world at that time is a wonder. But of course, any new idea that conflicted with the traditional teachings of the Church could undermine its authority and make its proud leaders look foolish to the common people. After all, they believed they were the keepers of God's Word, and they insisted that God's Word was clear that the sun moved around the earth. Of course, no such scripture can be found, and even at that time scientists had known for centuries that the earth was not the center of the universe. And so, on April 12, 1633, the church leaders stubbornly took Galileo to trial for his teachings of "heresy." Galileo agreed not to teach such "nonsense" anymore, and for his confession, he spent the rest of his life under house arrest. It wasn't until much later that the Church finally admitted that Galileo was right.

Should we be surprised? The Bible prophesied that a super religious power would rise in the Dark Ages to persecute God's people and try to change times and laws. That its leaders tried to suppress the gospel by persecuting the saints was one thing. That they tried to suppress science was another. But then again, the Bible truths and science aren't so far apart. After all, the God who created the universe is the same God who gave us the good news of the gospel of Jesus.

Miracle Storm

*As they fled before Israel on the road down from Beth Horon
to Azekah, the Lord hurled large hailstones down on
them from the sky, and more of them died from the
hailstones than were killed by the swords of the Israelites.
Joshua 10:11, NIV.*

Have you ever heard of the Hundred Years' War? Kind of a strange name for a war, especially since it lasted more than 100 years. The war actually lasted 116 years, and some very unusual stories came out of that era. One battle was fought in which a strange miracle took place. Here's how it happened.

The Hundred Years' War between England and France was already over 20 years old, and once again the English had invaded France. King Edward III wanted to engage the French in open combat, but they wouldn't come out from behind their fences and fight like "men." Instead they stayed entrenched behind their barricades all that winter while the English pillaged the countryside. But the French were a praying people. Many among them felt that God must come to their rescue or they would be overrun and destroyed by King Edward's army in the spring.

In April of 1360, King Edward's forces attacked Paris and burned much of it to the ground. Then the British moved on to the town of Chartres. On the night of April 13, while they were camped outside Chartres, a sudden storm hit the countryside. Lightning struck repeatedly, killing several people, and then hailstones showered down on the soldiers, scattering their horses. While trying to marshal the forces, military officers died where they sat on horseback, and panic set in among the troops. In the open air no one could find shelter from the storm, and soldiers began dying right and left. The French saw the heavy losses to the English as a direct sign from God that He was with them, fighting for their cause. They believed that surely the presence of God had been in that place in answer to their prayers! King Edward quickly negotiated peace with the French, and a treaty was signed not long after that gave them a few years' rest from war.

God has promised us that when we need Him, He is there to comfort us and to sometimes even work miracles to rescue us. It may not always be in ways that we expect or want, but He will be there just the same.

Lincoln Assassinated

There is a way that seems right to a man, but in the end it leads to death. Proverbs 16:25, NIV.

One of the most tragic of days in American history was the day John Wilkes Booth shot and killed President Lincoln. It happened on this day in 1865, while the president was attending a play in Ford's Theatre in Washington, D.C.

Booth was an actor and Confederate sympathizer who was living in the North at the time. His original plan was to kidnap the President and take him to Richmond, the Confederate capital. However, on March 20, the day of the planned capture, President Lincoln failed to appear at the spot where Booth and his six fellow kidnappers lay in wait. And then, two weeks later, the Civil War ended on April 8 when Richmond fell to Union forces, and General Robert E. Lee surrendered at the Appomattox Court House in Virginia.

With Confederate armies near collapse across the South, Booth hatched a new plan to save the Confederacy. On April 14, he would assassinate Lincoln while the president was attending a play at Ford's Theatre. Booth's co-conspirators, Lewis Powell and George Atzerodt, would kill the vice president and secretary of state. Booth carried out his part of the plan, entering the theatre box and shooting the president from behind with a single bullet to the head. To escape, Booth jumped to the stage below but broke his leg in the fall. He did manage to escape on horseback, but he had no way of knowing that his two co-conspirators had failed in their attempts. The president, badly wounded, was carried to a lodging house opposite the theatre where he died the next morning.

Meanwhile, Booth fled Washington but was pursued by the army and was finally cornered in a barn near Bowling Green, Virginia. No one knows exactly how he died, whether it was from a bullet in his own gun or from the smoke and flames from the barn that the army burned to the ground around him. Eight people were eventually charged with conspiracy to assassinate the president. Four were hanged and four jailed.

If you had asked John Wilkes Booth, he would have told you he had a good reason for doing what he did. The way that seemed right to him, however, led to the death of one of the United States' most popular presidents, and to his own demise.

McDonald's Gets a Jump-start

When you eat or drink or do anything else, always do it to honor God.
1 Cor. 10:31, CEV.

McDonald's is one of the most successful businesses in world history, but without a traveling milk shake mixer salesman, it may never have bloomed into the worldwide corporation that it is today.

In 1940, Richard and Maurice McDonald started a small hamburger joint in southern California. Looking to expand, they didn't know how they should go about it. When Ray Kroc walked into the small restaurant hoping to sell them a milk shake mixer, he was surprised when the brothers purchased, not one, but several! Curious, Ray inquired why they wanted so many, eventually offering them his services as their business agent. With his sharp business sense, Ray suggested they expand their presence. On April 15, 1955, Ray opened his own McDonald's in Des Plaines, Illinois, a suburb of Chicago, and the business became the McDonald's Corporation. Ray did so well that after a few years he bought out the founding McDonald brothers for 14 million dollars.

Ten years after opening that Chicago restaurant, more than 700 sites had sprung up all over the country. By the 1980s Ray had built McDonald's into a multibillion dollar, international burger empire. And by 2009, over 31,000 restaurants were serving over 58,000,000 customers in 118 countries! Kroc's golden arches at the original restaurant in Des Plaines, Illinois, is still the company's logo.

Fast food. It's fast and convenient, nobody can deny that. It's perfect for anyone who's goal is to inhabit a body for a very few years and then let it die, exhausted from overuse of its components. Fast food is a great way to squeak by, sitting around doing nothing, surviving an empty existence.

But why hobble through life when you can feel the wind in your face riding the rollercoasters of a challenging mission? Why tiptoe through a fearful field of unrealized dreams when you can soar on wind currents of lasting fulfillment? You can change this world for the better! God made you for an abundant life, a life oozing with action, adventure, and meaning. But you're definitely going to want to walk past those golden arches. Your mission requires quality fuel that won't leave your engine sputtering—fuel to help you honor God.

Great Train Robbery

Be sure your sin will find you out.
Numbers 32:23, NKJV.

One of the most daring robberies of our time was Britain's 1963 Great Train Robbery. Through a series of well planned logistics, Bruce Reynolds and his gang of thieves managed to stop a Royal Mail train loaded with cash from banks in Scotland and England. Boarding the train, they commandeered it, forcing the driver to stop it at a location where they could unload the sacks containing money valued at $56,000,000 in today's economy. Most notable train robberies happened in the days of the old west, with robbers chasing the trains on horseback. Not this time! Amazingly enough, the 15-member gang disappeared, leaving a trail of unanswered questions behind. Who were these men? How did they pull off the robbery of the century without the use of a single gun? How did they escape?

Initially, police were completely perplexed, overwhelmed by the staggering amount of money involved as well as by a lack of credible leads. But just a few days into the investigation, an anonymous tip led them to a farmhouse close to the scene of the robbery. The gang had used the place as a hideout, paying a man wads of currency to clean the farmhouse of any evidence of their stay. The man was glad to take their money but double-crossed them, leaving behind many telltale clues of their presence, such as a Monopoly game board covered with their fingerprints. The investigation came together rapidly and one gang member after another was handcuffed. Twelve of the 15 robbers were sentenced to prison on this day in 1964, with prison terms totaling more than 300 years! Reynolds, considered the mastermind of the heist, evaded arrest for a few years but was finally brought to justice in 1969. The years after the robbery for these men were tumultuous. Most languished in prison, staring every day at the same drab walls. Others were able to escape, only to be recaptured. The ones who were not caught were forced to constantly look over their shoulders, living in constant fear of capture. Was the money worth it? Was it truly rewarding to trade their freedom for bags and bags of cash?

When we really get to know our Creator and the incredible freedom He offers us, the last thing we'll want to do is jeopardize that freedom, which comes only through friendship with Him. Living in the confidence and security He provides, we never have to experience the truth that our sins will find us out.

Ben Franklin Dies

*So don't worry about tomorrow, for tomorrow will bring
its own worries. Today's trouble is enough for today.*
Matthew 6:34, NLT.

"Why put off 'til tomorrow what you can do today?" You've heard that line before, and you may think your mom or dad came up with it. Turns out they only borrowed it from Benjamin Franklin, who coined the phrase. He also came up with other famous American proverbs, like "God helps those who help themselves" and "Early to bed and early to rise, makes a man healthy, wealthy, and wise." Today Benjamin is still one of the most famous Americans in all our history, and with good reason. The man could do just about anything. At just 12 years of age he became a printer and later started one of the most successful newspapers in the country. He also secured a contract to print Philadelphia's paper money.

As his wealth grew and his fame spread, he became active in local government, helping Philadelphia start its own library, police force, volunteer fire department, post office, and an academy that later became the University of Pennsylvania. He was a key player, not only in local government, but also in national politics. He helped draft and signed the Declaration of Independence and the Constitution. He was witty and conversational, liked by people at home and abroad. Becoming an ambassador to France, he charmed both common folks and royalty alike. And with all his experience and famous contacts, he was a big help in writing two treaties with the British. We even put his face on the American $100 bill.

If all that weren't enough, he also ventured into the field of science, discovering faster ways to sail ships across the Atlantic, inventing bifocals, and designing an ingenious Franklin stove that is still sold today. But he is perhaps best remembered for his work with electricity, the picture of him flying a kite in a thunderstorm emblazoned in many American minds.

So when the famous printer, newspaper man, politician, scientist, and inventor finally died at 84 years of age on April 17, 1790, the whole world mourned. It was a big loss indeed, and every major newspaper in the world carried the news.

You may not have five careers to juggle, but life can seem pretty unmanageable at times, can't it? Today's text gives us surprisingly simple advice in balancing it all from Someone infinitely wiser than even Mr. Franklin: take one day at a time.

Earthquake and Fire

*After the wind there was an earthquake, but the Lord was
not in the earthquake. After the earthquake came a fire, but the
Lord was not in the fire. And after the fire came a gentle whisper.*
1 Kings 19:11, 12, NIV.

It's just after 5:00 in the morning, and you're snuggled in your bed when you feel your bed begin to move. Your eyes blink open, and you expect to see your little brother gripping the bed frame and grinning from ear to ear. But he's not there. Instead you hear him crying in the next room. You jump out of bed and are immediately thrown against the bookcase as your entire room shifts back and forth. Staggering into your brother's room where pictures are dropping to the floor and toys are sliding off shelves, you snatch your brother out of bed and stand with him in the doorway of his room, waiting for the frightening motion to stop.

When the motion finally did stop on that early morning of April 18, 1906, 500 blocks of San Francisco's downtown area were leveled. Buildings had been toppled, rubble had covered the streets, and gas lines had been ruptured. At a magnitude of 7.7-7.9, the temblor caused $400,000,000 worth of damage ($8.2 billion in today's currency). More importantly, modern estimates put the loss of life at around 3,000, with 225,000 people left without homes. San Francisco lies at the north end of the San Andreas fault, where the subterranean Pacific and North American plates meet. The ground on the Pacific Ocean side of the fault began moving toward the north, in some places as much as 21 feet, causing the horrific earthquake.

With the city of San Francisco reeling from the hideous loss of life and tragic widespread destruction, the country's worst natural disaster was immediately followed by an unwelcome and even greater destructive force taking it by the throat as a fire ripped through the mangled wreckage. Possibly helped along by some whose insurance policies covered fires but not earthquakes, flames caressed the city with melting fingers of smoking destruction for four days.

What really caused the earthquake and the fire? Some would have you believe that God was behind them both; after all, many insurance policies speak of natural disasters as "acts of God." Today's text says that God was not in the earthquake that shook the ground around Elijah, nor was He in the fire. While God has the ability to unleash earthshaking fireworks, His heart is not in them. The heart of God is in the gentle whisper of His most powerful feature—His love.

Oklahoma City Bombing

And do not fear those who kill the body but cannot kill the soul.
Matthew 10:28, NKJV.

Today we live in a world of fear. Everyday we hear new stories about people who have killed in large numbers. We hear about religious fanatics who go on suicide missions to kill "infidels." We hear of people burning churches, about troubled psychotics who walk into schools and gun down children, and madmen detonating bombs in planes and palaces.

On April 19, 1995, we heard yet another horrific story about death and dying, and it happened in the peaceful town of Oklahoma City, Oklahoma. Tragically, 168 people died in that blast, including 19 young children in the day care center housed in the building. It was the worst terrorist tragedy in our country up to that time.

Timothy McVeigh was the one who was finally brought to trial for the conspiracy and the deed. How did he pull it off? A Ryder van loaded with 5,000 pounds of explosives was driven into the basement parking garage of the Alfred P. Murrah Federal Building. The diesel fuel and fertilizer mixture was easy to buy—and easy to detonate. No one saw it coming. It was a foolproof plan, engineered down to the last detail, and the driver of the van got away undetected.

However, amazingly enough, only a little over an hour after the explosion, a state trooper stopped a car without license plates in the town of Perry. The trooper noticed a bulge in the driver's jacket. It was Timothy McVeigh. He was arrested for concealing a gun, and the FBI later decided to hold him in jail as a suspect in the Oklahoma bombing charges. Three of Timothy's friends were also arrested for their part in the bombing, and it was their testimony that sealed Timothy's fate. Timothy was convicted and executed for his act of mass murder.

Timothy McVeigh had a grudge against the American government, and bombing the Federal Building was his way of evening the score. Unfortunately, he killed a lot of innocent people in the blast. Our enemy used Timothy for his evil purposes—to bring death to the victims and suffering to the families of those who died. It is a sad story, but for those of us who trust in Jesus, we don't need to fear death. One day Jesus will resurrect those faithful believers who have suffered in this world of sin.

Electron Microscope

Oh, magnify the Lord with me, and let us exalt His name together.
Psalm 34:3, NKJV.

When is an eyelash 16 feet thick? When you look at it through an electron microscope. Vladimir Zworykin, co-inventor of television, immigrated to the United States from Russia in 1919, eventually going to work for *RCA*. An electronic whiz, he became interested in improving the electron microscope, and on this day in 1940, he demonstrated the first model in the United States. Invented in Russia by Ernst Ruska in the late 1920s, Zworykin greatly improved the device, giving us the ability to examine objects 100,000 times closer than we could with the naked eye. Apparently, in order to see tiny objects, the machine had to be mammoth, because the microscope he and his RCA team demonstrated in Philadelphia was 10 feet high and weighed half a ton! The idea behind the electron microscope was to get closer to objects than regular optical microscopes could take us—only 2,000 times closer than the naked eye. Instead of using optical lenses, like eyeglasses, the electron microscope uses an electric field or a magnetic coil to focus a beam of electrons at the item being examined. Looking through this focused beam, the object is greatly magnified.

Using an electron microscope, we can peer into living cells, possibly find a cure for cancer, determine the genetic makeup of a chromosome, or simply be amazed exploring a microscopic world. In this world where an eyelash is monstrous, it becomes clear that God took the time to create the microscopic in the same way He created everything else: with organization, contrast, and beauty. Apparently God didn't spend a lot of time painstakingly sculpting, arranging, smoothing, and coloring some things, and then hurriedly throwing other things together just to be reasonably acceptable for when company comes over. He thinks so much of us that, when creating our world, He thought, Hmmm . . . someone might develop the ability to see this tiny cell someday, so I'm going to make it as breathtakingly beautiful as I can.

What an awesome Creator God we have! And what a shame that most people in the world don't see and appreciate Him. We can show our awesome Lord to the world around us. How? When we, only tiny electrons, focus on what He has done for us, focus on sincerely seeking Him daily, and focus on coming together to appreciate Him, we magnify His name for all the world to see and appreciate.

First Firehouse Pole

I will save you; you will . . . escape with your life,
because you trust in me, declares the Lord.
Jeremiah 39:18, NIV.

Catch this news flash in a Chicago newspaper of April 21, 1878: "Thinking Fast, Firefighter Slides Down a Pole." That makes sense. It's something firefighters do all the time, right? Well, it is today, but back in 1878 it was a first.

This is how it happened. On this particular day firefighters at Engine Company 21 were unloading hay for the horses that pulled their fire engines. When the bell rang, George Reid was up in the hayloft on the third floor. A long binding pole that was used to secure the hay to the wagon stood nearby. Instead of running all the way down two flights of stairs, George grabbed the pole and quickly slid down it to the waiting fire engine below. Good thinking, George!

His captain liked the idea of a pole and asked the chief if he could cut a hole in the second floor to install a permanent pole. The fire chief agreed as long as the captain paid for the repairs to the ceiling if the idea didn't work. The crew then made a three-inch pole from Georgia pine, sanded it, varnished it, and waxed it with paraffin. Not surprisingly, the sliding pole worked perfectly. Engine Company 21 soon got a reputation for being the first crew at the scene of fires. The fire chief, instead of docking the captain's pay for the hole in the ceiling, ordered poles for every firehouse in Chicago.

Today fire poles are sometimes considered safety hazards, believe it or not, and new firehouses are often built without them. Single story firehouses are more common now to avoid having firefighters fall and injure themselves on the way down a fire pole. The last thing you want is for a firefighter to get hurt before he's even out of the building. But it's all about saving people—with or without a pole.

Jesus arrived on the scene of our burning world that would have destroyed us from sin inhalation. He knew that unless He risked His own eternal existence, lived dangerously close to the life taking smoke of sin, and experienced the skin searing flames of the cross, we would perish, never to be revived. Without Him, there is no escape from our burning building; there is nothing we can do to save ourselves. Our only hope is to simply say yes to our rescuing Firefighter.

Bike Trip Around the World

I can do all things through Christ who strengthens me.
Philippians 4:13, NKJV.

On April 22, 1884, at 8 a.m., Thomas Stevens embarked on a bicycle trip around the world, the first person ever to attempt such a momumental plan. He began his trip in San Francisco, riding east on a bike that was known in those days as a high wheeler. Stevens set out with only the bare necessities. In his handlebar bag were socks, a spare shirt, a raincoat that doubled as both tent and bedding, and a .38 Smith & Wesson pistol. Thirty-seven hundred miles later, after bouncing around on wagon trails, railroad beds, canal towpaths, and public roads, he finally reached Boston on August 4. It was the first transcontinental bicycle trip on record.

He spent the winter in New York, and then rode a steamer to Liverpool, England, where he was met by enthusiastic bicycle fans. He continued his world journey through England, France, Germany, Austria, Hungary, Slavonia, Serbia, Bulgaria, and Turkey. Thomas was worried about bandits in this part of the world but bravely set out on the dangerous roads through the middle east. God protected him from seen and unseen dangers, and he spent that second winter with the shah of Iran.

The authorities in Afghanistan kicked Thomas out of their country, so he took a Russian steamship across the Caspian Sea, and then on to India. He took another steamer from Calcutta to Hong Kong. Setting out for eastern China, he got lost and had great difficulty getting directions because he couldn't pronounce the words in their language. At one point a Chinese official saved him from an angry mob. His pedaling finally ended in Yokohama, Japan, on December 17, 1886, and in January of 1887, he took a steamer across the Pacific to San Francisco. He had bicycled 13,500 miles.

What an amazing feat of determination and endurance! Thomas Stevens had something else in his handlebar bag—persistent strength. Bouncing around on the roads of life, there are times when we feel overwhelmed by our small progress and the seemingly boundless expanse of forbidding terrain ahead. There are moments of fear when we are surrounded by threatening guilt, self-hatred, or temptation. You are not left to navigate your life journey alone. If you look up, you will see the tire tracks of Someone who has ridden your route before you. Reach into your handlebar bag and you will find, day in and day out, persistent strength from Him.

Amazing Skin Transplant

I will praise You, for I am fearfully and
wonderfully made; marvelous are Your works.
Psalm 139:14, NKJV.

Your skin is the largest organ of your body. It serves as the first and best of the body's defenses against invading disease and infection. In one square inch of skin, there are: three yards of blood vessels, 36 heat sensors, 75 pressure sensors, 600 pain sensors, 1,300 nerve cells, 900 nerve endings, 100 sweat glands, and three million cells total. With all those pieces of anatomy fitting into a tiny square inch of skin, it's amazing that our skin can even heal at all! But it does. The skin's ability to heal itself is one of the most amazing miracles of the human body. The clotting of blood, the immune system working overtime to keep infections down, and the ability of the skin to heal without a scar—amazing stuff.

People with serious injuries to the skin, such as burn victims, often have skin grafts. Doctors remove skin from other parts of the body to cover the wounded area. When a wound is so large that the doctor can't find a suitable area from which to take the skin, she may choose to cut off small pieces of skin from several places and, like a puzzle, piece them together over the wound.

What happens, though, if the doctor just can't find enough skin to cover a wounded area? The answer to this dilemma was found in a mixture of cowhide, shark cartilage, and plastic—artificial skin. This "skin" was developed by a team of researchers at Massachusetts Institute of Technology and, on April 23, 1981, was successfully transplanted to 10 severely burned patients, three of whom would have died without the procedure. Imagine all the tears of these patients and their families, thinking they were probably going to die, or else live a very bitter existence as a result of these severe burns. And then imagine the relief and joy flooding their bodies as this amazing new skin was attached, leading them to new lives.

Our amazing Creator, who shaped us with His very own hands, created us with a covering that heals itself! And even in the carnage of our existence marred by trauma and disease, He gave us the capacity to heal even the most extreme cases. You can be assured that the Great Physician, who can heal the most severely damaged skin, can also heal the most severely damaged heart.

First African-American Basketball Player Drafted

Now these are the gifts Christ gave to the church: the apostles, the prophets, the evangelists, and the pastors and teachers. Their responsibility is to equip God's people to do his work and build up the church, the body of Christ. Ephesians 4:11, 12, NLT.

Can you imagine professional basketball today without African-Americans playing? Imagine the National Basketball Association (NBA) without Michael Jordan's historic flight from the free throw lane to a spectacular slam dunk. Imagine watching games devoid of Magic Johnson's amazing assists, Kobe Bryant's fadeaway jump shots, or LeBron James' spectacular jams. Today 80 percent of pro basketball players are African-Americans, and with good reason. They have ratcheted up the athletic aspect of the game several notches, and the NBA is indebted to them for the success it has enjoyed.

Unfortunately, for years race discrimination kept African-Americans off the court, but on this day in 1950, Charles Cooper became the first African-American player to break through the race barrier and wear a jersey for a professional team. Drafted by the Boston Celtics, he eventually became an all-star player in the sport. The dominance of African-American players in the NBA has continued to increase during the last several decades. By 1994, of the 124 franchise players in the game, 86 were African-Americans, and 35 were European-Americans. When the NBA named its 50 greatest players from its first 50 years, 31 were African-Americans and 18 were European-Americans. In 2001, not surprisingly, 34 of the 111 NBA Hall of Famers were African-Americans.

The presence of African-Americans on NBA teams has made such a positive impact on the game that it is difficult to imagine the sport without these stars. The presence of Christian players makes a huge positive impact on the game, as well, not only in professional arenas, but also on college, high school, and playground courts. When someone fouls you hard, and you resist the urge to start a fight, the other players will admire your God-given integrity. When you help an opposing player up off the asphalt, you are showing the silent strength of a Christian champion. And when you play with a constant mindset of bringing glory to God, you are an evangelist for Him! Let's hope we never have to imagine basketball without the presence of true Christian stars.

First United States Guide Dog

You have eyes—can't you see? You have ears—can't you hear?
Mark 8:18, NLT.

What would it be like to be blind? Imagine not being able to see the fluorescent yellow, orange, and red leaves of fall clinging to their branches in an autumn wind, a seagull soaring alongside a ferry boat, or the twinkling stars against the purple blanket of a night sky. More than missed beauty, if you have poor eyesight, or night blindness, you understand better than most the dangers that dim vision can bring. And if you are legally blind, you are the expert and should be writing today's devotional!

Fortunately, society has made some adjustments to accommodate those living with blindness. Some intersections have audio signals that announce when it is safe to cross the street, braille messages can be found on the doors and elevators of government public buildings, and guide dogs are available for those who qualify. A visually impaired person can take her guide dog into restaurants, buses, and even football stadiums. A guide dog and his owner are a team. The dog is trained to guide his owner around obstacles in the path, but being color blind, Fido cannot differentiate the colors of stoplights and warning signs. The owner is the other half of the team and is the one who chooses the destination. Like a navigator on an airplane, she must know how to get from one place to another, but must rely on the dog to be the pilot and get them there safely.

The idea of guide dogs being teamed with visually impaired humans began in Germany after World War I, to help returning veterans blinded in combat. Great Britain also put together such a program, and in the 1930s the United States finally got on board with seeing eye dog training schools. On April 25, 1938, the first North American guide dog went to work.

One winter, on a sidewalk in England several decades ago, a blind man was walking with his guide dog. Suddenly, the dog stopped and wouldn't move. After repeated attempts to nudge him forward, the blind man heard footsteps and asked the person passing by what the trouble might be. "You are a blessed man," said the stranger. "There are huge icicles hanging from the roof edge just ahead, and if you had taken just a few more steps, you most certainly could have been killed."

God offers His Holy Spirit to guide us around unseen dangers. Thank you, Lord!

Grasshopper Prayer

And I will rebuke the devourer for your sakes,
so that he will not destroy the fruit of your ground.
Malachi 3:11, NKJV.

The 1870s were very hard times for family farms all over the Midwestern states. Rocky Mountain locusts, more commonly called grasshoppers, were swarming over the plains every summer, eating everything in their path. They came in such hordes that people were sure the grasshopper plague in ancient Egypt couldn't have been much worse. As each summer passed and the crops upon which they depended for food were once again eaten up before they had a chance to ripen, many people began to abandon their farms and homesteads. Some stayed on, though, hoping things would be better the following summer. But the next season the plague of hoppers would return in even greater numbers. As spring turned to summer, like clockwork, the swarms would arrive and consume all the developing produce in the long rows.

Desperate to get rid of the grasshoppers, some farmers tried burning their crops just to kill the spring-loaded critters. Others would drag heavy objects over their fields to crush the insects. But as many as they killed, even more took their place. They filled the wells and clogged the roads. Trains sometimes couldn't climb hills because of the floods of grasshoppers covering the tracks.

For Minnesota farmers in the spring of 1877, the grasshopper plague came to a head. The farmers had planted their wheat crop, knowing that they couldn't last another season with more grasshoppers on the horizon. Something drastic had to happen, and they knew it would take a miracle from God to save them. On April 26, 1877, Minnesotans all across the state set aside this day for prayer, asking God to deliver them from the scourges of locusts. In their minds God had to intervene because they couldn't take one more season of grasshoppers depleting their food supply. And wonder of wonders, their prayers were answered. Miraculously, the plague of grasshoppers ended that summer.

God is willing to help us when we call on Him. Sometimes He says, "Yes, I'll get right on it." Other times He says, "No, that's not the best thing for you." And then there are the times He simply says, "Wait awhile. I want you to grow in grace and learn to trust me."

Teatime

When all Israel saw that the king refused to listen to them, they answered the king: "What share do we have in David, what part in Jesse's son?"
1 Kings 12:16, NIV.

There was trouble brewing in Boston between the newly formed colonies and their mother country of England. England needed to replenish its revenues from its costly wars and assert its right to tax the colonies. The colonies argued that it was not fair for them to be taxed without having representation in British Parliament. On this day in 1773, Parliament passed a law that applied a small tax on any tea sold to the colonies by any company other than the struggling East India Company. It was called the Tea Act, and Britain thought for sure the colonies would love it, because it actually lowered what they would pay for tea. It also never thought the colonists could do without their tea. Instead of fixing the problem, the Tea Act resulted in angry resistance from the colonies. To the colonists, it wasn't as much about the money as it was about their right to independent free trade. That was the source of their prosperity, and they weren't about to give it up.

Months went by with the colonial leaders protesting the tax and the British government not budging. When three British ships loaded with tea from the East India Company docked at the Boston harbor, the colonists demanded that the tea be returned to England. When the British governor refused, a group of colonists called the Sons of Liberty, led by Samuel Adams, planned a little tea party. On a dark December night about 60 men disguised as Native Americans crept up the gangplanks of the ships and dumped $27,000 ($14 million in today's value) worth of tea into the ocean. As you can imagine, England had a fit, and the simmering tension between the colonies and the mother country increased until it finally boiled over into the Revolutionary War.

When ancient Israel's King Rehoboam consulted with his older, wiser counselors at court, they advised him to lower public taxes. Unfortunately, he decided instead to take the counsel of his younger, more immature private advisors, who insisted that he tax them more. Rehoboam's decision led to the permanent division of his nation. Big decisions require a very precious commodity that should be the top priority of governments and individuals alike—diplomacy.

Mutiny on the *Bounty*

All who take the sword will perish by the sword.
Matthew 26:52, NKJV.

You've no doubt heard about the mutiny on the *Bounty*. Books have been written and movies made about this story brimming with conspiracy, treachery, and murder. Most sailors in those days were not a very nice bunch. They swore, drank, gambled, and fought—all the time. These ships at sea were like little cities with their own governments. The captain was both king and executioner. He could have you flogged if he didn't like the way you looked at him, and he could make you walk the gangplank if he suspected you of mutiny.

Captain William Bligh of the *HMS Bounty* was that kind of man. Endeavoring to bring a shipment of breadfruit saplings from Tahiti to the West Indies, he had made too many enemies on board his ship. After spending four or five months on the beautiful island of Tahiti, the captain ordered the men to return to the ship and prepare to sail. Fletcher Christian, however, had other ideas. On April 28, 1789, he and 25 sailors mutinied, taking control of the ship. In retaliation for the horrible treatment they felt they had received from Captain Bligh, they set him adrift in a lifeboat with 18 of his supporters. Then they set off to find a home in paradise.

Sixteen crewmen decided to stay on Tahiti, even though the risk of capture by British authorities was high. Christian and eight others, along with 18 Tahitian men and women, went in search of a place in the tropical islands of paradise where they would never be found. Pitcairn Island seemed to be the ideal place, nearly 1,000 miles east of Tahiti. After burning the *Bounty*, they settled on Pitcairn in 1790, but their troubles were not over. Sickness plagued them, and when they began making liquor on the island, they did nothing but drink and fight. As they fought over the women they had brought with them, they killed each other off one by one. Finally, there was only one man left of the original mutineers—John Adams. In 1808, sailors from a whaling vessel came ashore and found Adams and a community of women and children. The mutineers' dream of finding a place in paradise where they could live like kings, had vanished. Each had paid the price for his sins, and Adams himself was an old, broken man.

For those of us who would fool ourselves into believing that we can sin and not pay the price, this story is for us. Jesus said to His disciples that all who live by the sword will die by the sword. The men from Pitcairn Island are a perfect example of Jesus' words come true.

April 29

Zip 'er Up

And Nathanael said to him, "Can anything good come out of Nazareth?" Philip said to him, "Come and see." John 1:46, NKJV.

Most fasteners used on clothing today, such as buttons and shoelaces, have been around in some form for thousands of years. But the zipper was invented much more recently, by an American named Whitcomb Judson of Chicago. Whitcomb had a friend who suffered from a stiff back and couldn't tie his shoes. To help his friend, Whitcomb started thinking and came up with a sliding fastener that could be opened and closed with one hand. Such gadgets are common in our world today, but back then, when you either tied your shoes or pulled them on, it was a rarity indeed.

Whitcomb called the device a clasp locker and thought it showed such promise that he took out a patent on it on this day in 1893. Compared to the zipper on your backpack or jeans, it was quite clumsy and often got jammed. But he had high hopes for it and proudly presented it at the 1893 World's Fair in Chicago. It bombed. People hardly even noticed it, and the clasp locker never did make Whitcomb any money. Gideon Sundback, one of Whitcomb's employees, took the idea and came up with the idea of interlocking teeth, calling it a hookless fastener. The B. F. Goodrich Company took notice and began selling rubber boots using Gideon's hookless fastener. The invention was catapulted into true success when it was marketed with the slogan, "Zip 'er Up." Goodrich called the boots zipper boots, and that's how the invention came to be called a zipper. Today, after years of rejection, the zipper has found its way into everything from plastic pencil cases to sophisticated space suits. And it all started with a guy who wanted to help his friend.

After centuries of persecution, Christianity has become the most influential religion in the world. "Can anything good come out of Nazareth?" Nathaniel asked. Like the zipper, Christianity had a slow start, and most people could hardly believe that something so wonderful could be so simple. And that's the best part about Christianity—it is simple, yet profound. And are we surprised? After all, its inventor is Jesus Christ, a Man with a great idea who just wanted to help his friends.

Louisiana Purchase

I will drive out nations before you and enlarge your territory.
Exodus 34:24, NIV.

What a moment in United States history! In one day the size of our country doubled, thanks to President Thomas Jefferson and his Louisiana Purchase. The Louisiana Territory contained all of the present-day states of Arkansas, Missouri, Iowa, Oklahoma, Kansas, and Nebraska, and parts of Minnesota, North Dakota, South Dakota, New Mexico, Montana, Wyoming, Colorado, and, of course, Louisiana. The land, originally named by two French explorers in honor of King Louis XIV, sat unused in French hands for nearly 100 years. Selling it to Spain as part of the terms of a treaty in 1762, France got it back in another treaty in 1801. The vast Louisiana Territory continued to collect dust as the French did nothing to develop it, and when President Louis-Napoléon Bonaparte of France needed money, he gladly sold it to the United States for about $13 million. On April 30, 1803, the deal was official, and President Jefferson had pulled off the biggest purchase in American history. Explorers plodding west in their covered wagons may have shaken their heads at the sight of this great american desert, but now it is impossible to imagine our country without its geographical heart.

Amazing! The French and Spanish, and then the French again, did nothing with it all those years, but within nine short years after the purchase, the U.S. began carving out new states from the territory. Today those states serve as the breadbasket for much of the world. The grain supplies alone from these midwestern states can feed the world, providing 50 million tons of grain annually. That's a hundred billion pounds of wheat, oats, and barley! God blessed the United States in 1803 when he helped us get our hands on land costing mere pennies per acre, and that, over 200 years later, is still providing an abundance for us and the world.

God can help you make good business decisions in your life, as well. He is hoping against hope that you will consult with Him about which school to attend, which career to pursue. He would love to be involved in every decision you need to make. You can trust Him as your business partner because He is the wisest Being in the universe, and He has already shown His care for you in providing everything you need to survive and thrive. A business partnership with Someone who helped a nation double its size in one day—what a deal!

First American Climbs Everest

For I can do everything with the help of Christ
who gives me the strength I need.
Philippians 4:13, NLT.

Nineteen sixty-three was an American year on Mt. Everest. Unlike the present day, with multiple expeditions from different countries and a thousand climbers on the slopes of Everest during the climbing season, 1963 saw one expedition, and that one from America.

Despite running out of oxygen, Jim Whittaker, along with Sherpa Nawang Gombu, reached the summit of Mt. Everest on May 1, Jim becoming the first American to stand atop the world. Whittaker jammed a U.S. flag in the ground, and the stars and stripes whipped in the wind at the peak of this icy monster. The successful ascent of Everest brought fame to the American climber, capped off by President John F. Kennedy awarding him the *National Geographic Society*'s greatest honor, the Hubbard Medal, in a ceremony at the White House Rose Garden.

This accomplishment was not the result of just one person. The expedition included 19 Americans, 37 Sherpas, and 907 porters, was preceded by months of preparation and weeks of logistical maneuvering, and carried a price tag of $400,000. Why this monumental expense in time, resources, and personal comfort, to go where no one can live? We can attribute this sort of sacrifice ultimately to the human need of doing something original, which sometimes includes the need to test one's strength—even in the face of death.

To accomplish great things, the concerted effort of more than one person is required. Much, much more is accomplished when we learn to work together. Our personal goals take on more meaning as we work together with others, helping them reach their goals while they help us reach ours. Working in conjunction with others also helps us conquer the time factor, bringing projects to be planned and executed alone out of the impossible realm and into the possible. Working with others, we can experience the concept of synergy, when the accomplishment of the team is even greater than its parts.

What creative goal do you have? What mountain will you climb? What team will you join? What will it cost you? If you strive for high goals, are willing to climb any mountain, will work with others, and are ready for it to cost you everything you have, you have a supernatural Teammate who has promised His strength to accomplish the mission.

Stonewall Jackson Killed

There is a way that seems right to a man, but in the end it leads to death.
Proverbs 14:12, NIV.

Who's the toughest person you've ever heard of—a WWF wrestler who weighs 342 pounds and can body slam you into next week? Or how about someone like Ray Lewis of the Baltimore Ravens, who can hit you so hard that you think your ancestors probably felt it?

Well, tough as those people may be, Thomas Jackson would beat them all. Nicknamed "Stonewall" Jackson in the Civil War because he was so tough, he was one of the most successful generals in the war because he trained his men to stand like a stone wall when they were under attack. Jackson won so many battles this way that he became a hero in the South.

He was also very strict about the ground rules of warfare. One of the commands he gave to his men was that a soldier couldn't afford to be too careful. "If you see a man coming toward you in battle, don't wait to identify him as friend or foe. Shoot him first, before he shoots you."

Unfortunately, that one basic rule was what killed Jackson. One of his own men did just that and shot General Jackson to death on May 2, 1863, in the battle of Chancellorsville.

The Civil War was fought over many things. Slavery in the United States was one of the big questions being settled, as was the right of states to make their own laws. The Southern states wanted both. Jackson and his soldiers felt that the South was right about a state's right to make its own laws, even if it meant that slavery would still be allowed.

In the end, however, the South lost the war. Slavery was wrong, and states did have to give up their rights about such things. It didn't matter whether General Jackson and his men thought the South was right about slavery, they were wrong. And as a result of the War, nearly a million lives were lost.

Sometimes we think our way is right, and we want to win no matter what the cost. But Solomon warns us that this attitude isn't wise. No matter how right we may think we are, if we make bad choices they will always come back to bite us.

Lock the Church Doors

I would rather be a doorkeeper in the house
of my God than dwell in the tents of wickedness.
Psalm 84:10, NKJV.

On May 3, 1675, a Massachusetts law was passed that required church doors to be locked during the worship service. Why? Because the services were running so long that people were leaving early. The services were running too long, no doubt, but is it also possible that the sermons were a bit boring, too? Not only were you trapped inside the building during a long, boring sermon, but if you tried to escape by nodding off, a deacon would walk to your pew with a long pole and bop you on the head!

How we worship has always been an issue for Christians. In some places, like the Boston of 1675, people have been punished if they tried to leave church. In others, they have been punished for reading the Bible. In some cultures, women have been told to keep quiet during services. People have been told what kinds of clothes to wear, and what not to wear. They have been asked to wear a head covering, to not wear a hat, to pray kneeling down, to pray standing up, to look heavenward when they pray, to bow their heads instead, to shout loud amens, and to pray in the reverence of silence.

In Jesus' day people loved to go to church and parade themselves around in all their finery. They loved to pray out loud and brag about all the good things they were doing. They made a point of keeping their faces long so people would know they were fasting and suffering for God. They liked to walk in with bags of coins and pour them slowly into the metal offering boxes so that everybody within earshot could tell how much they were giving. And some people spent huge sums of money to adorn their temples and synagogues so that they could be assured of a place in Heaven.

Jesus loves to meet you at church every Sabbath, but He certainly does not expect you to go to the most expensive cathedral wearing the finest of clothes and bringing the largest donation of everyone. Just give Him your heart in humble worship and praise Him while you're there. That's all He asks. After all, church is all about Him, and our worship is merely a sincere response to Him who loved us first.

The Three Stooges

Even in laughter the heart may ache, and joy may end in grief.
Proverbs 14:13, NIV.

The Three Stooges are one of the funniest trios in entertainment history. Their brand of slapstick comedy has made people laugh for decades. When you think of the Three Stooges, the names Larry, Moe, and Curly no doubt come to mind. Who's the dumb one? Larry. Who's the mean one? Moe. Who's the funny one? Curly.

Their funniest episodes include pie fights, bull fights, and adventures in the jungle with headhunters. And they've had just about every job under the sun. They've been plumbers, dentists, barbers, wallpaper hangers, salesmen, soldiers, and pest exterminators. The Stooges made 190 short comedy flicks and more than 20 feature-length films.

Moe and Curley Howard were brothers, born in Brooklyn in 1897. Another brother, Shemp, played in the comedy series alongside Larry Fine, but Moe was always the ringleader of the trio, in his sarcastic, abusive role. His distinctive hairstyle came about as a boy when he snipped off his long hair with a pair of scissors, giving himself the famous ragged, bowl-shaped look. He never changed his hairstyle for the rest of his life. Developing a strong interest in acting while quite young, he skipped school many times to watch theater plays. Moe had an unusually good memory, which made memorizing lines especially easy for him, and it was this that got him a career in acting.

The Three Stooges productions lasted for four decades, but as they say, all good things must come to an end. Moe Howard grew ill with lung cancer, and on May 4, 1975, he passed away, the last of the Howard brothers. But his memory and that of his partners in comedy remain a hit even today. Three Stooges reruns are still going strong on cable television networks.

The Three Stooges were a comedy act, and everybody loved them for it. But that was all you ever saw of them, because that is what they were hired to do. Like them, some of us like to be the funny one all the time. It's great being the life of the party, but what happens when the music fades and the last person leaves, and you're the only one left to clean up the confetti and take down the balloons? Life is made up of laughter, tears, and even some pain. Please remember that there is Someone who loves you even when you're not funny.

Japanese Bomb Kills Six on American Soil

*Wicked men are overthrown and are no more,
but the house of the righteous stands firm.
Proverbs 12:7, NIV.*

You're out playing with your friends in the woods behind your house. Maybe it's capture the flag, or hide-and-seek, or storm the tree house. And to make it even better, one of the kids' has brought over some chocolate chip cookies. The morning couldn't get any better! Then as you're sneak around the back side of some bushes to scale the wall and capture the tree house fort single-handed, you discover something in the bushes that looks like a giant balloon with a long narrow tube attached. You call the rest of the kids together to stare at it, and decide to drag it home where you can have a better look. And that's when it happens. *Kaboom!* And you're all dead!

Sound farfetched? It really happened just like that in a place called Lakeview, Oregon, on May 5, 1945. World War II was almost over—but not quite. The kids and a mom discovered a Japanese balloon in the woods near their home. Unfortunately, when they tried to drag it home, it exploded, killing them all. The balloon had been part of a Japanese military bombing strategy to attack America. Some 6,000 balloons with bombs in tow had been set adrift from Japan to ride east across the Pacific Ocean and land in the United States, but none of them ever hit urban targets. Amazingly, this was the only recorded killing of Americans on American soil during WW II. Four years later Congress awarded the woman's husband $5,000 as compensation for the death of his wife, Elsie. The parents of the dead children— Edward, Jay, Ethel, Richard, and Sherman—each received $3,000.

World War II was a tough time when the bad guys really wanted to win. Japan, Italy, and Germany had set out to rule the world, and it seemed they would stop at nothing to do so. Of course they lost, just as the Bible had predicted. According to Daniel, after Rome no empire would ever rule the world again. The evil guys of Japan's Imperial government are gone. The Nazi Gestapo and their killing machine are gone. And America still stands. Thank God for the country we live in! We are still safer, freer, and more blessed than most nations in our world, and that's because God has called us to take the gospel message everywhere. Wanna help?

Manhattan Island Bought for $24

*For which of you, intending to build a tower, does not sit down
first and count the cost, whether he has enough to finish it.*
Luke 14:28, NKJV.

On May 6, 1626, Peter Minuet and his fellow Dutch settlers bought
Manhattan Island from local Native Americans. Peter paid the legendary
sum of 60 Dutch guilders—$24 worth of beads and other handy items that
the Indians might need, such as kettles, axes, hoes, wampum, and drilling
awls. Until then, Peter had been an employee of the Dutch West India
Company, which had plundered over 120 million guilders from Spanish ships,
giving us perspective as to what kind of businessman he was. And now he
was to be the head honcho of the New Netherland Colony located in the bay
area of today's New York City.

The deal was a bargain as far as he was concerned. At home that night,
he and his men probably shared a few good laughs over the whole trade,
thinking how they had swindled the native Americans out of the choice piece
of property. The natives had no idea what land was worth in Europe, or how
much the Dutch settlers really would have paid for it. So, the newly-pur-
chased land came to be known as New Amsterdam, and its 270 residents
continued trading European goods for furs to be sold back in the
Netherlands.

So the Native Americans were really duped, right? This land deal represented the clash of two cultures with very different values. The Dutch settlers' goal was to purchase the land for as little as possible, creating the
opening for making more money. The native American philosophy was that
no one can truly own land, that it is part of the ongoing landscape of time,
loaned to us by "the great spirit." The contrast between the two perspectives
set the stage for hearty laughter at the "heist" Peter Minuet pulled off on the
unsuspecting Native Americans.

But who was truly the unsuspecting party? Although Peter and his pals
laughed into the night, the truth is that the Native Americans knew something
of which Minuet and the settlers were completely clueless. They knew that
grassy, wildflower-speckled meadows, majestic mountain peaks, and
sparkling streams can't truly be bought or sold by anyone. They knew that
the land they "sold" to Peter had not belonged even to them, that it was
merely on loan from a higher power.

In a way, it looks like it was Peter and the settlers who got duped.

Giant Pearl Found

Again, the kingdom of heaven is like a merchant seeking
beautiful pearls, who, when he had found one pearl of
great price, went and sold all that he had and bought it.
Matthew 13:45, 46, NKJV.

Pearls are some of the most beautiful things to grace this planet. Their glistening white sheen can catch the radiance of morning sunlight or the glow of candlelight. Much of the beauty of pearls is found in their rarity, and seeing a natural one is a memorable experience, because they are not easy to find.

On this day in 1934, the largest pearl on record, the Pearl of Lao-tze, was discovered on Palawan Island, in the Philippines. Pulled from a 160-pound giant clam, it was over nine inches long and weighed about 14 pounds. In 1936 Wilbur Dowell Cobb received the pearl as a gift from the chieftain of Palawan because Cobb saved the life of the chief's son. In 1980, the family sold it to a jeweler in Beverly Hills, California, for $200,000. And how much is it worth today? The San Francisco Gem Laboratory has put a price tag of $40 million on it. Wow! That's a lot of pearl!

The story of how pearls are made in nature is truly remarkable. When a clam or oyster accidently gets a speck of sand in a joint or muscle, it immediately begins to build a hard, white coating around the offending grain of sand with nacre, which is the pearly substance. This keeps the sand from irritating the creature. Then, over months and years, the pearl grows, and the longer it grows, the bigger it gets. So instead of helplessly griping about the grain of sand causing its discomfort, it chooses to react positively by building something rare and beautiful out of it.

Jesus said our search for Him should be like a search for a beautiful pearl. If we really want a pearl, we will leave no clam unopened until we find it. And if we really want to know Jesus, we will leave no page of the Bible unturned until we find Him. The merchant in Jesus' parable found an astonishing pearl like none he had ever seen before. It was worth more than he could really afford, but he just couldn't pass up such a promising investment. He wanted it so much that he sold everything he owned to buy it. Nothing is more valuable than knowing Jesus, the Pearl of Great Price.

American Bible Society

All Scripture is inspired by God and is useful to teach us what is true…
It corrects us when we are wrong and teaches us to do what is right.
2 Timothy 3:16, NLT.

The Bible is the most published book in the history of the world and is now available in the local language to at least 98 percent of its population. This sacred volume is made up of 66 books—39 in the Old Testament and 27 in the New. Interestingly, the word Bible does not occur anywhere in Scripture. Members of the early Christian church used the term to refer to the Old Testament until about 200 A.D. when the New Testament stories of Jesus and spiritual letters between Christians were accepted as God's Word and added.

In 1450 Johann Gutenberg began work on a printed copy of the Bible using a new invention he called block printing. In 1950, on the 500th anniversary of Gutenberg's invention, it was estimated that over two billion Bibles had been printed. In 2008, that number had doubled, with four billion copies having rolled off the presses in thousands of languages and editions. These numbers make the Bible the undisputed best seller of all time.

On May 8, 1816, delegates from 35 Bible societies met in New York City to form the American Bible Society. At that time Protestant Americans felt the United States was being called by God to preach the gospel to the world and to get the Scriptures out in as many languages as possible. In the American Bible Society's first year, 6,140 Bibles were given out to people on the streets of New York City or sent to overseas missions. By 1900 it had given away over 60 million copies of Scripture. That's enough Bibles to make a stack 900 miles into the sky!

Bible societies the world over are working together to get the Bible printed in as many languages as possible. As of this date, the Bible has been translated into 680 languages in Africa, 590 in Asia, 420 in the Pacific Islands, 420 in Latin America, 210 in Europe, and 75 in North America. In 1999, Wycliffe Bible translators announced that by 2025, they were planning to have begun a Bible translation in every single remaining language. Today they estimate that 2,251 languages need a Bible translation and that, out of a world population of nearly 7 billion, only 193 million don't have a Bible in their language—about the size of Brazil's population.

Inspiring numbers for an inspired book!

I've Got My Eyes on You

*The eye is the lamp of the body. If your eyes
are good, your whole body will be full of light.*
Matthew 6:22, NIV.

What would we do without our eyes? Seeing is vitally important and in many ways the most important of our senses. Sure, you need to be able to hear. Music certainly wouldn't be the same without your ears. And you need to be able to feel. Can you imagine not being able to feel the basketball in your hands, a kiss on your cheek, or a tack in your foot? And you need to smell and taste. A smoothie just wouldn't be the same without those two senses—cold, but very, very boring!

But without your eyes, well, the list of things you couldn't do very well—or at all—without them is almost endless. You couldn't zoom down a hill on a bicycle, do a rail slide at a skate park, or practice parallel parking a car. Without your eyes you couldn't read or write, study your Biology textbook, take notes in class, type a research paper, play video games, watch a movie, bowl, snowboard, or play footfall, basketball, or soccer. Get the point?

So once you lose your eyes, your life's over, right? Wrong. Many people go on to live fairly normal lives with no eyes—alright, except maybe the skateboarding or snowboarding part, but they can certainly "watch" movies, read, and even take notes in class if they have the right equipment.

There was a day when people who had lost their eyesight could only dream of getting a chance to see again. Cornea transplants, as well as complete eye transplants were science fiction ideas—that is until May 9, 1944. On that day, North America's first eye bank opened at New York Hospital in New York City. An eye bank is an organization that receives eyes from people who have recently died, either by consent of the donor before death, or with the consent of living relatives. Drs. Richard Paton and John McLean were responsible for getting the eye bank set up, and 21 local hospitals in the New York City area began sending eye donations to the bank.

Have you ever thought about donating your eyes to an eye bank, should the time come when you don't need them anymore? Just think! Your eyes could bring the light of sight to someone long after you are gone. Now that would be the best gift ever!

Transcontinental Railroad

In his days the righteous will flourish; . . . He will rule from sea to sea.
Psalm 72:7, 8, NIV.

On this day in1869, the eastern half of the United States was finally connected to the western half by a transcontinental railroad. The rail line had begun in Omaha, Nebraska, in the east, and Sacramento, California, in the west, meeting in the middle at Promontory, Utah. After failing to hit the spike on his first attempt, California governor Leland Stanford raised the heavy sledgehammer again and gave the golden railroad spike completing the track a solid blow. A great shout went up from the spectators. For the first time in American history, east and west were linked together, the realization of a dream that had begun two decades earlier.

Congress began considering how best to support the building of a transcontinental line in the late 1840s. The discovery of gold in California in 1848 made the issue all the more urgent: only a transcontinental railway could effectively tie that far off region to the rest of the nation. Northern and southern politicians, however, disagreed over where the line should be constructed, and the project stalled for more than a decade. It wasn't until the Civil War that funding and location were finally resolved.

The two tracks connecting in northern Utah marked the beginning of a dramatic transformation of the West. A 3,000 mile journey that had previously taken months to complete could now be made in just days. More importantly, the abundant resources of the West could be shipped quickly and profitably to insatiable eastern markets, greatly spurring the development of the western economy. Perhaps more than any other single event, the completion of this railroad enabled the American conquest and settlement of the West.

Today there are approximately 150,000 miles of railroad track in the United States for freight trains, with another 80,000 for passenger services. As the cost of fuel rises for the trucking industry, as well as for private automobiles, there may be a renewed interest in railway travel.

The history of the transcontinental railroad is an example of the productive union that can be achieved when people build with each other in mind. If you want to experience a productive union with God but feel that He's too far away, just start building with Him in mind. Sooner or later, He will meet you in the middle.

Dust Bowl

Who shall separate us from the love of Christ? Shall trouble or hardship or persecution or famine or nakedness or danger or sword?
Romans 8:35, NIV.

Our planet is constantly pelted with storms. Rainstorms, snowstorms, thunderstorms, hailstorms, lightning storms, dust storms. Dust storms? Unless you live in a place where there's lots of sand, you've probably never seen one. Dust storms can be pretty bad, especially if you don't know what to do when you find yourself surrounded by one.

In the old days the Great Plains were covered by prairie grass, which held moisture in the earth and kept most of the soil from blowing away, even during dry spells. By the early 1900s, however, farmers had plowed under much of the grassland with the newly invented tractor. Farmers planted so much wheat in the 1920s that wheat production increased by 300 percent!

During this period, a severe drought spread across the region. As crops died, winds began to carry dust from the over-plowed and over-grazed lands. And it got worse. The number of dust storms jumped from 14 in 1932 to 28 in 1933. The storms increased in strength, giving the United States some of the worst destruction our farmland has ever seen. On May 11, 1934, a massive dust storm sent millions of tons of topsoil sweeping across the parched Great Plains. Over a period of two days, heavy winds carried some 350 million tons of silt all the way from the northern Great Plains to the eastern seaboard, reaching New York, Boston, and Atlanta. Unfortunately, the swirling whirlwind forced thousands of families from their homes in Texas, Arkansas, Oklahoma, and Kansas, causing them to pull up stakes and migrate west. The discouragement of the storm reflected the times. Our nation wallowed in its worst economic depression and would soon enter World War II, arguably the most destructive planetary event in the history of the world. Americans were weary, fearful, and hungry.

But there was something about the American spirit that just wouldn't give up. Storms and hunger couldn't diminish the pride we all felt to be living in this great country. And when World War II began, danger or sword couldn't shake our faith in the American dream, either. We were living in a free country blessed by God, and we would make it through the hard times of dust bowls, depression, and danger. And we did it because God never separated Himself from us.

Law Against Spitting

If you will listen carefully to the voice of the Lord your God and do what is right in his sight . . . then I will not make you suffer any of the diseases I sent on the Egyptians; for I am the Lord who heals you. Exodus 15:26, NLT.

On this day in history the Department of Health introduced a new law in New York City. The year? 1896. The law? No spitting! No spitting? After some thought, it seems like a reasonable law. No one wants to step in spit on sidewalks and subway floors. No one wants to sit in it on the steps of a public building, or smell it on a hot summer day. But that wasn't the reason for the law. Nope! And the law wasn't written because spitting was considered uncivilized, even in a spittoon. (That's nasty, too!) The law was drafted and put into effect because city and health officials were trying to keep contagious diseases like tuberculosis, influenza, cholera, dysentery, and typhoid fever from spreading. They realized that spit contains some of the worst bacteria in the human body.

One of the worst epidemics in human history struck in the early 20th century. Influenza swept the world, causing 20 million deaths, including 500,000 in the United States. This disease killed more people in our country than any war ever did, and victims worldwide were dying at a faster rate than even famine could kill. And now, AIDS has caused an epidemic that affects about 33 million people and is killing millions each year as you read this. These horrible epidemics show just how disastrous infectious diseases can be.

In the United States deaths from infectious diseases have declined considerably during the last 100 years. Decreases in the death of babies and children have had a lot to do with the drop. In 1900, 30 percent of all deaths occurred among children less than 5 years of age. In 1997, that percentage was down to 1.4. In 1900, pneumonia, tuberculosis, diarrhea, and diphtheria caused one third of all deaths. Today only 4.5 percent of deaths are caused by these diseases.

God is saddened by all the epidemics that destroy His beloved human family. Someday He will come again and bring an end to it all. Until He appears in the eastern sky, there are some things we can do to stay healthy, like eating well, getting enough exercise, and not spitting in public.

Polk Declares War on Mexico

*He shall judge between the nations, and rebuke many people;
they shall beat their swords into plowshares, and their spears
into pruning hooks; nation shall not lift up sword against
nation, neither shall they learn war anymore.
Isaiah 2:4, NKJV.*

On this day in 1846, President James Polk declared war on Mexico. Relations between the two countries had consistently deteriorated during the eight years since Texas had won its independence from our neighbor to the south, joining the United States as its 28th state. Polk sent a diplomatic mission to restore relations and to help settle disputes between Texas citizens and Mexico. The mission failed and war broke out. After nearly two years of fighting, peace was finally established with the Treaty of Guadalupe Hidalgo. The Rio Grande was made the southern boundary of Texas and California and New Mexico were ceded to the United States. In return, the United States paid Mexico the sum of $15 million and agreed to settle all claims of U.S. citizens against Mexico.

War conjures up sickening images of bloodied soldiers watching their buddies hit by enemy fire, soldiers losing their arms, legs, and lives, and soldiers coming home to an unappreciative country. William T. Sherman, a Union general in the U. S. Civil War, summed it up well when he muttered, "War is hell." What is it that causes nations to arm themselves and kill each other? As in Polk's war with Mexico and most every other war in our planet's history, people's rights are at stake. War is the method that imperfect beings have chosen to purchase rights to land, to prosperity, and to freedom.

As Americans we sometimes forget just how much it has cost to be able to enjoy what we have in this country—the right to freedom. Could the same be said of our salvation? As much as we hate war and what happens to people during war, we are in a spiritual war. Just as it costs a great deal to wage war between countries, it also cost a great deal to engage the enemy of our salvation.

Do you ever feel like no one knows what you're going through in the battles you are fighting? There is a Soldier who really understands, for He experienced more horror, greater temptations, and more sustained assaults than you ever will. He did it, not for any rights for Himself, but for freedom for you.

United States Army Camels

And God said, "Let the earth bring forth the living creature after his kind, cattle, and creeping thing, and beast of the earth after his kind," and it was so. Genesis 1:24.

Camels are some of the most unique animals in God's wildlife zoo. Before the days of trucks and trains, camels were used to haul people and goods to market. They were also ridden into battle. Certainly not as fast as horses, people relied on them not for their speed but for their endurance. Plodding through the seemingly endless deserts of the Middle East, they could travel for weeks with very few complaints. Camels store food and water in their humps, some with one and others with two, and can live off this fuel for very long stretches. They can last for days, even weeks, on very little food and water.

And that's the reason why the U. S. Army decided to use camels as vehicles to explore and settle the American Southwest. Following the California gold rush of 1849, there was a growing need to facilitate safe travel for the thousands of Americans moving across the great american desert. Efforts to build a transcontinental railroad had stalled, so the military brass from Washington suggested that the Army experiment with camels to transport supplies and people across the rugged wilderness. It was thought that camels, in the dry climate of the west, would be more durable and less expensive than horses.

So they sent Major H. C. Wayne on a trip to the Middle East to bring back a load of camels. On this day in 1856, 53 camels arrived at Indianola, Texas, to report for duty. At first the camel recruits appeared to do well, and, as everyone expected, were reliable, needed little water, and were content to forage on scrubs and tough grasses. However, it soon became clear that the camels' padded feet couldn't hold up on the rocky terrain of the Southwest. Also, they spooked the horses and Army soldiers grew tired of dealing with the stubborn creatures. After the Civil War, some of the camels were auctioned off, a few escaping into the west Texas desert, where they lived out their post-Army lives.

Camels are not the only creatures God made to have incredible endurance. Some fish can live dormant in the mud of dried-up ponds and stream beds. Albatrosses can fly for weeks over the open sea, living only on the few fish they can catch. Do you think we can learn character traits from God's great wildlife zoo?

Keedoozle Store

If you, then, though you are evil, know how to give good
gifts to your children, how much more will your Father
in heaven give good gifts to those who ask him!
Matthew 7:11, NIV.

One of the most unusual stores ever built was the Keedoozle Store that opened for business in Memphis, Tennessee, on this day in 1937. Sample merchandise was displayed behind rows of tiny glass windows. When customers wanted to buy something, they made purchases by putting a notched rod into a keyhole beside the little window that contained the item they wanted to buy. The machine recorded the selections they made, collected each item, and wrapped it before dropping it on a conveyor belt. When the key was pushed into one final slot to purchase the items, all the packages were released down a little shoot into a box. The store operated like a giant vending machine, which is exactly what it was—the ancestor of today's vending machines. The name keedoozle was a coined word for key-does-all.

Some people think of God as a vending machine. They ask Jesus for things, thinking that if they're lucky or blessed He'll give them what they want. But God is not a vending machine; He's our heavenly Father. He's always with us, caring for us, and loving us as only a Father can. It's not like we have to be good enough for Him to pay attention to us. He's always paying attention to us, and He always wants what is best for us.

Sometimes we're stubborn and want to do things our way. We're so wrapped up in this world that we're able to see only the small picture. Like the little windows in the Keedoozle Store, we can't see everything in the store so we end up making our selections in life, one at a time.

God wants us to stop for a moment at the beginning of each day to take a look at the big picture ahead of us. He says, "Trust Me. If an earthly father wants to give good gifts to his children, don't you think I'm as anxious to do the same for you?"

His best gift for you is His Holy Spirit. Why not ask Jesus to give you a double portion today? That's one request Jesus will never deny.

SpaghettiOs

You are like babies who need milk and cannot eat solid food. For some-one who lives on milk is still an infant and doesn't know how to do what is right. Solid food is for those who are mature, who through train-ing have the skill to recognize the difference between right and wrong. Hebrews 5:12-15, NLT.

What's your favorite kind of pasta? Spaghetti? Lasagna? Fettucini alfredo? How about SpaghettiOs? SpaghettiOs are to spaghetti what ice cream cones are to ice cream; they make the spaghetti easier to handle. One of the most reconizable brand names of any food product, they were born on May 16, 1965, and now line store shelves in several varieties, such as SpaghettiOs Meatballs, SpaghettiOs Plus Calcium, SpaghettiOs RavioliOs, and SpaghettiOs Sliced Franks.

The concept for SpaghettiOs originated in Pozzuoli, Italy around 1884 by a family that later emigrated to Brooklyn, New York. They sold the original recipe to a family friend who worked at Campbell Soup Co. as a food prod-uct developer. Originally sold under the Franco-American brand, the little rings of cooked pasta in a sweet tomato and cheese sauce has lined grocery store shelves for over 40 years. "Uh-oh, SpaghettiOs!" is the advertising jin-gle that made them famous. "The neat round spaghetti you can eat with a spoon! Uh-oh! SpaghettiOs!"

But as good as SpaghettiOs are, there's certainly not as much nutrition in them as a plain old lettuce, tomato, and cheese sandwich assembled with whole wheat bread. We like SpaghettiOs, and we want to have a snack in the house that the kids can fix and is also half-way healthy for them, but SpaghettiOs are probably just that—a snack.

Spiritual things are like that. Paul said that when we are spiritual toddlers, it's right that we would want to drink the milk of God's Word. But as we ma-ture, we begin to desire the lasagna and fettucini alfredo of the Bible—the real, solid food that will help us grow from being toddlers into spiritual adults. But what if we don't want to grow up? What if we want to continue eating only spiritual SpaghettiOs? In that case, we cannot expect to get the very most out of life by becoming the people God wants us to be. And so it is at church. Many churchgoers enjoy soft, squishy, snack-like sermons from their pastors and push away nutritious, solid food. Why not ask your pastor to give you solid spiritual food? After all, you don't want to be a toddler forever.

Ra II

Look to Me, and be saved, all you ends of the earth!
For I am God, and there is no other.
Isaiah 45:22, NKJV.

Have you ever wondered how people crossed the oceans in ancient times? How did the first inhabitants of the Hawaiian Islands arrive there? How did the original dwellers of Australia reach their new home? How were ancient people transported from Africa to the New World? Did they sail on long, sleek boats like the Phoenicians, or in boats with long rows of oars like the Romans, or in long, wide, sloping ships with heads of monsters on the bow like the Vikings?

In the 1930s, world-renowned explorer and archaeologist Thor Heyerdahl set out to answer these questions. Noticing distinct similarities between Mediterranean peoples and civilizations in Central and South America, such as the penchant for building pyramids, he made bold assertions about how the ancients migrated to new lands over vast expanses of ocean.

In 1947 Heyerdahl tested his unpopular theory that the first humans to arrive in Polynesia had sailed across the Pacific Ocean from Peru on prehistoric rafts made of balsa wood. Hoping to prove the skeptics wrong, he built such a raft, called it the Kon-Tiki, and safely completed the 4,300-mile voyage in only 101 days.

But how did ancient humans first reach the Western Hemisphere? On May 17, 1970, Thor and a multinational crew of seven set out to prove his theory that the ancient travelers crossed the vast Atlantic Ocean, not in ordinary boats, but in reed boats made of papyrus, like those that had been floating up and down the Nile River for years. Contemporary scientists mocked this theory, arguing that the reeds would get waterlogged after less than two weeks at sea. With the help of Aymaro Indian boat builders, he constructed a 39-foot replica of an ancient Egyptian papyrus vessel and successfully reached the Western Hemisphere from the Eastern through the widest part of the Atlantic in 57 days.

Since time began God's people have been going to far off places to take the gospel to the world. Some walked and some probably rode on camels or horses. No doubt many took boats like the ones Thor Heyerdahl built. Someday in Heaven, when someone asks how the gospel got from your town to the ends of the earth, you will have a good travel tale to tell.

Mount St. Helens Erupts

The sky was rolled up like a scroll, and all of the
mountains and islands were moved from their places.
Revelation 6:14, NLT.

Few things on earth have as much destructive power as exploding mountains—volcanoes. Volcanoes are mountains with conduits, or vents, that leak magma up to the surface of the earth. Sometimes volcanoes ooze or spout relatively low levels of lava-producing magma. We see these in the Hawaiian Islands and other islands of the western Pacific. And sometimes a volcano lies dormant for a very long time, and finally builds up enough pressure to produce a tremendously powerful explosion.

This is exactly what happened to Mount St. Helens in the state of Washington at 8:32 a.m. on May 18, 1980. After decades of lying dormant, the volcanic peak suffered a massive eruption, flattening some 210 square miles of wilderness and killing 57 people. Not since the 1850s had there been any real action on the mountain, but when it erupted after 125 years of dormancy, it shot 500 million tons of ash 16 miles into the air—enough debris to cover an area the size of a football field 150 miles deep. Temperatures from the blast exceeded 800 degrees Fahrenheit!

The explosion caused the largest landslide in recorded history, a landslide that surged down the mountain and buried the Toutle River valley below for a distance of 13 miles. Roads, bridges, and parks were destroyed, and an estimated 10 million trees were killed. Ash from the eruption drifted far and wide, falling on Northwest cities and towns like snow and darkening the sky east of the volcano for more than 125 miles. The eruption is said to be the most economically destructive volcanic event in the history of the United States, causing $300 billion worth of damage.

The book of Revelation tells us that our earth is growing old, and one of the signs of its last chapter include enormously destructive natural catastrophes. In vision John the Revelator saw mountains being moved. Well, that's exactly what happened to Mount St. Helens, and the huge crater left on the side of the mountain is a living testimony that it's nearly time for Jesus to come. Bring it!

Dark Day

Immediately after the tribulation of those days the sun will be darkened, and the moon will not give its light.
Matthew 24:29, NKJV.

For more than 100 years Seventh-day Adventists (and many other students of Bible prophecy) have identified the Dark Day of May 19, 1780, as an event marking the beginning of the world's last days, directly fulfilling Jesus' prophecy in Matthew 24:29. Some people have disagreed, saying that it had no such significance. Did this day in 1780 fulfill prophecy by opening a doorway pointing to the end, or was it just another day?

Some say that the Dark Day most likely had some natural cause and that any event springing from a natural cause cannot be a direct fulfillment of prophecy. However, most of the other signs that Jesus mentioned in Matthew 24 spring from natural causes, such as wars, love growing cold, famine, and disease. So the cause of the sign does not reduce its prophetic value.

The timing of the Dark Day is very important. Jesus said it would come after the tribulation of "those days," referring to the persecution of the Dark Ages. In 1780, the world was just emerging from medieval suppression of spiritual truth. Bibles were more easily obtained and Bible prophecy was gaining greater attention and understanding. Spiritual darkness was diminishing and in its place came enlightenment, not only spiritually, but also in other areas. It is reasonable to conclude that the Dark Day fulfilled Jesus' words by pointing out this significant societal shift.

The Dark Day took place during the birth of the United States, in the very heart of its painful delivery from its mother country of Great Britain—the Revolutionary War. Built on an entirely different foundation than the other nations of the world—democracy and religious liberty—the United States' emergence would change the earth's political landscape forever.

George Washington wrote about the Dark Day in his personal diary while staying in New Jersey. "The sky grew so dark that even Mother Nature was fooled into thinking that night had come at midday; flowers curled their petals, and night animals began to stir."

How would you have felt if you had experienced this strange day? If it happened again, how would you react? We can rejoice that we have a God who cares enough about us to inform us of what's coming next!

First Ticket and Arrest for Speeding

The chariots storm through the streets, rushing back and forth through the squares. They look like flaming torches; they dart about like lightning. Nahum 2:4, NIV.

Jacob German, a taxicab driver, became the first person in the United States to be arrested for speeding. On May 20, 1899, Jacob was stopped by a traffic cop because he was driving at the "breakneck" speed of 12 mph on Lexington Avenue in Manhattan. But the traffic cop didn't stop at giving him a ticket. He booked him and held him in jail for a few hours at the East Twenty-second Street station house. However, Jacob was not asked to hand over his license and registration, because in those days such papers weren't required. Not until two years later did the state of New York begin making such requirements of its drivers. It seems fitting that our country's first arrest for reckless driving should be leveled at a New York cabbie! In most of our big cities, cabbies have developed a reputation for speeding and recklessness.

Compared to today, Jacob's speeding was not really speeding at all—people on foot can run faster than he was going. Today we travel on highways at death-defying speeds in convertible sports cars that have about as many safety features as an egg. Sure, they have air bags, bumper pressure sensors, and security systems to alert the owner of a car thief's intentions, but they have no protection for the head and hardly any weight. They're also low enough to the ground that when they are confonted by an unexpected tractor trailer, they'll go right underneath. Some would say that we're crazier than ever to travel at ridiculous speeds.

In today's Scripture verse we can almost see the wild traffic the prophet Nahum is describing in one of the ancient cities of his time—probably Nineveh, according to most Bible commentaries. "The chariots storm through the streets, rushing back and forth through the squares. They look like flaming torches; they dart about like lightning." That sounds more like one of our cities today!

Every day of our lives, cars, trucks, trains, and jets race around our country, cruising at breakneck speeds on hectic schedules. We need to slow down and think of safety, both physical and spiritual. We're always in a hurry so we can get to where we are going, so we can get back home to do something else we're trying to squeeze into our day. It's difficult to hear a whisper from God at 120 miles per hour.

Septuplets Born

Then God blessed them, and God said to them,
"Be fruitful and multiply; fill the earth and subdue it."
Genesis 1:28, NKJV.

It has been said that seven is the perfect number. Seven days make a perfectly complete weekly cycle, God gave the children of Israel victory over their enemies by having them march around Jericho seven times, and Revelation's seven churches represent the complete body of Christ's followers. But giving birth to seven babies at once seems to break the pattern.

The first record of septuplets being born was in the fifteenth century. The parents were Thomas and Edith Bonham of Wiltshire, England. They were described as having "seven children at one birth" several years after becoming the parents of twins.

Having that many babies simultaneously is rare, but it seems to be happening more often now with the coming of fertility drugs. Much more recently, in the 1980s, Sam and Patti Frustaci, who already had a healthy son named Joseph, wished for more children. Following a physician's recommendation, they used a special drug to help them realize their dream. But the dream turned out to be a nightmare. On May 21, 1985, at Children's Hospital in Orange, California, Patti Frustaci gave birth to septuplets, and what began as the hope for a larger family quickly became an ordeal of illness, expense, and unwelcome media attention.

The Frustaci septuplets, four boys and three girls, were born by Cesarean section 12 weeks premature. Christina was stillborn. The other six infants ranged in weight from 1 pound, 1 ounce to 1 pound, 13 ounces. Over the next several weeks, three more of the infants, David, James, and Bonnie, died from a disease that causes the lungs to collapse after each breath. At the age of two, the surviving children, Richard, Patricia, and Stephen, were found to have cerebral palsy. And a year later, there was more bad news: The children were also diagnosed as mentally retarded.

Amazingly, and controversially, assisted reproductive technology has since led to the so-far successful birth of octuplets—eight babies born at once!

God created parents, especially mothers, with an insistent, deeply meaningful sense of love for their newborn children, and it is difficult to imagine the intense pain of losing them so early in their little lives. How God must look forward to bringing His human family through the pearly gates, where not only their tears will finally dry up, but also His!

First Revolving Restaurant

I saw the Lord seated on a throne, high and exalted,
and the train of his robe filled the temple.
Isaiah 6:1, NIV.

The first ever revolving restaurant opened on May 22, 1961, in Seattle, Washington. An engineer named John Graham designed the skyscraper-restaurant as a landmark attraction, and it was completed just in time for the 1962 World's Fair. The restaurant, built at the 500-foot level of the 600-foot steel and glass tower of the Space Needle, contains 260 seats. Every hour it revolves 360 degrees, giving a wonderful view of the city. From the observation deck that's located above the restaurant a person can see all the way into Canada!

Now that's a restaurant! High-in-the-sky, kind-of-tall, whether it's revolving, or not. But its nothing like what we'll see someday when we reach heaven. God has planned mansions for us in the sky. He's designing them right now, one for each of us that is exactly what we were thinking it would look like. Remember, God can read your mind. However, if you talk to Him about it you can be sure that He'll be glad to add a few custom features just for you. Maybe you'd like a house that's 12 stories tall, made of pure glass, with a see-through aquarium that runs the distance from the basement to the roof. Or how about a bubble house that floats anywhere it wants across the fields and forests of heaven?

And to top it all off, every Sabbath we'll be able to visit the sea of glass and worship Jesus and the Father. Isaiah saw that picture. We can only imagine with him through his word-picture in our verse today. The Lord is sitting on His throne, lifted high up above the holy city. Seraphim, each with six wings, worship Him in humble reverence because He is so glorious. His power fills the temple. The floors and walls shake as iridescent colors of blue and red and fiery yellow stream across the temple floor and out into the streets of heaven!

That description was written about 2,700 years ago, but the promise is still a good one. One of these days Jesus will come and take us home to live with Him in the sky where everything revolves around His throne on "needles" in the sky.

Won't that be neat?

First Successful Limb Reattachment

I will praise You, for I am fearfully and wonderfully made; marvelous are Your works, and that my soul knows very well.
Psalm 139:14, NKJV.

What would you do if you lost your arm? To be involved in a terrible accident would be bad enough, but to lose an arm in the process must be awful! And that's exactly what happened to a boy names Red Knowles of Somerville, Massachusetts, on May 23, 1962. Red was trying to hop a freight train when he was thrown against a stone wall that ripped his right arm off cleanly at the shoulder. He walked away from the tracks, stunned, but able to hold his right arm inside his bloody sleeve. It wasn't until an ambulance rushed the boy across the Charles River to Boston that emergency room staff discovered the real extent of his injury.

A team of 12 doctors, led by Dr. Ronald Malt at Massachusetts General Hospital, immediately went to work reattaching the severed arm. All of the techniques they used that day had been used before, but never for the purpose of restoring an entire limb. Doctors rarely have the ideal candidate to do such a thing. Conditions have to be just right before they start—even before the real work begins. The doctors attached the bone with a special pin, reconnected the arteries, replaced four major nerves in Red's arm, and grafted skin and muscle together. Then, while waiting to see whether the operation would take, they were relieved to watch Red's hand regain its healthy pink color and to feel a pulse in his wrist. It was the first successful reattachment of a human limb in history.

Dr. Malt and Red Knowles became celebrities overnight. During the weeks that followed, Red, a Little Leaguer, got souvenirs and letters from Major Leaguers all over the country, and the country watched Red's progress. A few weeks after the operation, he began complaining of severe pain in his arm—a very good sign! After a year, Red could move his fingers and could feel someone touching them, as well as heat and cold. Finally able to bend his wrist, he began playing first base, but only with his one good hand. A year after that, he was back to playing baseball as before, and after four years of recovery, the boy had complete use of his right arm and hand as a natural lefty.

The doctors did an incredible job of putting Red Knowles back together, but the credit goes to God. Our amazing capacity for healing shows that we truly are brilliantly designed!

Outlaw Sheriff Elected

But Jesus said to him, "Put your sword in its place,
for all who take the sword will perish by the sword."
Matthew 26:52, NKJV.

On this day in 1863, the townsfolk of Bannack, Montana, elected Henry Plummer as their sheriff. They had no way of knowing that he had a long history of violence, robbery, and murder.

Born and reared in Maine, Plummer went west in 1852 and settled in the California gold mining town of Nevada City. There he opened a bakery and became active in politics. Well-spoken, friendly, and ambitious, Plummer won election to the office of sheriff in 1856 and again in the following year. Later in 1857, he was convicted of second-degree murder for killing an unarmed man in the line of duty. The jury believed the witnesses who testified that the true motive for the murder had a connection with the murdered man's wife.

Plummer served six months in San Quentin prison and was then pardoned by the governor. Returning to Nevada City, he won reappointment as an assistant marshal. In 1861 he fatally wounded a man in a brawl and fled to avoid prosecution. During the next several years, he wandered through the gold country of Nevada and Idaho, eventually taking up with a band of desperados who were robbing and killing miners in Idaho. When the evidence against him became too great, he packed up and fled the area.

When Plummer arrived in Bannack, Montana in October 1862, the people of the booming little mining town knew nothing of his record and elected him as their sheriff in May of 1863. He then reorganized his former band of outlaws.

Plummer's office of sheriff was the perfect cover for operating an effective and deadly criminal ring. He provided his henchmen with information on the movements of gold shipments and ensured that they avoided capture. After more than 100 people were robbed or murdered, the settlers organized a vigilance committee of nearly 2,000 members in December 1863.

Discovering Plummer for what he was, the Montana vigilantes destroyed him and his gang in a surprisingly short time. Early on a bitterly cold Sunday morning, January 10, 1864, they arrested Plummer and two of his lieutenants. While his cronies swore and resisted, Plummer reportedly wept and begged to be spared, but to no avail. All three men were hanged. Thus ended the life of a gifted man who had used his genius for selfish and ruthless gain.

Grizzly Bear Endangered

Then God said, "Let the earth bring forth the living creature according to its kind: cattle and creeping thing and beast of the earth, each according to its kind;" and it was so. Genesis 1:24, NKJV.

On May 25, 1975, grizzly bears were officially classified as a threatened species. Once the undisputed king of the western wilderness, the grizzly now has federal protection under the Endangered Species Act.

Before the Anglo-Americans began invading their territory, grizzly bears inhabited most of the country west of the Mississippi from Mexico to the Arctic Circle. Its only serious competitors for food were the Native Americans, who sometimes hunted the big bear as a test of strength and to have its long claws, prized as a status symbol.

Because of the grizzly's fearsome size and aggressive nature, early European explorers of the West made note in their journals of their encounters with the beasts. During their expedition to the Pacific, Lewis and Clark fought and killed many of the bears and were awed by their impressive speed and power.

With the settlement of the West, the hunting of the grizzly, along with the destruction of its habitat, caused a great reduction in the number of bears. In the days when California adopted its state flag adorned with an image of a grizzly, the state was estimated to have been home to 10,000 grizzlies. Since then, they have diasppeared from the state, also fading away from their native homes in Texas, Nebraska, Oklahoma, Kansas, Arizona, New Mexico, Oregon, Utah, the Dakotas, and likely Colorado and Washington. By the 1970s, outside of Alaska, small populations of bears remained only in a few isolated wilderness areas and national parks in Montana, Wyoming, and Idaho. Probably fewer than 1,000 grizzlies remain in the lower 48 states. While it is easy to understand why government plans to reintroduce the species into two wilderness areas in Idaho and Washington have met with controversy, the future of grizzly bears will depend on our willingness to share our habitats with them.

The grizzly bear is on its way back from extinction, but other creatures have not been so fortunate. As you consider the extinction of such creatures as dodo birds, Carolina parakeets, and passenger pigeons, what do you consider important to this earth and its inhabitants?

John Wayne Born

A friend loveth at all times, and a brother is born for adversity.
Proverbs 17:17.

Born on May 26, 1907, Marion Michael Morrison, now known as John Wayne, was to become an actor who epitomized the American West.

Wayne was 6 years old when his family moved from Winterset, Iowa, to Glendale, California. As a teen, he rose at four in the morning to deliver newspapers, and after school he played football and made deliveries for local stores. When he graduated from high school, he hoped to attend the U.S. Naval Academy. When the school rejected him, he accepted a full scholarship to play football at the University of Southern California in Los Angeles.

In the summer of 1926, Wayne's football coach found him a job as an assistant prop man on the set of a movie directed by John Ford. Ford continued to use Wayne as an extra, eventually trusting him with some larger roles. In 1930, Ford recommended him for a movie western called The Big Trail. Wayne won the part, but the movie did poorly and Ford let him go.

During the next decade, Wayne worked in countless low-budget western films, sharpening his talents and developing a distinct personality for his cowboy characters. Finally, his old mentor John Ford gave him his big break, casting him in the 1939 western, Stagecoach. Wayne played the role of Ringo Kid, giving the character such appealing traits that his role in movies was forever changed. Now everybody couldn't get enough of his toughness, clear-eyed honesty, bravery, and steady manner. Besides Westerns, Wayne also acted in war films. It was a small step from playing the simple cowboy to playing brave World War II fighters.

By the late 1960s, although he had proven more likable than they expected, some Americans tired of Wayne and his predictable patriotic characters. But as he went on to other—even Oscar-winning—roles, even his severest critics couldn't help but admire his toughness, clear-eyed honesty, bravery, and steady manner.

During his final screen role, he acquired a critic that he couldn't win over. Lung cancer invaded his body, and he died three years later. To this day, public polls identify John Wayne as one of the most popular actors of all time.

How do you act during adversity?

First Witch Execution

Then the Lord said to Cain, "Where is your brother Abel?"
"I don't know," he replied. "Am I my brother's keeper?"
Genesis 4:9, NIV.

On this day in 1647, the first recorded execution of a witch in the United States took place in Salem, Massachusetts. Many find it difficult to comprehend this kind of thing happening in our country. In the century leading up to our founding fathers' establishment of the freedoms and rights we now expect, our country learned a lot about what it means to be our brother's keeper.

The Salem Witch Trials were part of a notorious episode in New England colonial history that led to the execution of 14 women and 6 men on charges of witchcraft. The trials began as a result of the bizarre and unexplainable behavior of two young girls afflicted by violent convulsions and strange fits that seemingly rendered them unable to see, hear, or speak. After a medical examination and a review by Puritan preachers, the girls were judged to be victims of witchcraft. That summer, in the resulting hysteria, nearly 200 people were accused of witchcraft and imprisoned. Although the Salem Witch Trials have been portrayed as examples of religious zeal in New England, they were not a normal part of life in the rest of the American colonies. Charges of witchcraft were far more common in Europe during this period, particularly in Germany and Switzerland. From the fourteenth to the eighteenth century, some 110,000 people were tried for witchcraft in Europe, and anywhere from 40,000 to 60,000 were executed. In contrast, the only executions in colonial America were the 20 during the sensational trials at Salem.

We look back on the Salem Witch Trials and shake our heads at the townspeople's reactionary accusations that resulted from the young people's bizarre behavior. They panicked because they couldn't explain what they thought they saw. We also see a weak Massachusetts legal system that relied on hearsay testimony, encouraged accusations, and provided no chance for a defense. While we enjoy a legal system that, despite its flaws, currently safeguards against large-scale hysteria, do we follow the lead of the witch-hunters? Do we judge people before we know the whole story? Do we depend on hearsay testimony? Or do we take our duty as our brother's keeper seriously and treat each other with respect, logic, and fairness?

Monkeys in Space

Then God said, "Let us make human beings in our image,
to be like us. They will reign over the fish in the sea, the birds
in the sky, the livestock, all the wild animals on the earth,
and the small animals that scurry along the ground."
Genesis 1:26, NLT.

On this day in history, May 28, 1959, two monkeys took a ride into space and came back to tell about it. Alright, they didn't actually talk about it, but if they could have talked, they would have had a lot to say. Their names were Able and Baker, two females weighing a pound each, one a rhesus and the other a spider monkey. The flight lasted only 15 minutes, but it was enough to send the monkeys 50 miles into space at speeds up to 10,000 mph. The capsule cone was recovered 90 minutes later, floating in the ocean off the island of Antigua 1,500 miles away.

The monkeys were weightless for nine minutes and were monitored throughout the flight for changes in heartbeat, muscular reaction, pulse velocity, body temperature, and rate of breathing. A spokesman from the U. S. Army's Medical Research and Development Command said the monkeys returned to earth in perfect condition. The research was done to determine what effect space flight might have on a person. However, animal rights groups complained that sending Able and Baker, and animals in general, into space was a cruel thing to do. And maybe they were right. Although a thorough post-flight examination revealed that Able had suffered no negative effects from her trip into space, a few days after the trip, she died from a reaction to anesthesia during surgery to remove an infected medical electrode. Her body was preserved and is now on display at the Smithsonian Institute Air and Space Museum. Baker survived a similar operation, lived a healthy life to the age of 27, and was buried on the grounds of the United States Space and Rocket Center in Huntsville, Alabama.

The United States was not the first country to send animals into space. Between 1957 and 1961, 13 dogs were part of spaceflight experiments by the Russians. One such experiment occurred on November 3, 1957, when the Russians sent a Siberian husky named Laika into orbit. Unfortunately, days into the flight the dog died.

What do you think? Should animals be rocketed into orbit, dissected in science class, put on display in museums?

Pop-up Toaster

The Israelites were puzzled when they saw it. "What is it?"
they asked each other.... And Moses told them,
"It is the food the Lord has given you to eat."
Exodus 16:15, NLT.

On this day in 1919, the pop-up toaster was invented. Charles Strite of Stillwater, Minnesota, designed it so that bread could be heated and then ejected when it had been toasted properly. A small fire inside the toaster did the trick for him in those days, but, of course, today's toasters use little electrical wires to heat the bread. Now, who would have ever thought it would be worth the bother to invent a little machine that would hold a piece of bread, brown it on both sides, and then shoot the slices out at just the right time?

We have all kinds of machines in our homes that are designed to do little things that we are either too lazy to do ourselves, or that we just want to do faster—like handheld ice crushers, electric can openers, toaster ovens, food processors, and microwaves. And where exactly did we get the idea for Pop-Tarts? A toaster, of course! We designed them to fit in a toaster that we invented because we didn't want to take the time to toast the bread in an oven like our ancestors have done for thousands of years. Sooner or later someone will invent a machine that makes the Pop-Tarts and then puts them in the toaster for us.

When the Israelite masses scurried out of Egypt and began wandering in the wilderness, their stomachs began rumbling, and they asked God for food. He invented something for them—something entirely new for earthlings. We don't hear of it ever having been used before the wilderness wanderings, and we don't hear of it being used after. Far from normal fare that had to be prepared and cooked, it was instant, ready-to-eat food! When they put it in their mouths, it was nothing like they had ever tasted, so they called it manna. In their Hebrew language, manna actually means *what is it*. Now that's what you call a great breakfast! It would fit into our culture just fine today, along with the electric can openers, food processors, and Pop-Tarts.

Sometimes we expect God to be a pre-packaged, bite-sized, instant source of fulfillment for us. We impatiently wait for Him to give us what we want and to fix all our problems when we want them fixed. But God is not a ready-to-eat, supernatural shortcut for our convenience. He took His time creating us, and we were made for *His* fulfillment.

Joan of Arc Martyred

They will lay hands on you and persecute you, . . . and you will be brought before kings and governors, and all on account of my name. Luke 21:12, NIV.

Joan of Arc was a teenager when she claimed that she had received messages from God through visions. She was just a 16-year-old peasant girl, but she was so sure of herself that she went to the crown prince of France and told him she had a message for him. Saints and angels had visited her, she said, giving her messages about how the French army could win against the English in the hundred year's war.

Prince Charles didn't know whether or not he should believe her, but he finally gave her a small army to lead into battle. And her predictions came true. Though she was wounded several times, she fought bravely, stubbornly refusing to retreat with her army, and won many important cities back for the French.

She was finally captured by the English and tried in a court of law as a heretic. In spite of being treated badly by the church, she remained firm in her belief that God had spoken through her.

But the story doesn't end very nicely. On May 30, 1431, Joan of Arc was burned at the stake because the Church of England said she was a heretic. In those days a heretic was someone who believed or taught religious ideas that were different from what the government church said was right.

Joan of Arc was an amazing hero in medieval history. Whether or not she was the real thing will probably never be known. Psychologists today think she was probably schizophrenic because she heard voices. Some theologians suggest she simply used her religious experience to gain fame. Whatever her reasons for sharing the messages she received, perhaps God did indeed use her to help liberate the French. Whatever the truth is, she was willing to give her life for God and France.

Jesus was also martyred because He was considered a heretic. He too was treated badly, and eventually He was crucified on a cross. He died for you and me and everyone who loves Him, so that we could live forever with Him. Why not accept Him again today as your Savior?

Worst Flood in United States History

Then the dragon tried to drown the woman with a flood of water that flowed from his mouth. But the earth helped her by opening its mouth and swallowing the river that gushed out from the mouth of the dragon. Revelation 12:15, 16, NLT.

What could be worse than looking up to see a wall of water coming toward you at 40 miles per hour? Not much! If this were a catastrophe happening at sea, or on a beach somewhere, it would be shocking enough, but a flood in the mountains? Unthinkable! Yet that's exactly what happened on May 31, 1899. The South Fork Dam on the Conemaugh River in Johnstown, Pennsylvania, burst, sending a wall of water 75 feet high and half a mile wide down the corridor of the narrow mountain valley. The water smashed into the town like a tidal wave, destroying it and killing over 2,200 people.

It all started with heavy rainfall that spring, and when a violent storm on May 30 dumped six to 10 inches of water, the creeks flooded, and the Conemaugh River rose to a dangerous level behind the South Fork Dam. By 10:00 the next morning, the water rippled a perilous 12 inches from the top of the dam. The spillway screens were clogged with trees and debris, making the water rise even higher, and the dam bowed dangerously in the middle. Workers tried to pull the debris away from the spillway screens. They dug trenches on the hillside to divert the water away from the dam and then threw more dirt on the dam in hopes that this would help buttress it. But it was too little, too late. At 3:10 that afternoon, the intense pressure of the extra water in the reservoir was just too much. The dam finally collapsed, flooding the valley and town with 20,000,000 tons of water and causing $17 million worth of damage. Today that figure would be more like $2 billion.

Fortunately, a new organization called the American Red Cross, led by Clara Barton, got right to work bringing relief to the injured in the area. Thankfully, support for victims came from all over the United States, as well as from 18 foreign countries.

The enemy would like nothing more than to destroy God's people with an overwhelming wave of temptation or tragedy. The rains of trials have been pelting us for millennia, and storms dump extra pain on us regularly, sometimes causing our spiritual dams to break and threatening to drown us. Fortunately, we have a Savior who died on a blood-red cross to heal the injured.

Super Pigeon

What is the price of two sparrows—one copper coin? But not a single sparrow can fall to the ground without your Father knowing it. Matthew 10:29, NLT.

On this day in 1845 a homing pigeon made an amazing trip from Namibia in southern Africa to London, traveling over 6,600 miles in 55 days. That's a long trip! What a bird! Homing pigeons can fly at speeds of up to 60 miles per hour and are sometimes called messenger or carrier pigeons because they are often used to carry messages. A message is written on thin, light paper, rolled into a small tube, and attached to the bird's leg.

Carrier pigeons were used as early as 1150 in Iraq, and also later by the brutal barbarian, Genghis Khan. During war time in Europe, pigeons were used to deliver messages home to military headquarters. During World War I, a famous homing pigeon named Cher Ami was given a medal for his bravery in delivering 12 important messages, despite having sustained severe injuries.

When a homing pigeon is taken to a location and released, it has a natural ability to find its way home over extremely long distances, even in unfamiliar territory. Most likely, pigeons use their sense of smell, as well as visual landmarks, to guide them when they fly. Homing pigeons have been observed taking 90-degree turns when coming upon a main road intersecting the road they were following.

Swallows and plovers are well-known for their ability to migrate long distances. So are ducks, geese, and swans. But when it comes to migration, arctic terns have a wing up on their flying counterparts. They have been known to fly as many as 11,000 miles to reach their summer or winter destinations!

God created birds with the ability and instinct to find their way. Some think it's a small piece of metal embedded in their skulls that serves as a beacon for magnetic forces, much like a compass. Others think it's just the Spirit of God working in them, a sixth sense given them at creation. Birds provide us with many lessons about God's care. As small as they are, God still cares for them daily, protecting them and giving them food. If He can do this for them, make no mistake about it—He can do it for us.

Greatest Show on Earth

And what do you benefit if you gain the whole
world but are yourself lost or destroyed?
Luke 9:25, NLT.

On this day in 1835 P. T. Barnum took his famous circus on its first tour. And what a show it was—even in those days. In the 1800s people didn't have movie theatres, TVs, or even radios, so a circus coming to town could draw crowds by the thousands, and his certainly did. Barnum made it no secret that his one goal in life was to accumulate wealth. He was a businessman and entertainer, probably the first show business millionaire.

While still a young man, Barnum worked as a storekeeper, learning how to haggle, strike a hard bargain, and use deception to make a sale. In 1836 he organized a traveling show called *Barnum's Grand Scientific and Musical Theater*, which later became *Barnum's American Museum*. His live exhibits included albinos, giants, midgets, "fat boys," jugglers, and magicians. A dwarf, Tom Thumb, became one of his most popular attractions. By late 1846, Barnum was drawing 400,000 visitors a year. He even toured Europe, entertaining royalty in many countries.

When he started his famous traveling circus, Barnum became one of the great show masters of all time with his hoaxes, bizarre side shows, and sensational demonstrations of acrobatics under the big tents. His traveling animal zoo became a great attraction for children and adults alike. One of the most famous animals of all time was a giant African elephant named Jumbo. Barnum's traveling show eventually became known as *Ringling Brothers and Barnum & Bailey Circus*. Not surprisingly, he claimed his circus was "The Greatest Show on Earth."

Barnum was the first circus owner to move his circus by train, and the first to purchase his own train. Given the lack of paved highways in America, this turned out to be a good business move that made him very successful. He became incredibly wealthy, sometimes quadrupling his investments in a single show. However, several times in his life he lost everything, and bad marketing deals, train wrecks, fires, and bankruptcy all haunted him.

Jesus asks us a very important question. Even if we become incredibly wealthy, what's the point of it all if we lose our eternal life? That's a very good question, and like P. T. Barnum, we would be wise to think about it.

Hudson Taylor Dies

But he who is greatest among you shall be your servant.
Matthew 23:11, NKJV.

China is one of the most fascinating nations in the world. Over one billion people live in the country, and its population is still growing. Modern China grew out of an ancient civilization, its culture going back thousands of years. The Chinese were the first to use many things that we take for granted today, including matches, gun powder, fireworks, silk, paper, wheelbarrows, the decimal system, dominoes, sundials, porcelain china, the pottery wheel, paper money, the compass, seismograph equipment, dominoes, jump ropes, kites, tea, folding umbrellas, ink, printing, the abacus, wallpaper, the cross-bow, ice cream . . . The ancient Chinese were very inventive! We owe them a lot!

About 150 years ago, Hudson Taylor became fascinated with China and decided to go there as a British Protestant missionary. In 1865 he started the China Inland Mission and spent the next 51 years there doing what he loved most: being a witness for Jesus. Taylor realized that to be effective as a missionary he was going to have to eat, dress, and travel like the Chinese, something that was rare for missionaries to do at the time.

When he died on June 3, 1905, he left a great legacy for Christian missions. In his lifetime God helped him start 300 mission stations and 125 schools. He brought 850 missionaries to China, established a network of 125,000 Chinese Christian workers in the mission organization, and was directly responsible for the conversion of 18,000 Chinese Christians. Besides this, his mission's active fight against the opium trade made him especially welcome by the Chinese government.

It has been said that no other missionary in the 19 centuries since the apostle Paul had a wider vision and carried out a more effective plan of evangelism over a larger area than Hudson Taylor.

Like Paul, Hudson Taylor was most happy being a missionary for God. And he wasn't one to complain. He was willing to work tirelessly to help spread the gospel, and he did it as few missionaries have done it since. He was a great man, but the thing that made him truly great was his willingness to first become a servant. Because of his humble ways, Hudson won the hearts of the people.

Women Vote

*Who can find a virtuous and capable wife? She is
more precious than rubies. When she speaks, her words
are wise, and she gives instructions with kindness.
Proverbs 31:10, 26, NLT.*

On this day in American history, June 4, 1919, women finally won the right to vote. The right to vote! Can you believe that? It took the 19th Amendment to the United States Constitution to give American women the right to vote! After 300 years of women taming the wilds of a new America with their families, the U. S. government finally got smart. After loaning their brothers, husbands, sons, and fathers to fight in the Indian wars, the Revolutionary War, the War of 1812, the Civil War, the Spanish-American War, and World War I, we finally recognized our sisters, wives, daughters, and mothers for all the painful sacrifices they made. After decades of helping fight against alcohol, slavery, and child labor in our nation's factories and coal mines, they were finally getting rewarded for all their hard work as citizens.

We've come a long way since 1919. Now women can enlist in the military and fight side by side with men. They can go to any college—something that was not possible for a long time in much of the U. S. And they can live single lives without society looking down on them.

However, there are a few things we still need to address when it comes to women's rights, such as equal pay for equal work. Many jobs in America still pay more for a man's contributions. And women still receive much more discrimination and harassment than men. If a woman takes her car to be repaired at a garage, the odds are that she'll end up paying more money for more unnecessary work.

Women deserve the best that America has to offer its citizens. After all, they certainly do their share of the work. Especially our moms. Many moms get breakfast ready for the family every morning, sometimes making separate lunches for each child. Moms send dad off with a kiss, get the kids off to school, and then head to work themselves. Moms do all kinds of errands after work—the grocery shopping, a trip to the library for homework on penguins, a piano lesson, and soccer practice. That's why we call them soccer moms. Then its home to make supper, do the laundry, and help the kids with homework.

And we waited until 1919 to give women the right to vote? Shame on us! Let's begin today showing our moms how much we appreciate them. Saying "I love you" is a start.

Klondike Gold Digger

Choose a good reputation over great riches;
being held in high esteem is better than silver or gold.
Proverbs 22:1, NLT.

If you could have anything you wanted, what would it be? A winning ticket in the lottery? A large inheritance from a long lost uncle? Striking it rich while panning for gold in a mountain stream?

George Carmack was just such a man. Who was he, and what did he do? He was the man who became famous for discovering gold along the Klondike River, in Canada's Yukon Territory. His father had been a California 49er years before, so Carmack came by it naturally. When he was in his early 20s, Carmack went to the Yukon Territory of northwest Canada and married a Native American woman. At first he didn't seem all that interested in searching for gold, but then things changed. In the summer of 1896, he was fishing with two Native American friends on the Klondike River when he decided to explore Rabbit Creek. It was there that he saw gold pieces so large that he didn't even need to pan for them. Some pieces were as large as his thumb!

Carmack's discovery inspired the last big gold rush of the century. Historians estimate that over 100,000 people set out to try their luck at panning for gold. Some took everything they would need to live and work there for years. Others took little more than the clothes on their backs. Sadly enough, half of the would-be prospectors never even reached their destination. Few were experienced gold miners, and many had to turn back because of sickness, starvation, and the bitterly cold weather.

But Carmack had better luck. He struck it rich several times, and when he retired from mining in 1898, he was now a million dollars richer (today he would be worth 125 million). Unfortunately, he left his wife, moved to Vancouver, B.C., where he remarried, this time to the daughter of a rich tycoon. And on this day in 1922, at only 61 years of age, he died. He was rich, but in the end he died just like everyone else, taking nothing with him but his reputation and the suit he wore in his coffin.

Apparently, it's more worthwhile to seek a sparkly reputation than a few sparkly chunks of gold.

D-day

Thus says the Lord to you: "Do not be afraid nor dismayed because of this great multitude, for the battle is not yours, but God's."
2 Chronicles 20:15, NKJV.

On June 6, 1944, the Allied forces of Europe and the United States invaded the coast of France, where German forces were firmly entrenched. We called that event D-day. Nearly 200,000 troops in 6,000 boats and 800 aircraft made the 26-mile trip across the English Channel to attack the beaches of France. We landed in wave after wave on the beaches of Utah, Omaha, and Normandy. Ground troops marched in under a hail of bullets, and 18,000 paratroopers blanketed the countryside like a cloud. Thirteen thousand more aircraft were later sent in to provide air cover and support for the invasion. Wow! The D-day invasion was one of the planet's most massive invasions in thousands of years.

It's hard to imagine such numbers all moving in the same direction, coordinated to achieve one thing—overwhelm the Nazi Germans and break the strangling hold they had on Europe during the waning years of World War II. Within three months, northern France would be freed and the Allied forces would enter Germany, where they would meet the Soviet forces moving in from the east.

Hitler had been expecting us, and he guessed that we would arrive in the spring of 1944. For months he had been building bunkers along the beaches so that his men would be able to repel an invasion by sea. But he had no idea of the numbers that would arrive. When we finally did arrive, the German defenders couldn't hold us back, and shortly after dawn, Gold, Juno, and Sword Beaches were captured. Although losses were high for the Allies, with thousands dying at Utah and Normandy Beaches, D-day was a success. By the end of June, 850,000 Allied troops and 150,000 vehicles were taking control across Europe.

The soldiers who fought on D-day gave their lives for freedom everywhere. Today we still speak about the heroism and bravery of soldiers in battle and pilots in the sky. Books have been written. Movies like *The Longest Day* and *Saving Private Ryan* have been made. The faith of Americans and other Allies ran high. They knew that God was on their side, going before them into battle. And many claimed the promise, "Do not be afraid nor dismayed because of this great multitude, for the battle *is* not yours, but God's."

Pirate Port Destroyed by Earthquake

For the Lord knows the way of the righteous,
but the way of the ungodly shall perish.
Psalm 1:6, NKJV.

Jamaica is one of the finest tourist spots in the Caribbean today and its rich culture adds to its appeal. However, it has some very intriguing history, too. European conquerors sailed to its shores of paradise, pirates chose its exotic ports in which to hide out, and for hundreds of years the Christian Church has battled its dark forces of superstition and spiritualism.

One Jamaican town became a famous haven for piracy, smuggling, and voodoo witchcraft—Port Royal, an island off the coast, where Kingston stands today. In the seventeenth century it was described as the most wicked and sinful city in the world. And when a massive earthquake devastated the seaport town, many people, not surprisingly, felt the quake was a direct judgment from God.

Earthquakes on the island are common but are usually only small tremors. On June 7, 1692, however, three powerful quakes struck Jamaica, and a large tsunami hit soon after. This put much of Port Royal under 40 feet of water. The waters rose so high that one boat was carried from the harbor and deposited on the roof of a building! Since the small island did not have much bedrock, the quakes caused the soil to cave in, causing buildings to sink into the ground. In the end, every building in the city was destroyed, including two forts. Thousands died during the quakes and tsunami, and then in the landslides that continued in the aftermath. One of the most gruesome sights was that of corpses from the cemetery floating in the harbor alongside recent victims of the disaster. Widespread looting began, and thousands more died in the following weeks due to sickness and injury.

So was the quake really a judgment from God? Only God can say for sure, but one thing is certain. Port Royal did have hundreds of treacherous pirates living there, rough men who had robbed and killed all across the Caribbean. And it was full of the darkest forms of spiritualism known to man. Like the biblical cities of Sodom and Gomorrah, Port Royal was not a place where angels loved to be. Even so, God in His mercy preserved the lives of many, and today Jamaica has one of the strongest Christian populations in the world.

Mohammed Translated

Why are you standing here staring into heaven? Jesus has
been taken from you into heaven, but someday He will
return from heaven in the same way you saw him go!
Acts 1:11, NLT.

One of the most influential leaders in the history of the world was
Mohammed, father and prophet of the Muslim religion. Muslims believe
that on June 8, 632 A.D., he was translated to heaven. Legend says that he
ascended to heaven from the Dome of the Rock in Jerusalem. Today, a holy
Muslim shrine and mosque sit over the Dome of the Rock, considered by
Muslims to be one of the holiest spots in the Islamic Empire.

Mohammed was born in a humble home in Mecca and married a wealthy
widow when he was 25. The story goes that in 610 A.D., he was in a cave
north of Mecca where he received a vision from God. An angel commanded
him to become a prophet of the only true religion, after which he and others
began compiling the writings of the Qur'an. And thus the Islamic religion was
born. Mohammed regarded himself as the last prophet of Judaic-Christianity,
and according to Muslim tradition, was translated without seeing death.
That's the stuff of legends. Then there's reality.

Actually, Mohammed did what all mortal men do in old age. He died.
History tells us he spent his last moments in the arms of Aishah, his third and
favorite wife, and was buried in Medina, Saudi Arabia. The only thing alive
and well about him today is his tomb.

We know of only two people in the history of the world who were translated to heaven without having to die. There was Enoch, the son of Jared,
seventh in the antediluvian line from Adam. He walked with God, and then
one day he disappeared because God took him. With his extremely close
friendship with God, he was more fit for heaven that he was for this world.
The other person to be translated without seeing death was the great prophet
Elijah, a revolutionary leader and reformer in ancient Israel. He was taken up
to heaven in a chariot of fire.

But the most inspirational story of all is the story of Jesus ascending to
heaven, and His disciples witnessed it all there on that Judean hillside. He
died on Calvary, rose again, and today is in heaven preparing a home for everyone who believes. And best of all, He will come again. Isn't it wonderful
to serve a God who doesn't have to make up any stories?

A Dictator Dies

Blessed is the man who walks not in the counsel of
the ungodly . . . He shall be like a tree . . . The ungodly are
not so, but are like the chaff which the wind drives away.
Psalm 1:1-4, NKJV.

Nero Claudius Caesar was only 16 when he became emperor, and he was one of the most arrogant, cruel, extravagant rulers Rome ever saw. He never wore the same robe twice, had his mules shod with silver shoes, and used gold thread for his fishing nets. He was evil and cruel and was disliked by Roman citizens and government leaders. Not surprisingly, Nero murdered members of his own household, including his mother and his wife. It was Nero to whom Paul appealed for a fair trial, but the emperor never looked favorably upon the mistreated apostle.

When a fire burned most of Rome to the ground, rumors began to fly. Many were saying that Nero himself had started the fire to clean out a large section of Rome where the riffraff lived and that the fire had gotten out of control. Historians assure us that this story is probably not true, but nonetheless, Nero feared for his safety and fought back by blaming the Christians, which sparked an era of horrific persecution. Nero loved the games of sport and brutality in the Roman Coliseum, and it was there that he now made an example of Christians, slaughtering them by the hundreds. They were tortured and crucified. They were covered with animal skins and then thrown to the wild beasts. And when the sun went down, they were set on fire as torches to light the evening festivities in the arenas. Tradition tells us that both Peter and Paul died during this time as martyrs. Peter died by crucifixion since he was a Jew, and Paul was beheaded.

In the end, Nero alienated the entire nation, and when several Roman governors revolted, he had precious few supporters. Even his own bodyguard abandoned him, and he finally fled the city. Rather than be captured and executed by his enemies, he decided to take the coward's way out. On this day in 68 A.D., Nero Claudius Caesar, emperor of Rome, took his own life by drinking poison.

But in spite of Nero's horrible persecutions, God's church grew by leaps and bounds during and after his reign. The blood that the deaths of Paul and Peter planted, along with the blood of all the other saints, did indeed become the seed of the church. And Christianity, the very thing that Nero despised, grew and grew, blooming throughout the world.

Alcoholics Anonymous

Wine is a mocker, strong drink is raging:
and whosoever is deceived thereby is not wise.
Proverbs 20:1.

Let's imagine what it's like to be an alcoholic. You drink all the time. You want that beer early in the morning, maybe even before you go to school or work. It's a quick swig you swallow along with your breakfast glass of milk. Then you take some more with you in a water bottle or a thermos so you can have it at lunch. It's a long wait until after school or work, and then you can finally go to a quiet park and have a few beers you've stashed in your back-pack. Or maybe you'll go "study" at a friend's house who's got the problem too. At home you spend more time in your room than you'd like, watching some TV maybe, and hoping that your family won't think it strange that you're just not the person you used to be. If you're an adult, it's legal. If you're a minor, you wonder how you've managed to hide it this long.

More and more kids today are alcoholics. They get introduced to the habit by watching mom or dad drink, or Aunt Millie or Granddad. Or maybe they get turned on to alcohol by friends. Whatever the reason, there's hope, thanks to Alcoholics Anonymous. The Twelve Step organization was started by Bill W. and Dr. Robert Smith to help people who want to be free from alcohol. That was more than 70 years ago, on June 10, 1935. Today group sessions offer members a chance to take responsibility for their weakness. The organization teaches alcoholics that they need a higher power to help them escape the clutches of the bottle. More than 100,000 AA groups are now operating in 150 countries, with a worldwide membership of 2 million. The organization Bill W. and Dr. Smith started has helped millions kick their old habits through prayer and sharing, because that's exactly what their organization is all about.

And there are organizations around to help people with other addictions too: Narcotics Anonymous, Cocaine Anonymous, Gamblers Anonymous, Sex Addicts Anonymous. Like an army these organizations provide support and power for kicking the habits of addiction.

Jesus wants to help addicts. He can heal alcoholics of their terrible curse. He is the higher power to which each AA member—and anyone else—can turn. Only through Him can anyone truly overcome the habits of this sinful old world.

Praise God for a hope like this!

Lung Transplant

As long as my breath is in me, and the breath of God is in my nostrils, my lips will not speak wickedness, nor my tongue utter deceit. Job 27:3, 4, NKJV.

Have you ever fallen and gotten the wind knocked out of you? Do you have asthma, allergies, or another respiratory problem that makes breathing difficult? Have you ever been swimming and felt like you were going to drown? There's no doubt that our lungs are among the most important organs in the body. It's said that we could exist without our arms, legs, eyes, ears, tongue, much of our stomach and intestines, one kidney, and most of our liver, but without our lungs, we would die almost immediately. We can last about four weeks without food, four days without water, but only four minutes without air.

Our lungs are also among our most fragile organs. A normal adult lung is about nine to 10 inches long, and pound for pound, is the lightest organ in the body. Dried specimens look like Styrofoam and are just as light, consisting of tiny, paper-thin air sacks called alveoli. Because of their fragility, lungs do not take trauma well and can get infected easily. They can fill with fluid and can go into shock due to a puncture or collapse.

Diseases of the lungs can be deadly. Every year hundreds of thousands of people die from emphysema, fibrosis, and lung cancer, caused primarily by smoking or breathing chemicals in our air. Even people who don't smoke can suffer from secondary smoke in the air around them.

However, there is good news. Every year medical teams discover new ways to save people's lives and help the human body live longer. And today is the anniversary of one of those days. On June 11, 1963, the first successful lung transplant in the United States was performed, and the staff at the University of Mississippi Medical Center were excited. They had just made history! In a three-hour operation, Dr. James Hardy led a team of doctors in replacing the left lung of John Russell. Unfortunately, due to kidney failure, the patient survived for only 18 days.

It is our lungs that give us air to breathe and speak and sing, and we should praise God for these complex, fragile, life-sustaining gifts. As long as we are alive we should be shouting from the rooftops our gratitude to Him for giving us life and for making us with such sophisticated bodies.

Nicole Brown-Simpson Murdered

You may be sure that your sin will find you out.
Numbers 32:23, NLT.

O. J. Simpson was one the most famous football players of all time. His accomplishments paralleled his rushes carrying the football—they went on and on and on. His most celebrated achievements include the following: He was an all-American collegiate player, won the prestigious *Heisman Trophy* award, made the Pro Bowl all-star team, was the NFL's Most Valuable Player, held the single-season rushing record, was named *Pro Football Monthly's* NFL Player of the Decade, made the College Football Hall of Fame, and made the Pro Football Hall of Fame.

But take away the bright lights, the goal posts, the crunching of colliding helmets, his teammates, the field, and the cheering fans, and a very different man appeared. It is said that he had serious problems with anger, likely one of the causes of his marriage falling apart. Then, on June 12, 1994, the entire nation and much of the world gasped as news reports flooded the airwaves that Ron Goldman and Simpson's ex-wife, Nicole Brown-Simpson, had been brutally stabbed to death outside Nicole's home in Brentwood, California. The real question remains—was O. J. Simpson guilty of their murders? Did he hold the bloodied knife himself? Did he hire someone to do it for him? Was he innocent altogether? Although a court officially found him not guilty, we may never really know. Today, with many of those questions still unresolved, that tragedy and the trials that followed remain among the most highly publicized events of the twentieth century.

While many people think he was innocent, many people think he was guilty and got off easy for heinous crimes. One thing is for sure: If he is guilty, he will pay for his sins. Even if he escaped the judgment of an earthly courtroom, he will not escape the judgment of the heavenly one.

When we lead hidden lives of sin, we are only concealing a powder keg that is sure to blow sky high sooner or later. Like a cancer growing deep within the tissues, sin eats its destructive way until the damage becomes irreparable. But Jesus can deliver us from the power of sin. He can make us strong to resist temptation if we will call on Him to help us.

Peasants Revolt

*God overlooked people's ignorance about these things
in earlier times, but now he commands everyone
everywhere to repent of their sins and turn to him.
Acts 17:30, NLT.*

The year was 1381, and the bubonic plague was sweeping Europe. One third of Europe's population had died from the fatal disease. In those days people were ignorant about the causes of bubonic plague, or the black plague, as it was commonly called. No one knew that it was the fleas on the rats that were carrying the disease.

Sanitary conditions were poor in those days, making the rat population multiply uncontrollably. People threw garbage into the streets for pigs and dogs to eat, and it was common for people to throw the contents of their chamber pots into the village streets every morning. Flies crawled on the animal waste in the streets, and then on the foods the people ate. And to make matters worse, when people got sick with bubonic plague, they fled, taking the disease and the hitchhiking fleas with them to other towns.

Because so many had died, workers were in short supply. Peasants were on the move in search of jobs, and this made common folks more educated about the world around them. It also gave them new goals and dreams of better things to come.

But government leaders resisted the changes that such a crisis was bringing on Europe, and they refused to listen to the peasants in their cries for reforms. They wanted to return to the ancient system of feudalism where people could be bought and sold with the land they farmed as serfs. Besides all this, the royal treasury was short on money, and when taxes were raised, the peasants' discontent erupted into anger, and they revolted. On June 13, 1381, a mob of peasants marched into London and proceeded to trash the city. They started fires, looted stores, and destroyed several government buildings. They broke prisoners out of jail, and a judge was even beheaded along with several dozen other leading citizens.

What a terrible time in which to live! People were ignorant about the most basic things of life, such as hygiene and sanitary conditions in their streets and homes. Thankfully, God overruled the basic ignorance under which Satan had confined society, and we have more common sense today. The gospel story of Jesus can bless society even more by bringing truth and light to those in need. Let's help spread the good news!

Stars and Stripes Forever

We will rejoice in your salvation, and in the name of our God we will set up our banners! May the Lord fulfill all your petitions. Psalm 20:5, NKJV.

Since ancient times flags have been very important to clans and tribes and nations. They have flown over cities and castles, have led armies, and have helped generals celebrate victory. In 1776, during the American Revolution, the colonial Continental Army flew a flag that had 13 red and white stripes. According to legend, Philadelphia seamstress Betsy Ross designed a new flag at the request of General George Washington. It consisted of 13 red and white stripes, and a circle of 13 stars on a blue background, which soon became known as the Stars and Stripes. The stripes represented the 13 original colonies, and the circle of stars was supposed to represent a new constellation for a new country. On June 14 of 1777, the Continental Congress adopted the new flag for the United States of America.

Since then, there have been 27 versions of the American flag. In 1960, we came out with the flag we have now—still 13 stripes, but also 50 stars for 50 states. Nicknames for the flag include the Stars and Stripes, Old Glory, and the Star-Spangled Banner, a term prominent in our national anthem.

The United States flag is one of our nation's most common symbols and is displayed almost everywhere, on government buildings, schools, restaurants, and even private homes. The flag stands for many things, but among the most important are the freedoms given to us by the Declaration of Independence, the U. S. Constitution, and the Bill of Rights, and for the tremendous sacrifices of those who have purchased those freedoms at the high cost of their time, labor, and lives.

God has given us so very much in this great country of ours. We are wonderfully blessed to live in neighborhoods where we can expect to be protected by our police and firemen. We drive on good roads, have plenty of food and clothing, and rarely have to go without electricity. We have schools and libraries where our children can learn, and jobs that enable us to provide a good living for our families. We even have time and money for leisure and entertainment. On top of this, we can worship when and where we want and send missionaries to the ends of the earth. And we have the privilege of flying the Stars and Stripes in our gratefulness.

Magic Rubber

Whatever your hand finds to do, do it with all your might.
Ecclesiastes 9:10, NIV.

Magic Rubber. That's what they should have called it. It did all the things that rubber was supposed to do, under all kinds of weather conditions, and for long periods of time. On this day in 1844, Charles Goodyear of New York City, took out a patent on what would become the magic substance of the century. Quite by accident, he had stumbled upon the answer that many had been desperately seeking.

Rubber had been known for quite some time, but no one could ever get it to become stable, and therefore, useful. Whoever could conquer the substance and make it usable in everyday life, stood to make a lot of money. Latex, the white liquid sap from rubber trees, had all the potential of becoming the wonder product of the future. But no matter which combination of chemicals it was combined with on a trial and error basis, nothing ever seemed to work. The treated and heated sap would just get all gooey and eventually disintegrate.

And then a freakish accident jumped off the pages of fate. Once in a century, a quirky slip of fate does this for an inventor and hands him the dream discovery of his life. Goodyear had been investing years into the rubber project. He had spent all his money, sacrificing even his family's well-being to solve the puzzle and reach the prize. One day while he was working with the latest latex compound, a bit of it slipped off the utensil he was using to spread it on a piece of material. The blob of latex fell onto the top of the heated stove, and when he picked it up, it had a new feel to it. It was firm and yet springy to the touch, like a sponge. *Voila!* He had stumbled upon a discovery that had eluded inventors and chemists for years. Unfortunately, Goodyear never realized the wealth that should have been his for his success. Greedy industrialists and manufacturers used his ideas without ever paying him for what the prize was worth.

Even when things don't turn out as you wish they would, take heart and continue to do your very best. God will reward you and give you a blessing simply because you persevered to reach your goal. And if you choose to serve God, you know you will suffer disappointments. Satan will see to that. But if you take God as your partner, you can't go wrong. God has never failed in a business venture.

Helicopter Born

Who are these that fly along like clouds, like doves to their nests?
Isaiah 60:8, NIV.

Helicopters are one of the most incredible inventions of the twentieth century. They are used to carry military personnel and mountain skiers, emergency rescue teams, and tourists on sightseeing trips. Although they do need lots of fuel and are dangerous in high winds, they don't need runways, and they don't need wings.

On June 16, 1922, Henry Berliner presented a primitive helicopter to the United States Army at College Park, Maryland. The copter raised itself up to the height of seven feet, three separate times. It had two lifting propellers in the front and a propeller in the rear that could be tilted to make the machine move forward.

The helicopter is about as close as humans can get to complete mobility. We do have military jets now that can move up, down, forward, backward, and sideways, but the size and weight of these machines require massive amounts of fuel, making helicopters more efficient. It seems impossible that a helicopter could lift itself off the ground with the simple whirling of a blade, and this wonder is all the greater when we see military copters lifting tanks off the ground!

While even successful human wonders of flight are blighted by inefficiency, nature's are not. Take hummingbirds. These tiny aircraft are the smallest of birds. They lay eggs the size of a pea in a nest no bigger than a walnut shell. And like the helicopter, they can fly in every direction by a simple tilting of the wings and a dipping of the tail feathers. However, they move so quickly that the naked eye cannot possibly follow their wing movements, and they take very little fuel to operate!

The most ingenious flying machine of all is arguably the bumblebee. Scientists are stumped at how the bumblebee can maneuver itself with its incredibly disproportionate wing size to body weight ratio. In other words, the wings are way too small to be able to move its large body as it does. We will probably never be able to build flying machines as efficient as the hummingbird or bumblebee, but we can certainly sit in awe at the wonders of God's creation. Only He could put together the paper-thin wings of a bumblebee and the delicate strands of muscle needed to power a hummingbird. Absolutely amazing, is what we must say in praise to our Creator God for His incredible flying machines!

Strongest Man on Earth

*Better a patient man than a warrior, a man
who controls his temper than one who takes a city.
Proverbs 16:32, NIV.*

In 1957, on the 17th of June, Paul Anderson of Toccoa, Georgia, became the strongest man on earth when he lifted over 6,000 pounds in a dead lift. Paul was a trained weight lifter and had entered many strongman contests, lifting enormous weights, but this test of brawn stole the show. In an almost super-human effort, he back lifted a table holding heavy automobile parts and a safe full of lead. The total weight was actually 6,270 pounds. With that feat of strength he broke every record that had ever been set by a man. Many were saying that he had to be the strongest man who ever lived. And we would have to agree—almost.

Sampson is a biblical legend for the history books. Scripture tells some pretty phenomenal stories about his superhuman strength. He was chosen by God for a special mission in life—to deliver the tribes of Israel from the Philistines. His parents had dedicated him to serve God as a Nazarite, and as part of his vows to God, he was never to drink wine or cut his hair.

He was still a young man when his amazing strength first became evident. While walking down the road to Timnath, a lion sprang out of the vineyards and pounced on him. In that instant God's Spirit possessed him, and he ripped the lion's jaws apart as though they were a piece of goat meat. Another time he went to battle against 3,000 Philistine soldiers and killed 1,000 of them with nothing but a donkey's jawbone. A third time, as he stayed overnight in the Philistine city of Gaza, the Philistine leaders thought they had him, but Samson had the last word, capping off his victory by lifting the two city gates, with posts and bars attached, and carrying them several miles up into the hills. Most of the scrapes Samson got himself into were because he was not keeping his promises to God, and yet amazingly, God still gave him the strength to fight his battles.

When Samson flirted with danger a final time and revealed the secret of his strength to Delilah, she betrayed him. The Philistines cut his hair, put out his eyes, and chained him to work in the prison. He had a change of heart, but his days were numbered. A few months later, on a pagan feast day, he pulled down the Temple of Dagon, and died in the process. What a sad end to a spiritually weak man who was undoubtedly the strongest man on earth!

First American Woman in Space

Charm is deceptive, and beauty does not last; but a woman who fears the Lord will be greatly praised. Reward her for all she has done. Let her deeds publicly declare her praise. Proverbs 31:29-31, NLT.

Women have been competing with men for jobs since . . . who knows when. Today they compete as professional musicians, CEOs, fashion designers, and athletes. Women like Danica Patrick have competed and won in sports contests against men. Just look at her performance as the first woman to win an Indy-style auto race.

On this day in 1983, Dr. Sally Ride became the first American woman to travel into space on the space shuttle *Challenger*'s second mission. An astrophysicist from Stanford University, her job on the six-day mission was to operate the shuttle's robot arm, which she had helped design.

Twenty years before, almost to the day, a cosmonaut named Valentina Tereshkova from the Soviet Union, became the first woman ever to travel into space. That was on June 16, 1963. The United States had screened a group of female pilots in 1959 and 1960 for possible astronaut training, but later decided to limit space missions to men. However, in 1978, NASA finally changed its policy and announced that it had approved six women to become the first female astronauts in the U. S. space program. The new astronauts were chosen out of some 3,000 original applicants. Among the six was Sally Ride, who set a new space record in 1996. She stayed in space longer than any woman had ever done before—188 days. That's over half a year! Most people can't even stay on vacation at the beach that long, and she did it orbiting the earth on the Russian space station *Mir*.

So ladies, what do you really want in life? Charm? Beauty? Musical ability? Athletic ability? Political power? Solomon warned us that charm can be deceptive and beauty will eventually fade away, but those who learn to love and serve God deserve the real places of honor in our society. Because honesty and faithfulness accompany everything they do, they deserve the most prestigious jobs and the most honored places in our society. We would do well to have more women—and men—like them on our racetracks, in our space shuttles, and everywhere!

Batter Up!

We know that the law is good if one uses it properly.
1 Timothy 1:8, NIV.

For decades baseball was called America's favorite sport, and along with hot dogs and apple pie, came to be one of America's unofficial symbols. Baseball came to mean a day of relaxation with the family at the ballpark on a hot summer's day. No doubt you've heard the words to the famous song: "Take me out to the ball game, take me out with the crowd. Buy me some peanuts and cracker jack, I don't care if I never get back. Let me root, root, root for the home team, if they don't win it's a shame. For its one, two, three strikes, you're out, at the old ball game."

All across America kids still love to play baseball. It isn't the favorite pastime it once was, but it's still popular, especially among Little Leaguers. Church leagues and summer leagues are a fun way for adults to enjoy the game, too. There's nothing like a good game of baseball to bring a group together.

The first baseball game as an official sport was played on June 19, 1846, in New York. The New York Nine, an informal team of weekend warriors, defeated the New York Knickerbockers. The score? Twenty-one to four in four innings of ball. The umpire was Alex Cartwright, who wrote the first set of formal rules for baseball. He also laid out the diamond-shaped field, and set up the nine playing positions on the field: pitcher, catcher, first, second, and third basemen, shortstop, and three outfielders.

In a game of baseball one man is the boss. It's the umpire. He makes the decisions on what's a strike and what's not. He decides who's out and who's not. He's the one who shouts, "Safe!" or "You're out-a-there!" He interprets the rules of the game, and he has the final word.

God is kind of like that. He made the rules, as that first umpire, Alex Cartwright did, and if we love Him, we'll live by the rules. But His rules were made, not to throw us out at home plate, but to bless us with a happy and meaningful life. As the lyrics to the song say, "The law of the Lord is perfect, converting the soul. The testimony of the Lord is sure, making wise the simple. More to be desired are they than gold, yea than much fine gold. Sweeter also than honey and the honeycomb." God's law is like baseball. If we love His law and stick to the rules, it makes for a very good game.

Look at Him Run!

*Don't you realize that in a race everyone runs, but only
one person gets the prize? So run to win! All athletes are
disciplined in their training. They do it to win a prize
that will fade away, but we do it for an eternal prize.
1 Corinthians 9:24, 25, NLT.*

What's the fastest creature on earth? Dogs and cats can run at speeds of about 30 miles per hour. An ostrich's top speed is 43, horses can gallop at about 50, and antelopes have been clocked at 60. What is the fastest land mammal? You guessed it—the cheetah, who can sprint at 70 miles per hour! But the fastest creature on earth is a bird, the peregrine falcon, who can dive at the blistering speed of 217 miles per hour! Now, while all this information is correct, if you want to get technical, for it's size, the Tiger Beetle is really the fastest creature on earth. Its top running speed is from 5 to 7 miles per hour, but if it were the size of a human being, that would be about 300—as fast as most any racecar!

How fast can a human being run? Well, in 1936, Jesse Owens was clocked at about 36 miles per hour. On this day in that year, he won a gold medal in the 100-meter dash at the Olympics in Berlin, Germany. Beating the previous record by one tenth of a second, he set a new record at 10.2 seconds. Jesse was such an outstanding athlete that he went on to achieve international fame by winning three more gold medals in the Olympics that year: the 200-meter dash, the long jump, and the 400-meter relay. He became the first American to win four Olympic gold medals in track and field.

As they say, records are made to be broken, and Jesse's 100-meter dash record has been broken 13 times over, the most recent being in 2005 when Asafa Powell of Jamaica set the newest record at 9.77 seconds.

Do you like to run races? Do you like competing in track and field events? Competition like that can be fun, but can you imagine what it's like to compete at the Olympic level? Even more importantly, is there any greater challenge than to compete for a crown of life? Fortunately, we can all win one. Paul reminds us that we need to persevere like athletes, though, and press on to the finish line as if we were the only ones in the race. Sometimes it really does feel like that, but we draw strength from the fact that Jesus, Who ran the perfect race, also felt alone at times. Don't give up—He'll cross the finish line with you.

Royalty on the Run

Enter not into the path of the wicked, and go not in the way of evil men.
Proverbs 4:14.

It was the height of the French Revolution, and the whole country was up-side down. King Louis XVI and Marie Antoinette were hiding behind closed doors while the peasants rioted in the streets, war between the "haves' and the "haven nots." The "haves" were the rich and famous, of course, and the "have nots" were the dirt poor peasants, so poor they couldn't afford a piece of land even the size of a postage stamp. The only dirt a peasant owned was on the bottoms of his feet. Most of the peasants were themselves owned by a wealthy baron or count. When land was sold, peasant workers usually went with it, along with the dirt floored, grass thatched hut they called home.

And now the royal couple knew the jig was up. On June 21, 1791, they hatched a plan to flee from Paris and escape the angry mobs. The plan was to reach the fortress of Montmedy in northeastern France where they had supporters. But they had some problems. The coach they chose for the ride was too elegant to be disguised—luxurious green with yellow trim, with a ridiculous white velvet interior, and a leather toilet. Probably the six horses pulling the coach were a giveaway of their true identity, too. Word spread like wildfire that the king and queen were on the run. One thing after another went wrong, and finally, just 194 miles outside of Paris, at a place called Varennes, they were captured.

Things weren't looking good for the royal couple. King Louis had always been uppity and arrogant and too extravagant, always spending money on himself. He cared nothing about the subjects of his kingdom and even less for the good of France. He and his queen had showed little compassion in their lifetimes, and even less mercy. And now none was shown them. The government was now in the hands of the peasants, and they acted swiftly. Following the capture of the royal family, King Louis XVI was put on trial and sent to the guillotine. Marie Antoinette received the same fate nine months later.

What a sad ending for two rulers who could have been so much more! They had every advantage. God warns us to avoid choices that put people down. Sooner or later the poor will have the last word with the rich. Why not determine that you will have the heart of Jesus, acting with compassion and love to all His children?

Henry Hudson Disappears

They refused to obey, and they were not mindful of Your wonders that You did among them. But they hardened their necks, and in their rebellion they appointed a leader to return to their bondage. Nehemiah 9:17, NKJV.

Have you ever felt rebellious—angry enough to do something drastic? If so, you're not alone. Lots of people feel that way when they have a hard time getting along with others, especially in the middle of a trying situation. That's what happened to Henry Hudson.

This is how the story goes. The year was 1611 and Henry Hudson was on a voyage for England to see if he could find a trade route to Asia by sailing north around Canada. He was one of the first modern explorers to enter these uncharted waters so he had no reliable maps to guide him. And he had no idea how severe the weather could be. After three months of exploration along the northern coasts of Canada, his ship was caught too far from open sea when winter arrived, and the crew was forced to haul the ship ashore and set up a winter camp. The sailors had very little food, and they suffered miserably in the piercing cold. Many of the men blamed him for their predicament. When summer came and Hudson wanted to continue his explorations, his crew mutinied against him. On June 22, 1611, they set him adrift, with his son and seven supporters, in a small, open boat.

The crew later returned to England and was arrested for the mutiny. Unfortunately, Henry, his son, and the others in the boat suffered a worse fate. They were never seen again, and most explorers gave up the idea of finding a passage through the Northwest. Did anything good come from this tale? Hudson's discoveries did give England its claim to the rich Hudson Bay region, which meant a foothold in the New World. Today, we owe in part our English heritage in North America to the brave Henry Hudson.

Like Hudson's crew, ancient Israel grew tired of wandering in the wilderness. They failed to remember all the miracles God had performed for them—the miraculous delivery from the 10 plagues in Egypt, the jaw-dropping parting of the waters of the Red Sea, the manna, and the water from the rock. But God didn't mutiny and set them adrift to fend for themselves. He stuck with them, cared for them, and led them all the way to the Promised Land.

Secret Service Begun

Some trust in chariots and some in horses,
but we trust in the name of the Lord our God.
Psalms 20:7, NIV.

On June 23, 1860, the United States federal government started a new department that was to be in charge of security. It was called the Secret Service, but it wasn't created to protect the president or other important government leaders. It was started to get the problem of counterfeiting under control. The Treasury Department was having a particularly hard time keeping criminals from illegally making counterfeit coins and paper money.

Today, if you really want to keep your money safe, you can hire professionals in the security business. They can install window and door sensors, hidden video cameras, infrared detectors, and alarm systems. You've probably seen movies featuring some of these high-tech devices. Security is big business because banks have a lot of money on hand at any one time. But a bigger problem for banks today than bank robbers in ski masks breaching physical security barriers, is the danger of criminals hacking their way into the computers and stealing money electronically. Much of the money a bank uses doesn't really exist. It's simply a system of credits and debits, a list of dollar figures in electronic files. The money you have in the bank is usually safe, as it is insured by the federal government up to $100,000. If a bank robber breaks into your bank at gunpoint and steals some of your cash, or hacks into the bank's computer systems and transfers funds illegally, you won't be out a dime—up to a hundred grand.

After the assassination of Lincoln, the Secret Service took on some new responsibilities, that of guarding the life of the president. Today, Secret Service guards are dispatched to protect the president and family, the vice president, former presidents and their wives, widows of former presidents unless they remarry, minor children of former presidents until they reach the age of 16, major presidential candidates, and foreign government representatives and ambassadors.

When Jesus came to earth He had no Secret Service officers to guard Him day and night. However, I can imagine that ten thousand angels probably offered their services the day He left for His special mission. He didn't trust in security systems, Secret Service officers, or even angels. He trusted only in the name of His Father.

First Europeans on Mainland North America

They went in and took possession of the land. . . Even the Canaanites, who inhabited the land, were powerless!
Nehemiah 9:24, NLT.

Who were the first people to set foot on mainland North America? On June 24, 1597, the first European explorers since the time of the Vikings set foot on the North American mainland. King Henry VII had sent John Cabot and his English crew west across the Atlantic to find a spice trade route. Their goal was Asia and the East Indies, but they had no idea they must first get past a huge and wild continent. Cabot arrived on the coast of Newfoundland, or possibly Maine, and what he found made him wonder. Here was a wild and untamed land with few inhabitants—free for the taking! After planting the English flag, he and his men tramped through the woods to explore the area surrounding the landing site.

But they weren't the first people to arrive here from a foreign land. Many people had come and gone, and the evidence is here to tell the story. The Vikings stumbled upon North America around 1000 A.D., leaving their huts, weapons, and altars to prove they had been here. One of them, Leif Ericson, was amazed at the richness of the continent and reported seeing abundant wildlife, such as wild turkeys and white-tailed deer. But there were others even before them. Ancient peoples arrived as many as 2,500 years ago, from places like Egypt and Phoenicia. The writing on cliff walls along the Mississippi River valley is proof enough, and the copper mines they abandoned showed they came from a well-developed, sophisticated culture.

So who were the first people to set foot on mainland North America? We just don't know. Maybe Noah's sons or grandsons came during the days following the flood, when they were exploring the new landforms of earth. Ancient Israel faced the challenges of a new land when they first entered Canaan, just as Cabot and his men did when they disembarked on the east coast. The Israelite tribes were excited, but they were also afraid. They had heard stories of giants in the land, and it terrified them just thinking about having to fight the monsters. But God had promised to be with them, driving out the enemy with hornets, wild lions, and violent hailstorms. Even the sun became a tool of deliverance in God's hand, when it stood motionless in the valley of Adjalon for over 24 hours. What a God we serve!

Custer's Massacre

Pride goes before destruction, and a haughty spirit before a fall.
Proverbs 16:18, NKJV.

One of the most lopsided military defeats in the history of the West occurred on this day in 1876. Historians call it Custer's Massacre, and it was simply a military mismatch, with the odds overwhelmingly in favor of the Indian tribes in Southern Montana. Because of the United States government's broken promises, Sioux chiefs Sitting Bull and Crazy Horse refused to stay on their reservations. Both chiefs wanted nothing more than for their people be left alone to simply live the life of plains Indians, but a confrontation was inevitable. By late spring of 1876, more than 10,000 Indians had gathered in a massive camp along a river in southern Montana called the Little Big Horn.

The United States Cavalry was called in to deal with the Indian uprisings, but it had no idea of the massive numbers of its Indian enemy. Colonel Custer, an ambitious young officer from the Civil War years, hoped to make his mark as a hero in the Indian wars and use a sensational victory to launch a campaign to become president of the United States. On the morning of June 25, while on an expedition into the Little Big Horn valley, Colonel Custer and his 7th Cavalry regiment received warnings from their scouts that a massive Indian gathering lay ahead in a nearby valley, but Custer dismissed it as unrealistic. He and his 215 men proceeded up the valley and within minutes found themselves surrounded and under attack by as many as 3,000 armed braves. Within the hour it was all over. Custer and his standing regiment were wiped out to the last man.

The Battle of the Little Big Horn was a great victory for the Indians, and a horrible defeat for the U. S. Army in the long and bloody Plains Indian War. The victory for the Indians was sweet—but short. Within five years, the Sioux and Cheyenne nations would be confined to reservations forever.

If Colonel Custer had lived he might have learned a valuable lesson. "Pride *goes* before destruction, and a haughty spirit before a fall." Custer died a bloody death short of that lesson, and short if his dream to become a hero. If he had only listened to his scouts . . . Let's learn from Custer's mistake by listening to God's warnings and by bringing all our ambitions into line with His plan.

June 26

Smallpox Inoculation

Let all that I am praise the Lord; may I never forget the good things He does for me. He forgives all my sins and heals all my diseases. Psalms 103:2, 3, NLT.

In our world's short history major disease epidemics have swept through villages, cities, and even countries, killing untold millions. Smallpox was one of those diseases. It is believed to have originated in Africa thousands of years ago, then spreading to India and China. The first smallpox epidemic on record was in 1350 B.C. during a war between the Egyptians and Hittites. By the fifth century A.D., smallpox had reached Europe, eventually becoming a critical disease in nearly every major country in the world. Closer to home, Americans were hit especially hard by the dangerous killer in the seventeenth and eighteenth centuries.

During these times of medical darkness, there were innovative people who were trying to find an answer to the disease. Dr. Zabdiel Boylston of Boston, Massachusetts, was one of them, and he found himself right in the middle of a smallpox epidemic. Fortunately, he didn't back away from the almost impossible challenge. On the 26th of June, 1721, he was finally successful in developing a primitive vaccine and cure for smallpox. Because smallpox was such a deadly disease at the time, this discovery was a real breakthrough. Dr. Boylston used his 6-year-old son and two servants as guinea pigs, and then went on to successfully inoculate 247 other people. His new ideas about disease control were accepted in Massachusetts largely because of a famous Boston preacher named Cotton Mather, who was also a scientist. Mather was sure Dr. Boylston was on to something. The advances in disease control we have today are due largely to men like Mather who supported Boylston and insisted he go on with his experiments in spite of the public's doubt and disapproval.

In 1967 the World Health Organization started a worldwide campaign to eradicate smallpox, and by 1977 the last major smallpox outbreak occurred in Somalia, Africa. On May 8, 1980, the World Health Assembly declared the world officially free of smallpox.

In this old world we will never be completely free from the effects of disease, but we should take heart. Jesus has given us the innovation to find healing from our physical diseases, and even more importantly, He wants us to find spiritual healing. Let us never forget that, whether now or in the future, He will indeed heal us of all our physical and spiritual diseases.

Wonder Woman

I can do all through Christ who strengthens me.
Philippians 4:13, NKJV.

Life would be hard if you couldn't see. There would be no way you could watch TV. No chance for you to be on the tumbling team at school or in a computer graphics class. No chance of going to a football stadium to watch a game between the Dallas Cowboys and the Pittsburgh Steelers. Now, what if you couldn't hear, either? Most activities at school or after school would be out of the question, too.

There are people who have lived that life. Helen Keller was one of them. Blind and deaf almost all her life, yet she became one of the most famous women in American history. By the time she was an adult she was a celebrity. She is known for many things that she could do, but it is what she could not do that made her a legend.

She was born on this day in 1880, a normal child, but before she was 2 years old she got a bad fever and lost both her sight and hearing. Because she couldn't see or hear, she couldn't learn to talk either. That is, until she met Alexander Graham Bell. In addition to his interest in inventing things (think telephone), Mr. Bell studied ways to teach deaf people how to talk.

Helen was 6 years old when Mr. Bell arranged to have Annie Sullivan, a partially blind woman, come live with her. Annie had been to a special school where she learned how to use sign language to teach blind and deaf students to communicate. Because Helen couldn't see or hear, she was a very frustrated little girl, but eventually she learned to trust Annie. Before long, Helen learned to spell her first word, water, by feeling cool water run over her hand while Miss Sullivan spelled the word into her other hand using sign language.

Helen went to several schools in Boston and New York City and learned how to speak and read by putting her fingers on her teacher's lips and throat. Later, she went to college and even wrote several books. She became a famous speaker and traveled all over the world. She once wrote, "I seldom think about my limitations, and they never make me sad."

We have been promised that with God's help we can accomplish anything we set out to do. Like Helen, we should never let bad experiences keep us from being happy and successful in life. If we give Jesus a chance to help us, we can turn our troubles into stepping-stones for our future.

Cholera Epidemic

Therefore, these plagues will overtake her in a single day—
death and mourning and famine.
Revelation 18:8, NLT.

The year was 1832. The dreaded Asiatic cholera had been spreading over the world, and though desperate attempts had been made to keep it out of North America, it arrived in Canada anyway. Quebec was the first point of the cholera attacks in the spring of that year, probably brought by immigrants from Ireland. The plague traveled up the St. Lawrence River and soon reached Buffalo, New York. Everyone in that city was terrified—and with good reason. Within days of its arrival, people were dropping like flies.

On June 28, 1832, the epidemic hit New York City, spreading its malicious fingers over the city through its unsanitary food and water supplies. Knowing virtually nothing about the disease and how it was carried, the people did not know to watch for the first ominous symptoms—diarrhea and vomiting followed by low blood pressure, shock, and eventually unconsciousness. The killer worked quickly. A child would appear to be in good health in the morning but be resting in his grave by nightfall, and this hideous scenario was common. Death carts patrolled the streets, and as they passed by homes, the driver would shout, "Bring out your dead!" It was not permitted for a body to lie unburied for more than an hour or two, and with dozens in every neighborhood dying daily, the death cart drivers stayed very busy.

Cholera's effect on the world was deep. It affected many countries, some of which had to devote entire cemeteries to hold its victims. Sweden was one of those countries, suffering through 11 cholera epidemics from 1834-1873 and losing 37,000 people in 1853 alone. Although the footprint of cholera's impact has been greatly diminished, largely through the emphasis on clean food and water sources, cholera remains a threat to people traveling to third world countries and those eating raw or undercooked food from contaminated sources.

Before Jesus comes, disease and death will become a serious part of earth's final crisis. According to the book of Revelation, death and mourning will overtake the world in a single day. But for those of us who can see past the gravestones to the bright, healing atmosphere of our promised heavenly home, God's salvation will happily infect us just as quickly.

Pricey Painting

And we know that God causes everything to work together for the good of those who love God and are called according to His purpose for them. Romans 8:28, NLT.

On June 29, 1987, a famous painting called Le Pont de Trinquetaille sold for over $20 million at an art auction in London. Wow! $20 million! Who was this artist that his painting of a bridge would sell for that much?

His name was Vincent Van Gogh, born in 1853 in the Netherlands. While still a young man, he became an art dealer, and then a teacher, but neither of these professions satisfied him. Then he was offered a chance to be a preacher for a congregation in a small community, but that didn't seem to work for him either. He liked the prestige the job provided him, but he had a hard time making it financially. Blessed with a soft heart, he was giving away most of his salary to people in need. One day he received a visit from an officer in his church who asked him why he didn't dress in nicer clothes. When he confessed that he was donating his money to the poor, the officer told Van Gogh that he wasn't properly representing the church. Disappointed that he was not doing the job they had hired him to do, church leaders soon gave him his walking papers.

This was a real blow, and Vincent became severely depressed. It seemed to him that he was a failure in everything he tried to do in life. In 1880, at just 27 years of age, he decided to become an artist. He moved around Europe, teaching himself to draw and paint, until finally his brother arranged for him to meet professional artists in Paris. Before long his work began to show real promise and he began to turn out some real masterpieces.

Today Van Gogh's work is well-known, and his paintings hang in museums all over the world. Not surprisingly, his work brings fabulous sums of money wherever it sells. But it would never have been, had he remained an art dealer, or a teacher, or a preacher.

God is hoping against hope that we will keep Him in mind as we search for our path in life. If we are not successful in one area, we should not be discouraged. Like Van Gogh, we need to find our sweet spot, our passion, the thing in life we really enjoy. We may not know what it is, and it may take time to find it, but God has known from the day of our birth, and we can trust Him completely to lead us to it in His time and way.

Daredevil Stuntman

Do not be a fool—why die before your time?
Ecclesiastes 7:17, NIV.

On June 30, 1859, a Frenchman by the name of Charles Blondin did something no human being had ever done before. He walked across Niagara Falls on a tightrope two inches in diameter and 1,100 feet long, stretched 160 feet above the raging cataract. The daredevil, wearing pink tights and a spangled tunic of yellow silk, performed the feat before a crowd of about 10,000 people. In the months that followed, Blondin did the stunt many more times. One time, he dared to walk across while carrying his manager on his back. Another time he pushed a loaded wheelbarrow, and he even tried the trick while walking across in a sack. Other stunts included walking across blindfolded, and on stilts, and sitting down midway across to cook and eat an omelet.

In the Bible we read of many characters who took risks, and they paid a heavy price for their sins. Adam and Eve ate the forbidden fruit and lost their Eden home. Rebekah convinced Jacob to deceive Isaac and steal the birthright. Because of it Jacob had to flee from home and she never saw him again. David dared to have an affair with a married woman and reaped the consequences many times over. His sons tried to steal his throne and his nation lost respect for him. Solomon married too many pagan women and they stole his heart away from God. Gehazi dared to ask for gifts from Naaman against Elisha's command and he contracted leprosy for his selfishness. Judas betrayed Jesus and his guilt drove him to suicide. The Sanhedrin crucified Jesus and went to their graves burdened with the guilt of murdering the Son of God.

But there were others who took calculated risks *for* God, and they received an abundant return. Noah built an ark at great personal and social expense and God saved his family because of it. Ruth left her homeland and became the grandmother of King David. Elijah was brave enough to enter Ahab's royal palace to warn of a coming drought and God provided for him during the famine. Shadrach, Meshach, and Abednego refused to worship Nebuchadnezzar's golden image and were spared miraculously from the fiery flames. Daniel prayed three times a day in defiance of the king's decree and God's angels shut the lions' mouths. Jesus' disciples left everything and got to spend three years walking and talking with the Creator of the Universe. And most importantly, Jesus died on the cross and saved you and me for all eternity.

Yeah, Gideon!

I have hidden your word in my heart that I might not sin against you.
Psalm 119:11, NIV.

W hat if," three men asked each other, "travelers at any hotel in the United States could find a Bible, if they wanted one?" John Nicholson, Samuel Hill, and William Knight were salesmen, so knew hotels. They knew what it was like to drag into yet another hotel after a hard day pounding the pavement, wanting something to do or something to read. "Bibles should be available for anyone who wants to read one," they said. And so Gideon International, a Christian professional organization dedicated to personal evangelism, determined to make Bibles available for travelers wherever they stayed. They chose the name Gideon for they thought of themselves as Gideons—willing to do whatever God asked of them.

At first they thought they'd put a Bible at the front desk of each hotel, but in 1908 decided to put Bibles in every room of every hotel in the United States. By now the Gideons have placed Bibles in 175 countries. Every year they place more than 56 million Bibles in hotel rooms and schools across America. They get financial support from churches of many denominations, and now they place Bibles in hospitals and doctors' offices, jails and prisons, schools, colleges and universities, and even military bases. Countless people have been blessed by finding a Bible nearby just when they needed it most. Today you can choose just about any kind of Bible you want—from everyday English to serious research versions. The wonder and blessing of the Bible is how the Holy Spirit speaks through it to give you exactly what you need when you need it.

Check out a few psalms, for David's writing is as real as it gets. He was a man on the run when he wrote "How many are my foes!" (Ps. 3:1) and "when I am afraid, I will trust in you," (Ps. 56:3). Guilt weighed heavy on him when he wrote "Create in me a clean heart . . . do not cast me from your presence" (Ps. 51:10, 11), and he must have been happy writing Psalm 103 with its theme of "Praise the Lord!" Then go to the New Testament. Meet Jesus—again—in the Gospels. Thrill to Luke's stories of the early Christian church. Hear the courage and triumph in Paul's voice as he faces death (2 Timothy 4:6-8). Open your Bible. Read it every day. Ask God to help it speak to you.

Now That's a Wild Ride

For he will command his angels concerning you to guard you in all your ways; they will lift you up in their hands, so that you will not strike your foot against a stone.
Psalm 91:11, 12, NIV.

It's a bird."

"No . . . it's . . . not . . . It's . . . uh, it's—an alligator!"

On this day in 1843, an alligator fell from the sky during a Charleston, South Carolina thunderstorm. No one knew for sure exactly how an alligator got into the sky so it could fall from the sky. Obviously, it didn't fall from a plane. Planes hadn't yet been invented. A kite? Nah. It's likely that the funnel of a tornado swirled it up into the atmosphere then let go, and the poor dizzy creature shot back down to earth. I can imagine it shaking its head, thinking, *Where I am and why am I spinning* before it landed back on terra firma and drunkenly headed back toward the water where it belonged.

A girl named Freda lived in a Midwest farming community many years ago, and attended a small country school. One afternoon her teacher noticed dark storm clouds billowing up in the distance and feared they were in for a severe storm. With one eye on the clouds and another on the clock, the teacher hoped the storm would pass over before school was out, but it didn't. Just as school let out the storm was almost upon them. The teacher asked the students to stay and wait it out because of the danger they'd be in if they walked home. Everyone agreed, but Freda.

"Please, you must let me go," she begged. "My mother will be so worried about me. I'll run really fast." The teacher protested, but finally against her better judgment let her leave. The girl hadn't been gone five minutes when the storm slammed the school in all its fury. A terrible roaring like a freight train told them it was a tornado. Ordering the children to take cover under their desks, the teacher implored God to take care of Freda. Without a doubt, she would be killed. And Freda? She unknowingly walked right into the tornado's path. In an instant it lifted her off the ground and high into the dark, swirling clouds. Then carrying her across fields and forests it gently set her down right near her front door. An alligator. A little girl. God can do anything, can't He!

Idaho Statehood

The Lord is . . . not willing that any should perish,
but that all should come to repentance.
2 Peter 3:9.

Idaho. When you think of Idaho, do you think of potatoes? Think again, for this United States state has another claim to fame that I think is even better. Idaho is a virtual jewel box of precious and semi-precious stones. Of the 72 types and colors, which include diamonds, rubies, sapphires, jasper, opals, and garnets, some are found nowhere else in the world. You might say that God reached down into some heavenly valley, scooped up a double handful of stones, and tossed them all across this state. Rock hounds love it. Every year thousands of people come to pan for gold and search for gemstones.

Idaho has a fairly small population—only 1.4 million—and Idahoans don't mind at all. They love all the open spaces. Eleven mountain peaks in Idaho are higher than 12,000 feet and 50 are higher than 10,000. That makes for a lot of good hiking and climbing as well as wild, wonderful views. What we now call Idaho was the last of the U.S. territories to be explored by Caucasians. The exploration and settlement of North American was mostly inward from the oceans and northward from Mexico. Spanish, French, British, and early Americans pushed north and inward as explorers, trappers, and missionaries. Even so, as late as 1805, Idaho Indians such as the Shoshone had never even seen a White person. Then everything changed the summer of 1805. Explorers Lewis and Clarke and their party of 33 passed through the Northwest Territory across what is now a 120-mile strip of land in present-day Idaho. With the help of Shoshone Indians and their horses, it took the expedition eight days.

It was inevitable. Fur traders and trappers followed a few years later, and so did missionaries and hardy settlers. And of course thousands hurried into Idaho with the news of a major gold strike in 1860. Merchants and farmers then followed, ready to make their fortunes "mining the miners." By 1890, more than 32,000 lived in the southern section of the territory, and on July 3, Idaho became the 43rd state in the Union.

Names on the Line

Free those who are wrongly imprisoned; lighten the burden of those who work for you. Let the oppressed go free, and remove the chains that bind people.
Isaiah 58:6, NLT.

A nation was born on this day in 1776 when the first of the men who signed the U.S. Declaration of Independence wrote their names at the bottom of that document. One by one, during several weeks time, 54 delegates to the Continental Congress in Philadelphia, Pennsylvania, figuratively stood up to England, saying: "We'll pay no more taxes without representation. We'll accept no more tyranny! No more English soldiers quartered in our homes! We pledge our fortunes, our lives, and our sacred honor." Patrick Henry spoke for them all when he summarized their stance, saying, "Give me liberty or give me death!" Unfortunately many citizens of the 13 original colonies would do just that—pay for their freedom with their lives. Already 442 days had passed since the first shots of the Revolutionary War were fired in Lexington and Concord, Massachusetts. At first the other colonies had watched while Massachusetts bravely resisted the British, starting their own revolutionary government, and raising their own army. Most thought of this as a kind of civil war in the British Empire. King George III saw it as just another colonial rebellion, but to many Americans it was a struggle for their rights as British citizens. But the British wouldn't negotiate a truce of any kind. Instead they hired an army of German mercenaries to help crush the rebellion.

The Declaration of Independence is probably the most important document in U.S. history, beside the United States Constitution. "We hold these truths to be self-evident, that all men are created equal, that they are endowed by their Creator with certain unalienable Rights, that among these are Life, Liberty and the pursuit of Happiness." Pretty powerful words.

Jesus came to earth to give you and me a declaration of independence too. Jesus came to free us from sin and Satan. He knew that when He died for us, we could be forever free from sin's deadly clutches. In the coming world we'll have no worries, guilt, loneliness, or pain. But for now it's our job to share this good news with anyone who needs it. Give them a smile. Tell them Jesus loves them and came to set them free.

Hello Dolly!

Man who is born of woman is of few days and full of trouble.
Job 14:1, NKJV.

Hello, Dolly. Welcome to the world. You're the first cloned mammal ever born."

I don't know for certain, but I imagine that like newborn lambs everywhere one of the first things little Dolly did was bump her head against her mom's udder to get her first taste of milk.

July 5, 1996, was a big day in the scientific world—the day Dolly's birth proved the first successful cloning of a mammal. Her original code name was 6LL3. She was born at the Roslin Institute in Scotland, and named after singer and actress Dolly Parton. When Dolly's birth was announced in 1997, it kicked up brought a storm of controversy. Some argued that cloning was great and would lead to important medical discoveries. Cloning, they said, would provide organs for people who needed transplants. A diseased heart could be repaired with cloned healthy cells. Stem cells, harvested from cloned fetuses, could be used in research for such nerve diseases as Alzheimer's and Parkinson's. And cloning would make it easier to preserve endangered species.

No, protested the other side. Cloning is not good. We don't know how safe it is. Besides, it's unethical. There's too much we don't know about cloning. We could be creating problems down the road that will be much worse than the ones facing us now. And you can't harvest stem cells without destroying the fetuses. That's wrong, since they're already living creatures.

Eventually it became obvious that some of the problems in cloning don't show up for months and even years. Autopsies on cloned animals showed high rates of pneumonia, liver disease, and cancer, and evidence of defects in their immune systems. (Dolly developed arthritis and lung disease and finally she had to be put to sleep.) Another challenge is that the life span of cloned animals is less than what is normal for their species. All the researchers agreed that Dolly's problems and the problems found in other cloned animals should be a warning to anyone who wants to clone humans.

No matter which side you agree with, there are real issues. The benefits of cloning must be weighed against the problems. But we must be very cautious about trying to play God.

Name Your Price

God bought you with a high price. So you must honor God with your body.
1 Corinthians 6:20, NLT.

Money! Who can live without it? Most of us can't, and we'd like to get as much of it as we can. It's what makes the world go round. Or does it? Well, in a way it does.

On this day in 1785, the Continental Congress of the newly formed United States of America decided on the unit of money that we would use. The dollars would be the standard unit, with the smallest coin being of copper, worth one 200th of a dollar. That would be a half-penny, but of course pennies today are worth one 100th of a dollar. Early on, most money was made out of metals. Only since 1862 has paper money been used, and in 1933 the U.S. recalled all gold coins from general use.

What jobs have you had for money? Most kids have done a little babysitting. Maybe you've cleaned houses or raked leaves for a few dollars. Perhaps you've even worked in a store. What would you do for money? Maybe a more important question is, What would you not do, no matter what you were paid?

Think about that. People get paid to do some pretty nasty jobs, but it's honest work and as they say, someone has to do it. Would you clean bedpans for money? Mop up throw up? Would you play a joke on your best friend for $20? On your grandma? Would you play a mean joke on your grandma—for $100? For a $1,000? Would you cheat on a test to get a scholarship? Do you have a price? Most of us think we don't, but sometimes our "price" isn't money. It can be as simple as wanting to belong, or wanting a class office, or even wanting a certain friend. You need to make the decision now, whether you have a price. Whether you'd ever want something so badly that you'd compromise your principles to get it.

People. They're what make us truly rich. If that wasn't so Jesus would never have come so far and given so much to buy us back. And be assured, He would have given all the gold and silver in the universe to do it. But that wasn't what it cost. It cost His life instead—the life of the eternal Son of God. We shouldn't be surprised. After all, He is our Brother.

He Just Kept Rolling

But he who endures to the end shall be saved.
Matthew 24:13, NKJV.

What's the scariest roller coaster you've ever been on? The highest? The longest ride? Well try this. On July 7, 1980, Jim King put one in the record books—the most hours riding a roller coaster. Jim's ride in the Miracle Strip roller coaster lasted 368 hours. That's more than 15 days of continuous up-down, round and round. Of course, he didn't do the entire 15 days without stopping though there were hours of riding without a stop. He must have taken time out to use the restroom. Maybe he caught catnaps as he rode. Whatever it took, it gives me a headache just to think about it. Jim got himself in the record books, but honestly, did it get him a better job? Probably not. Did it made him a few inches taller? Nope. It might have given him some gray hairs and made him older in the process, but aside from a bit of publicity, that was it.

God's people have been on a roller coaster ride of their own. It began back in Eden when Eve and Adam made the choice to trust a snake instead of God. It continued on in the wars between the sons of God and the sons of Cain. The roller coaster of sin and violence took the world to the brink of annihilation when Noah's catastrophic flood swept all but eight survivors into oblivion.

The roller coaster began to roll in God's favor when the nation of Israel was born. He delivered them from slavery, placed them in Canaan, and made them His chosen people. But it seems they never met an idol they didn't like and at last they came full circle—carried away, again, into Babylonian slavery. And then Jesus came to earth, and changed the course of history. His death showed us the Father and brought heaven nearer than it had ever been before. The Christian church was born and the roller coaster began to pick up speed. The Dark Ages slowed salvation's progress, but the Reformers brought the pendulum back up again. Today the Three Angels' Message is going to all the world. Churches, schools, hospitals, and publishing houses proclaim the message of a crucified, risen, and soon coming Savior. Satan still claims this world as his own, but radio and satellite television bring the gospel to millions.

When Jesus comes again, the roller coaster ride will end. Until then, hang on to Him for dear life.

Killer Weapon

In all circumstances hold faith up before you as your shield;
it will help you extinguish the fiery darts of the evil one.
Ephesians 6:16, NAB.

On July 8, 1856, Charles Barnes took out a patent for a machine gun, a new weapon that promised to revolutionize the way wars were fought. Barnes called it an "improved automatic cannon." It was actually a type of Gatling gun that operated by turning a crank; the speed of firing depended on how fast the crank was turned. Unfortunately, or fortunately, depending on which side of the battlefield you were on, if you turned the crank too long at a time the barrel got so hot you couldn't touch the gun. Some machine guns could fire up to 350 rounds a minute. Horrible! Absolutely horrible that people could invent a machine so terrible that it improved the odds of winning a battle by mowing down more soldiers in a shorter amount of time!

Four years later the machine gun got its first real test in the Civil War, and what a lot of damage it did, just as its inventor predicted. More than half a million men lost their lives during the Civil War—thousands and thousands of them due to the machine gun. The machine gun became even more common during World War I. These guns were so big they had to be mounted on tripods and manned by a crew of four to six operators. They were designed to fire as many as 1,000 rounds per minute, through a fabric belt. The machine gun became so valuable that some military experts said its firepower was as great as 100 rifles. During World War II the machine gun really became versatile as a killing machine. Lighter more powerful submachine guns were now being used, like the AK-47.

The devil has spent his existence finding new ways to invent pain. War is just one of them, but with more and more deadly weapons being invented every year, the world is truly filled with his misery. But Jesus came to help, and show the world Satan's true colors in this battle between good and evil. When on earth He healed diseases, gave sight to the blind, and even raised the dead. Today He wants to protect us from the devil's Gatling gun of flaming darts. "Take up your shield of faith!" Paul advises us, so "you can extinguish all the flaming darts of the evil one." Sounds like a plan to me.

The Pope Stampede

You shall have no other gods before Me.
Exodus 20:3, NKJV

On this day in 1980, seven people died in a stampede in Brazil—trampled to death by hundreds of feet. So what kind of a stampede could do that? A buffalo stampede? A cattle stampede? A stampede of people trying to get out of a burning building? Nope! A stampede to see the pope. What a tragedy. So many were so eager to see the famous head of a world church that they trampled the fallen bodies of men and women, killing them.

Millions of people revere the pope—not just as God's representative on earth—but as one who stands in the place of God. Modern statements from the Catholic church stress that the pope is God's representative, but the message doesn't always get through. God is very clear about such things. "You shall have no other gods before Me."

No man or woman should accept worship and reverence. Only God should receive that.

In Acts 14, Luke tells a story about Paul and Barnabas on one of their missionary journeys. They were in the city of Lystra and, like they did everywhere they went, they began to preach the gospel. While they were preaching a man crippled from birth stared intently at Paul. Paul could see that the man had faith to be healed so he called to him, "Stand up!" The man jumped up and began walking. When the crowds saw the miracle they went wild, shouting, "These men are gods in human form!" Immediately they brought bulls and wreaths of flowers to the city gate and started preparations to offer sacrifices to honor Paul and Barnabas.

Horrified, Paul and Barnabas tore their clothes and ran among the worshippers. "Why are you doing this?" they shouted. "We are merely human beings—just like you! We have come to bring you the good news that you should turn from these worthless things and worship the living God." But strangely enough, when Jewish troublemakers came to town a few days later, they turned the crowds against Paul and Barnabas, stoning Paul and leaving him for dead.

Paul and Barnabas knew better than to accept such adoration and worship. They stood for Jesus, no matter what. Could you be this true to your convictions if the opportunity were given you? You may be asked to do just that some day.

Monkeying Around

Then God said, "Let us make man in our image, in our likeness."
Gen. 1:26, NIV.

Where did we come from? That's a philosophical question as important as the question What are we doing here and where are we going? Thinking people have asked those questions for thousands of years. Were we created by God? Are we nothing more than evolved creatures that were once apes, as Charles Darwin would have put it? Or someday will we end up living among the stars? Does it make a difference what we believe?

Well, the picture got a bit more confusing for some on this date in 1925, when John Scopes, a high school science teacher in Dayton, Tennessee, was taken to court for teaching Darwin's theory of evolution. In March, 1925, the governor of Tennessee had signed a law stating that no teacher in any public school or university in the state of Tennessee, could "teach any theory that denies the story of the Divine creation of man as taught in the Bible." But John, who strongly believed in reason, decided to do it anyway. He was fined $100 for breaking the law and taken to court.

The well known William Jennings Bryan was the prosecuting attorney for the State, and Clarence Darrows was John's defense lawyer. It became the most celebrated trial of the century, dubbed by all the newspapers as The Monkey Trial. It was broadcast live over the radio, and the world listened intently to the showdown between faith and reason. The trial also drew thousands of spectators, and was finally moved from inside the courthouse to the front lawn for fear that the weight of the crowd would collapse the main floor of the courtroom. Surprisingly, Scopes won his case, though he was fired from his position as teacher in the high school.

Since then, state courts have given their verdicts many times. Some favor the exclusive teaching of evolution, while others feel that schools should present both evolution and creation and let students decide for themselves. How about you? What is your stand on the subject? Will you be brave enough to speak up for God when it comes to the creation of the earth and the origin of life on earth? Do you know why you believe as you do? Why do you think it makes a difference?

Long, long ago Jesus stood up for you. Will you do the same for Him?

Dueling Diplomats

Choose a man and have him come down to me. If he is able to
fight and kill me, we will become your subjects; but if I overcome
him and kill him, you will become our subjects and serve us.
1 Samuel 17:8, 9, NIV.

On this date in history, a U.S. vice president shot and killed his longtime political opponent in a daring duel. Whaaaaat? The year was 1804, and that's the way some "gentlemen" settled arguments in those days. You see, Vice President Aaron Burr was running for reelection and his political enemy, Alexander Hamilton, attacked him in the newspapers. Burr challenged Hamilton to a duel—at that time often called an "affair of honor." Hamilton didn't want to duel, but politics seemed to leave him no choice. If he admitted Burr's charge was true, he'd lose his honor. If he refused to duel, the result would be the same. So despite the fact that dueling was being outlawed in the United States, on July 11, the longtime enemies met on a dueling ground near Weehawken, New Jersey.

Hamilton shot first. Now historians don't agree on whether he intentionally or accidentally aimed his shot above Burr and into a tree. There were strict guidelines for dueling (in most duels no one was even hurt) and it's still being argued whether Burr followed them when he shot back. However, most agree that he was within his rights when he returned fire, hitting Hamilton in the belly. The bullet struck Hamilton's spine and he died the next afternoon. The nation was outraged by the killing, and Burr was charged with murder.

Because a few days remained in his term as vice president he could not yet be prosecuted. When he left office he fled Washington and all but disappeared. Perhaps his punishment was that he dropped into obscurity. Today, most people today don't know his name and wouldn't recognize his face. But the face of Alexander Hamilton, Secretary of Treasury of the United States, is on the U.S. $10 bill.

It's interesting that in ancient Israel one champion would challenge another and often the outcome of battles were decided by the winner. David and Goliath faced down in such a duel with the weapons of the day. Goliath might as well have said, "Choose your weapon!" because that's exactly what David did. And he won—with a sling, five sling stones, and the help of his God.

July 12

Heat Kills

But the day of the Lord will come as a thief in the night,
in which the heavens will pass away with a great noise,
and the elements will melt with fervent heat; both the
earth and the works that are in it will be burned up.
2 Peter 3:10, NKJV.

Warning: Heat Wave. On this day in 1995, Chicago radio, TV, and newspapers warned that record breaking heat was on its way. "Prepare for the worst," people were told, but many didn't take the warning seriously. Hot summers were common in the Midwest, but few had experienced anything like this. By the time the heat broke a week later, nearly 1,000 people in Illinois and Wisconsin had died from heat prostration.

Why? How could this happen in North America in this day and age? Well, first, it was hot! The temperature hit 106 degrees Fahrenheit, and with the high humidity it felt more like 120. The heat buckled blacktop pavement, and train rails warped so badly that some commuter trains had to shut down completely.

Most of the people who died were elderly, many were bedfast, and most lived alone. In fact, lack of a social network was one of the main causes. Without close friends or family there was no one to look in on them, no one to make certain they were drinking water and caring for themselves in other ways that could have saved their lives. Many lived in low income, crime ridden apartments and were afraid to open their windows. And some of the elderly simply didn't want to run their fans or air conditioners because of the cost of electricity.

Hundreds of children were hospitalized, too. Within two days area hospitals were unable to keep up with the victims of heat stroke. Bodies began to pile up in the morgues, and refrigerated trucks were brought in to help with the overflow.

Some day another heat wave is coming, one so hot that the elements of earth—everything that seems permanent like the rocks, and dirt, and mountains—will melt. And the cities with their buildings, factories, military bases, and missile silos will melt too. What will you be doing on that day? I hope you'll be looking to Jesus.

Fighting Tanks

And I saw them as they went up on the broad plain of the earth and surrounded God's people and the beloved city. But fire from heaven came down on the attacking armies and consumed them. Revelation 20:9, NLT.

The largest tank battle in history happened on this day in 1943, near the city of Kursk, Russia. Six thousand tanks lined up in a battle formation that stretched 150 miles wide. Two million men and 5,000 planes joined in to help push back the German army. The Germans fought valiantly, but the Soviets had better tanks and air support, and eventually destroyed about 40 percent of the German ground forces including the new Tiger tanks. The tide of the battle turned in favor of the Soviets, and soon the Germans were in retreat.

A tank is an armored fighting vehicle with rotating tracks to propel it forward. It is designed for frontline combat, and if it has armored plates, can do quite well in battle. Tanks can pull left or right, depending on which way you break, and usually have a turret with cannon that can rotate 360 degrees. Tanks can be dropped by parachute, can be amphibious, and can race along at pretty fast speeds.

Tanks are a fairly new weapon in the history of warfare. They were first introduced in World War I by the British. To conceal them on the battlefield, the British disguised them as water carriers, or "tanks," short for "water tanks."

World War II was the first war in which armored vehicles helped bring real success on the battlefield. After the War, the U.S. Army hired the Chrysler Corporation to design and build tanks at the Detroit Arsenal. Today, America's armor forces are the fastest, best equipped, and most lethal in the world.

Some glorious day the New Jerusalem will descend from heaven, and God will raise all the wicked to life for judgment. Satan will be allowed to gather his forces one last time for a gigantic army. Brilliant generals will be there taking charge of armies. All the weapons ever used will be made ready for the attack on the city and God's people inside. In a moment of delusion, spurred on by Satan's challenge, the army will swarm around the Holy City to take it by storm. Will they have tanks? Yes, perhaps millions of them. But it won't matter. Jesus will be all the firepower we need, and then the battle will be over.

July 14

The Death of a President's Son

For God loved the world so much that he gave his one and only Son, so that everyone who believes in him will not perish but have eternal life. John 3:16, NLT.

July 14, 1918. World War I. On this day in history a president's son was killed by two machine gun bullets. The United States was in the middle of World War I. For months former President Theodore Roosevelt had urged that the U.S. should enter the war. He'd even volunteered to go as head of a volunteer division. When President Wilson refused to let Roosevelt go, his son Quentin volunteered to go instead. Actually Quentin was too young to be drafted, but as the son of a president he was expected to volunteer, and he did. He signed up as a pilot in the Air Service and was soon sent to Europe.

The president's three other sons—Ted, Archie, and Kermit—had also volunteered to serve in the army. They teased Quentin for wanting to go so young, but that just made him all the more determined. He did get to be a pilot and fly missions against the enemy. He did get to see some of Europe. But he didn't get to return home to his family or to marry his fiancé. For Quentin, the youngest of the four Roosevelt brothers, gave his life for our country.

Once upon a time another Father gave His Son to die for us too, and it was His only Son.

Jesus left His Father's throne with the rainbow of glory arched overhead. He left the adoring gaze of countless millions of angels. He left the golden streets, and walls of jasper, and those gates of pearl. He came to this dark world, degenerated by 4,000 years of sin. Born in a stable to poor peasants, a manger his bed, during a time when the Jewish nation was oppressed by the Roman government, He grew up in an obscure town. He never got a fancy education, or went very far from home, or held public office. He ministered to thousands giving them food and sight and life, but most never seemed satisfied or grateful. The tide of public opinion turned against him when he was still a young man. His followers deserted him, he was put on trial for crimes He never committed. He was beaten, scourged, and crucified on Calvary, and buried in a borrowed grave. However, when He arose Sunday morning, no one doubted the gift His Father had given the world!

The Beast that Picked Up Body Parts

Then God said, "Let the earth produce every sort of animal, each pro-
ducing offspring of the same kind—livestock, small animals that scurry
along the ground, and wild animals." And that is what happened.
Genesis 1:24, NLT.

On this day in 1922, the Bronx Zoo displayed a creature that had never before been seen in the United States. One bystander thought it looked something like a beaver, because of its tail, only smaller. Another thought it looked something like a duck because of its bill. Still others thought maybe it was related to an otter because of its feet. But then they learned that it had barbed spurs-like-stingers on its legs with lethal poison that could be injected into its enemies. The plaque over the cage said it was a platypus and had fur like a mammal, fed its young with milk, but laid eggs like a bird or reptile. So which was it? A mammal? A bird? Reptile? Beaver, duck, otter? Poisonous lizard? None of the above? All of the above?

Now a platypus is rather strange because it doesn't look like anything you've ever seen before. Today we know a lot more about the platypus, but we still don't know why God gave us an animal with such a hodge-podge of body parts. Maybe He just loves variety. Some would say that the platypus is a product of evolution, picking up body parts of various species as it developed. But our text from Genesis is quiet clear about God's boundaries for that kind of thing. He said that every sort of animal should produce offspring of the same kind.

Actually, our wonderful world is filled with strange creatures. (And no, I'm not talking about your little brother.) There's the narwhal—most males sport an eight-foot tusk that they use, among other things, for determining the saltiness of the water. Then there's the tiny star-nosed mole whose weird nose helps it sniff out food extra fast. And the Yeti crab that lives among the hydrothermal vents along a ridge deep in the Pacific Ocean. It's arms are thickly covered with pale yellow hair.

God created these strange creatures, and many, many more. New species are being discovered all the time. Some of us humans look pretty strange too—look at your parents' old yearbook photos, or even yours in 20 years.

Aren't you glad that God likes us the way we are!

City On a Swamp

Then I, John, saw the holy city, New Jerusalem, coming down out of heaven from God, prepared as a bride adorned for her husband. Revelation 21:2, 3, NKJV.

On this day in 1790, the young American Congress declared that a swampy, humid, muddy, mosquito-infested site on the Potomac River between Maryland and Virginia would be the new permanent capital of the United States. Benjamin Banneker, a free African American, was appointed architect of the new city's design. Among other things Banneker was an astronomer, mathematician, surveyor, almanac author, and farmer—but the thing he is most remembered for is his design of Washington, D.C.

"Washington," named after George Washington, the military leader of the American Revolution and the country's first president, became the federal "District of Columbia." The capital is not located in any one state, but exists much like the Vatican as a city state all its own. Thus the title D.C., District of Columbia. It was General Washington who saw the area's potential economic advantages and its potential as a nation's capital because it lay near a large navigable river. Washington had been in office as President of the United States for just over a year when the capital site was chosen. He asked a French architect and city planner named Pierre L'Enfant to design the capital.

When we say Washington, D.C., we often think of the White House, and that makes sense for it is where one of the most influential men in the world lives and heads the U.S. government. Three years after Washington, D.C., was established as our nation's capital, the first cornerstones of the president's mansion were laid. George Washington, however, never lived in the mansion, as it was not finished until 1800. Thomas Jefferson moved into the White House in 1801, and was the first President to spend his entire administration there.

We sing "God bless America," and pray that He blesses all of North America and the rest of the world too, but someday a much more famous city will become the center of this planet. It is called The New Jerusalem, and Revelation 21:2 says so. In fact, The New Jerusalem will become the headquarters of the entire universe, and God will be with us here on earth for the rest of eternity. Now that's exciting!

Mickey Lives!

But as it is written, Eye hath not seen, nor ear heard,
neither have entered into the heart of man, the things
which God hath prepared for them that love him.
1 Corinthians 2:9.

On July 17, 1955, Disneyland opened its doors to the American public. Never before had a theme park captured the imagination of so many people! Even adults loved the attractions, the rides, and the live shows. It was like they could become children again and go out to play. The 160-acre theme park in Anaheim, California, cost $17 million, but soon brought in staggering profits. Today, Disneyland has 14 million visitors a year, and brings in nearly $3 billion.

The designer and creator of the park was Walt Disney, a commercial artist in Los Angeles. He wanted Disneyland to offer family entertainment, but he also wanted it to be a source of education for adults and kids. Construction began in 1954, and in the summer of 1955, special invitations were sent out for its grand opening. Unfortunately, the pass was counterfeited and on July 17, opening day, thousands of uninvited people poured into the park. Disneyland wasn't ready for such a crowd and food and drink ran out, and a near disaster occurred when the Mark Twain Steamboat almost capsized from so many passengers.

But the people loved the new concept in entertainment. Early attractions to Disneyland included the Castle, Mr. Toad's Wild Ride, Snow White's Adventures, Space Station X-1, Jungle Cruise, and Stage Coach. There were so many different things to do and see that people couldn't get enough of it. Special celebrity guest appearances were scheduled, and continual building of new attractions encouraged people to come back again and again. In 1971 a new sister theme park and resort called Disney World opened near Orlando, Florida, and today it is Florida's number-one tourist attraction. In 1983, Japan opened its own version called Disneyland Tokyo, and in 1992 EuroDisney opened in Paris, France. The most recent Disneyland in Hong Kong opened in September, 2005.

Theme parks are fun and exciting, but God has promised us a home in heaven that is beyond anything we can possibly imagine. Eye has not seen nor can we even imagine all the amazing attractions He has in store for us.

A Bubblin' Crude

*Understanding is a fountain of life to one who has it,
but the discipline of fools is folly.
Proverbs 16:22, NASB.*

You remember the old episodes of the Beverly Hillbillies and their unusual rise from rags to riches. It was a story "'bout a man named Jed, a poor mountaineer barely kept his family fed." He was out shootin' game one day and must have missed the squirrel and shot the ground, for bubbling up came a pool of "crude." A bubbling spring of oil was the cause of their new status in life. And that's exactly what happened in Cuba, New York, in 1627, just seven years after the Pilgrims landed at Plymouth Rock, Massachusetts.

On July 18, 1627, Roche-d'Allion, a Jesuit priest wrote a letter describing that an oil spring had been discovered. In the letter he mentioned two other Jesuit priests who were doing missionary work, and discovered the oil spring by following the directions on a secret map they had received from yet another friend of theirs in Canada. Amazing! As usual, "X" marked the spot. Sounds like one of those exciting old stories about pirates searching for buried treasure using a secret map. Of course. in those days no one knew the potential value of oil. There were no cars or truck or factories that could burn the stuff at that time. It as just a novelty—dark, greasy, a little smelly. It would be more than 250 years later, in 1879, when finally someone seemed to have a use for it.

And that's a lesson for us. Many people don't have much use for God. In fact, it might be a good idea for you to think out your own ideas about God. Sometimes we like Jesus pretty well but we're not too sure about God. He can seem a little scary, what with all that fire and brimstone stuff. If you're not too sure about God, I challenge you to get into the books of Isaiah and Jeremiah. You'll see that God's chosen people turned their backs on Him again and again, doing terrible things in their idol worship, even sacrificing their own children to heathen gods (see Jer. 32:35). But then you read, "Call to me and I will answer you" (Jer. 33:3). God begging His sinful children to return to Him.

Can you hear God calling your name?

floating Hospital

Jesus answered and said to them, "Those who are well have no need of a physician, but those who are sick." Luke 5:31, NKJV.

Some of the most amazing hospitals in history float. On July 19, 1875, a floating hospital made a trial trip up and down the east coast of the United States. *The Emma Abbott*, as she was called, was nicknamed the poor children's yacht because it served children from families that could not afford medical treatment. The 215-foot-long ship cost $20,000 to build. It had three decks with dispensaries for treatment, and even a dining room to feed the children wonderful meals they would never forget. The hospital operated out of New York City, usually only during the summer months, and treated thousands of children each year.

During the summer of 1862 a hospital boat called the *City of Louisiana*, was launched on the upper rivers of the Alleghany Mountain region in the United States. The U.S. Government supplied the hospital boat with medical supplies and 500 beds. That summer the boat treated and transported more than 3,300 patients.

In 1994, Yves Marre, a Frenchman, sailed an unwanted barge from France to Dhaka, Bangladesh, to donate the boat to a worthy cause. His plan was to then return to Paris and continue on with his life as an airline steward. Well, that was the plan, but today 15 years later, he is still in Bangladesh running a floating hospital with his wife, Runa. The barge hospital provides medical care for some of Bangladesh's poorest people.

Floating hospitals are especially helpful because they are mobile. They don't have to wait for sick people to come to them—they can go to those in need. Christians should be more like these floating hospitals. They should seek out those who are ill, and lonely, and destitute. You can be sure that's what Jesus would do.

Jesus said that those who are well don't need a physician. It's the sick who need a doctor. That's why He came to this world—to seek and to save those who need a spiritual doctor. Of course, some sick people don't want or need a Savior at all. But everybody needs the Great Physician. No one can survive without the life-giving blood of Jesus.

July 20

Captain Kirk Said It Best

How beautiful are the feet of those who preach the gospel of peace,
who bring glad tidings of good things! Rom. 10:15, NKJV.

July 20, 1969. A man first set foot on a mysterious shining body 238,855 miles (384,400 km) from earth. Ten years before it seemed impossible. Then on their black-and-white TVs people watched Neil Armstrong's first step and, "That's one small step for man, one giant leap for mankind." For years the United States and the USSR had been racing to conquer space. Since then, however, both nations have worked together developing the expensive technologies for joint research in space. In today's multi-nation space lab scientists are exploring how to slow down the aging process, how to develop new cures for diseases, and ways to make outer space less a battleground of weapons, and more of a opportunity to explore a new frontier. "The final frontier," as Captain James Kirk always said in Star Trek, "is limitless."

After the U.S. made a few more trips to the moon money for such projects began to dry up. Americans had become bored with the venture (such a short attention span!). We had beaten the USSR to the moon, and now NASA found it more and more difficult to get money from Congress. The last to walk on the moon were part of the *Apollo 17* mission, a costly program involving about 400,000 engineers, technicians, and scientists. In today's dollars it cost nearly $100 billion.

The moon is a very small part of the heavens but it's a favorite. It shines huge above the horizon, then two weeks later is a pale thin curve. We've now walked on its surface, but that's not our greatest accomplishment. With God's help Christians have taken even bigger steps. In just two centuries we have taken the gospel around the world. That's the good news. The sad news is that, even so, billions have yet to hear the name of Jesus. The Joshua project* lists 16,309 distinct people groups—and 6,653 have not been reached with the Gospel.

This is the most exciting time in earth's history. I know that's what they always say, but it's true. Between education and ease of travel, countless ways exist for you to share God's message with people who might never know Him. It is the grandest, most satisfying frontier in the world.

---

* A research initiative to highlight the ethnic people groups of the world with the least followers of Jesus.

World's Strongest, Most Lovable Dog

For the Son of Man has come to seek and to save that which was lost. Luke 19:10, NKJV.

What's the biggest dog on record? Some claim it's a seven-foot-long Great Dane. Others say it's Hercules, a 282-pound English Mastiff. Russian Wolfhounds are pretty big and so are St. Bernards. They're probably the strongest known dogs in the world, because of their massive size. On July 21, 1978, the world's strongest dog on record, a St. Bernard that weighed 80 kilograms, pulled a 2,909-kg load, 27 meters. In other terms, this 176 pound dog pulled a 6,400 pound load for 87 feet. Now that's a strong dog!

In 980 AD, Bernard de Menthon, a monk, built a wayside hospice at 8,000 feet in the Italian and Swiss Alps. His mission: to rescue travelers who were lost or stranded in the deep snows of that mountain pass. To help, he used a gigantic breed of dog that became known as a Saint Bernard. The huge bodies of these magnificent dogs seem immune to cold temperatures and they have an incredible sense of direction and smell.

The story is told of one of the Saint Bernards that worked for a monastery in the Swiss Alps. He was well known for his bravery and stamina in rescuing stranded victims from the killing temperatures of such high altitudes. Daily he was sent out to patrol the trail that passed by the mountain monastery, searching for anyone in distress and in need of care and warm lodging. On one particularly cold night he found a man lying motionless face up in the snow. As he'd been trained to do, the dog nestled himself down beside the man and began licking his face to revive him. When the man didn't respond, the St. Bernard crawled on top of him to give him additional warmth. When the man finally opened his eyes he was terrified to see a gigantic animal hovering over him. Fearing for his life, he grabbed his knife from his belt and plunged it into the animal. Only then did the man realize that he'd stabbed the one who'd come to save him.

The parallels between this story and the sacrifice of Jesus are obvious. Some question whether this particular incident actually happened, but there is no question that Jesus lived and died to save us. Our hearts are touched by the senseless killing of a dog who'd come to save a man. How do we respond to the death of a Man who died to save a whole world?

July 22

The Sad Short Life of John Dillinger

The truly righteous man attains life, but he who pursues evil goes to his death.
Proverbs 11:19, NIV.

His mom died when he was 3. His dad was harsh and sometimes cruel. He skipped school and didn't obey authority. His sister raised him til his dad remarried. He joined the Navy but didn't like it, so deserted a few months later. John Dillinger.

At 21 he was imprisoned for a hold-up. There he became friends with some guys who taught him the bank-robbing trade and promised to make him a member of their gang if they all escaped. After he was released he helped make the plan that sprung some of his prison friends out of jail, and they made good on their promise. Life was exciting. Life was good! At least that's what Dillinger thought. He became one of the most famous gangsters in American history and eventually was declared Public Enemy Number One by the U.S. attorney general.

Dillinger and his gang pulled off a series of bank holdups in broad daylight. In one case people actually stood on the sidewalk and watched with smiles (in admiration as well as horror?) as the gang pretended to be part of a film company scouting locations for a bank robbery scene—and made off with a bunch of money. It's estimated that in 11 heists the gangsters stole about $300,000 (more than $6 million today)—and this was during the depression when most people weren't certain where their next meal was coming from. And, oh yes, counting gang members and people the police shot by mistake, 26 people died while Dillinger and his gang were rip-snortin' their way from one bank to another. On July 22, Dillinger and two friends went to a movie. Some guessed that it wasn't that they wanted to see the film but the fact that the theatre was one of the few places in town that was "air-cooled." At any rate, one of the women with him had tipped off the police and more than 20 officers were waiting for him when the movie ended and he walked out into the street. Five shots were fired. Two struck John Dillinger. One of them killed him.

Handsome guy. Famous outlaw. Admired by many. Hated by more. Dead at 31. A tragic example of a life lived without God.

Backward All the Way

Salvation is found in no one else, for there is no other name under heaven given to men by which we must be saved.
Acts 4:12, NIV.

What's the most fun trip you ever took? Camping? A trip to Disney World? Surfing the waves, or exploring museums in Chicago or Washington, D.C.? Well, how about a 3,000-mile road trip? Charles Creighton and James Hargis took one, but not the kind you'd expect. Cross-country trips weren't big news, not even in 1930. But on July 23 the trip Charles and James finished made the headlines. Why? Because they drove their 1929 Model A Ford from New York to Los Angeles—and back again—in reverse.

Why'd they do it? Because they could? To put their home town, Maplewood, New Jersey, on the map? Because they were nuts? The round trip took 42 days, driving the entire 7,180 miles in reverse. Well, that's some way to set a record, and one not likely to be repeated. What's the point? No doubt Charles and James did it as a gag, just to get into the record books. Now you can travel across the country by car, plane, train—or even kayak if you can find enough rivers and streams. You can walk, or ride in a wheelbarrow, or even drive the whole way in reverse, though I'd hate to do that over the mountains. But to get to heaven—there's only one way to do that—through Jesus.

In Acts, Luke tells the story of the first Pentecost in the early Church. Jesus had ascended to heaven just 10 days before, and now His disciples were preaching up a storm in the temple complex. Thousands of Jews had come from every country in the Roman empire. Peter led the way, pulling out all the stops with his fiery message of a crucified and risen Savior. This angered the temple leaders so much that they arrested him and John and kept them in prison overnight. The next morning they brought out the two disciples and demanded they stop preaching in Jesus' name. But nothing could stop Peter now. A few weeks before, when Jesus was on trial, Peter had denied that he even knew his Lord. But now, with an opportunity to make up for his cowardice, Peter was ready to suffer anything for Jesus' sake. To Peter, witnessing for Jesus was pure joy. Jesus was the only way to heaven, Peter preached, and he'd follow Him forever—even if it meant dying on a cross.

Machu Picchu Discovered

Remember the days of old; consider the generations long past. Ask your father and he will tell you, your elders, and they will explain to you. Deuteronomy 32:7, NIV.

History tells us that the ancient Inca Empire located in what is now modern-day Peru was one of the richest civilizations in the world. The empire stretched all along the Pacific coast of South America, and high on the peaks of the Andes the Incas built a fortress city called Machu Picchu. Surrounded by steep cliffs, and entered by a single narrow path, it was a place of retreat and refuge for Inca aristocracy as well as a perfect place for viewing the heavens, the sun and stars—the deities of the Incas.

And then Machu Picchu was abandoned. Sociologists and historians still aren't certain why. Were they conquered by an unknown enemy? Did they die from an epidemic such as smallpox? Or was it abandoned simply because other places were built and became popular?

By the sixteenth century when Spanish Conquistadors invaded the land, the mountain city was already covered with trees, vines, and other growth. The Spaniards discovered the Incas had gold and lots of it, and in their greed they nearly wiped out the entire Inca civilization.

In the centuries that followed, only the peasant farmers living in the region knew about the secret mountain retreat. But that changed on July 24, 1911, when an American archeologist, Hiram Bingham, first saw the ancient stone terraces of the mountain Machu Picchu.

Today it is one of the world's top tourist attractions. Every year more than 300,000 people tramp through Machu Picchu, fighting crowds and potential landslides to watch the sun set over the Sacred City. It remains one of the world's most famous and yet mysterious, man-made wonders.

We don't know what became of the people in this high mountain dwelling, but God knows. He lives from forever in the past to forever in the future. He understands our dreams and our heartaches, our pain and our loneliness. He knows what you need now, and what you will need tomorrow. And He knew what the people of Machu Picchu needed. He knows what happened to them. Even though the memory of the Inca people in Machu Picchu has been lost in the ancient winds of time, God knows their story.

First Test Tube Baby

As you do not know the path of the wind, or how the body
is formed in a mother's womb, so you cannot understand
the work of God, the Maker of all things.
Ecclesiastes 11:5, NIV.

It's a girl! Her name was Louise Joy Brown, and her July 25 birth made head-lines around the world—the world's first baby conceived through in vitro fertilization. The world's first test-tube baby. Of course she didn't spend nine months in a test tube! Rather, her mom's egg was fertilized by her dad's sperm "in vitro," that is in a Petri dish, under very special conditions. It's a kind of last resort for infertile couples. It's pretty amazing when you under-stand that normal conception is a fairly hit and miss proposition. The mom's egg must exit the ovary, then swim across an open space into the fallopian tube above the uterus, before it can meet up with the sperm waiting to fertil-ize it. The odds of everything lining up perfectly are fairly slim. And yet, it happens thousands of times each day.

So you see a test-tube baby is a miracle indeed. That scientists have been able to pull it off is a marvel of our modern age. After in vitro fertilization, the egg must be implanted in the mother's uterus. None of this comes cheap. The cost is close to $13,000 for one cycle, with no guarantee that it'll even take. All that work to make something happen that seems so natural otherwise. Yet, what a blessing it is for those who long to be parents. And here's an up-date. Louise Joy has a younger sister, Natalie, who was also a "test-tube baby." And Natalie was the first test-tube baby to give birth herself—the old-fashioned way. Eight years later Louise Joy made news again, when she had a baby boy. In vitro fertilization is common now. Since 1978 hundreds of thousands of children have been born through the procedure. After Louise Joy was born, doctors monitored her closely to see if she'd develop problems because of her "test-tube" birth. But she was just a normal, happy little girl.

That God can make us all in His image is incredibly mind-boggling, but that He has made us with the ability to make little copies of ourselves in His image too, is really cool! I can't wait to see what else He has in store for us when we reach heaven.

The FBI

For the Lord's sake, respect all human authority—whether the king as head of state, or the officials he has appointed. For the king has sent them to punish those who do wrong and to honor those who do right. 1 Peter 2:13, 14, NLT.

Would you like to be part of a Secret Service organization like the CIA, or the NSA, or maybe even the INS? The CIA works mainly with crime or criminals that are outside the United States. The NSA deals with problems that might affect national security, and the INS handles immigration and naturalization of people who aren't U.S. citizens.

And then, of course, there's the FBI. If you learned that an FBI agent wanted to talk with you, you might get a funny feeling in the pit of your stomach. And with good reason. They work with police on crimes that are committed in the United States on a local level.

The FBI (Federal Bureau of Investigation) was born on this date in 1908 when the Federal Department of Justice hired 10 former Secret Service agents to work for them to solve serious criminal cases. It grew quickly. J. Edgar Hoover began working for it in the 1920s and under his leadership the agency got very technical. He brought modern technology to police work including a central fingerprint file and forensic laboratories. In 1935 he helped found the FBI, and remained its director until his death—48 years later. (It is because of Hoover's long reign that FBI directors are now limited to 10-year terms.)

You may have heard stories about how the FBI agents tracked down big-time gangsters like Al Capone. How they hunted down outlaws such as "Machine Gun" Kelly, and John Dillinger. Trouble is, these stories sound much more exciting than real life, and don't take into account the people harmed and killed and the fact that every human on earth is precious to God, and He grieves over their crimes and their deaths.

Today's text reminds us that we should respect government organizations that work to keep us safe. We are blessed that there are people who dedicate their lives to keeping peace in the land. Whether it is your local police officer or a national security agent, the Bible tells us to respect their authority. They work to protect and honor the good guys among us, and to bring the bad guys to justice.

Bugs Bunny

And the Lord God formed man of the dust of the ground, and breathed into his nostrils the breath of life; and man became a living being.
Genesis 2:7, NKJV.

Bugs Bunny is one of the all-time favorite American cartoon characters. On July 27, 1940, Chuck Jones created the animated rabbit called "Bugs," and Mel Blanc provided the legendary voiceovers. Bugs made his first appearance in *A Wild Hare*, and the rest is history. Kids loved the wisecracking rabbit, but adults did too. Through the years (and with the skill of his creators) Bugs' personality just continued to grow and his famous carrot-chomping line, "What's up, doc?" became known around the world.

Animated cartoons first appeared in France, and were soon being used in America. They were an instant hit here, and with the development of sound in the late 1920s, cartoons became even more popular. Walt Disney created the Silly Symphonies series of cartoons, but it was Mickey Mouse and his gang that put Mr. Disney on the map. By the 1930s, feature length musical cartoons such as *Sleeping Beauty* were being created by the Disney drawing boards.

And then Warner Brothers developed its own set of cartoon characters, including Bugs Bunny, Tweety Bird, Daffy Duck, Porky Pig, and Yosemite Sam. Mel Blanc started with Warner Brothers in 1937, and not only did the voices for Bugs, but also Road Runner, Sylvester the Cat, Tweety Bird, and Yosemite Sam.

Cartoon characters who figure prominently alongside Bugs Bunny are the sarcastic Daffy Duck, the stuttering Porky Pig, and the eternally angry Yosemite Sam. But without fail, Bugs always gets the upper hand. He outsmarts, outwits, and outmaneuvers all of them, hands down.

When the earth was brand-new God created the very first man and woman. But He didn't use pen and ink, or watercolors, or computer animation techniques. He created Adam from the dust of the ground, and breathed into his nostrils the breath of life. That's what makes us way, way different from our own creations. And God's personal touch is what sets us apart from the other creatures on earth. We are God's creation in whom is the breath of life.

China Earthquake

And there will be great earthquakes in various places.
Luke 21:11, NKJV.

Minutes before the start of the third game in the 1989 World Series, an earthquake struck San Francisco. A Pacific Union College student who was there said, "If we'd known they were going to have an earthquake, we wouldn't have come."

California has about 10,000 small earthquakes a year. But every now and then there's a big one, like the Northridge quake in 1994 that killed 33 people and did $20 billion damage. Of course, even that wasn't *the* Big One—the California quake that will make all previous ones seem pretty small. Geologists know that a really big one is inevitable, probably during the next 30 years. So homes and skyscrapers are built with extra support even as they're made to handle a "little" movement, should the earth beneath them suddenly move back and forth.

An earthquake is probably the most devastating natural force on earth. Little more than a year ago, in May, 2008, a 7.9-magnitude earthquake hit a mountainous region in Western China, killing about 70,000 people and leaving more than 18,000 missing. That followed the 1976 quake in Tangshan, China—that killed 250,000 people! The day before that earthquake, rats were seen running in frightened packs, and chickens refused to eat. The quake that killed so many lasted only 23 seconds!

North America has had its share of big ones, too. Some have been recent, but one of the biggest was actually three earthquakes hitting almost at once. That was in 1811 in the Mississippi Valley. The ground literally rolled in waves. Thankfully, few people lived where it was the strongest so few people lost their lives.

The Bible tells us that before Jesus comes again disasters will devastate our earth. The earthquakes will be far worse than anything any of us has ever seen. Revelation 6 says that every island and mountain will be moved out of place. But Jesus has promised to be with us—even then.

Belle Boyd—Spy

Charm and grace are deceptive, and beauty is vain, . . . but a woman who reverently and worshipfully fears the Lord, she shall be praised! Proverbs 31:30, Amplified.

Belle Boyd was born 17 years before the start of the War Between the States, on a big plantation in Virginia's Shenandoah Valley. The war had hardly started when Union soldiers entered her home and wanted to fly their flag over the house. When one pushed her mother she pulled out a pistol and shot him. The Union officers questioned her and decided the shooting was justified. Soon after this Miss Boyd began spying for the Confederacy, using her father's hotel as a cover. Often while on her missions infiltrating enemy territory, she flirted and chatted with the Union soldiers and officers to get information about upcoming battles. Eventually, someone caught on and she was banished back to the South.

Two months later she was back at it again, braving enemy fire that put a bullet hole through her full skirts to deliver sensitive information to General "Stonewall" Jackson. This critical intelligence gave the Confederates the advantage and helped them defeat General Nathaniel Banks and his forces at the Battle of Winchester. Another time Miss Boyd turned two courteous Union cavalrymen over to Confederate pickets as prisoners of war. Their crime? They'd innocently escorted her back home across Confederate lines. On July 29, 1862, Belle Boyd was captured by the Union army and held in the Old Capitol Prison in Washington, D.C. It was the first time she was captured, but it wouldn't be the last. But when she was released one month later as part of a prison exchange program and sent back to Richmond, she soon began spying again.

Miss Boyd was arrested several more times. In 1864 she went to England where she met and married a Union officer. He died soon after the war ended. Not surprisingly, Belle became an actress. She also wrote a book and gave dramatic lectures about her years as a spy. Some people believe that extreme circumstances make lying and deception OK, but I don't believe that's how God looks at it. For all her bravery and accomplishments, Belle struggled with mental illness and in many ways lived a troubled life. Perhaps the characteristics that enabled her to sneak through enemy lines became her downfall. It's something to think about.

Happy Birthday, Henry

Thank you for making me so wonderfully complex.
It is amazing to think about.
Psalm 139:14, TLB.

Henry Ford made cars. Now he didn't start out making cars. Born July 30, 1863, his dad expected him to carry on the family tradition of farming. But Henry liked hoeing weeds about as much as he liked mucking out horse stalls! Even though his dad had given him 40 acres to get him started, Henry spent most of his time trying to build a farm locomotive and a steam carriage. Finally he moved to Detroit and an honest job, but still spent his spare time trying to build a petrol-powered motor car. And he did. Didn't have any brakes, but it ran.

As you already know, eventually Ford convinced enough people to invest in his ideas and he began making cars. Of course, his first two companies failed but finally he convinced enough investors that he truly could make a car that people would buy, and he tried again. The Model A was a success, and then in 1909 Ford decided to make only one model: the Model T. However, it took 13 hours to make, and selling at $850 the car was too expensive for most people to buy.

So Ford introduced the assembly line. It wasn't a totally new idea, but he's the first that really made it work. Here's how. The first few guys welded together the car's frame and other workers put on the wheels. Next the engine and other important parts were put in, then the metal body went on, followed by seats, doors, a coat of paint, and maybe even a horn. Cars that had once taken 12½ hours to make were now finished in 90 minutes. Then Ford decided to double the salaries of his employees from $2.50 a day to a whopping $5.00. His executives thought he was crazy, but Mr. Ford convinced them that if they made more money they'd buy cars of their own built right there in Ford's factory. And it worked. Other people bought them too! By 1927 Mr. Ford had sold more than 15 million Model Ts because he had gotten the price of a Model T down to only $260.

Ford's assembly line was great for making cars, but thankfully God didn't make you and I like that. If He did, we'd all look and act alike. Jesus has made each of us in God's image and no two of us are exactly the same. Aren't you glad!

Sunken Treasure

If you look for it as for silver and search for it as for hidden treasure, then you will understand the fear of the Lord and find the knowledge of God.
Proverbs 2:4, 5, NLT.

Do you dream of finding buried treasure? That's pretty unlikely, but there are sunken treasure ships still to be found and people continue to search for them. On July 24, 1715, a fleet of 11 Spanish ships left Havana, Cuba, for Spain. Known as the 1715 silver treasure fleet, the 11 ships were carrying tons of gold and silver coins worth about 14 million pesos—around $500 million in today's market. It was already hurricane season so the ships stayed close to Florida to protect them in case of storm.

Just days later, on July 31, a violent hurricane hit almost without warning. Of course, the captains struggled to save them, but one by one the ships went down. The *Nuestra Senora de la Regla* sank with 200 people and 120 tons of coins on board. The *Santa Cristo de San Ramon* went down with 120 sailors aboard. It's estimated that 1,000 people lost their lives close to what is now Cape Canaveral. However, there were some survivors. Eventually word reached Havana and emergency supplies were sent back. Salvage crews came too, and about 80 percent of the gold was recovered. The rest of it wasn't discovered until nearly 250 years later. Even today, silver artifacts and coins still wash up on Florida beaches from time to time.

Now, that's a story to send shivers down your spine—those wooden ships breaking up on the reefs with all those men on board. It was dangerous business anyway. Pirates prowling the open waters. Illness caused by the terrible hygiene, awful diet of biscuits and salted pork, and tropical disease. Hurricanes to tear apart your ship. It's no wonder that the sailors were so superstitious. And that's to say nothing of their fears of giant sea monsters and the edge of the world.

If we value God's Word as much as people value jewels and gold, we'll give anything to get it and keep it, even going so far as to risk our lives for it. Thousands have done just that through the ages. The Bible has been safeguarded at great cost. It has been translated and shared in the most remote areas of the earth. Truly its value is far above rubies or silver or gold.

Mr. Perky's Breakfast

Then God said, "Look! I have given you every seed-bearing plant throughout the earth and all the fruit trees for your food."
Genesis 1:29, NLT.

What do you get when you cross a paper shredder with a farm product of Middle-America? Shredded wheat.

OK. That's lame, and I know it. But shredded wheat is kind of lame. It doesn't snap, crackle, or pop. It's not candy coated. It doesn't glow in the dark nor is it named after a monster (think Frankinberry). Unlike 60 percent of 100 breakfast cereals examined in a certain survey, one serving of shredded wheat doesn't have as much sugar as a jam doughnut. In fact, it has no sugar at all. It just lies there in the bowl with its natural protein, awaiting your milk and a little sugar, ready to start your day.

Its inventor's name: Mr. Perky. (No kidding.)

In the early 1890s Henry Perky who had trouble with his stomach, saw a man eating a bowl of boiled wheat with cream. He couldn't get that combination out of his mind. He took his idea of a product made from boiled wheat to a friend, William Ford, who was a machinist. Together they developed a machine for making what Perky called "little whole wheat mattresses," and on August 1, 1893, got a patent for the idea. Now this is where it gets confusing. Perky wanted to make and sell the machines that made the biscuits, so he began handing out the "little mattresses," hoping that people would want to buy the machine so they could make them themselves. Instead, they wanted the biscuits. A few years later Perky moved to Boston and opened his first bakery, making what by then was called shredded wheat.

Perky had strong beliefs about food. John Harvey Kellogg and Charles Post are much better known for their invention of dry cereals, but Perky was the first pioneer of cookless breakfast foods and he was the first to mass-produce ready-to-eat dry cereal. By 1898 shredded wheat was being sold in North and South America and Europe.

Today shredded wheat is being marketed as a simple, honest brand, and one of the healthiest foods in the cereal aisle. That makes it anything but lame.

Wild Bill

For when they say, "Peace and safety!" then sudden
destruction comes upon them, . . . and they shall not escape.
1 Thessalonians 5:3, NKJV.

"Wild Bill Hickok . . . gunfighter . . . murdered in a saloon in Deadwood, South Dakota." In the days that followed August 2, 1876, such headlines screamed in many newspapers across the young United States.

It's hard to separate fact from fiction in James Butler's life. What most historians agree on is that Butler—known as Wild Bill Hickok—got a reputation as a gunfighter when he and two fellow employees shot three unarmed men who'd come to collect money owed them by the company where Hickok was working. They pleaded self-defense and were not prosecuted. During the Civil War Hickok served the Union forces as a wagon master, scout, and spy. After the war, while gambling, Hickok killed a man, a former Confederate, in a shoot-out in a public square. Again he was tried for murder. Again, acquitted. Shortly afterward *Harper's Magazine* published a wildly inflated story of the gunfight, and suddenly Hickok was known everywhere.

His reputation as a marksman in desperate encounters with outlaws made him a frontier legend. There were other gun battles, and sometimes innocent people were killed. He served as deputy U.S. marshal in Fort Riley, Kansas, a rough town with serious problems between discontented soldiers and emigrant train scouts. One day when things seemed about to explode, Hickok bellowed, "This has gone far enough!" Even the most unruly of the mob were shocked into silence. But when that tactic didn't stop a quarrel, his fist or pistol barrel did. Some historians say that eventually Wild Bill lived off his famous reputation instead of weapons.

Hickok was quite a gambler and often lost. For a while he toured with Buffalo Bill's Wild West Show, but he hated it. Through the years he'd made enough enemies that he always sat with his back against the wall to keep anyone from sneaking up on him. But one day in Deadwood, South Dakota, he forgot. A young gunslinger walked up behind him as he sat in a poker game and shot him in the back of the head. Hickok was only 39.

Bill thought he could live out his days in peace, retired from his reputation as a gunslinger. But it finally caught up with him. In the end, no matter where he went, he couldn't escape.

Off Track, New World

Then the Lord appeared to Abram and said, "To your descendants I will give this land." Genesis 12:7, NKJV.

You remember the rhyme: In 1492, Columbus sailed the ocean blue, leaving on August 3, in search of a shorter trade route to the West Indies, China, and India.

He had a fleet of three ships—The *Nina*, the *Pinta*, and the *Santa Maria*—a commission he had received from King Ferdinand and Queen Isabella in Spain. Two months and nine days later, on October 12, he reached Watling Island in the Bahamas, went ashore, and claimed the new land for Spain. He named the peaceable people who lived there Indians, because he thought he'd found India.

Columbus, like most people of that time, had no idea how big the world is. Sailing on, when he saw Cuba, he thought it was mainland China. In reality, China was 8,531 miles (13,729 kilometers) away. Columbus believed that Hispaniola, which is now Haiti, might be Japan. He planted the Spanish flag there, started a small colony with 39 sailors, and then returned to Spain with gold, spices, and Indian captives. He received a royal welcome and the highest honors the Spanish court could offer. Not because he had discovered a new world! They didn't know he had. They simply thought he'd found a new trade route to the East Indies. They had no idea that Columbus had discovered the Americas.

That's the irony of it. He had no idea how truly amazing his discovery was! He had rediscovered the western hemisphere, and that would change the history of the world. What a privilege! What an opportunity! He was totally wrong about where he was on the planet, but so very right in discovering it. Unfortunately he never benefitted from his incredible discovery. He died in 1506, still unaware that he had discovered a new hemisphere—one that probably had not been visited by Europeans since the times of the Vikings nearly 500 years before.

Thousands of years ago, God sent Abraham in search of a new country, and like Columbus, Abraham had no idea where he was going. But by faith, he went anyway. Why not be like Abraham? If you ask God to go with you, you can't go wrong.

Diary of a Young Girl

The Lord is my shepherd; I shall not want.
Psalm 23:1, NKJV.

Anne Frank didn't set out to write a book. All she was doing was writing down her thoughts in a small notebook she took with her when she went into hiding.

Anne and her family moved to Amsterdam after the Nazis came to power in Germany. By then Germany was deadly for Jews, but no one expected that Holland would be captured by the Nazis. But in 1940 the Germans invaded the Netherlands and little by little a noose tightened against Jews living there. Small freedoms were taken away from them a little at a time. Anne's father, Otto Frank, wrote to relatives, friends, and officials trying to find a way for his family to leave Holland for someplace safe, but no one could help. Finally, in July, 1942, the Frank family made a decision. They walked up a stairs and behind a secret bookcase into a small annex above Mr. Frank's office. They would live there with another four Jews for the next two years, helped by neighbors of the Otto family who lived below and smuggled in food and other supplies.

But their days were numbered. A Dutch informer told the Gestapo about the Jewish refugees and on August 4, 1944, the Nazi secret police raided the place. All were arrested and sent them to Auschwitz—concentration camps in Poland. There they endured starvation, humiliation, and even torture, all the while hoping the war would end. But Anne didn't make it. She died of typhus in March, 1945, just months before the camp was liberated by the Allies.

Back in Holland friends searched the rooms where Anne and her parents had been hiding, and found Anne's diary. Anne's father survived the war and had the diary published in 1947 as *The Diary of a Young Girl*. Since then it has been translated into more than 50 languages. Suppressed people all over the world are encouraged by Anne's courage during suffering. This famous line in the diary shows her hopeful spirit: "In spite of everything, I still believe people are really good at heart."

Today the Franks' hiding place behind Mr. Frank's store has been turned into a museum. People from all over the world come to see the place where a girl wrote out her testimony of faith despite incredible, inhuman cruelty. Someday those true to God may suffer such persecution, but that should not be our greatest concern. God has assured us that He will be with us through those times.

Stop! Light

Thy word is a lamp unto my feet, and a light unto my path.
Psalm 119:105.

What must it have been like to ride in a buggy or wagon down a busy city street in the old days? And how about streetcars and horses and bicycles and people walking? How did everybody keep from running into and over each other? In those days there were no traffic lights, or lines on the road to tell people which way to go.

It must have been really challenging to keep everyone going in the same direction on the same side of the street. Or did they do that? Did oncoming traffic stay on the left? Did small vehicles give way to big ones? It must have been chaotic. When accidents and traffic began to increase with the invention of cars, it soon became evident that some rules of the road would be needed.

On August 5, 1914, the very first traffic light was installed in Cleveland, Ohio, on the intersection of Euclid Avenue and East 105th Street. Some people probably didn't like it, but it probably did make things more organized on the busy streets of Cleveland.

Today traffic lights signal traffic when to go and when to stop. The most common traffic light is the three-tiered signal with green, yellow, and red lights. Green for go, yellow for caution, and red for stop.

What other kinds of traffic lights do we have on our roads? Left turn-right turn signal lights, pedestrian crossing lights, railroad crossing signals, blinking lights on construction signs. And then there are the moving lights: screaming siren lights on police cars, ambulances, and fire engines. And of course our cars, trucks, and vans come with lights, too, lights that help keep us safe in traffic. Headlights, fog lights, taillights, brake lights, back up lights, and turn signals.

Psalm 119 reminds us that God's Word is a lamp to our feet, and a light to our path. It serves as a guiding light to all who are walking the rough and rocky road to heaven. Like a lighthouse, it offers a beacon to ships that travel too near the rocky shores of spiritual tragedy.

Like traffic signals, we should hold up our lights—our faith and trust in God—so that others may see our Father who is in heaven. Our example may be just the thing that encourages someone to begin their journey to Jesus and accept Him as their Savior.

Bombing of Hiroshima

For nation will rise against nation, and kingdom against kingdom.
Mark 13:8, NKJV.

World War II was all but over. Italy had long since gotten out of the war, Germany had collapsed, but the Japanese were still holding out. They continued to wage war against the Allies in the Pacific. Finally on August 6, 1945, the United States tried to force a Japanese surrender by dropping an atomic bomb on Hiroshima, Japan. It was the first of its kind to be used on a nation during time of war. The bomb weighed five tons and had the same amount of power as 15,000 tons of TNT. The terrible blast flattened four square miles of the city, instantly killing 80,000 people. Three days later, when Japan had not surrendered, a second nuclear bomb was dropped over Nagasaki.

These bombings brought the end of World War II and, many believe, ultimately saved thousands of lives. However, in some ways they were the start of the United States' Cold War with the Communist Soviet Union. Within four years the Soviets had built a nuclear bomb of their own—and so the nuclear arms race began. Today there are still more than 30,000 nuclear missiles and bombs in the world, with most of them being in Russia and the United States. Besides those two countries, France, Great Britain, Israel, China, India, and Pakistan all have nuclear weapons. And several more countries are also on the verge of making them. It is estimated that right now there are enough nuclear bombs on earth to destroy the world several times over.

Jesus said that before He comes again there will be wars and rumors of war, and that the heart of people will fail them for fear of what is coming on the earth. He said that nation would rise against nation, and kingdom against kingdom. Today we are living with that prophecy being fulfilled before our very eyes. Rational men and women are doing everything possible to prevent nuclear war. Even so, should it happen, there is nowhere we can run to get away from its horrors.

What we can do is trust Jesus during these troubling times, until He comes again to take us home.

We Love Speed

Many shall run to and fro, and knowledge shall increase.
Daniel 12:4, NKJV.

On this day in August of 1915, Dario Resta broke all records for speed in an automobile. No one had ever seen anyone go this fast, except by train. Today we would think nothing of it, but in 1915 it made newspaper headlines.

Dario set this new record in an automobile race in Chicago. An incredible 100 miles per hour was fast back then. The first successful car had been invented by two men in Germany only 30 years before, in 1885. In those days automobiles looked more like a horse carriage than a car.

But hey, we don't have a monopoly on speed. Long before we learned how to make a motor that would drive the wheels we'd attached to a frame, God created creatures that could move fast. For example, a pronghorn antelope can run up to 60 miles per hour. Greyhounds can run as fast as 40 miles per hour, and cheetahs can run for short distances at about 70 miles per hour. Others creatures fly like the wind, with honeybees sometimes clocking in at 100 miles per hour, peregrine falcons zooming up to 180 miles per hour, and bald eagles diving at speeds between 75 and 100 miles per hour.

And here are a few other racers. The desert sun spider is the fastest creature on eight legs, sometimes zipping along at 10 miles per hour. Go to the sea and you might see the sailfish flying along at 110 kilometers, or 68 miles per hour.

It's great to be able to go fast, but speed isn't everything. Just because God moves faster than the speed of light, doesn't mean we have to—at least, not yet. Yes, fast is fun. It just feels good. But there's a time for everything. Do you ever see the small crosses and little shrines of flowers and teddy bears placed along roads and highways? Traveling a few weeks ago, it seemed I saw them every few miles. Far too many teens are killed in cars that were going much too fast. Of course, life is fast. If you're a teen you're likely involved in so many things that it's easy for you to lose track of who you are. It's also easy to lose track of God.

Slow down. Sit down. Wind down. Catch your breath. Think about what you want in life. Think of what God means to you. Fast is good, but sometimes slowing down is even better.

The fall of a President

The Lord detests lying lips, but he delights in those who tell the truth.
Proverbs 12:22, NLT.

Have you heard of the Watergate Scandal? Your parents surely have. Accusations and denials. Evidence, and denials. Suspicion, crimes, and corruption—the front pages of U.S. newspapers were filled with it for months. But let's back up. The Watergate Scandal started when five men were arrested for breaking into the Watergate Complex of the Democratic National Committee headquarters in Washington, D.C. Further investigation uncovered that this burglary was one of many illegal activities authorized and carried out by U.S. President Richard Nixon's staff.

The Republican Party was using telephones and other surveillance equipment illegally to listen in on conversations of other government leaders. Then it was discovered that Nixon had tape recordings that might reveal the truth about the whole scandal, and everyone wanted to hear them. When Nixon refused to turn them over, the U.S. Supreme Court demanded that he do so. Nixon fought every way possible to survive. Even today people re-member his statement in the November 17, 1973, interview: "I am no crook." But slowly and surely the truth was discovered. One by one men in high lev-els of the U.S. government were forced to resign. At last Richard Nixon had to give up. And on August 8, 1974, he resigned as 37th President of the United States. Almost immediately Vice President Gerald Ford was sworn in as the 38th president. One important lesson of Watergate is that not even the pres-ident of the United States is above the law.

In many countries today the passage of power from one government leader to another is not a pleasant thing. Kings, dictators, and prime minis-ters go through bitter feuds, bloody coupes, and violent assassinations. But in the Untied States, the outgoing president hands over the White House keys to the incoming president, as if he were handing over the keys to a car.

So what's the lesson for us in the Watergate Scandal? Honesty is the best policy. One lie requires another . . . and another . . . and another. Dishonesty never pays. Eve believed the serpent's lie, and think of the trouble that's caused. God's advice: Tell the truth, the whole truth, and nothing but the truth—so help you God.

Big Bad Barbarians

During the reigns of those kings, the God of heaven will set up a
kingdom that will never be destroyed or conquered. It will crush
all these kingdoms into nothingness, and it will stand forever.
Daniel 2:44, NLT.

On this day in 378 A.D. the Visigoth barbarians attacked a large Roman
army. It was a decisive battle for the barbarian hordes of Europe, and
spelled the beginning of the end for the Roman Empire. But we're getting
ahead of our story.

It had been nearly 400 years since the birth of Christ, His death, and resurrection, and the Christian Church had conquered the known world, including the Roman Empire. But the Roman Empire was falling apart. Economic
hard times coupled with corruption in the Roman government spelled disaster for the once invincible empire of iron.

The barbarian tribes to the west were already knocking on the door, and
the Roman army had grown too weak to successfully fend them off. The
Visigoths, Ostrogoths, and Vandals had been introduced to Christianity, but
they preferred their own kind of Christianity to that of the Church of Rome.
As a result they were soon being branded as heretics. This didn't help much
in their relationship with the Romans.

The Visigoths had gotten permission to settle south of the Danube River,
but were tired of the Romans and their oppressive tactics: tired of their taxes,
tired of their military restrictions, and tired of their religion.

Finally in early August the Visigoths rose up in revolt. So on August 9,
Valens, the Roman emperor of the east, ordered a hasty attack on the unsuspecting barbarians. He hoped to put down the Visigoths revolt as quickly as
possible. The Visigoth cavalry was off on a hunting trip, but returned in time
to meet the Roman army head on. The mounted barbarians thundered down
upon the fleeing Roman infantry, slaughtering 20,000 men. It was a disaster,
and Valens never saw it coming! In fact, Emperor Valens himself died in that
battle.

God showed Daniel that after the collapse of the Roman empire, God
Himself would set up a kingdom that would last forever. Any day now we expect Jesus to come riding through on the clouds of glory.

The Smithsonian

The fear of the Lord is *the beginning of knowledge,
but fools despise wisdom and instruction.*
Proverbs 1:7, NKJV.

Today, in 1846, the Smithsonian Institute was born. And now Smithsonian is the largest museum complex in the world. Here's how it happened.

In 1829, James Smithson of England left his entire estate to his nephew, and a legal will with a very peculiar request. If the nephew died without an heir, the estate would go to the United States of America. Smithson wanted the money to be used to build a museum of learning in America called the Smithsonian Institution. Why? everyone asked, and the story drew a lot of attention on both sides of the Atlantic. But despite his gift and influence on the history of American science, we know little of Smithson's early life. Information about it was burned up in the fire that destroyed the Smithsonian Institution building in 1865.

Six years after receiving the estate, Smithson's nephew did indeed die, and without children. In 1836, the U.S. Congress officially accepted Smithson's gift. Two years later the gift arrived in the United States: 11 boxes containing a fortune in gold worth $500,000. Today that amount would be more than $100 million. The first building, called The Castle, was built in 1855. Others soon followed. .

Today, the Smithsonian Institute has 19 separate museums and galleries and millions of exhibited items. This includes museums of African American History and Culture, Natural History, American History, Air and Space, a National Art Gallery, and the National Zoological Park. What an honor Smithson paid the United States with his gift, and what a testimony the museum became to the American dream that everyone deserves an education. Today John Smithson has been honored by entombing his body in the Smithsonian Building.

The Smithsonian Institution is one of the most visited museums in the world. A visit to Washington, D.C., is not complete without seeing at least some of it.

It reminds us that wisdom begins with God. In His omnipotence, He created all things. Because of His omniscience, He knows all things. The first step in learning, period, is recognizing this and bowing down to God. Only fools thumb their noses at such power and wisdom.

Now That's Hot

As long as the earth endures, seedtime and harvest, cold and heat, summer and winter, day and night will never cease.
Genesis 8:22, NIV.

On August 11, 1933, a world-record temperature of 136° F was recorded at San Luis Potosí, Mexico. Now *that's* hot! Can you imagine temperatures that hot all the time? Some places on earth endure temperatures near 120 degrees much of the year. Seattle, Washington, holds the record for a quick rise in temperature. A Chinook wind can bring warmer weather in a real hurry—47 degrees in 7 minutes is the record.

But some places get really, *really* cold. The lowest temperature ever recorded on earth was in Antarctica—minus 128 degrees Fahrenheit. And Browning, Montana, has the U.S. record for a 24-hour drop in temperature. On January 23, 1916, the temperature dropped 100 degrees in one day—from 44 degrees above to 56 degrees below zero. Now that calls for a heavy coat!

The earth has all kinds of climates at all levels of elevation. There's the tropical climate, usually near the equator where temperatures are pretty even and range only about 20 degrees year round. Then we have temperate zones where during a calendar year temperatures range from below zero to above 100 degree Fahrenheit. Most of North America is in the temperate zone.

And then there are the arctic regions where temperatures rarely rise much above freezing. In fact, they often drop near 100 degrees below zero. Temperatures at sea level are usually warmer than those at higher altitudes. And temperatures in dry climates usually feel warmer than the same temperature in a moist, more humid climate. Temperatures at night are usually cooler than those during the day. A large body of water will keep the air warmer longer in the evening.

One of the curses that sin brought to this world was extremes in heat and cold. But even in the antediluvian world the temperatures were pretty even. It wasn't until after the Flood that climate zones on the earth began to heat up and cool down drastically. When Eden is once again restored, the weather will always be pleasant. Praise God! It's possible that we'll never again have to wear a coat or use an air conditioner! Do you think you'd like that?

Let's Work

For the laborer is worthy of his wages.
Luke 10:7, NKJV.

On this day in 1955, the U.S. Federal Government set the minimum wage at $1.00—worth $10.80 today. Since 1955 the hourly wage has gone through several wage hikes. In May, 1974, it reached $2.00. In 1980, it was raised to $3.10, and in 1991, it was set at $4.25. As of July, 2008, the U.S. minimum wage is $6.55.

So what are your skills worth? What would you bring to a job? Good computer skills? Are you a fast typist? Do you know word processing programs? Are you good with children? Are you good at cleaning? Perhaps you're creative and do great lettering or even some art and design. Even young teens can get jobs, but sometimes they don't like the wages. Picking fruit or vegetables usually pays less than any kind of construction work, even just sweeping up. Babysitting usually brings in less than lifeguarding.

As you plan your life and your temporary job career (what you work at while you're still in school), focus on what you truly want. Are you working for spending money? Do you need to earn enough to buy a car? Are you helping to pay for your education?

As far as money goes, there's never enough of it. And cars cost a lot! Even used ones. Once you get the vehicle there's insurance, license plates, gas, and oil—and spare parts and labor when they inevitably break down. And education? If you're helping to pay for private education, you have really learned to count the cost.

All the research shows that kids who help with at least some of the costs of their education go further in life and accomplish more academically. And they're usually more successful in their careers, becoming supervisors, managers, private business owners, or professionals such as lawyers, professors, and doctors. Why? Because they have learned to manage themselves, their time, and their money.

Jesus says that a "laborer is worthy of his wages." Or at least he should be. If you're not doing your share of the work where you work, then you're probably not worth the wage you're being paid. Even while on his missionary journeys, Paul was proud to be working as a tentmaker so he could provide for himself financially. It's nice to be on your own, and it's nice to be taking care of your own finances. Just remember, no job is beneath you if it's done well.

August 13

Anyone Home?

Before they call I will answer; while they are still speaking I will hear.
Isaiah 65:24, NLT.

When was the last time you saw someone talking on a pay phone? When was the last time you even saw a pay phone? They are scarce as floppy disks. It's a shame. The tall, narrow phone booth played a supporting role in many a movie. They were so handy, especially the phones placed at car level so you could talk while sitting in your car. Then there were the phone booths in the basements of college dorms, good for ringing your girlfriend or making a collect call to Mom or Dad.

Invented on August 13, 1889, pay phone celebrates its 120th birthday in 2009. Of course, with the invention of cell phones, fewer and fewer people even need a pay phone. Almost as early as the telephone itself was invented, people figured a public pay phone would be a great way to make money. William Gray of Hartford, Connecticut, came up with the idea and got a patent for it. The pay phone was coin-operated, and installed in the lobby of the Hartford Bank. Soon they were found on street corners, in train stations, airports, and diners, grocery stores, and shopping malls.

But no more. Pay phones have gone the way of the reel-to-reel tape and black-and-white TV, while "everyone" seems to have a cell phone glued to their ear. They've truly changed our way of life. Remember in movies of just a few years ago, when the criminal (or hero) made a quick call to the police/their mother/girlfriend/boyfriend and there was a desperate attempt to keep the caller on the line so they could "trace the call." Does anyone "trace" a call anymore? Rather, the caller's name and/or phone number comes up on the screen and the "call-ee" can choose to answer—or not—depending on whether the caller is friend or nuisance. Phones are even programmed with specific tunes for certain callers. Of course, there are disadvantages to cell phones. Having to keep them recharged. And they're so easy to lose. Of course, you can always use someone else's cell to call yours, and you follow the sound of the ring.

What about calling God? He's there anytime you need Him, and it won't cost you a thing. And you don't have to worry about those roaming charges or a need for roll-over minutes. God gives you instant access anytime of day, any day of the week, and the reception will always be good. Most importantly, you don't have to worry about Him cutting out on the conversation.

Lights Out

Arise, shine, for your light has come, and the glory of the Lord rises upon you. See, darkness covers the earth and thick darkness is over the peoples, but the Lord rises upon you and his glory appears over you. Isaiah 60:1, 2, NIV.

Americans today know they are overly dependent on electricity. They use it for lights, electrical appliances, TVs, garage door openers, and just about everything, it seems, in our modern world. So what would we do if we suddenly had no more electricity? Well, we got a chance to find that out on August 14, 2003, when the largest blackout in North American history hit the northeastern United States and parts of Canada. Twenty-one power plants shut down, and 50,000,000 people were affected, with big cities like New York, Cleveland, and Detroit, being hit the hardest. It was over 24 hours before power could be completely restored.

The shutdown stopped trains and elevators too, and affected things as simple as cell phone service. But it affected things a lot more serious too. Surgery at hospitals had to be postponed in some cases, and flights at airports had to be suspended. In places like New York City, metro traffic stalled for over two hours. Restaurant refrigerators shut down temporarily and food spoiled. Water supplies were interrupted, and even amusement park rides stopped, stranding people in midair. New York City alone, estimated the cost of the blackout to be more than $500 million. Fortunately, very few crimes happened during this time.

At first we thought terrorists might be responsible for the blackout, but that wasn't the case. The hot weather had been overloading systems everywhere, as they often do in August, but that didn't really seem to be the problem either. No one could pinpoint the exact reasons why the power plants had shut down, and it gave us a chance to examine the major flaws in the country's outdated power grid. Finally, a task force traced the problem back to an electrical company in Ohio called FirstEnergy Corporation. Overgrown trees had come into contact with a power line, triggering a series of problems that led to a chain reaction of outages.

The incident has shown us just how dependent we are on our electricity. But we are even more dependent on God's power. If it wasn't for God, spiritual darkness would cover the earth completely. It's our job as Christians to let God's light shine out from our lives. Only then will others see the love of Jesus, and come to know the Father in heaven.

A Short Cut

*For who would begin the construction of a building
without first getting estimates and then checking to
see if he has enough money to pay the bills?
Luke 14:28, TLB.*

The first mention of a passage across the tip of South America was in the 1550s when the king of Spain ordered a survey done to look for a route through Panama that would ease the voyage for ships traveling to and from Spain and Peru. Finally in 1855 a railway was built across the 50-mile wide isthmus, but until the Panama Canal was completed in 1914 there was no way to get across Cape Horn on water. Government leaders and shipping companies from around the world had dreamed of building a canal across the isthmus. However, the task seemed impossible since much of the land was volcanic rock and was covered with thick steaming jungles and treacherous swamps.

The French were the first ones to try and build a canal through Panama, but the project ran into trouble. It's estimated that 22,000 workers died from diseases such as yellow fever and malaria during this attempt. Experts were called in to solve the problem of disease, but after nearly 20 years the project was abandoned. Then the Americans tried to start working on it, but they ran into the same problems. However, they began to make progress under the leadership of engineer John Frank Stephens who rebuilt the Panama railway and figured out a way that soil from the excavations could be hauled away by rail. Too, he had decent housing built for canal workers and he oversaw extensive sanitation and mosquito-control programs that eliminated yellow fever and other diseases. He also convinced U.S. President Theodore Roosevelt that the canal must be built with dams and locks to raise and lower the water that flowed through it.

It was a great day of celebration when the job was finally done, and the canal finally opened up for traffic on August 15, 1914. The Panama Canal was one of the toughest construction jobs ever undertaken. It cost the United States $380 million (about $7 billion in today's money), and took the lives of hundreds of people.

Jesus told us to count the cost before we begin a project. Like the building of the Panama Canal, the price tag can sometimes be high. Today let's ask God to help us count the cost before we make a decision that could cost us our health, our reputation, and even our eternal life.

Elvis Has Left the Building

For the wages of sin is death, but the gift of God is eternal life in Christ Jesus our Lord. Romans 6:23, NIV.

On this day in 1977, Elvis Presley died. He was only 42. People still call Elvis the king and somehow his music remains popular more than 30 years after his death. Elvis grew up in a small shotgun house in Tupelo, Tennessee. It's said of these narrow homes that "you could fire a shotgun through the front door and the bullet would go out the back." After high school Elvis became a truck driver, and at 19 he paid $4 to record a few songs for his mother in a Memphis studio. The owner was impressed with Elvis's voice—it had a new soulful sound—and asked him to sing with some local musicians. It's said that Elvis was afraid the music might be too worldly, but he needed the money. A year later he was back in the studio fooling around, and sang a blues song, "That's All Right." Sam Philips, the studio owner, recorded and released it. It shot to the top of the charts, and Presley's career took off with it.

Elvis became a real hit with fans in the South, and then RCA Records gave him a contract for $40,000—an unheard-of amount of money. Teens went crazy when he preformed on the Ed Sullivan show, but parents everywhere were horrified at the way he moved his hips when he sang. By the late 1960s, rock and roll had changed so much that Elvis was losing popularity, and in the 1970s, his health began to decline. He and his wife had divorced. He put on a lot of weight and developed a dangerous dependence on prescription drugs. He continued to perform on stage, but only sporadically. He looked bloated and sick, and on August 16, 1977, he was found lifeless in his large, beautiful home. Attempts to revive him failed. Elvis was dead.

Early in his career Elvis found that despite being popular and making tons of money he still wasn't happy. One time after visiting his home church, he wrote to the pastor. "I am the most miserable young man you have ever seen. I have more money than I can ever spend . . . but I am miserable." He went on to describe his struggle with right and wrong (*Last Train to Memphis*, Peter Guralnick, Back Bay books). As the years went by he often spent the hours after a wildly successful concert in his hotel suite singing gospel songs. His friend Joe Moscheo calls those times Elvis' church. It's a fact. "Having it all" is nothing if you don't have God.

Missionary Man

*And this gospel of the kingdom will be preached in all the world
as a witness to all the nations, and then the end will come.
Matthew 24:14, NKJV.*

On this day in 1761, William Carey, the great English missionary to India was born. He served God with a full heart, and probably did more to advance the cause of modern Christianity, than anyone since Martin Luther. While still a teenager William learned to read the Bible in six languages. He joined the Baptist Church in 1783, and soon began speaking of the need for missions. In 1793, he went to India as one of the first missionaries under the English Baptist Missionary Society. In 1801 he became a professor of Oriental languages at the newly formed Fort William College, and held the position for the rest of his life. The Serampore Publishing House that he helped start made the Bible accessible to more than 300 million people.

There have always been missionaries for God. Abraham is the first mentioned in Scripture to travel to a new land. His job? To establish a culture of people in the land of Canaan that worshipped the One True God. And then there was Joseph. Sold into Egyptian slavery, he witnessed for God in that pagan land. God told Jonah to go to the pagan country of Nineveh and preach a message of repentance. When Daniel and his three friends were captured and taken to Babylon God used their experience to help convert Nebuchadnezzar to the worship of Jehovah.

And, of course, the early Christian missionaries took the gospel to the Roman Empire and beyond. Led by Paul, they evangelized the then-known world. In the modern era, thanks to the Spirit of God and missionaries like William, the gospel message has spread to almost every land. There are more than 6,600 languages in the world today, and the Bible has been printed in more than 4,000 of them. According to Wycliffe Bible Translators, by 2025 they plan to have a translation project started in every language. Strangely enough, someone has even gone to the trouble to write a translation of the Bible in Klingon, an imaginary race of people in the Star Trek movie series. This almost seems sacrilegious, but it does prove an interesting point. Even secular script writers for the movie culture understand that God and His Word are the oldest and most influential forces in the universe.

Whatever Happened to Virginia Dare?

And a little child shall lead them.
Isaiah 11:6, NKJV.

The very first baby born of English parents in America was Virginia Dare. She was born on Roanoke Island, off the present-day coast of North Carolina, on August 18, 1587. Her grandfather was John White, governor of the colony. It's sad that only the first nine days of her life are known to history. Her parents were part of a group of 150 settlers that had sailed from England on three ships headed for the new colony. Two of the ships returned to England immediately and the third ship, with John White aboard, left for England a month later to get more supplies for the colony. Before he went, they all agreed that if the colonists had to leave the island they would carve their new location on a tree or post outside the fort. And if the move had to be made because of an attack by Indians, they were to carve over the letters a distress signal in the form of a cross.

Unfortunately his return voyage was detained for longer than he anticipated. The ship had to undergo repairs, and it was hard to raise the needed money for the trip. Three years passed before he could get back to the colony in 1590. The colonists had vanished, and their fort lay in ruins. Unfortunately, the only message he could find was the word "Croatoan." There was no cross or any other sign of distress. What happened? Did the colonists die of disease? Was their settlement attacked by Indian warriors? Were the colonists killed or carried off as captives? No one knows for certain, but history does have some interesting tales to tell us.

Years later it was reported that some of the people in the area Native American tribes had blue or green eyes. Where could that eye color come from? Most of the native people had dark brown or black eyes. It was a dominant trait among the local tribes. It just may be that the small Roanoke settlement was indeed sacked and burned, and the small children carried off as captives. Did they grown up, marry into the local tribes, and have children of their own? It's interesting to speculate and wonder.

Perhaps God preserved the memory of those colonists after all—through the lives of Virginia Dare and the other children in the colony. Some day soon Jesus will return, and when He does everything will be made plain. Mysteries like this one will be uncovered and secrets from the past will be revealed.

August 19

Balloon 19 Miles Up

Then we who are alive and *remain shall be caught up together with them in the clouds to meet the Lord in the air. And thus we shall always be with the Lord.*
1 Thessalonians 4:17, NKJV.

Have you ever climbed a mountain? What altitude? Have you ever been up in a skyscraper? How tall? Have you flown in a jet at 40,000 feet? Well, all of those are neat experiences, but climbing, walking, or flying at those heights is nothing compared to what a medical army officer named David Simons from Crosby, Minnesota, did.

On August 19, 1957, he broke all records for altitude by rising in a hot air balloon more than 100,000 feet into the stratosphere. He stayed up all night floating west into South Dakota, and said it was one of the most exciting experiences of his life.

Hot air balloons go way back. Pilatre De Rozier is considered the world's first balloonist. He sent a sheep, a duck, and a rooster up for the first ride in 1783. The ride lasted for 15 minutes before crashing to the ground. Two years later Rozier tried the same thing himself. Unfortunately, his balloon exploded half an hour after takeoff and he was killed. Evidently the design of the balloon and the flammable hydrogen were a bad combination. Two years later in 1785, Jean Pierre Blanchard and John Jefferies became the first people to successfully fly across the English Channel.

Experimental flights with hot air balloons continued for the next 100 years, and then in 1932 a Swiss scientist set a record for altitude into the upper stratosphere—52,498 feet. From that day on it has been a race to see who can go the farthest and fly the highest. In 1935 a gas helium model reached an altitude of 72,395 feet—more than 13 miles up. So high, in fact, that the pilots had to be in a pressurized chamber. It was one of the first real steps to future space travel. And then David Simons broke that record by nearly 30,000 feet, climbing into the air almost 19 miles. But in 1960 Joe Kittinger set the standard by jumping from a balloon 102,000 feet in the air. Even more amazing, as he was falling from the sky, he broke the sound barrier with his body!

Do you want to really fly? Then don't miss the biggest ride coming yet. When Jesus comes again, we'll be caught up together in the clouds to meet the Lord in the air. We'll wing our way to worlds unknown. Now that's a ride we can't afford to miss!

Yeah, Football!

Be of good courage, and let us be strong for
our people and for the cities of our God.
2 Samuel 10:12, NKJV.

On August 20, 1920, the Professional Football League was born. Jim Thorpe, legendry athlete in baseball and the Olympics, met with six other men in Canton, Ohio, to talk about football. The result was a football league with eight teams. If you happen to live in a cave you may not know that today the National Football League has two conferences—the American Football Conference and the National Football Conference—with 32 teams competing for the coveted Lombardy Trophy at the Super Bowl. Without doubt football has taken its place as America's favorite sport.

At the risk of sounding sexist, sports and competition have always been important to men. In ancient times they competed for land, power, and the love of a woman. Fighting battles for your tribe or city or country, was an important part of survival. The ancient Greeks created the Olympic games to test the strength and speed of their athletes. Roman gladiators fought each other and wild beasts for sport in their arenas and stadiums. Medieval men fought one another in hand-to-hand contests, and their holiday celebrations often featured jousting. May the better warrior win! The Vikings challenged each other in sword matches. The winner took the other's possessions. During the 1600s and 1700s, Europeans challenged one another to pistol duels, and for a while the Old West seemed to adopt that foolish sport.

Today sports are a favorite pastime—both to watch and to play. While people in the States favor football, Canadians love hockey and soccer. The games don't have much to do with survival, but they do seem to satisfy an urge to be stronger and smarter and better than the next guy.

But really, these games are of little importance compared to the life and death issues people have faced down through the years. In David's day, his people were fighting for the survival of their homeland and had to rely on God for help.

Use that inspiration to do your personal best for Jesus. Let's honor what matters most: our families, our church, and people everywhere—for we are all, all of us, God's beloved children.

Mona Lisa Missing

*Don't store up treasures here on earth, where moths eat them
and rust destroys them, and where thieves break in and steal.
Matthew 6:19, NLT.*

On August 21, 1911, an amateur painter discovered that the Mona Lisa
had been stolen from the famous Louvre Art Museum in Paris where it
was being displayed. The Mona Lisa was one of Leonardo da Vinci's favorite
paintings from the time of the Renaissance. Most art historians say he began
painting it in 1503 and finally finished in 1506. More than 500 years have
passed, but she continues to inspire art lovers everywhere. Why is she so appealing, many wonder? Is it her eyes that seem to magically follow the
viewer? Is it her shy smile?

More than six million tourists see the Mona Lisa each year. And yet,
amazingly, she was stolen from under the museum's careful watch. The entire nation of France was stunned. Experts guessed that this was not the work
of professional thieves, because selling the world's most famous painting
would be too dangerous. Some thought the Germans had stolen it to embar-
rass the French. Not! It was much simpler than that.

Vincenzo Perugia, a former employee of the Louvre, had done the job.
He had walked into the museum, removed the famed painting from the wall,
hidden it beneath his clothes, and walked away. But what would he do with
it? For two years he held the painting, and then an Italian art dealer reported
that he'd received a letter from a man who called himself Leonardo.
"Leonardo" said the painting was safe in Florence, Italy, and would be returned when a hefty ransom was paid. The time and place were arranged for
the payoff, and when "Leonardo" tried to collect, he was nabbed. It was
Perugia, of course. Fortunately the painting was unharmed.

If Jesus had been walking the streets of Italy in 1911, He would have had
some important advice: Don't put your stock into things of this world. Don't
hoard treasures of silver or gold, or collect expensive cars or yachts, or build
extra homes at the beach. These things are nice, but someone can always
burglarize or trash them, and then what have you got? An insurance claim at
best. Jesus advises us to put our treasure in heaven. No one ever steals from
the heavenly vaults where our treasure is stored. And a reward awaits us
there.

Angel Under Fire

I tell you the truth, whatever you did for one
of the least of these brothers of mine, you did for me.
Matthew 25:40, NIV.

The Red Cross is one of the most generous humanitarian organizations in the history of the world. During times of war they bring medical help to soldiers. They arrive with food and shelter for victims of fire. They bring medical treatment to people who have been through natural disasters like tornadoes, floods, and tsunamis. And through their blood drives they help millions with the gift of life.

On August 22, 1864, 12 nations from the Geneva Convention created this humanitarian organization. But it is Clara Barton who we remember when we think of the Red Cross, for Clara gave the Red Cross its real identity. History reminds us that she was one of the kindest, most selfless people in the world. During the Civil War she started an agency to help wounded soldiers. In 1862, she got permission to travel behind enemy lines, and eventually saw some of the worst battlefields of the war, giving aid to soldiers of both the North and the South. Here's one story about Clara's service on the battlefield:

Arriving near the bloody Antietam Battlefield, Clara saw surgeons using cornhusks to try to dress the soldiers' wounds. Army medical supplies still hadn't arrived, so Miss Barton gave the surgeons a wagonload of bandages and other medical supplies that she had been collecting for quite some time. Then she went to work. Bullets whizzed over her head as she tended the broken bodies of the men who had come to fight each other and been mowed down like grass. Artillery boomed in the distance as Clara carried water to the wounded, dying men. As she knelt to give one man a drink, she felt her sleeve quiver. A bullet had gone through her sleeve and killed the man she was helping.

What courage! What brave faith Clara must have had in those frightening hours. When all around her lay bleeding soldiers who would likely die from infections rather than bullets, she worked long days, trying to relieve the agony of those who suffered.

Jesus came to do that. No matter who came to Him for healing, He never turned them away. When the demoniacs and lepers cried out for mercy, He brought them just what they needed. Compassion, healing, and acceptance. What a Savior!

State Denied Admission

Wait on the Lord; be of good courage, and He shall strengthen your heart; wait, I say, on the Lord! Psalm 27:14, NKJV.

The Revolutionary War was over and things were beginning to get back to normal. States were gearing up to become part of what would be known as the brand new United States of America.

On August 23, 1784, a state calling itself "Franklin" was denied admission into the Union. Now, that's a strange story most people have probably never heard before. Weren't there only 13 original colonies that later became the first 13 states? Yes, and, well, there could have been 14 original states, but this is the rest of that untold story.

Franklin is a stretch of land between the Bald Mountains and the Holston River in what is now eastern Tennessee. For some reason, the people of Franklin got all excited about something and split from North Carolina to form their own state and state government with a regular senate and house of commons. They elected John Sevier as governor for a four-year term of office, with a salary of 200 pounds, or 1,000 deerskins, whichever was available. The new colony requested statehood from the Union, but was denied, and John was arrested on charges of high treason. He was later released, after which he served as the first governor of Tennessee when it was formed 12 years later and admitted into the Union as the sixteenth State.

This is a remarkable story. Franklin was denied statehood, and Sevier was denied the opportunity of being a governor of one of the first states in the United States of America. But he was patient and was later elected as the first governor of that very same territory when it was admitted into the Union as the state of Tennessee. Who would have thought that was possible? Probably not John Sevier.

That's the way things seemed to work out for King David, too. Even after being anointed as the next king of Israel, David had to be patient and wait for the Lord. King Saul chased him relentlessly, causing David to flee here and there, live in caves, eat off the land, and sleep on the ground.

But he trusted God, and that's what counted most. In the end, he won the prize.

Those Who Stayed, Died

For when they say, "Peace and safety!" then sudden
destruction comes upon them, as labor pains upon
a pregnant woman. And they shall not escape.
1 Thessalonians 5:3, NKJV.

Volcanoes are some of the most frightening natural phenomena on earth. Some call them an act of God, but that couldn't be further from the truth. Volcanoes are a direct result of sin and the aftershocks of the flood. And they can be devastating. .

At noon on this day in 79 AD, after sleeping for centuries, Mount Vesuvius in southern Italy, erupted. There was some warning, and some people fled. But thousands died when the Roman tourist towns of Pompeii and Herculaneum were buried under a thick layer of volcanic ash. These prosperous cities were never rebuilt and for 1,700 years lay forgotten. When they were rediscovered, Pompeii and Herculaneum were the talk of the archaeological world.

Twenty thousand people lived in Pompeii, a favorite tourist spot for rich Romans with its public Roman baths and gambling casinos. But the city's pleasure and prosperity came to an end when Mount Vesuvius exploded, shooting a cloud of ash and cinders into the sky. During the next 12 hours, ash and stones as big as three inches in diameter showered down on Pompeii, forcing people to flee in terror. Some stayed, hoping to wait out the eruption, but were killed the next morning when a cloud of poisonous gas poured down upon the city. The avalanche of rocks and ashes that followed caved in city roofs, covering them up to 17 feet deep.

In wasn't until 1982 that the preserved remains of 2,000 men, women, and children were uncovered at Pompeii. It is apparent that after the victims died from the heat and falling debris, their bodies were covered with ash. Later the bodies decomposed, leaving an empty space. When plaster is poured into these empty spaces in the ash and allowed to harden, you get a "statue" of the person or animal just as they were at death. Very, very sad.

The last major eruption of Mount Vesuvius was in 1631. Another eruption is expected in the near future, and would, of course, be devastating for the 2 million people who live in the shadow of Vesuvius. Mt. Vesuvius has a long history of eruptions, so the people living around it should know better than to trust it. Paul warns us that peace and safety are not guaranteed in this old world. In the end, destruction will come upon our earth due to war, disease, and natural disasters. Those who trust in themselves instead of God will not escape.

The Great Moon Hoax

For false Christs and false prophets will appear and perform great signs and miracles to deceive even the elect—if that were possible. Matthew 24:24, NIV.

Landing a space craft on the moon took a lot of mystery out of it, though much more remains. We live in an age of knowledge and exploration. Much of the whimsy of past years is gone, and that's not all bad. But a century and a half ago a lot of people believed some wild stories about the moon. For a little while, at least. This is how it happened.

On this day in 1835, stories began to circulate in United States newspapers that life had been discovered on the moon. Yes, the moon. It was hard to believe, but it was true! Most of the articles were reprints from the *Edinburgh Journal of Science.* Surely a science journal could be trusted. The articles said that Dr. Andrew Grant, a friend of the famous astronomer Sir John Herschel, had found evidence of life on the moon. Grant described strange animals like unicorns, two-legged beavers, and furry creatures resembling human bats. The articles described the moon's geography, including craters, huge amethyst crystals, raging rivers, and green vegetation. The New York *Sun,* a cheap tabloid paper something like today's *The Enquirer,* published all the hoax articles. When the first article was printed, sales of the New York *Sun* shot up immediately. The articles were exciting, and readers loved it. The problem? None of it was true, of course! And the *Edinburgh Journal of Science* hadn't even been published for years. Everything was made up, and Dr. Grant was a fictional character.

Who did it? Richard Adams Locke, a reporter from another newspaper was the most likely writer. The stories weren't meant to be taken seriously. Rather, they were meant to poke fun at earlier stories about aliens, especially those written by Reverend Thomas Dick, who once said that the moon alone had 4.2 billion inhabitants. But readers were so eager to believe that they failed to catch the joke, and were completely fooled. Even Yale University scientists were duped. Finally the *Sun* admitted the articles were a con, and referred to them as the "The Great Moon Hoax." Most readers thought the whole thing was funny, and kept buying the newspaper.

Before Jesus comes again, false prophets claiming to be Christ, "will appear and perform great signs and miracles to deceive even the elect—if that were possible." Are you one of the elect? Ask God to make the Scriptures clear to you today so you won't be fooled.

Woman's World

You must certainly give [women] property as an inheritance among their father's relatives, and turn their father's inheritance over to them.
Numbers 27:7, NIV.

Girls, can you imagine not being allowed to do something as simple as voting in an election? Did your mom vote in the last presidential election? Are you allowed to vote in school elections, are only the guys given that privilege? What a question! Of course, you can vote. Besides, women make up more than half the voters in American politics. But only recently have women had that privilege. Women were considered too emotional to vote. Too delicate to think about such serious matters. Women were not allowed to vote, they couldn't own land, or take a public office, or go to college with men. Women in the U.S. had none of these rights 150 years ago. Unfortunately, Canadian women lagged behind U.S. in gaining this important right.

The women's rights movement began in the mid-1800s when Elizabeth Stanton and Lucretia Mott showed up in Washington. They worked to get women the right to go to any college they wanted, and to get jobs that were usually given to men. But the right to vote was still a dream. In fact, it took another 50 years of hard work before things began to change. In the 1890s Wyoming became the first state to grant women the right to vote. By the beginning of the twentieth century, women's roles in society were changing. With the growth of cities women were working more outside the home and having fewer children. During World War I it was necessary for women to help in the factories because so many men were fighting, and that changed men's attitudes toward women. And then on this day in 1920, history did an about-face. On August 26 the U.S. Federal government passed the nineteenth Amendment. It was now every woman's constitutional right to vote.

Today women have more rights than ever. Women serve in the military, and own their own businesses too. But the U.S. still has some problems. In many places women still have trouble getting equal pay for equal work. As far back as ancient Israel, women have been working to get their rights. Four women came to Moses because their father had died and not left them an inheritance. That's the way it was in those days. Women couldn't own land. But God agreed with the four daughters and changed the laws of the land, giving the women permission to own their land. Isn't God good?

War

But there is no peace for the wicked, says the Lord.
Isaiah 48:22, NLT.

How many wars has the United States had since it declared its independence in 1776? At least 12. How many wars have there been in the history of the world? Who knows! How many wars are going on at any one time in the world today? Well, what defines a war? According to one definition, 1. It must involve armed struggle by at least one province or state against another. 2. It must be formally declared to be a war. 3. It has existed for at least six months. Fifteen years ago there were 27 active wars in the world. Today, according to that definition, there are 42 wars going on today. Tomorrow there may be less . . . or more.

The United Nations defines major wars as conflicts bringing 1,000 battlefield deaths per year. With that definition, in 1965 there were 10 major wars under way. In 2003 there were 15. As of 2005, there were eight major wars under way and about two dozen lesser ongoing conflicts. What makes these wars really bad is that most of the victims are civilians. Today, more than 75 percent of those killed or wounded during war are not even soldiers.

Africa has more problems with war than any other continent, and has had more than 20 major civil wars since 1960. Among these are Rwanda, Somalia, Angola, Sudan, Liberia, and Burundi.

No one in their right mind would really want a war, would they. In their right mind, is the key word here. But there are lunatics in this world, dictators who hold their countries ransom and crave the power and wealth war may bring them. Still, most governments and peoples of the world don't want war.

On August 27, 1928, a law was made outlawing war. It was called the Kellogg-Briand Pact, and was signed by 15 nations, including France and the United States. But good intentions can only go so far. Within 11 years major countries launched themselves into the most costly war the world had ever seen, both in money spent and in lives lost—World War II.

For those who are at war with God, there will never be peace. Jesus says that if we take up the sword, we must perish by the sword. That makes sense. Whether it's inspired by right or wrong motivations, war always costs something priceless. Peace. Security. Money. Our sons. Our daughters. One day there will be no more war, but for now, it's hard to wait.

The Foolishness of the Cross

For the message of the cross is foolishness to those who are perishing, but to us who are being saved it is the power of God.
1 Corinthians 1:18 NKJV

On August 28, 1938, a ventriloquist dummy was given a college degree. That's right. Ridiculous as it sounds, a well-known university of higher learning awarded a degree to a lifeless piece of wood. The dummy's name was Charlie McCarthy, and they gave him a degree titled "Master of Innuendo and Snappy Comeback." What were they thinking there at the School of Speech at the Northwestern University in Illinois! Of course, it was a joke. I think they should win the grand prize for the craziest academic award since higher education began.

Comedy is a popular form of entertainment and the reality competitions on TV are getting more and more common. But how many of them are worth your time? People you don't know doing foolish things, often lying and cheating, too, in the hope of winning some money. Turn on any of them and see how often they must bleep out the expletives used by the competitors. And comedy. It's rare to hear a really good comedian without a lot of crass language. But he or she is not a skilled comedian if they must rely on pottie language to get laughs. And the others: most can't manage without insults aimed at women or sex or race, and then of course there's the cursing that takes God's name in vain. Even Christians tolerate the stuff. People get used to the profanity and think less and less of it. "I don't even hear it. It goes right over my head," they'll say. Or: "It's just words." But it's impossible not to be changed by it. God takes it seriously, and I believe that He also takes seriously all the jokes about sex that deny the beautiful bonding experience between two people that God intended it to be.

Comedians must think that this is all people want to hear, but truly there are lots of people who'd prefer really good comedy without all the extras. But hey, if all this is so normal and there's nothing really wrong with it, why does the movie industry rate the shows as R or PG-13? Why schedule certain programs late in the evening so kids won't be up to hear it? Because they know its offensive, and not what we want our kids repeating. Paul reminds us that godliness and purity are not something the world really understands. He challenges us to choose the foolishness of the cross over the crass comedian any day.

Hurricane Katrina

But you are a tower of refuge to the poor, O Lord, a tower of refuge to the needy in distress. You are a refuge from the storm. Isaiah 25:4, NLT.

On August 29, 2005, Hurricane Katrina slammed into the Gulf Coast, causing billions of dollars in damage. The storm set off 36 tornadoes in Mississippi, Alabama, Georgia, Pennsylvania, and Virginia. Hurricane Katrina was a Category 4 storm, and the worst natural disaster in the history of the United States. The New Orleans mayor had ordered an evacuation of the city the day before, but more than 150,000 people didn't leave. Some just didn't want to, but many didn't have the money or the transportation to go elsewhere.

When it hit, the raging winds reached 145 miles per hour, cutting power lines, destroying homes, and turning cars into flying missiles. Before it was over, 80 percent of New Orleans was flooded to the rooftops.

Thousands found shelter in the New Orleans Convention Center and Superdome. Things got out of hand when food and water ran low. Tragically it took two full days for a full-scale relief program to begin. There were reports of looting and murder, but the police force had fled town too. Authority figures began pointing fingers at one another. Everybody blamed everyone else. Finally, military convoys arrived with supplies, and the National Guard was brought in to restore the peace. Bodies had to be identified, and the lowland levees had to be repaired.

It's estimated that the hurricane caused more than 1,300 deaths and up to $150 billion in damage to public and private property. Only about $40 billion of that total number was paid for by insurance. Because of the disaster, 400,000 people lost their jobs, and one million people had to leave their homes, something that had not occurred in the United States since the Great Depression. Fortunately, international aid poured in from all over the world, and $600 million were donated by U.S. citizens alone.

It was a tough time for everyone. Regrettably, it took far too long for the rest of America to come to the aid of the Katrina victims. God was with those who suffered through the hurricane and its aftermath, and if it hadn't been for this, many more people would have given up in despair. But sometimes it's important for God to have a human face and hands. Think of that the next time a disaster hits close to home.

Hitler's Siege of Leningrad

Hide me in the shadow of your wings. Protect me from wicked people who attack me, from murderous enemies who surround me. Psalm 17:8, 9, NLT.

World War II was the most costly war in world history. It involved more nations, more soldiers, and more loss of life than ever seen before in any war. Nazi Germany was the aggressor, and was soon joined by the Italian and Japanese governments. One of Hitler's main goals in the war was to penetrate Russia militarily and conquer the USSR.

On this date in World War II, German troops fully encircled Leningrad, in the USSR, cutting off all aid to the people of that city. That winter thousands fled east over frozen Lake Ladoga, though German shelling kept that to a minimum. Two hundred thousand Russian soldiers did their best to keep the Germans at bay, while every able-bodied person in the city helped build antitank fortifications.

They burned books and furniture in their homes to stay warm. By now they had eaten all the animals in the zoo, and next came household cats and dogs. They scraped the potato wallpaper paste off the walls, boiled their leather shoes, cooked grass, weeds, and pine needles, and even tried eating tobacco dust.

Tragically, some turned to cannibalism, and people were even murdered for their flesh. Near the end, people who lived in high rise buildings didn't even have strength to carry their dead family members down to the wagons coming to pick up the dead. They simply dropped the bodies out the windows to the ground below.

The siege lasted 872 days, and then in early 1944 Soviet forces finally forced the German army to retreat. On January 27 the siege was over, leaving at least one million soldiers and civilians dead. Many Christians in Leningrad lived through those hard times. Most of us will never be that cold or hungry, will never have to endure such terrible hardship. But whether it's needing a job or money, not having a place to live, a broken friendship, or loss of a loved one—everyone faces hard times. That's when it's especially important to hang on to God. Let Him be your shelter no matter what the storm.

Edison at it Again

Finally, brothers, whatever is true, whatever is noble, whatever is right, whatever is pure, whatever is lovely, whatever is admirable— if anything is excellent or praiseworthy—think about such things. Philippians 4:8, NIV.

On this day in history, Thomas Edison made history—again. On August 31, 1897, he took out a patent on an invention he had made called the Kinetograph, or what would later be called a movie camera. He wasn't the first one to develop all the ideas, but he was the one who put the pieces all together.

To build a camera, he needed several components—the camera part, a light bulb, a viewer, and of course the film to record the movie on. Edison's Kinetograph used a camera and celluloid film, both of which had already been invented by a photography pioneer named Eastman. And of course Edison invented the light bulb and viewer to be used in the projector part of the camera. Edison then built a small movie studio that could be rotated to give it the best possible sunlight.

The first movie cameras were based on still photography, which took the concept a step further in something called sequential motion. This was done, for example, by setting up 24 cameras attached to trip wires stretched across a racetrack. As a horse ran, he tripped each wire, making the shutters snap. The series of photos could then be projected in quick succession to resemble what looked like pictures in motion. Another idea of making movies was based on a rotating camera, something like the repeating Gatling gun, where pictures were taken in a rapid sequence by a rotating barrel cartridge.

Movies are just one of the legacies Edison left us with. Others include the light bulb, phonographs, and batteries. Most people are surprised to find out that Edison invented a version of the movie camera, but he was a talented and brilliant man. Of course he had no idea how much his movie camera would change the world of entertainment. Live stage shows were the thing of his day, but Edison's movie camera would begin to change that forever.

Most movies today are not worthy of our time and money. They aren't destined to become classics, and they are definitely not what Jesus and His disciples would have checked out at the local Jerusalem video store. Make a choice today to watch only movies that honor God.

The Ship Is Found

You will seek Me and find Me, when you search for Me with all your heart.
Jeremiah 29:13, NKJV.

Books have been written about it. Broadway shows have been performed. Movies have been filmed. Its story is one of the best known in America today. When the *Titanic* sank in 1912, it disappeared, gone forever to its watery grave. No one ever hoped to see it again, but that was before the age of high-tech submarines and video photography.

In 1985 on this day in history the famous ship was finally found buried beneath two miles of water. Robert Ballard and his team of scientists discovered the old ship where it had lain on the Atlantic Ocean floor for almost three quarters of a century. Seventy-three years before, on a spring day in April, the *Titanic* had left the British port of Southampton, England, on its maiden voyage across the Atlantic Ocean.

At that time it was one of the largest ships on the ocean and was almost like a floating city. All the newspapers of the day said that the *Titanic* was unsinkable because it had airtight compartments in the bottom of the ship. These compartments could be sealed off from the rest of the ship in case of an emergency. One official was heard to say, "Even God Himself couldn't sink this ship!"

Unfortunately, the ship did sink. After only a few hours at sea the *Titanic* entered a stretch of foggy, iceberg-filled waters, and side-swiped one, ripping a 300-foot gash in its bulkhead. In less than three hours the floating city settled in the water, broke into two parts, and then sank to the bottom of the Atlantic.

And that's where Mr. Ballard found in it 1985 by using special sonar equipment and a robotic submarine called Argo. The two large parts of the *Titanic* and many smaller pieces were lying just where they had sunk so many years before. At last, after many years of searching, the mighty *Titanic* had finally been found.

Jesus told many stories about things that were lost and later found—a sheep, a coin, buried treasure, a boy. Usually the more valuable something is the more we'll risk in finding it. Jesus said that if you want to find Him and get to know Him better you'll search for Him with all your heart. That doesn't mean Jesus doesn't want to be found; it just means He's worth a lot.

When London Burned

But a tiny spark can set a great forest on fire. And the tongue is a flame of fire. It is a whole world of wickedness, corrupting your entire body. It can set your whole life on fire, for it is set on fire by hell itself. James 3:5, 6, NLT.

On this day in 1666, the Great London Fire began. Thomas Farrinor, the king's baker, failed to properly put out the oven fire before going to bed.

But the Great Fire of London was a disaster waiting to happen. Someone should have seen it coming. London was a city of medieval houses made of oak timber. The walls of some poor homes from the lower side of town were covered with tar. This kept out the rain, but made them into tinder boxes should there be a fire. The streets were narrow, and houses were crowded close together, making it easy for fire to leap from one house to another. And the firefighting equipment? The only firefighting brigades were the ones that neighborhood people made themselves—lines of people armed with pails of water that had to be filled and refilled at ancient broken-down hand pumps.

And then it happened. In the early morning hours, smoldering coals ignite firewood that is stacked by the oven in the baker's kitchen. A fire breaks out on Pudding Lane near London Bridge, and leaps the street to the stables at the Star Inn. From there it soon spreads to warehouses on Thames Street that are filled with flammable materials like lamp oil, spirits, and coal. A strong easterly wind fans the flames, turning the fire into a blazing inferno. People rush from their homes by the thousands, dragging their families and possessions into the Thames River. The Great Fire of London was so big it could be seen 30 miles away. In the end it burned 13,000 homes, 90 churches, and 20 public buildings. One hundred thousand people were left homeless. Within days, King Charles II began rebuilding his capital. To prevent future fires, new houses were built of brick or stone. Streets and alleys were made wider, but even so, there were still no fire departments in London until the late 1700s.

The book of James compares a flame of fire to the human tongue. Words start small, but can become a raging inferno of pain and suffering to those they touch. Think of the words you use with your parents, and teachers, and even your friends. Could any of them start a fire? Give your tongue to Jesus today. He'll help you put out those fires before they get started.

Back to the Future

Then Joshua spoke to the Lord . . . , and he said . . .
"Sun, stand still over Gibeon; and Moon, in the Valley
of Aijalon." So the sun stood still in the midst of heaven,
and did not hasten to go down for about a whole day.
Joshua 10:12, 13, NKJV.

In 1752, England adopted a calendar change that moved the calendar ahead 10 days. The people went to bed on September 3 and woke up on September 14! This took care of 10 days the calendar had already gained. You see, a year is actually 365 and a quarter day long. After enough years have passed, whole days must be added to your calendar. Every four years an extra day in February takes care of the problem, but England hadn't come up with that solution yet.

If you gained an extra quarter day each year, and you never had a leap year, after 40 years you'd be ahead 10 days on the calendar. And thus the calendar change—a jump ahead into the future, and a drop of 10 days from the calendar. Can you imagine that! Most of us don't think about what that kind of change would do to our everyday lives. Maybe it wouldn't change things much for students, but for adults it would be disastrous. Kids would lose 10 days off the school year, and that might be cool, but adults (and some teens) would lose ten days of work. But credit card companies would still want their monthly payment. Banks would still want you to make your mortgage payment. It would be like one great big daylight-savings-time clock change, except we'd be moving our calendars ahead, instead of our clocks. Our calendars in our computers would have to be reset too.

There's a story in the Bible that tells about a time change. It happened in the days of Israel when they had just entered the Promised Land. Joshua and the Hebrew army were fighting a battle, but the battle wasn't yet over, and daylight was going fast. "Then Joshua spoke to the Lord . . . , and he said . . .' Sun, stand still over Gibeon; and Moon, in the Valley of Aijalon.' So the sun stood still in the midst of heaven, and did not hasten to go *down* for about a whole day."

Now isn't that incredible! Joshua asks God to freeze the sun in place, and God grants him the favor. The tribes go on to fight for another 24 hours, and they win the battle.

What a fantastic story! There has never been a day anything like it, because the Lord listened to the prayer of a man.

Great Was the Fall of It

Then the iron, the clay, the bronze, the silver, and the gold
were crushed together, and became like chaff from the summer
threshing floors; the wind carried them away so that no trace
of them was found. And the Stone that struck the image
became a great mountain and filled the whole earth.
Daniel 2:35, NKJV.

Humpty Dumpty sat on a wall / Humpty Dumpty had a great fall / And all the King's horses / And all the King's men / Could not put Humpty together again.

As far as we know no prophecy exists foretelling Humpty's great fall. We learn of his fate after the fact in a nursery rhyme. In the case of the empire of Rome (represented in the text above as iron mixed with clay) and for the three great ancient kingdoms preceding Rome (the bronze, the silver, and the gold), prophecy played a vital part in their stories.

Years before the four kingdoms fell, God Himself revealed their ultimate demise in a dream given to a young man, Daniel, living in the seventh century B.C. in the gold kingdom of Babylon. He wasn't a native Babylonian. He was a Hebrew, teen-aged captive of the Babylonians serving in the king's house. Early on he "purposed in his heart that he wouldn't defile himself." He wouldn't forsake the ways he had been raised to respect. Because Daniel trusted God with his life, God could trust Daniel with such a momentous prophecy.

Fast forward to the year 475 A.D. Six centuries have passed . . . Jesus Christ is born.

Then another five centuries go by; another teenager comes on the scene, this time in Rome. He's called Romulus Augustulas. At age 14 he's declared emperor by his father, the Roman general, Orestes, who, of course, has other political fish to fry and rules in his son's name for a year.

Then it was all over. Remember God's prophecy that was entrusted to the young man Daniel? The Stone he had spoken of so long before in chapter 2 struck the iron empire, and on September 4 in 476 A. D. Rome fell. A German barbarian named Odoacer defeated and killed General Orestes, took Ravenna, the capital of the Western empire, and carried away the young Romulus who died later as his prisoner. Romulus Augustulus is generally recognized by historians as the last emperor of the Western Roman Empire. Like Humpty Dumpty, the empire broke into many pieces and was never put together again. God's Word is true. You can take it to the bank.

A Good Reputation

A good name is rather to be chosen than great riches,
and loving favor rather than silver and gold.
Proverbs 22:1.

Jesse James, who was born on this day in 1847, probably would not have agreed right off with the above text. Or maybe he just thought he could have a daring reputation as well as silver and gold. There are some people who read the story of his life as a famous outlaw and say they think that he was a gallant Robin Hood—you know, stealing from the rich to give to the poor. Others see him as a vicious murderer. Whichever it was, few world characters have attracted such worldwide fascination as the legendary Jesse Woodson James.

Jesse and his older brother Frank had a troubled beginning. As young men, even before the American Civil War (1861-1865), they joined the Quantrill gang and raided border towns between Kansas and their home state of Missouri. After the Civil War Jesse and his brother continued their attacks along the line between the North and the South. Evil became part of their lives as they went on a wild rampage of stealing and killing that lasted for several years. They stole from banks, but it was the railroads that seemed to get hit the hardest. Contrary to rumors, the times they robbed payroll trains and then shared the loot with common country folks weren't as common an occurrence as folklore would have us believe.

Jesse went from bad to worse, driven on by the excitement and support of his partners in crime. Their reckless deeds eventually led to execution for many in the gang and for Jesse himself. But it's worse than that! Jesse wasn't even sure he could trust the men in his own gang, and with good reason. The men were all desperados, running somewhere, from someone or something. Jesse shouldn't have been surprised when Robert Ford, a member of his own gang, shot him in the back of the head in his home in Saint Joseph, Missouri.

Why would a member of Jesse's own gang want to betray a friend and partner in crime? The reward money of course. All $10,000 of it. The irony of it all is that blood money like this never did Jesse and his gang much good. And when Robert Ford went to collect the reward money for shooting Jesse, the authorities arrested him for murder.

To have a good name is like gold. If you choose to trust Jesus and love Him, He will help you build a good name and reputation that will stand the test of time and eternity.

September 6

Magellan Circles the Globe

And they shall wander from sea to sea, and from the
north even to the east, they shall run to and fro
to seek the word of the Lord, and shall not find it.
Amos 8:12.

What's the longest trip you've ever taken? Across the state? Across the country? To Europe or Asia? On this day in 1522, Ferdinand Magellan's convoy of ships—or what was left of it—arrived back in Spain from its voyage to circumnavigate the world. Actually, only one ship, the Vittoria, made it back in one piece. The others all were wrecked or abandoned along the way, and Magellan himself didn't make it. He was attacked by Philippine nationals and died there while on one of the islands.

But his famous voyage was the first of its kind. For nearly three years his fleet of five ships and 270 men had been at sea in search of a western sea route to the rich Spice Islands of Indonesia. In the process, Magellan also did something no one else had ever done in modern times—circumnavigated the globe. His ships sailed across the Atlantic from Africa to Brazil, down around the frigid southern tip of South America, and out across the endless ocean to the west. The waters of this sea were almost too calm to sail, so they called it the Pacific. He and his men endured starvation, scurvy, and attempted revolts by mutineers. By the time they reached the island of Guam, the men were out of food, had eaten all the rats on board ship, and were chewing the leather on their boots to keep themselves alive.

When Magellan died from a poison arrow in the Philippines, Elcano, one of Magellan's captains took charge of the two remaining ships and sailed on to Moluccas. After filling the ships with cargos of spices, one ship attempted unsuccessfully to sail back across the Pacific. The other headed west across the Indian Ocean, and down around the southern tip of Africa. Only Elcano, 17 sailors, and four Indians survived to reach Spain in September of 1522.

Some people think they must circle the globe in service for Jesus. But it's not always necessary. Seeking for God where you are can be just as effective, because God is right there beside you. Amos said that in the last days people will go in search of God from sea to shining sea, and from north to South. In desperation they will run everywhere looking for God, but they won't find Him, because the day of salvation will have passed.

Uncle Sam

*To him who overcomes I will give some of the hidden manna
to eat. And I will give him a white stone, and on the stone a
new name written which no one knows except him who receives it.*
Revelation 2:17, NKJV.

On this day in 1813, the United States gets its nickname, Uncle Sam. The name was borrowed from Samuel Wilson, a meat packer from Troy, New York, who hauled in barrels of beef to the United States Army during the War of 1812. Wilson stamped the barrels with "U.S." for United States, but soldiers began referring to the food as Uncle Sam's. Local newspapers picked up the story and eventually the name stuck. Uncle Sam became a trademark nickname for the U.S. Federal Government.

Fifty years later in the 1860s and 70s, a political cartoonist named Thomas Nast revived the popular image of Uncle Sam. Nast added a few touches to Uncle Sam's image by giving him a white beard and a stars-and-stripes suit that we see on posters of the character today. Nast is also famous for creating the image we now have of Satan Claus, and also the donkey and elephant symbols used by the Democratic and Republican political parties.

But probably the most famous image of Uncle Sam was one created by James Flagg. Flagg's image shows Uncle Sam wearing a tall top hat and blue jacket, and he's pointing straight ahead at the viewer. This portrait of Uncle Sam with the words "I Want You for the U.S. Army" was used as a recruiting poster during World War I.

Wilson was buried in his hometown of Troy, New York, which today proudly calls itself "The Home of Uncle Sam." Now that's a nice way to go out. In 1861, the United States Congress recognized Samuel Wilson as the father of our national symbol for Uncle Sam. It couldn't have happened to a nicer man.

Some day when Jesus comes again, we're all going to get a new image, and a new name. But unlike Uncle Sam, we won't look old and gray. We'll be young and attractive, and full of life. We won't remember all the bad times we had while here on earth. We'll only know that we are so glad to be with Jesus. Jesus himself will welcome us to heaven, and He will be the One to give us our new name. The name will describe us perfectly because we will have overcome through Jesus.

Star Trek

*When I look at the night sky and see the work of your fingers—
the moon and the stars you set in place—what are mere
mortals that you should . . . care for them?"*
Psalm 8:3, 4, NLT.

On September 8, 1966, the crew of the U.S.S. *Enterprise* took off on its first mission to "boldly go where no man had gone before." OK, they didn't really launch a space ship, but with the premiere of *Star Trek*, the sci-fi space television series, began.

And it wasn't that successful, lasting only three years and never rating better than number 52 on the network. But it was a hit with its fan base, and down through the years its popularity has grown by leaps and bounds. Gene Roddenberry, the creator of the series, had no idea what a gold mine he had, and no one would have predicted *Star Trek's* rise to fame—not the writers, not the producers, not the television networks, not even the fans who were loyal from the start.

So what's the big deal about *Star Trek*? The comical cardboard-foil sets and often silly subplots came to be less-than-serious trademarks of *Star Trek*, but it was the underlying message of the show that seemed to appeal to everyone. The space frontier, the gadgets of technology that allowed for transporting across time and space, the arguments between a stubborn Vulcan and crazy doctor, matching wits with creatures sometimes awesomely appealing and sometimes hideous . . . That was what kept everybody from writing off the show completely, and eventually inspired a series of cartoons. From there it built in intensity to trigger a series of spinoff movies—six in all. Then it was *Star Trek: The Next Generation*, and *Star Trek: Deep Space Nine,* and *Star Trek: Voyager,* and lots of movies and book deals to go around. The *Star Trek* books are now published in 15 languages, and *Star Trek* conventions for Trekies are held all over the United States. And the greatest honor of all? In 1992 the National Air and Space Museum in Washington, D.C., honored the original *Star Trek* TV series with exhibits of the 80 original costumes, props, and models from the show. The museum even displays Mr. Spock's pointy ears and a piece of the command deck from the *Enterprise*.

Unfortunately, *Star Trek* never left much room for God, the Creator of the universe. It fantasized more about the accomplishments of future man. God doesn't want us to become obsessed with a time and space that isn't reality. The far reaches of space should inspire us, but only because Jesus will someday take us there.

USA Gets Its Name

*"A good name is to be chosen rather than great
riches, loving favor rather than silver and gold."*
Proverbs 22:1 NKJV

On this day in 1776 the name, United States of America, became the official title of the united 13 colonies. The Second Continental Congress voted the new name in on that day—but at great cost. For the next eight years the newly formed United States fought a long, hard war for independence in which 25,000 lives were lost, and 25,000 more were wounded. It cost the U.S. federal government about $37 million, and the 13 states acquired another $114 million in debt. In today's dollars that would be about $62 billion.

The United States were free, but it was a weak, young nation with no political influence worldwide. It had no standing army, and very little experience in world trade. The 13 original colonies were now the 13 United States, but none of this would become official until well into the 1780s when the war was won.

Even after our independenc, we hardly knew what we were doing. It took nine years before the final draft of the U.S. Constitution was written, and another four years to get the Bill of Rights in hard copy. We had no major manufacturing industries except maybe ship building, and cotton and tobacco production in the South depended on slavery. And then to add insult to injury, the U.S. had to fight the British again in the War of 1812. For two years the British had remarkable success, and even managed to attack and burn the White House.

But God has blessed the United States beyond our forefathers' wildest dreams. We have grown from a few upstart colonies to the greatest nation in the history of the world.

Dreams are made in America. You can get a job and buy a house. You can get three jobs, if you want. Our military is second to none, and our court system is one of the best in the world.

Our freedoms are the envy of the world—freedom to speak our minds, freedom to own a gun, and freedom to worship—and God should get all the credit.

All this, and still we help other nations. We've helped fight two world wars, conquered Communism, and helped victims of earthquakes, hurricanes, and tsunamis. Today we need to get back the reputation we've always had for being a nation that helps. After all, it's the responsibility we carry for receiving such blessings.

Nathan Hale's Regret

*No one can take my life from me. I sacrifice it voluntarily. For I have
the authority to lay it down when I want to and also to take
it up again. For this is what my Father has commanded.
John 10:18, NLT.*

Have you ever wondered what it would be like to be a spy? I think that spying has bad connotations for Christians. Is it even possible to spy without living a lie? We think of espionage and all that word means. Spies can end up killing, or providing evidence that leads to an enemy's death. It's certainly not the glamorous role movies make it out to be. If you're spying for your country, you're considered a hero. If you're spying for the other side, you're a traitor!

Throughout America's history there have been many spies, and Captain Nathan Hale was just one of them. On this day in 1776, General George Washington asked for a volunteer to go on an extremely dangerous mission: to spy for the Continental Army in preparation for the coming Battle of Harlem Heights. Nathan did what any brave soldier during the Revolutionary War would do. He volunteered for the job and became one of the first American spies to operate behind the British enemy lines. Disguising himself as a Dutch schoolmaster, he successfully gathered intelligence about when and where the British troops were going next. Unfortunately Hale was captured while trying to cross back into American-controlled territory. When the British officers found incriminating evidence on him they knew he was a spy, and executed him.

Today Nathan Hale remains a national hero because he was willing to give his life so the United States could be free from British rule. He fought and died for his country so we could have freedom to assemble, freedom of speech, and freedom to worship God as we please. It's said that right before his death he told his captors, "I regret that I have but one life to give for my country."

A long time ago Jesus came to this world on a mission of mercy. He wasn't a spy, but He knew He would die for the mistakes others had made. In order to accomplish His mission, He would have to die for the sins of every person who had ever lived. His famous words still ring loud and clear nearly 2,000 years later. "No one can take my life from me. I sacrifice it voluntarily."

911

He shall call upon Me, and I will answer him; I will be
with him in trouble; I will deliver him and honor him.
With long life I will satisfy him, and shew him My salvation.
Psalm 91:15, 16.

This is the anniversary of 9-11, the day the United States was attacked on American soil for the first time since the War of 1812. On a clear Tuesday morning, a Boeing 767 and 20,000 gallons of jet fuel crashed into the north tower of New York City's World Trade Center. The impact tore a giant burning hole near the 80th floor of the 110-story skyscraper. It killed hundreds of people instantly, and trapped hundreds more on higher floors. At first everyone thought it must have been a freak accident, but 18 minutes later TV cameras captured the terrible sight of a second plane slicing into the skyscraper like a knife into butter—and suddenly it was clear that the United States was under attack.

It is thought that the attackers were Islamic terrorists from the Arab world, angry at America's over involvement in the Middle East. Some of the terrorists had even lived in the United States, and had taken flying lessons at a flight school. Others had slipped undetected into the country. It's believed that the young men used box cutters to hijack the jets and turned them into guided missiles.

That same day a third jet crashed into the Pentagon military headquarters in Washington D.C., and then a fourth jet crashed into a field near Shanksville, Pennsylvania. It is believed that the people on board the fourth jet may have regained control of the jet from the hijackers.

Back in New York City, the south tower and then the north tower of the World Trade Center collapsed in a huge cloud of dust and smoke. Nearly 3,000 people died as a result of the crashes, including 403 firefighters, paramedics, and police officers. Of the people still in the towers at the time of the collapse, only six survived. Almost 10,000 other people were injured that day, many of them severely.

We still mourn for the innocent people who died in this attack and for the brave firefighters and others who gave their lives to try to save them. We thank God that despite such tragedies He is in control. God has promised to be with us in trouble and to give us long life in heaven, if not now.

September 12

Pictures in a Cave

He is not here; for He is risen, as He said.
Come, see the place where the Lord lay.
Matthew 28:6, NKJV.

On September 12, 1940, four teens entered a cavern and made one of the greatest archaeological finds of the twentieth century: the Lascaux cave paintings near Montignac, in Southern France. They could hardly believe their eyes. The cave walls and ceilings were covered with paintings in vivid reds, yellows, browns, and violets. Holding a small lamp, they went through room after room. Herds of horses, oxen, and deer stampeded across the walls. There were stags and cattle, lions, bison, bears, and wolves. When experts came in and counted, they found more than 1,500 pictures in all, including some mythical creatures. Only one human figure is depicted in the cave: a bird-headed man. It's obvious that the cave was used as a center for hunting and religious rites. The paintings may be among the most beautiful examples of cave art in the world, and they're thousands of years old. But what was so shocking is the incredible detail and depth of movement portrayed in each one.

The Lascaux caverns were opened to the public in 1948, but closed in 1963 because artificial lights were fading the vivid colors of the paintings. Algae was even beginning to grow on some of them. A replica of the Lascaux cave has since opened, and tens of thousands of visitor go through it every year.

For centuries historians and anthropologists had thought cave dwellers were uncivilized ape-like barbarians, but this discovery gave them real doubts. It showed that despite modern thinking, these cave dwellers of the distant past were intelligent and culturally developed. It could be that they lived in this cave to escape an epidemic or war. Maybe they didn't actually live there, but used the cave for special events.

The world has seen many archeological discoveries, but the greatest of all time was found in an empty cave near Jerusalem 2,000 years ago. Then again it's not what was found in the cave, but what was *not* found. Jesus had been buried there, but now the angels said, "He is not here for He has risen." The world was excited when the Lascaux caves were discovered, but think how ecstatic the disciples must have been when they discovered the empty cave tomb!

Poor Henry

As for man, his days are like grass; as a flower of the field, so he flour-ishes. Psalm 103:15, NKJV.

Carole's mailbox was like a million others that sit atop a roadside post. Sometimes she or her husband stopped their car on the edge of the road and took the mail from it. But Carole was home today, so she walked up her driveway to get the mail. At the exact moment that she stood in front of the mailbox a drunk driver slammed into her. She died almost instantly.

The stats vary from year to year. But every year in Canada and the U.S. thousands of pedestrians are hit and killed by cars. Henry Bliss, a 68-year-old real estate broker in New York City, has the unfortunate distinction of being the first fatality caused by a car accident. It was September 13, 1899, and Henry was stepping off a streetcar at the corner of Central Park West and 74th Street, when he was hit by an oncoming taxi.

While Henry was taken to a nearby hospital the driver was arrested and held on $1,000 bail. Henry died of his injuries the next morning. Charges against the driver were dropped, as the death was ruled accidental.

Can you imagine someone being killed by a car in 1899! You wouldn't think cars could even travel fast enough to do any damage. The driver couldn't have been going more than 18 or 20 miles an hour—the average speed of cars in those days. OK, maybe for normal car drivers. Aaron was a taxicab driver, after all.

Every year in North America around 8,000 pedestrians die from being hit by moving cars, and another 100,000 are injured. How does this happen? Well, people jog on the streets in the early morning hours wearing dark cloth-ing. Pedestrians listening through headsets step off the curb or sidewalk into the street without thought. Or they get distracted while talking on their cell phones and don't take care to watch for traffic. And one study showed that 34 percent of pedestrians hit by cars had been drinking,

We need to remember that humans are pretty fragile. We're resilient, but we can get badly hurt—and even die—when hit by moving objects. David wrote that people are like grass and wildflowers—living today and gone to-morrow. Only God can preserve us.

Star Spangled Banner

Great and marvelous are your deeds, Lord God Almighty.
Just and true are your ways, King of the ages.
Revelation 15:3, NIV.

The night was cool and rainy, and Francis Scott Key was on deck a British ship trying to help arrange the release of a special American prisoner. The War of 1812 was in full swing. On shore, Fort McHenry was being bombarded by the British warships, their rockets lighting up the night sky. Now and then in the red flashes of the rockets, Mr. Key could see the American flag hoisted over the fort's walls. Its colors rippled in the stiff breeze blowing up off the ocean, and Francis wondered if it could last the night. Would the Fort withstand the steady shelling? Would the flag finally fall, shredded to pieces from the explosions? At dawn Francis went up on board and saw that the flag still flew over the fort. Its blue stars, and red and white stripes still waved proudly in the morning sunlight and Mr. Key's heart swelled with pride. The date was September 14, 1814. Fort McHenry had stood the test of battle, and the flag was there to prove it. Francis was so inspired that he sat down and wrote a poem that was destined to make history.

The words have become one of the best loved songs in America. "O! say can you see by the dawn's early light, what so proudly we hailed at the twilight's last gleaming. Whose broad stripes and bright stars through the perilous fight, o'er the ramparts we watched were so gallantly streaming. And the rockets' red glare, the bombs bursting in air, gave proof through the night that our flag was still there. O! say does that star-spangled banner yet wave o'er the land of the free and the home of the brave?"

In 1931 it became the national anthem of the United States. Ever since then it has been taught to immigrants and school children and sung at just about every professional sports event in the U.S. It couldn't have happened to a nicer song.

One day soon we'll all stand on the sea of glass and sing a national anthem to the Lamb. John saw it all in vision. Don't you wish you could have been there to see it too? The sea of glass mixed with fire. Millions of God's people standing on it, victorious over Satan. His temptations are a thing of the past. Everyone is so grateful, and now they are singing an anthem that soars into the heights of heaven, dedicated to Jesus the Lamb.

Darwin's Iguanas

In the beginning God created the heavens and the earth.
Genesis 1:1, NKJV.

How in the world did the idea of evolution ever get started, and how has it become such a strong part of our science program in the United States, a country that was started on Christian ideas? It's a long story and has caused a lot of trouble for Christians.

For thousands of years people believed that the gods were responsible for the creation of the world. And then came along the Renaissance, a time when people began to debate everything on the basis of science and logic. And Charles Darwin was one of those scientists. He had studied medicine and theology at the University of Edinburgh in England, but had lost interest in both. Then a friend invited Charles to sail with him on a five-year cruise of the Pacific to study wildlife from a scientific perspective. Darwin said yes, and he never looked back.

On September 15, 1835, they landed on the famous Galapagos Islands where Darwin would begin to develop his theory of evolution and natural selection. Darwin's book *Origin of Species* suggests that lower forms of life evolved over time into higher forms. His conclusions were based on his study of finches and iguanas, among other creatures. At the same time many other scientists were studying geology and biology, trying to answer the question Where did life come from? Sadly, they did not go to the Bible for their answers. During the last 150 years evolution has become almost universally accepted as is the basis for science as taught in many schools. However, the theory of evolution requires faith, the same as creation.

Now many public school districts are saying it is wrong to teach the theory of evolution without the option of teaching creationism too. State governments remind schools that teaching creation is illegal because it forces religion on kids who might not want it. Yet, more and more public schools are demanding that they be allowed to teach creation side by side with evolution.

It's encouraging to know that Darwin himself had doubts about his theory. And are we surprised? If you know the God of the Bible, it's much easier to believe that He created the heavens and the earth. And there's a perk here, too. The same God who created us, offers us an eternal home in the earth made new. Now that's a deal you can't refuse.

A Place for Freedom

And the woman fled into the wilderness, where God had prepared a place to care for her for 1,260 days. Revelation 12:6, NLT.

On this day in 1620, 102 passengers left England to sail for what they called the New World and Virginia (actually what is now New England) where they hoped to settle. Half of them were seeking religious freedom from persecution in Europe. The other half just wanted to make money. They'd planned to leave England in August but the *Mayflower's* companion vessel developed serious leaks and finally the *Mayflower* left for America alone. For the first half of the Atlantic crossing the ocean was calm. Then the 90-foot boat met rough seas and storms that blew it 500 miles off course. After a 66-day voyage, the ship and its passengers finally landed at Cape Cod, Massachusetts. It was to be the first permanent European settlement in New England.

Almost immediately, a party of armed men went ashore to explore and find a good location for settlement. To their delight they found cleared fields and plenty of fresh running streams. It wasn't until after Christmas that the Pilgrims began work on crude wooden huts with straw thatched roofs. Snow fell, the ground froze, and food was scarce, but there was no way they could know how bad things would get. During that first winter, half of the colonists died from disease.

The next summer their health and spirits improved as they built better houses and the Indians helped them plant gardens. The Pilgrims were amazed at all the game available for them to hunt—white tailed deer, black bears, and wild turkey. That fall they decided to have a feast of thanksgiving, and Governor Bradford invited the local Indian tribes to celebrate with them. The new colonists never had it quite as bad again.

In vision 1,500 years before, John the Revelator saw quite a sight. A woman was running for her life and fled into the wilderness. When she could run no more, she discovered that God had prepared a place for her to be safe from religious persecution. The American colonies provided a fulfillment of John's vision for the Pilgrims. Today we have come full circle and now take the gospel to other parts of the world where people want freedom of religion too.

Quick Draw Judge

This is what the Lord says: "Maintain justice and do what is right, for my salvation is close at hand and my righteousness will soon be revealed."
Isaiah 56:1, NIV.

On September 17, 1884, a California judge broke all records for the numbers of criminals sentenced. In six minutes he disposed of 13 criminal cases.

Judge Allen had a reputation for that kind of thing. And when he started swinging his gavel, defendants in Oakland's criminal court did not stand much of a chance of getting an appeal. In Judge Allen's 40-years as judge, only one defendant in 100 was acquitted. The following copy of a trial in 1895 was printed in the Oakland *Tribune:*

"I didn't think I was drunk, your Honor," said Gus Harland.

"Not drunk?" said the court.

"Not very drunk."

"How drunk?"

"Well—I could see the moon."

"It was raining hard Sunday night when I arrested that man," said the officer.

"Six dollars or three days. Next."

Judge Allen was known for being notoriously speedy in his sentencing, but that was not commonplace in the early days of American courts. In the early 1800s, criminal cases were often made to wait for more frivolous settlements that involved personal problems. For example, a man named Henry Blake in Philadelphia was taken to criminal court by his wife "for refusing to come to bed, and then making too much noise, preventing her from sleeping." Today's courts would almost immediately dump such a case, thinking it petty and childish.

Contrary to what many might think, American courts do offer one of the best judicial systems in the world. They're not perfect, and they are a bit slow, granted, but they do err on the side of leniency. Most people prefer it that way because they don't like the thought of courts making mistakes and sending innocent people to jail. Will the guilty sometimes go free? Yes, but in the end God will take care of everything. He'll settle all accounts with the bad guys. You can be sure of it.

Accidental Poisoning

But the tongue can no man tame the tongue.
It is an unruly evil, full of deadly poison.
James 3:8, NKJV.

On September 18, 1987, a strange incident occurred in Brazil that shocked the country and the world. Two years before, the Goiania Institute of Radiotherapy moved its operations 600 miles away to a new location in São Paulo. Unfortunately they neglected to report to medical authorities that left behind in their abandoned headquarters was an old machine that contained a lethal radioactive chemical called Cesium-137. The piece of equipment stayed there for more than a year before two thieves one day stole it.

On September 13, the two men sold it to a local junkyard where five days later some of the staff took the machine apart and removed the Cesium-137. The glowing blue stone fascinated them, and unaware of its dangers, they broke it into pieces and took it home to their friends and relatives. By this time the radioactive chemical had been spread around so much that it was found to be as far as 100 miles away.

Within days the junkyard owner's wife noticed that workers at the junkyard were getting sick, and so were her friends and relatives. When she sent the workers to a doctor, it was found that they were all suffering from acute radiation poisoning. Eventually four people died from exposure, including one child.

But that's not all. Dozens of other friends and relatives were hospitalized for treatment, and nearly 100,000 people in the city had to be checked for radioactive contamination. Besides all this, 40 homes had to be demolished because they were found to have high levels of contamination. And there's more. Many people suffered psychologically from the ordeal, and fear of contamination spread, making people in other cities shun the families that had been exposed.

What's the lesson? Small amounts of something that appears harmless can have a deadly effect. The tongue is like that. It's a very small part of our bodies but it can cause lots and lots of damage. In fact, ordinarily harmless words that are used in the wrong way, at the wrong time, can be horribly destructive and have long lasting effects. Ask God to help you tame your tongue today so you can use it only for good.

His Brother, Ted

Deliver me, O my God, out of the hand of the wicked,
Out of the hand of the unrighteous and cruel man.
Psalm 71:4, NKJV.

In the 1990s the newspapers often ran reports about someone who sent homemade bombs to people through the mail. The killer's victims innocently open a package addressed to them—and set off some kind of a device that would trigger a homemade bomb. For 17 years he had continued on his killing spree, and by now the newspapers were calling him the Unabomber. His trademark signature as a criminal had been established in cities all over the United States.

A wave of national terror seemed to grip the country. People were genuinely frightened. Where would he strike next, and who would he kill or maim? How did he choose his targets?

Then one day he sent a paper he'd written to the New York *Times* and Washington *Post,* asking that these large newspapers publish it. If they did, he promised to stop mailing the bombs. On September 19, 1995, the Washington *Post* and New York *Times* printed the paper, hoping that someone would recognize the style of writing. Amazingly, someone did identify the writing style as that of Ted Kaczynski. It turned out that Ted graduated from Harvard, and got a Ph.D. in math from the University of Michigan. After buying some land in Montana, he'd built a cabin on the spot, and it was there that he had been building his bombs.

And who turned Ted in? His own brother, David Kaczynski. Knowing he had no other choice, David finally contacted the FBI. In January 1998, Ted was convicted. He was put in prison without the chance of parole. He had murdered three people with his bombs and caused injury to 23 more.

Sometimes we feel powerless to fight against evil. It surrounds us and makes our lives miserable. We want to cry out like David, "Deliver me, O my God, out of the hand of the wicked, out of the hand of the unrighteous and cruel man." And God can do that. He loves us so much that when we pray for deliverance, He's there to hear every word. Some day we will see everything clearly. We will know why there is so much suffering, and why criminals like the Unabomber have been allowed to live lives of evil and murder and mayhem. But for now we must live our lives as Jesus did, trusting that the heavenly Father will work things out for our good. Be assured, He has a plan, and we'll like it when we finally see it.

RR Land Grant

Don't let the wise boast in their wisdom, or the powerful boast in their power, or the rich boast in their riches.
Jeremiah 9:23, NLT.

Do you ever play Monopoly? Some of the favorite properties to own in Monopoly are the railroads: the Reading, Pennsylvania, B&O, and Short Line. Well, of course Monopoly is just a game by Parker Brothers, but the railroads in the old days of the western frontier were for real.

At that time the only way to get around was by wagon, buggy, or carriage, all powered by oxen and horses, of course. Public transportation along the rivers was by paddleboat steamer, and on land, stage coaches were the rage of the day. But it was the railroads that were really becoming successful. Miles of railroad ties and fingers of steel reached further into new territory every year, and maybe that was because they got some help. On September 20, 1850, President Millard Fillmore signed the first Federal railroad land grant act. This land grant worth 2.5 million acres was designed to encourage railroad companies to build railroads on the western frontier. The land for the railroads spanned several states and into western territory.

It worked like this. The government gave the railroad companies whole sections of land that checker-boarded the railroad lines through the western states. This was designed by the government so that the railroad companies would push west and conquer the frontier. It worked well for the big railroads, but the small farmers began to suffer for it. The railroads had all the power because they owned monopolies on the transportation of the day. When farmers and ranchers wanted to send their grain and cattle to market in the east, they had to pay to have it shipped. The railroads could charge any price they wanted, and if the farmers couldn't afford the price, too bad. By the turn of the century, railroads were among the most powerful companies in the U.S. When President Teddy Roosevelt came to office, he set out to break up the railroad monopolies, and fortunately he was successful at it.

Sometimes even today, it seems that the rich get richer and the poor get poorer. And that seems to make sense. It takes money to make money. But even if we have money, we shouldn't brag about it, and we should use it wisely. God is the one that gives us all our blessings. If we abuse or misuse these blessings, He could very well take them away.

Congress Prints a Bible

Your Word I have hidden in my heart, that I might not sin against You.
Psalm 119:11, NKJV

Sometimes we get so used to something that we don't think much about it. Like the Bible. Bibles are everywhere, and in so many versions. We take it for granted that we'll always have one. Or maybe we think that if we had to, we'd get along fine without it. Really? How much do you read your Bible? What difference would it make if it was gone and you couldn't get it back?

America was at war with the British. It had been going on for about three years, and had cut off many of the supplies Americans had been getting from Europe.

Printed Bibles were just one of them.

The situation had gotten so bad that in the fall of 1777, Congress asked the United States Committee of Commerce to see if it could import 20,000 Bibles from "Scotland, Holland or elsewhere." But there was war on the high seas, and no one was able or willing to take the risk. Three years passed. Then in January of 1781, a Philadelphia printer named Robert Aitken came up with an idea. He wrote to Congress, offering to print a copy of the Old and New Testament, and asked the United States government to officially endorse the project. If they would give him their blessing, he would be willing to print the Bible at his own expense.

On September 21, 1782, the United States Congress passed a law officially authorizing the printing of a Bible: "We highly approve the . . . undertaking of Mr. Aitken . . . and recommend this edition of the Bible to the inhabitants of the United States." Their desire was that it be used in the army and schools to help teach right from wrong. Not surprisingly the news made headlines on the front pages of all the newspapers. "Aitken's Bible Endorsed by Congress."

Now that's as close as our country ever came to endorsing one religion over another. The U.S. Government has never recommended one religion over another. But they did endorse a printing of the Bible, and that is worthy of praise. Printing was very expensive back then, and if you were going to print something, you had to be sure it would sell. Well, the Bible has proven time and again that it is a best seller. In every age it has been popular, and the early days of America were no different.

Conquistador Coronado Dies

But seek first the kingdom of God and His righteousness,
and all these things shall be added to you.
Matthew 6:33, NKJV.

On September 22, 1554, Coronado, the famous conquistador in search of the fabled cities of gold, died without realizing his dream. Twenty-five years earlier Coronado had begun a search for the Seven Cities of Cíbola that were said to have incredible wealth. All the legends said the walls of the houses in these cities were made of gold and filled with priceless gems. Too outlandish a tale to chase? Maybe not. Try reading about Cortez and the incredible wealth he found with the Aztecs.

For years Coronado explored much of the Southwest, but had been disappointed time and again. And then one day he reached the border between what is now New Mexico and Arizona, where he actually did find Cíbola. But of course it wasn't what he thought it would be. After winning a brief battle against a tribe of Zuni Indians, he found that he had conquered a small village built with adobe mud. There were no golden walls. Either he had still not found the legendary cities . . . or the stories were totally untrue. He was quite discouraged and thought he might abandon his search. And then while exploring the area of the Rio Grande, another officer in Coronado's army came forward with a tempting tale. His slave kept telling him about a mysterious city of treasure far to the north and east. It was his homeland of Quivara, and the slave would lead them to it if they would give him his freedom.

Excited again, Coronado led his troops off in search of Quivara. They covered territory in Texas and Oklahoma, and on up into Kansas. But again, when Coronado discovered who the Quivara Indians were, he was furious. They lived in simple huts and, like the Zunis, had nothing of value Coronado wanted. No gold. No silver. No precious gems. Coronado ordered the slave executed, gave up his quest for treasure, and headed home to Europe. He never did find the legendary cities of gold, and he died believing that he had been a shameful failure.

Jesus said that our focus should be more on the Kingdom of God and His righteousness than on money or gold. If we trust in Him, we won't have to worry about having enough things in this world. There are far more important things to possess, like a home in the heavenly City of Gold. It's just waiting for us in the sky. All we have to do is follow Jesus and stake our claim.

Billy the Kid

A good name is to be chosen rather than great riches . . .
A prudent man foresees evil and hides himself,
but the simple pass on and are punished.
Proverbs 22:1-3, NKJV.

You've heard stories about this guy. He went by several names—Henry McCarty, Henry Antrim, and William Bonney—otherwise known as Billy the Kid. On this day in 1875, the infamous Billy the Kid was arrested for the first time. His crime? Robbing a bank? Killing a sheriff or U.S. Marshal? No. For hiding a bag of dirty laundry.

Evidently, an older friend of his had stolen a bag of clothes from a Chinese laundryman and convinced the fun loving Billy to get in on the joke. Billy hid it for him, but when a policeman literally caught him holding the bag, he was thrown into jail to teach him a lesson. Back in the 1800s there was no leniency just because one was a young orphaned teen. While in jail Billy discovered he had a real phobia for confinement. After two days he managed to find a way up the jail's chimney, and escaped. Billy was so mad about being jailed for such a small thing that he vowed from then on he'd always be on the wrong side of the law. It's sad that he had no one to befriend him and help him get back on track. Unfortunately, his future crimes would be far worse than hiding a stolen bag of laundry.

Billy was born in the slums of New York City, and life for him was shaky at best. He never knew his father, and he and his mom moved often. She was said to be "a jolly Irish lady, full of life and mischief." But she had tuberculosis, a fatal disease in the 1800s, and died when Billy was only 14. After that, he was on his own. After the death of his mother he'd decided that he would be honest and work hard to get ahead. He was an unusually friendly young man. Billy's boss at a hotel where he worked said he was "the only kid who ever worked here, who never stole anything." Only after his unfair treatment for hiding a bag of dirty laundry did William Bonney, a good-natured boy, become so hardened that he became a ruthless murdering outlaw called Billy the Kid.

Billy would have been wise to contemplate where his life decisions were taking him. At only 21 he died leaving nothing but his legendary life of crime. What reputation are you making for yourself? Is your good name more important to you than money or fame? Pray that it is.

September 24

United States Supreme Court Began

As I looked, thrones were set in place, and the Ancient of Days took His seat. . . . The court was seated, and the books were opened.
Daniel 7:9, 10, NIV

Has anyone in your family ever been to court, maybe to serve on a jury, or even to testify? Perhaps they went to settle a small claim. Lots of people go to court to do that.

Courts in the United States run at the local, state, and federal level. The United States Supreme Court is one of the most important courts in the world because it sets the example about how a court system should be run. It decides which laws are right in the United States, and which ones are wrong.

On September 24, 1789, the Supreme Court of the United States was first formed. Six judges were chosen by President George Washington to serve on the Supreme Court, and later, in 1869, that number was increased to nine members.

Now, having to go before a judge is kind of scary. If you've ever gotten a speeding ticket you know that sometimes you have to go before a judge. If you go to court to settle an argument with your neighbor, it's likely that a judge will hear your case. And if you commit a crime and have to go to trial, a judge will no doubt pass sentence on you.

In the book of Daniel God is portrayed as a judge. Daniel saw Him in vision as the Ancient of Days, coming to sit on His throne of judgment. Daniel says there were thousands of created beings in that courtroom, watching as the books of good deeds and bad deeds were opened. The whole thing sounds scary, when you think about it. Here's a court that has accurate records of everything we've ever done. How does He do it? Electronic chips with digital readings? Superman-type crystals? Really now, if anybody would have a good memory, it would be God!

But we don't have to worry about being afraid of the judgment. Moses tells us that we serve a God who is merciful and full of goodness and truth. We also have the Bible as a guidebook to tell us what is right and wrong, and the Holy Spirit to help us obey. Best of all, God loves us so much that He forgives us when we sin and disobey the rules. Let's thank Jesus today that He's our redeemer, judge, and coming king. We can't ask for a better deal than that!

It's Not Really Red

The heavens declare the glory of God;
and the firmament shows His handiwork.
Psalm 19:1, NKJV.

On September 25, 1992, NASA launched a space probe to Mars called *Mars Observer*. It was yet another of 30 probes that have been sent since 1960 to help develop the space program. NASA's goal? To find out if the planet Mars can support human life. Unfortunately, before even a year had passed, NASA lost contact with the probe. To this day no one knows what happened. It was a real blow to all the efforts and money NASA had poured into the project.

Countless movies and sci-fi stories have been produced about alien life from outer space, and a majority of them, it seems, focus on the planet Mars. Of all the planets in our solar system, Mars is the most intriguing, and in some ways the most mysterious.

Did you know that although Mars is known as the red planet, it's actually not red at all? It's more butterscotch in color.

Did you know that Mars has the largest canyon in the solar system? If the giant gorge were on earth, it would be as wide as the distance from Los Angeles to Chicago.

Did you know that Mars has the largest volcano in the solar system? The gigantic cone is 341 miles (550 km) wide, and covers an area the size of Arizona. But that's not all. It's nearly 16 miles (27 km) high, compared to Mt. Everest on Earth, which is only about five and a half miles (nine km) high.

Did you know that mars has polar ice caps like the ones we have on earth at the north and south poles?

Did you know that it would take six months for a spacecraft to get to Mars, but the crew would have to wait a year and a half before returning? Mars and Earth are usually quite far apart in their orbits, but every two years the planets line up.

God created our planets for us to look at in our night sky, but He must have created them for some other purpose. Surely He intended for them to have some other function than to be mere heavenly bodies orbiting the sun. Did He, in fact, create them with the future plan that we would one day inhabit them when earth had run out of real estate. Some day we'll ask Him.

Death of Daniel Boone

Now therefore, arise, go over this Jordan, you and all this people,
to the land which I am giving to them. . . . Every place that
the sole of your foot will tread upon I have given you.
Joshua 1:2, 3, NKJV.

On this day in history, Daniel Boone died at age 86. He was probably the most famous frontiersman of his time. The year was 1820, and no man had become a greater legend in American folklore than Boone. He experienced untold hardships hacking his way through the forests of the Cumberland Gap, narrowly escaping attacks by wild animals, and fighting in hand-to-hand combat with the native Americans. On one occasion he hid in the loft of a tobacco barn when they were stalking him. His quick thinking saved his life. Boone was hiding in the loft, while the Indians waited on the floor below. Suddenly he jumped, armfuls of the tobacco leaves in his arms, surprising the Indians and choking them with clouds of tobacco dust.

Boone was born in Pennsylvania, into a Quaker family. He and his family moved to North Carolina, where Daniel began his lifelong adventures in the wilderness. He never learned to read or write much, but he quickly became an expert marksman, hunter, and woodsman. He and five friends crossed over the Cumberland Gap to explore what is now the state of Kentucky. He blazed a famous trail through the mountains called the Wilderness Road, and later settled in a place people called Boonesborough.

But there was never enough room for the pioneer. "Elbow room," said Daniel Boone. You may have heard those words, and they became Daniel's slogan in life. He honestly felt crowded if a neighbor built his cabin within sight of the Boone home. Daniel's wife, Rebecca, couldn't have been pleased too much with this unusual philosophy.

As an explorer and frontiersman Daniel Boone helped conquer a new land. Like Joshua in the Bible, he carved up the wilds of the frontier so that people could move on to a new life. Today we are challenged by God to get ready to go to the Promised Land of heaven. However, this time Jesus Himself has blazed the trail for us. He's already traveled the way before us, walking that road to Calvary, so we wouldn't have to. Thank Him that He did.

Radar Invented

For the eyes of the Lord are on the righteous,
and His ears are open to their prayers.
1 Peter 3:12, NKJV.

Radar! Cops use radar to catch speeders. Astronomers use radar in giant telescopes to receive messages from outer space. The military uses radar for surveillance of our enemies.

Radar was invented September 27, 1922.

Albert Taylor and Leo Young were technical scientists at the Naval Radio Aircraft Lab in Washington, D.C., and what they came up with was quite astounding! The two men had been working on the project for quite some time, when they finally discovered a way to help the Navy detect the approach and passage of ships or planes. But the really amazing part was that it could be done even in dense fog, darkness, or smoke screens. This was done through a machine that could transmit a signal, bounce it off an approaching object, and then pick it up later like an echo. You've seen radar equipment in movies. The signal can be seen as a blip on a screen to show how near the moving object is. When we use this technology under water we call it sonar. Submarines use sonar to help detect how close they are to the ocean bottom, and how close they might be to other submarines or ships in the water.

Some amazing animals use radar too. Bats use something like radar, called echolocation, to navigate and detect their prey. They use their vocal chords to make sounds, then listen for the echo to return to them from any object that may be in their flight path. It's why they can fly in dark caves without hitting anything. It also helps them know where insects are in the dark so they can catch and eat them. Dolphins and whales also use echolocation to communicate, travel at high speeds, and hunt in dark, murky waters. They do this by producing rapid clicks with their larynx through the cavities connected to their blowhole.

Radar is a lot like prayer. We send out our prayers to God so we will receive strength and encouragement from Him. But there's one major difference. Even if we don't feel like we're getting messages back, He's still there. He will never abandon us, even if we don't always follow His advice, and He always answers our prayers. Sometimes He says, "Absolutely," sometimes "No way," and sometimes, "I'm going to have to think about that one."

Deadly Epidemic

*And there will be famines, pestilences, and earthquakes
in various places. All these are the beginning of sorrows.
Matthew 24:7, 8, NKJV.*

September 28, 1918, marked the beginning of one of the worst disease epidemics in American history, and a parade in Philadelphia seems to be where it all started. A highly contagious strain of influenza had struck America, and it was proving to be deadly. Influenza is a virus that attacks the respiratory system, and then mutates very quickly to keep from being destroyed by the human body. The very old and very young are the ones most likely to die from it. This specific strain of flu had been gaining strength in the United States for several years, but it was not until 1918 that the rest of the world found out just how lethal the flu could be. The virus most likely came from a bird or farm animal in Midwestern American. It may have traveled among birds, pigs, sheep, moose, or even elk. Sooner or later, however, it mutated into a strain that could be spread among humans.

That fall the epidemic spiraled out of control. In the U.S., Philadelphia was hit the hardest. Its city morgue had been built to hold 36 bodies, and now was faced with hundreds of arrivals in just a few days. The best estimates say that five out of every 1,000 people in the United States died from the flu.

It appears that the flu reached Europe when 200,000 American troops arrived on the continent to fight in World War I. Not surprisingly the port cities of the world were the first to be affected. In Latin America, one in every 100 people died. In Africa, it was 15 per thousand, and in Asia the death toll was as high as 35 per thousand. Twenty million people died in India alone, and by the time it was all over, official estimates reported that worldwide, 30 million people were dead. In fact, more people died from this flu epidemic, than from all of the battles of World War I combined.

We would like to think that we can eradicate any disease, but it's not possible. In fact, as the earth continues to deteriorate the worst disease epidemics are yet to come. Whether it's swine flue, or avian flu, or AIDS, or a mutated form of tuberculosis, disease is part of Satan's plan to destroy God's creation. But God will triumph in the end and put a stop to sin and death.

Tylenol Murders

He shall call upon Me, and I will answer him; I will be
with him in trouble; I will deliver him and honor him.
With long life I will satisfy him, and show him My salvation.
Psalm 91:15, 16, NKJV.

September 29, 1982, began a string of bizarre poisonings that were called the Tylenol Murders. But the murders were not typical, if any murder can be considered typical. The first victim was a 12-year-old girl in Elk Grove Village, Illinois, who'd been sick, and took an extra-strength Tylenol capsule to feel better. Tragically, she died later that day. The capsule she took had been laced with cyanide poison. And then a triple tragedy: two relatives of one victim also died from the poisoned Tylenol, because they'd developed headaches because of the grief surrounding the other family member's funeral. During the next few days seven people died, all from the Chicago area.

Investigators soon decided that the Tylenol capsules hadn't been tampered with in the factories where they were made. That meant that someone on the street had taken the Tylenol bottles from store shelves, laced them with poison, and then put them back on shelves where they were later purchased. The drug company, Johnson and Johnson, urged people not to take the medicine, and offered a $100,000 reward to anyone that could give them information about the Tylenol terrorist. Then they recalled 264,000 bottles, and quickly put tamper-proof caps on a newly designed bottle. By the time the whole thing was over it had cost Johnson and Johnson more than $100 million dollars. Before the deaths, Tylenol was the number one over-the-counter drug in North America. Most people thought Johnson and Johnson would never recover from the disaster. However, within months, Tylenol was back on store shelves with a new safety seal.

God hasn't promised us that we won't die in this world. That is what living in a sinful world ultimately offers us. But if we give our hearts to Jesus and dedicate our lives to Him, we don't need to worry about it. Jesus has promised to be with us during times of crisis, and He can save us. All we need to do is call on Him. "He shall call upon Me, and I will answer him; I will be with him in trouble; I will deliver him and honor him. With long life I will satisfy him, and show him My salvation."

Meet the flintstones

A cheerful disposition is good for your health;
gloom and doom leave you bone-tired.
Proverbs 17:22, Message.

On September 30, 1960, the animated TV series, *The Flintstones*, premiered on the ABC television network. William Hanna and Joseph Barbera created the half-hour show, giving Americans a look into the lives and antics of two prehistoric families. It was new. It was funny. And the series was an instant success. In the series, Fred and Wilma Flintstone and their best friends, Barney and Betty Rubble, live in a prehistoric city called Bedrock. The couples face the everyday problems of a working family. Fred and Barney work at the rock quarry, and Wilma and Betty are stay-at-home moms.

The men drive a foot-powered car with stone wheels, and a canopy for a roof top. After hours the families do typical things with their friends—go bowling, watch movies, and attend the "Water Buffalo" lodge. They even have pets—a pet baby dinosaur and a saber tooth tiger. In 1962 and 1963, Pebbles and Bamm Bamm appeared as the daughter and adopted son of the Flintstones and Rubbles respectively.

The *Flintstones* went on to become the longest running, animated, situation comedy in prime-time television. It premiered on 30 September, 1960, and gained very high ratings in its first season, proving that prime-time cartoons could indeed be successful on TV. Rather than just for kids, *The Flintstones*, which was patterned after *The Honeymooners*, was created to appeal to the whole family. It was very popular with teenagers, and when it began to go down in the ratings in 1967, it was rebroadcasted as a form of "children's television." Cartoons are usually only a few minutes long, but the Flintstones changed that tradition too, lasting a full half hour.

It's fun to sit and watch a movie with the family once in a while. It's not a good idea to make TV the center of family life, but a few, well-chosen shows can help a family have fun together. Unfortunately, the average American family watches TV too often and too much. God knows that laughter is like medicine and can help us be healthy, but too much of a good thing can be harmful too.

The Miracle of the Seagulls

"Your crops will be abundant, for I will guard them from insects and disease"... says the Lord of Heaven's Armies. Malachi 3:11, NLT.

Statues of people are pretty common in the United States. Animal statues are less common, though war memorials often feature a man on horseback. But a seagull? On this day in October 1913, an unusual monument was unveiled on Temple Square in Salt Lake City, Utah. Dedicated to the seagulls of the Great Salt Lake, the statue was designed by Mahonri Young, a grandson of Brigham Young who was the leader of the pioneer Mormon settlement in Utah. But why a seagull?

In 1848 a plague of crickets attacked the first wheat crop the Mormon settlers planted in the area, and they feared the worst. They desperately tried to fight the hordes of insects, but it was useless. They could do nothing but stand helplessly by as the food that meant their survival was destroyed. When all else had failed and there was seemingly nothing they could do to stop the insects, they prayed, trusting that God would come to their rescue. And then it happened. A white cloud of seagulls flew in and began devouring the crickets. It was a miracle, and the settlers never forgot it. Seagulls did not live near the inland lake, and the fact that they showed up when the settlers needed them most, was truly a godsend and a sign that God was watching out for the Mormon pioneers.

But one of the strangest things about the whole story was the way the seagulls ate the insects. The birds would gorge themselves with the crickets, regurgitate the partially digested bodies, then once again gorge themselves with another cricket meal. This strange behavior allowed the seagulls to eat and destroy many more crickets than is possible for one bird. Apparently this is quite common for seagulls, but the fact remains that the birds came when the settlers prayed. Not surprisingly the seagull has since been named the state bird.

In spite of miracles such as this, there are always naysayers who try to explain away miracles of this sort. But that's OK. We will always have the doubters among us. However, we should never let them make our own faith weak. Instead we must be strong and continue giving our testimony of what Jesus has done for us.

The Meaning of forgiveness

But I say to you, love your enemies, bless those who curse you, do good to those who hate you, and pray for those who spitefully use you and persecute you.
Matthew 5:44, NKJV.

On October 2, 2006, Charles Roberts, a 32-year-old milk truck driver from a nearby town, entered an Amish school in Nickel Mines, Pennsylvania, and shot five Amish children before shooting and killing himself. He planned it well, bringing an arsenal of weapons, ammunition, tools, and other useful items in case of a long standoff.

He entered the one-room schoolhouse at around 10:30 a.m. and forced 15 boys and several women with infants to leave the building. Then he lined the 11 girls up against the blackboard.

Of course, as soon as the boys and women left the classroom they contacted the police. When they arrived a short time later they discovered that Roberts had barricaded the school doors with boards he'd brought with him. He had also tied up his hostages.

Then he talked to his wife for a few minutes by cell phone. Roberts said he was upset with God over the 1997 death of his baby daughter. He also confessed to several crimes that his wife knew nothing about. Roberts and his wife had three children. He had no criminal history or record of mental illness.

At approximately 11:00 a.m., Roberts spoke with a 911 dispatcher, saying that if the police didn't leave, he'd start shooting. Seconds later, he shot five of the students. When authorities stormed the schoolhouse, Roberts shot himself in the head. Two of the survivors told their parents that 13-year-old Marian Fisher, one of the slain girls, asked to be shot first. Apparently she hoped that by killing her, Roberts would change his mind and let the younger girls go.

The world looked on in amazement at the actions of the Amish. They visited and comforted Roberts' widow, parents, and parents-in-law. Some even attended his funeral. It was reported that an Amish man held Roberts' sobbing father in his arms for as long as an hour, trying to comfort him. The Amish set up a charitable fund for the family of the killer. And a grandfather of one of the murdered girls was heard warning some young relatives not to hate the killer, saying, "We must not think evil of this man."

What an incredible example of loving behavior after being spitefully used.

Attack of the Tiger

Stay alert! Watch out for your great enemy, the devil. He prowls around like a roaring lion, looking for someone to devour"
1 Peter 5:8, NLT .

Roy Horn and his magician partner, Siegfried Fischbacher, from Germany, met in 1957 on a cruise ship. Horn had actually smuggled a cheetah aboard the ship, which prompted Siegfried to suggest they become partners. Their show, which made two white tigers disappear and reappear, was one of most famous and well-attended shows in Las Vegas. The two had performed at the Mirage Hotel since 1990, earning an annual income of at least $57 million.

On October 3, 2003, a 380-pound tiger named Montecore mauled Horn during a performance. It just happened to be the animal trainer's fifty-ninth birthday. Not a very nice birthday gift, was it?

According to witnesses, Montecore, who had performed with the act for six years, bit Horn on the hand, pulled him to the ground, then grabbed his neck and dragged the performer offstage. Once offstage, the crew was able to subdue the tiger by spraying it in the face with a fire extinguisher. A stunned member of the audience recalled, "We just heard all this commotion behind the curtain, and you could hear Roy scream." Thinking the attack to be one of the show's illusions, people were slow to come to his aid. Shortly after the attack, his partner, Siegfried, informed the audience that the show was indeed over.

Horn, suffering massive blood loss, was rushed to a nearby hospital for treatment. He remained conscious in the ambulance and pleaded that Montecore's life be spared. He said that he was sure the tiger hadn't meant to hurt him. Horn suffered a stroke after the attack, and in the following months continued to have physical therapy while making a few appearances in a wheelchair. Unfortunately, Siegfried and Roy's show was closed permanently soon after the attack. They had given 5,750 performances. Montecore was quarantined for a time to make sure he didn't have rabies, and then released to live with the other animals the two partners keep in Las Vegas.

Do you like taking spiritual risks? Remember, the devil is like Montecore, just waiting to attack those who are unsuspecting.

White House Under Attack

A thousand may fall at your side, ten thousand
at your right hand, but it will not come near you.
Psalm 91:7, RSV.

On this day in history a military siege on the White House ended. After several days of fighting, tanks stopped firing, soldiers put down their guns, and both sides began to talk. Now, we're not talking about the White House in Washington, D.C. This White House is in another capital far away: Moscow, Russia. White House is a nickname the Russian people have given their government parliament building because it's painted all white.

The Communist government had collapsed two years before and everything was in chaos. Everybody wanted control of the new government that was forming, but the old regime from the Communist party wasn't going quietly. Two of the hardliners and their supporters had barricaded themselves inside the White House in downtown Moscow, refusing to even talk with President Boris Yeltsin, the new boss.

But it was all a show. After being shelled by tanks for 10 hours they finally surrendered on October 4, 1993. When the tanks started shooting it was scary for everyone, especially for Americans and other foreign workers living in Moscow. No one knew if a civil war might begin, or if foreigners would be safe. When it was all over, the famous building was now blackened where the explosives had hit it.

When times really get scary, Jesus says don't worry. He has promised us that He'll be with us no matter what happens. We don't need to be afraid. Today's scripture reminds us that thousands may fall at our side, but because God is always near us; we don't need to worry.

A mother hen hovering over her chicks is a pretty good illustration of what God wants to do for us. We're a lot like baby chicks, fragile and weak, just as the Communist leaders were who were fired on by the tanks. We humans don't have any real weapons to fight against Satan, but inside God's protecting hand we are safe forever. Today let's once again thank God for His protection.

World Walk About

I have fought the good fight, I have finished
the race, and I have remained faithful.
2 Timothy 4:7, NLT.

On October 5, 1974, an American named David Kunst became the first person to complete a round-the-world journey on foot. The trip took four years, wore out 21 pairs of shoes, and covered 14,500 miles to cross four continents. David had begun the trip in June 1970 in his hometown of Waseca, Minnesota.

After walking from Waseca to New York City, David dipped his hand in the Atlantic Ocean as a symbolic gesture. Then he flew across the Atlantic to Lisbon, Portugal, and continued across Europe and Asia to Calcutta, India. When he finally reached the Indian Ocean, he flew to Perth in Western Australia, and then walked clear across the continent to Sydney. A flight across the Pacific Ocean took him to Los Angeles, California, where he began the last leg of his journey. He walked from California back to Waseca, Minnesota, the place where the whole thing had started.

David carried a plastic scroll with him on his trip to document the walk. He had the mayor of every city and town where he spent the night, stamp and sign the scroll. By the end of the walk he had six 1' by 5' scroll sheets totally covered with stamps and signatures of officials from around the world.

David's brother John accompanied him on the first half of the journey. Bandits attacked the boys in the foothills of the Hindu Kush Mountains of Afghanistan, no doubt thinking they would collect a lot of money. David was wounded and John was shot and killed. After recuperating with the help of the American Embassy, David and another brother, Pete, started at the exact spot where John had been killed, and continued into Pakistan.

During his walk across Australia David met an Australian schoolteacher named Jenni. They fell in love and after completing his walk around the world, David returned to marry her.

Like David, you have been challenged to take an historic walk, but this one is for Jesus, and its effects will last for eternity. David won a bit of fame for his adventure—and a wife. When you complete your trek for Jesus, your reward will be a crown of life.

Tyndale Martyred

More to be desired are they than gold, yea, than much
fine gold; Sweeter also than honey and the honeycomb.
Psalm 19:10, NKJV.

On this day in 1536 William Tyndale was burned at the stake for his work in translating Bibles and smuggling them into England. Fifteen years before, he had become interested in the work of Erasmus and Martin Luther, both of whom were reformers in the translation of the Scriptures. A few Bibles had been printed in Europe, but most copies were still in Latin, a dead language that only the priests, monks, and bishops of the Catholic Church could read. More than anything, Tyndale wanted the common people to have the Bible to read in their own language. After studying Hebrew, Greek, and German, he went to work translating the Bible into English. On one of his trips to smuggle Bibles into England via a merchant ship, Tyndale was betrayed by a so-called friend and was thrown into prison where he endured the most inhumane treatment.

When the church finally gave him a trial 500 days later, it was a ridiculous charade. He was tried and convicted by the church for heresy, and sentenced to be executed in the prison yard. Can you believe it! The church, which was ordained by Jesus to spread the Gospel, was going to execute a man who was making copies of God's Word! Unfortunately, King Henry VIII, a Christian himself, did nothing to stop the execution.

Tyndale's last words were "Lord, open the eyes of the King of England." And God did. The reformer's prayer was answered three years later when King Henry VIII eventually did see the light.

William Tyndale, the father of the English reformation, the apostle of England, and a brilliant scholar, was used by God to profoundly change history. He bravely led the way for the reformers who followed him. Thomas Cromwell and Thomas More would continue Tyndale's work shortly after the martyr's death. And others, such as John and Charles Wesley in the 1700s, became even more influential in bringing the gospel to the common folks of England. God has always had His champions to shed the light of the gospel on the pathway to heaven. Time and again, when the way has seemed darkest, the light of truth has broken forth to bring the dawn. Don't be afraid to stand up for God. You can do great things for Him!

Worst Fire in U.S. in History

And did not know until the flood came and took them all away, so also will the coming of the Son of Man be. Matthew 24:39, NKJV.

Temperatures so hot they blister your skin. Winds like a blast furnace. The loud roaring as the flames rush toward you. You hold your breath until you're desperate for air. When, at last, you take a deep gasp the super-heated air scorches your windpipe and sears into your lungs, and you drop to the ground with just seconds left of life. The date: October 7, 1871. The place: Wisconsin. The conditions: extremely dry. Trees had dropped their leaves. Swamps and peat bogs had dried up. Fires were breaking out everywhere.

No one knows where the fire started. Perhaps in the dense Wisconsin forest or in the tinder-dry peat beds. It first spread to the small village of Sugar Bush, where every resident was killed. Such a fire creates its own hurricane-force winds, and this one sent 200-foot flames roaring through forests where the trees exploded from the 2,000 degree flames. Peshtigo, Wisconsin, its every building made of wood, was right in its path. It took 24 hours for the fire to reach it, but with the lack of communication, no one saw it coming. Two hundred people crowded into a tavern, hoping they would be safe, but all died. Others drowned when they fled to a nearby river. The next day rescue parties buried 350 people in a mass grave because they couldn't identify the charred bodies. Town after town was swallowed up until it had burned an area twice the size of Rhode Island. The blazing inferno killed between 1,500 and 2,000 people and destroyed approximately two billion trees. Because of the loss of human life, it is still considered the most devastating fire in American history.

During the months of extended drought preachers had shouted that the end of the world was upon them all—that they must repent because hellfire was coming. This message kept many from seeking refuge in time to save their lives. Believing that this was the end of the world, they awaited their fate.

Christ's coming to the world will be unannounced, just as the fires of Wisconsin. "As it was in the days of Noah," thousands in Wisconsin were unaware of the danger until it was almost too late. You and I know that Jesus is coming soon. Let's make certain that we're ready to meet Him.

One Day is *Not* as Good as Another

There are six days when you may work, but the seventh day is a Sabbath of rest, a day of sacred assembly. . . . it is a Sabbath to the Lord.
Leviticus 23:3, NIV.

On this day in 1990, the state of South Dakota decided to celebrate a Native American Day instead of the usual Columbus Day. Because Native Americans were here long before Europeans landed on this soil, and because it was one of the natives, Squanto, who taught the newcomers how to establish friendly relations with the Indians and how to plant crops, fish, and trap mammals for the fur trade, people decided it would be good to celebrate their contribution.

Of course, we might ask why any Native Americans would want to celebrate the coming of Columbus. His arrival was the beginning of the end of their way of life. When Columbus landed on the Bahamas in the Caribbean, he claimed the new lands for Spain and captured some of the Indians to take back to Europe. The explorers who followed him into the New World, enslaved the Indians, forcing them to work in mines and farm their plantations. All told, half of the Indian tribes that were conquered in the Caribbean, died from problems related to slavery.

However, when South Dakota chose to celebrate a substitute day for Columbus Day in honor of the Indian tribes and their rich history, that didn't actually make that particular day special. In reality, no day is more special than another just because a person says it is. The day they chose in 1990 was not an anniversary of any kind. It was just a day of celebration.

Something similar has happened with Sunday, the first day of the week. It has become a substitute for the Sabbath, God's special day. Many people worship on Sunday out of ignorance; they don't know about the true Sabbath. Some observe Sunday because that was the day Jesus rose from the dead. For some, Sunday is more convenient. And some worship on Sunday because they think it really doesn't matter. But it does! Exodus 20:8-11 tells us that God set apart the seventh day and made it holy. No matter the reason, it's impossible for a human to change God's holy day. The Sabbath simply *is*. No person can change what God established.

Vinland

Now the Lord had said to Abram: "Get out of your country, from your family and from your father's house, to a land that I will show you." Genesis 12:1, NKJV.

On this day in the year 1000, Leif Ericson discovered a place he named Vinland (or Wineland, because of the grapes and other vegetation). There is strong evidence that Ericson was the first European to set foot on North America, long before Columbus, but it's not certain where he actually landed. Newfoundland? Maine? Massachusetts? Ericson wasn't sure what he had found, and surely had no idea that he'd found a new continent.

Ancient stories told of a land far to the west, but no one in Viking history had ever seen it. Ericson was fascinated by the stories, and in 1000 set off with a crew of 35 men to explore. It's likely that they first reached Labrador and Newfoundland. They kept sailing south and stopped in a land Lief described as rich, fertile, and forested, where grapes grow. He and his men spent several weeks in "Vineland," then returned to Greenland with their ship filled with riches from the new land. Ericson described Vinland's weather as fairly warm with green grass everywhere. Was it a particularly warm year in North America? Was Leif further south along the eastern coast than historians have previously thought? Or was the weather then quite different than it is today? Maybe. In 1000, Greenland's climate, much further north than where Ericson landed, was warm enough for farming.

It wasn't long before more Vikings with their strange looking ships came to the New World. Today archaeological digs still find the remains of Viking settlements in Canada and the United States. Crude Viking huts have been unearthed, and stone altars chiseled with ancient Viking inscriptions to their god Thor.

Centuries ago, God called Abraham to travel to a new land of which he knew nothing. Like Leif Ericson, Abraham may have been an adventurer and ready to face the risks of the unknown. But unlike Ericson, Abraham worshipped the One True God, the Creator of heaven and earth. He had no fear of the ancient gods. Not Chemosh, or Molech, or Baal, or Ashtoreth. Abraham served the Living God who can make a delicate lily or the giant leviathan, who created billions of stars and newborn babies. And He can change hearts too. Through His Spirit He can bring us to repentance, and make us more like Him every day.

October 10

800 Children Die at Auschwitz

For God will bring every work into judgment,
including every secret thing, whether good or evil.
Ecclesiastes 12:14, NKJV.

On October 10, 1944, 800 gypsy children were murdered in the gas chambers of Germany's Auschwitz. World War II was nearing its end, and Hitler's hate of specific people groups led him to slaughter gypsy boys between the ages of 9 and 14.

Gypsies had been singled out early on for brutal treatment by Hitler's regime. He considered them as disease carriers and lazy people who were unwilling to do useful work. So they were marked for extermination, along with the Jews of Europe, from the earliest years of the war. Many of them roamed the countryside in caravans, earning their living as musicians, peddlers, and fortunetellers. To Hitler, the gypsies and their wandering ways were not at all like the hardworking Nazis. During the course of World War II he ordered that nearly 1.5 million gypsies to be murdered.

Auschwitz was made up of a group of camps, designated I, II, and III, as well as 40 smaller "satellite" camps. It was at Auschwitz II in October 1941 that the SS Gestapo created a monstrous killing machine, comprised of 300 prison barracks, four bathhouses used to gas the prisoners, corpse cellars, and cremating ovens. Thousands of prisoners were used for medical experiments.

A mini-revolt took place on October 7, 1944. While several hundred Jewish prisoners were being forced to carry corpses from the gas chambers to the furnace to dispose of the bodies, they blew up one of the gas chambers and set fire to another, using explosives smuggled in by Jewish women who worked in a nearby weapons factory. Of the 450 prisoners involved in the sabotage, about 250 managed to escape the camp during the ensuing chaos, but they were all found and shot. Those coconspirators who never made it out of the camp were also executed, as were five women from the weapons factory, after they were tortured for information on the smuggling operation. None of the women talked.

Someday in the earth made new there will be no more sadness or pain or death. The Gypsy boys who died at Auschwitz will run and play and experience the happiness Jesus meant for them to have as children. And God will wipe all tears from their eyes. What a day that will be!

Yellow Fever in Philadelphia

He will shield you with his wings. He will shelter you with his feathers. His faithful promises are your armor and protection. Psalm 91:4, NLT.

On October 11, 1793, yellow fever broke out in Philadelphia, Pennsylvania, in epidemic proportions. The death toll hit 100 that day, and by the time it ended 5,000 people were dead.

The first yellow fever outbreaks in the United States occurred in the late 1690s. Yellow fever, or American plague, as it was known at the time, is a viral disease that begins with fever and muscle pain. Next, its victims may become jaundiced, or yellow, as their liver and kidneys stop functioning normally. Some even suffer worse symptoms. Besides turning yellow, patients can vomit with bleeding. Many victims become delirious before dying.

In 1793, Philadelphia, with a population of 55,000, was America's largest city and its busiest port. That summer had been unusually dry and hot, and Philadelphia had all the necessary ingredients for an unprecedented health disaster. By July people were talking about the unusual number of flies and mosquitoes that swarmed around the docks.

That same month refugees from the Caribbean Islands increased to thousands as ship after ship unloaded them at the Philadelphia docks. A yellow fever epidemic was raging in the Caribbean at that time, and within weeks people throughout the city were experiencing symptoms.

By midOctober 100 people were dying from the virus everyday, and bodies were everywhere. Caring for the victims had put such a strain on the hospitals and mortuaries that the city government collapsed. Philadelphia was the capital of the United States government at the time, but congressmen fled the town like everyone else.

Like malaria, the yellow fever virus was carried and transmitted by mosquitoes. When a cold front finally killed the mosquito population, the death toll fell to 20 per day. Today there's a vaccine available that prevents yellow fever in much of the world.

Sin is our worst disease, but Jesus has provided the vaccine that can save you. The question is, are you willing to accept His solution to your sin problem?

Unlikely Hero

But Daniel resolved not to defile himself with the royal food and wine, and he asked the chief official for permission not to defile himself this way. Daniel 1:8, NIV.

War is a terrible thing! With tanks rolling across the battlefield, bombs exploding, and bullets flying around, things can get pretty scary. But when your country calls you to fight, you don't usually have a choice. Despite the war Americans are fighting in Iraq, most of us have never even been near a war. But in times past it was different. During World War II, with Germany and Japan trying to take over the world, many, many Americans were drafted or enlisted—in all, more than 16,000,000. And Desmond Doss was one of them.

Drafted into the Army, he refused to use a gun to kill the enemy and it caused him all kinds of trouble. He entered the military under the category of conscientious objector. Doss, however, preferred the term conscientious cooperator, because he did everything he could to cooperate with the military officers and soldiers. However, he also would not work on the Sabbath. It's not surprising that he was mocked and harassed by the men in his unit. But like Daniel in Babylonian times, Doss was faithful to his convictions, and because of that he was able to witness for God in a remarkable way.

As a medic, he was under fire in many battles. In one battle, atop a blood-soaked escarpment on the island of Okinawa, Doss lowered 75 men to safety, all the while under Japanese fire. During those long hours as he rescued one man after another, Doss kept praying, "Lord, help me get just one more. Just *one* more." Only when the last man was evacuated did Doss get himself to safety. Through this experience, and many others, the name Doss became a symbol throughout the 77th Infantry Division for outstanding gallantry far above and beyond the call of duty

When it was all over, on October 12, 1945, Desmond Doss was given the Congressional Medal of Honor, the United States' top military award, for noncombat achievements in the Second World War. It was the first time that a conscientious objector was given the nation's highest military award. And when Desmond was honored, God was honored, because Desmond had stood for what he knew was right, and depended on God to protect Him while he was doing it. Now that's inspiring!

Beatle Mania Begins

You shall have no other gods before Me.
Exodus 20:3, NKJV.

A sensation called Beatle Mania took hold of England on this day in 1963 when the Beatles appeared at the London Palladium, a local theater where groups could come and show off their talent to British TV audiences of up to 15 million people. Competition at the Palladium was fierce, and the Beatles knew this might be their one chance at stardom. After their first song at the beginning of the show it was announced "If you want to see them again, they'll be back in 42 minutes."

And indeed they were. The Beatles topped everything that had been done that night by closing the hour-long show with Paul McCartney asking the audience to clap and stamp their feet as they began singing "Twist and Shout." Newspaper reporters wrote breathless front-page stories about the screaming fans.

Although The Beatles' popularity had been growing steadily in England throughout 1963, their appearance at the Palladium suddenly launched them into the spotlight of the international mainstream media. Overnight, Beatlemania was the word being used to describe the mobs of screaming fans that would give the Fab Four fame and fortune for years to come in radio, TV, and newspapers. Their first album was followed by a string of 23 consecutive albums in the top ten of the pop music charts, and that record has never been broken since.

John Lennon told a London reporter, "Christianity will go. It will vanish and shrink. I needn't argue about that. . . . We're more popular than Jesus Christ now." In John Lennon's eyes they had become like God. So what finally became of the Beatles? Well, John Lennon was shot dead December 8, 1980, outside his New York apartment. George Harrison died November 29, 2001, of a brain tumor. The aging Ringo Starr and Paul McCartney have continued writing songs and performing their music on stage and in movies.

The Beatles are gone, but Christianity hasn't died. Our God still reigns. He's done a lot more impressive things than standing up to sing at the London Palladium or going on the Ed Sullivan Show or singing on American Idol. God's been busy for ages doing things such as walking on water, raising the dead, and creating the world. Now, that tops the Beatles any day, don't you think?

October 14

Cuban Missile Crisis Begins

And you will hear of wars and rumors of wars. See that you are not troubled; for all these things *must come to pass, but the end is not yet.* Matthew 24:6, NKJV.

On October 14, 1962, the Cuban Missile Crisis erupted when the United States discovered Russian missile sites under construction in Cuba. Photographs taken by a high-altitude U-2 spy plane offered undeniable evidence that Soviet-made missiles, capable of carrying nuclear warheads, were now stationed 90 miles off the American coastline in Cuba, and the two nations teetered on the brink of nuclear conflict.

Tensions between the United States and the Soviet Union over Cuba had been steadily increasing since the Bay of Pigs invasion when Cuban refugees, trained and armed by the United States, landed in Cuba and tried to overthrow the government of Fidel Castro. Though the invasion didn't succeed, Castro was convinced that the United States would try again. So he set out to get more military assistance from the Soviet Union. During the next year the number of Soviet advisors in Cuba rose to more than 20,000, and rumors began circulating that Russia was also moving missiles and strategic bombers onto the island.

Maybe Russian leader, Nikita Khrushchev, believed that the United States was indeed going to invade Cuba and so provided the weapons to stop it. Maybe it was a way to get the support he needed of the hard-line members of the Communist party back home in Moscow. Or maybe he had always been unhappy that the U.S. had nuclear missiles stationed near the Soviet Union, and putting missiles in Cuba might have been his way of balancing things out.

Two days after the pictures were taken they were analyzed by the CIA and presented to President Kennedy. This was a new sort of threat for the United States, who had fought most of its wars on foreign soil. During the next two weeks the United States and the Soviet Union would come as close to nuclear war as they ever had, and a fearful world awaited the outcome.

Wars and rumors of war are in the media blogs and on TV every day. Jesus warned us that it would be like this. He also told us not to worry, whether it's the Soviet Union or China or the terrorists of Arab nations. This just means that Jesus' coming is very near.

Better than the Belmont

*In my Father's house are many rooms; if it were not so, I would
have told you. I am going there to prepare a place for you. And
if I go and prepare a place for you, I will come back and take
you to be with me that you also may be where I am.*
John 14:2, 3, NIV.

What's the biggest apartment house you've ever seen? Nine stories? Ten?
Cities in metropolitan areas today have some pretty big ones that can
include many buildings. Some apartment complexes are made up of dozens
of structures that cover lots of acres. And the skyscrapers in the business sections of town that stretch 80 and 90 stories into the air, sometimes have
apartments in the upper levels. Today's architects design some remarkably
impressive structures, but building codes usually restrict how big an area one
building can cover.

One of the biggest apartment complexes ever built was in New York
City. It was a 12-story apartment house the size of a city block. Called the
Belmont Apartment House, it opened for business on this day in 1909. At the
time it was the biggest apartment house in the world with 178 suites. The
building had more than 64,000 square feet. Every apartment in it opened
onto a large inside court. Typical apartments had seven to 11 rooms, with
two to four baths. All of them had windows that opened on city streets or to
the inner court. The price: they started at a whopping $175 per month, or
$4,200 in today's market. If you could pay for it, the Belmont House was *the*
place to live!

Someday soon we're going to take possession of our new apartment
complexes in the sky. Some might prefer to call them condos, and Jesus
would probably agree. John tells us of a conversation Jesus had with His disciples just before He died. "Don't worry about the future," He reassured these
men who had spent three years with Him in ministry. "Trust the Father as
you have trusted Me." He went on to explain that at this very moment, in His
Father's giant apartment complex in the sky, there were many rooms for
each of them.

"Believe Me," He said. "It's true! I wouldn't tell you such a thing just to
impress you. And the best part is that I'm going there soon myself, to get everything ready so you can come and join Me there."

Prehistoric Hoax

For a time is coming when people will no longer listen to sound and wholesome teaching. They will follow their own desires and will look for teachers who will tell them whatever their itching ears want to hear. 2 Timothy 4:3, NLT.

One of the biggest hoaxes in archaeological history got its start in Cardiff, New York, on October 16, 1869. It happened like this.

George Hull, a tobacco farmer in Birmingham, Alabama, hired a sculptor in 1868 to carve a block of gypsum in the form of a 10-foot-tall giant. Then he had it shipped to Cardiff, where he buried it secretly on William Newell's farm, a friend who was in on the hoax.

On October 16, almost a year later, the statue was "discovered" by a workman who had been hired to dig a well. Hull and Newell spread a rumor around that the giant was a petrified man from Bible times. And from there the hoax took off and became quite a sensation far and wide.

The giant was shipped around to exhibits in cities on the east coast—Syracuse, Albany, New York City, and Boston. They charged crowds $1 a head to see it, an exorbitant amount in those days. Thousands came to see the giant, and they made ridiculous amounts of money.

Of course it was only a matter of time until someone figured it out and blew the whistle on the boys. The hoax was exposed by Othniel Marsh, a paleontologist from Yale University, who told everyone that the statue was of a very recent origin and nothing but humbug. Today the Cardiff giant is on display in the Farmers' museum in Cooperstown, New York.

Sometimes it seems that people will believe almost anything to be entertained and to give themselves a buzz. Some folks are by nature skeptics, but most people are probably more followers than leaders, and that can get them in trouble spiritually.

Remember, if it sounds too good to be true, it probably is. Paul said you need to be wise. Don't fall for every brand of teaching that comes along. Be suspicious in a healthy sort of way. Be willing to investigate, and you will be rewarded for your good judgment and common spiritual sense.

San Francisco Earthquake

*I watched as the Lamb broke the sixth seal, and there
was a great earthquake. The sun became as dark as
black cloth, and the moon became as red as blood.
Revelation 6:12, NLT.*

On October 17, 1989, a devastating earthquake hit the city of San Francisco, the deadliest earthquake since 1906. It lasted for 15 seconds, and measured 7.1 on the Richter scale. Its aftermath was witnessed on live television by millions of people who were watching a World Series game of baseball between the San Francisco Giants and the Oakland Athletics, at Candlestick Park. The tremor hit moments before the start of the game, and sportscasters were soon performing the duties of news anchors as they reported on the resulting pandemonium in the stadium. The earthquake killed a total of 63 people, while 3,000 others were injured, and more than 100,000 buildings were damaged. Freeway bridges buckled, and traffic snarled as rescue vehicles struggled to respond to the calls for help.

The Great 1906 San Francisco earthquake, which had happened more than 80 years before, ranks as one of the most devastating earthquakes of all time. Of course in those days we didn't have the kind of knowledge we now have about plate tectonics, and we didn't have the kind of equipment we have today, either.

But there's no mistaking the terrible effects of that morning more than 100 years ago. At almost precisely 5:12 a.m. local time, a foreshock hit with enough force to be felt throughout the San Francisco Bay area. The biggest quake broke loose some 20 to 25 seconds later, with an epicenter near San Francisco. Violent shocks kept coming on and off for the next 45 to 60 seconds. The series of earthquakes were felt from Oregon to Los Angeles, and east to Nevada.

The death toll from the earthquake and resulting fire, was more than 3,000, and was the greatest loss of life from a natural disaster in California's history. Its economic impact has been compared with the more recent Hurricane Katrina.

Earthquakes remind us that our earth is getting old. The world will end, but we shouldn't worry. When it does, Jesus will be here to save us.

Thomas Edison Dies

And men of all nations, from all the kings of the earth who had heard of his wisdom, came to hear the wisdom of Solomon. 1 Kings 4:34, NKJV.

One of the most prolific inventors of all time passed away at the age of 84 on this day in 1931. Thomas Alva Edison registered the first of his 1,093 successful U.S. patent applications when he was just 21. In addition, it is estimated that he filed between 500 and 600 unsuccessful applications.

Born in Milan, Ohio, in 1847, Edison received little formal schooling, which wasn't unusual for most Americans at the time. He developed serious hearing problems at an early age, and this disability provided the motivation for many of his inventions. At age 16 he found work as a telegraph operator and soon was spending much of his time and ingenuity on improving the telegraph system itself. By 1869 he was working full time on his inventions, and in 1876 moved to a laboratory and machine shop in Menlo Park, New Jersey.

Edison's experiments were sparked by his scientific instincts, but he also employed lab assistants who helped him with the mathematical and technical skills he lacked. Edison continued his work on the telegraph at Menlo Park, and in 1877 he stumbled onto one of his greatest inventions: the phonograph. Originally, it was designed to record telephone communication, and public demonstrations of the phonograph made Edison world famous.

The discovery of a way to record and play back sound guaranteed Edison a place in scientific history. However, it was just the first of several Edison creations in the late 1900s that would change American life forever. Other famous inventions included the first practical incandescent light bulb in 1879 and a version of the movie camera and projector we use today.

Probably Edison's greatest gift to our world came from his work in electricity. He developed a complete electrical system for light and power, and set up the world's first power plant in New York City. He invented the alkaline battery, the first electric railroad, and scads of other inventions that use electricity in today's busy world.

God has used—and continues to use—His creativity to bless His creation. You are made in His image. Always use your creativity to bless others.

Mile High Wedding

*Blessed are those who are invited to the wedding supper of the Lamb!
Revelation 19:9, NIV.*

Weddings are special, and it's especially nice when the couple includes things that are meaningful to them. I saw wedding photos of the couple standing in a flowing mountain stream. But I think the mile-high wedding in a hot air balloon is the wildest one I've ever heard of.

It happened on this day in October, 1874. Sound bizarre? It was. Mary Walsh and Charles Colton got hitched a mile into the sky above Cincinnati, Ohio, with 50,000 people as witnesses. Actually it was a stunt put on by the famous circus entertainer, P.T. Barnum, and Mary was a horseback rider in his circus. The balloon held 62,000 cubic feet of air. That is equivalent to a balloon 30 feet in diameter and more than seven stories tall.

That must have been quite an event! An unusual wedding ceremony like that would certainly be one to remember. But, of course, after such pizzazz, the couple had to live with the marriage. I hope Mary and Charles' life together was as memorable as their wedding ceremony, but life is not often like that. After the excitement of their high-flying wedding they had to come down to earth, so to speak. But all couples do, no matter how exciting or mundane their ceremony. Did Mary and Charles laugh together? Did she cry when they argued? Did they buy a house and have kids and a dog or cat? Did he handle all the money? Did she create surprises for him? Did they love each other 'til death did them part?

Many people today are casual about marriage. Too many say "I do," with the thought that if it doesn't work out they'll just get out. Today's husbands may help with the housework more than they did in 1874, and women may provide half the income. But when almost half of all marriages end in divorce you know something's seriously wrong.

Marriage is no stunt. It's a wonderful gift from God, but it takes a lot of dedication—from both the man and woman. It requires a ton of time and energy. Not that it can't be fun and exciting and fulfilling. It's all that and much more. But you've got to be committed to it. You must be in for the long haul.

Someday when all the worries of this life are over, there'll be a wedding in the sky. It will be a wedding to end all weddings, between Jesus and His Church, and we're all invited. Even if you're not much into weddings, you're going to like this one. I guarantee!

Flower Vending Machine

Does the Lord delight in burnt offerings and sacrifices as much as in obeying the voice of the Lord? To obey is better than sacrifice. 1 Samuel 15:22, NIV.

On October 20, 1961, a refrigerated vending machine designed to dispense fresh flowers was set up in Grand Central Station in New York City. That sounds cool, but I can't believe that the flowers would be in very good shape. Besides, getting flowers from a machine sounds about as cheesy as buying a can of soda.

It's amazing the things we try to do with flowers. We use them to celebrate baby dedications, graduations, banquets, dates, engagements, weddings, anniversaries, and to remember our loved ones who have passed away. We go through life trying to do the right thing for the right motive, but sometimes we do things just for show, because it seems the right thing to do at the time. And as important as flowers are, we can't afford to do things halfway.

Take flowers for a girlfriend or Mother's Day, for instance. Better not go cheap there. Better not buy them from a guy selling wilted bunches on the street, not if you want to impress anybody. Or flowers for a funeral. If you buy a really cheap bouquet the family of the deceased will think that's all they're worth in their time of sorrow. Actually, the person who died would probably have preferred getting flowers when they were alive. An old poem says it perfectly: "I'd rather have one flower now, than a truckload when I'm dead."

When King Saul made excuses for disobeying God's command in his battle with the Amalekites, Prophet Samuel scolded the king for thinking that sacrifices were more important than obedience. God wants us to give Him our best too; He wants to be important in our lives. But sometimes we do things for all the wrong reasons as the Israelites did in the old days when they offered sacrifices to pay for their sins, and it became a ritual. God told them that sacrifices were important, but He'd rather they just stopped making all those dumb mistakes again and again, and then offering sacrifices to pay for them.

Confessions are nice but, like the flowers for a girlfriend, they would be more impressive if they weren't being given to pay for our dumb mistakes!

First Kamikaze Pilot

For scarcely for a righteous man will one die; yet perhaps for a good man someone would even dare to die. But God demonstrates His own love toward us, in that while we were still sinners, Christ died for us. Romans 5:7, 8, NKJV.

What would you die for? What a question. We don't like to think about dying. Most of us have a strong sense of self-preservation—something inside that keeps us from knowingly causing ourselves harm. Would you die for God? If it would save their lives, would you die for your parents or your brother or sister? For a friend?

Would you willingly go to war for your country if you knew—without a doubt—it would cost you your life?

Today, in 1944, the first kamikaze pilot flew his Japanese Zero plane into an Australian ship in the Pacific. That was a test run, and it worked. Four days later scores of kamikaze pilots made an all-out attack on a fleet of ships in the Philippines. The kamikaze squadron at this battle was composed of 24 volunteer pilots. The first America ship attacked was an escort carrier called *St. Lo.* It sank in less than an hour, killing 100 Americans. Tragically, more than 5,000 Japanese kamikaze pilots died in the gulf battle that day, taking down 34 ships and more American lives.

These pilots had but one mission: to dive bomb into Allied ships, destroying as many as possible. It was late in the war. The Allies were becoming stronger, and the Japanese were becoming desperate. Motoharu Okamura, a Japanese naval captain said, "I firmly believe that the only way to swing the war in our favor is to resort to crash-dive attacks with our planes. . . . There will be more than enough volunteers for this chance to save our country."

The great controversy between good and evil has been raging for thousands of years, but when Jesus died Satan knew he had lost the battle. But like the kamikaze pilots, Satan hopes that one last stand against God might turn the battle in his favor. He'll use whatever he can to take our minds off God. TV, the Internet, music, sports, video games, our friends, shopping, and dating are all fun, but if they take us farther away from God, then they're like the kamikaze crash-dive attacks from the Japanese war planes. Instead, let's focus on Jesus and the fact that He has already won the battle between good and evil.

Great Disappointment

*Then I took the little book out of the angel's hand and
ate it, and it was as sweet as honey in my mouth.
But when I had eaten it, my stomach became bitter.
Revelation 10:10, NKJV.*

It was the spring of 1844, and many New Englanders were excited. William Miller, a local farmer, was preaching that Jesus was coming soon—and using biblical prophecy to prove it. His message was spellbinding. His prophetic charts, full of horrific beasts right out of the Old Testament, convinced many of the thousands who came to hear him explain the 2300-day prophecy of Daniel 8. The end of the world was at hand, said Miller. According to his calculations, the prophecy would end on October 22, 1844. When it did, the world would end in a judgment of fire, and Jesus would come to take His children to heaven. Of course, many thousands did not believe it, but still the message took New England by storm. Churches were holding camp meetings all up and down the eastern seaboard, and Miller had more invitations than he could accept. People left their businesses to come listen to him, and all-night prayer meetings often followed. By the end of the summer, emotions were running so high that people would weep when they heard Miller's message.

What a wonderful hope it was! In that time, few families were untouched by death. But when Jesus came, the righteous dead would awake. The old, the crippled, the weak would receive new, strong bodies. The saved would be taken up to heaven, to be with Jesus forever.

Believers left their crops in the field that fall. What was the point of harvesting them? As the date drew near, people spent whole days in prayer meetings. Early on the morning of October 22, hundreds gathered on a hillside behind Miller's barn, to wait for the Savior. They waited all day. They waited on into the evening, and some even stayed until past midnight. But Jesus didn't come. It was a dreadfully disappointing experience, and a bitter pill for the believers to swallow.

Where had they gone wrong? What had they missed? After much study and prayer they discovered their error. They'd misunderstood the prophecies of Daniel and Revelation. It did not predict the coming of Christ. Rather "the cleansing of the sanctuary" referred to a special judgment to begin in heaven. It was a life-changing experience, but God helped His people get through this crisis. Today Jesus, our High Priest, is in the Most Holy Place of the heavenly sanctuary reviewing the lives of the living. And when He is finished, He will come.

Unknown Soldier

Then he said, "Jesus, remember me when you come into your kingdom."
Luke 23:42, NIV.

Do you ever feel like a nobody? I hope not. No one should feel that way. But sadly, in wars that span thousands of years, many "nobodies" have died far from home and no one even knew their name. Their families never learned how they died or where they were buried. During the Revolutionary War both British and German soldiers died fighting here and are buried in American soil in unmarked graves. Only God knows their names.

This happened again during World War I. American soldiers valiantly gave themselves for their country, but being so far from home, no one could identify their remains. More than 77,000 United States soldiers died along the western front of the war, and most of their bodies never got to go home. With so many dead in one place, they had to be buried in a hurry. What a sacrifice they made! What a sad shame to pay with their lives and get no recognition for it.

Then someone had the idea of making a monument to all the unknown soldiers who died in World War I. On October 23, 1921, in the French town of Chalons-sur-Marne, an American officer chose the body of an unknown soldier to symbolically honor all those thousands of Americans that had died. No one knew the soldier's name. He had no dog tags on him to indicate his name or rank. And no one knew the date of his death. Today that soldier is buried in the Tomb of the Unknown Soldier at Arlington National Cemetery, near Washington, D.C. That soldier is everyone's son, everyone's brother. That tomb represents all the American soldiers who died for the cause of freedom.

Jesus died nearly 2,000 years ago for a much bigger cause than a world war. He died to save all people of all time from their sins. Jesus was buried in a borrowed tomb, and wonder of wonders, He rose again from the grave. No one knows exactly where Jesus was buried. Tour guides will take you to a tomb that resembles a typical grave Jesus might have been buried in, but the real site has been lost in the mists of time.

But it doesn't' matter. Jesus gave His life so that you and I would not have to die and be buried in unmarked graves for eternity. Like the thief on the cross, we are promised, "You will be with Me in paradise."

October 24

Barrel Over Niagara

So be careful how you live. Don't live like fools, but like those who are wise.
Ephesians 5:15, NLT.

What's the scariest thing you've ever done? Sky diving? Bungee jumping? Snorkeling in shark-infested waters? Doing pushups in a rattler pit? How about going over Niagara Falls in a barrel? Sound crazy? Well, it is, but it was a risk a schoolteacher named Annie Taylor was willing to take. What's even crazier, she was 63 years old at the time. She claimed she was in her 40s, but genealogical records later showed she was 63. But that was in 1901, when the life expectancy for Americans was 47 years, so maybe she thought she had nothing to lose. Here's how it happened:

After her husband died in the Civil War, Taylor lived in many places before settling in Michigan around 1898. In 1901, while reading an article about the Pan-American Exposition in Buffalo, she learned of the growing popularity of two enormous waterfalls located on the border of upstate New York and Canada. Strapped for cash and seeking fame, Taylor came up with the perfect attention-getting stunt: she would go over Niagara Falls in a barrel.

Taylor wasn't the first person to try the plunge over the famous falls. In 1829 Sam Patch, known as the Yankee Leaper, survived jumping down the 175-foot Horseshoe Falls on the Canadian side of the border. More than 70 years later, Taylor chose to take the ride on October 24, her birthday. With the help of two assistants, Taylor strapped herself into a leather harness inside an old wooden pickle barrel that was five feet high and three feet in diameter. With cushions lining the barrel to cushion her fall, Taylor was towed by a small boat into the middle of the fast-flowing Niagara River and cut loose.

She was knocked violently from side to side by the rapids and then propelled over the edge of Horseshoe Falls. Some 20 minutes after her journey began, Taylor reached the shore a bit battered but alive. After a brief flurry of photo ops and speaking engagements, Taylor's fame cooled, and she was unable to make the fortune for which she had hoped.

Annie Taylor was foolish. But there is something worth risking your life for. Peter, Paul, John—and all the disciples of Jesus—knew this. And the reward of living for Him is infinitely greater than all the fortune and fame the world can offer.

Picasso Is Born

I have made the earth, and created man on it . . . My hands—
stretched out the heavens, and all their host I have commanded.
Isaiah 45:12, NKJV.

Without doubt the most famous artist of the twentieth century is Pablo Picasso. In his lifetime he produced more than 50,000 works of art—paintings, drawings, engravings, sculptures, and ceramics.

Picasso was born in Malaga, Spain, on October 25, 1881, and his father, a professor of drawing, trained his son for a career in academic art. Picasso had his first exhibit at age 13, and later quit art school so he could experiment full time with modern art styles.

He went to Paris for the first time in 1900, and in 1901 was given an exhibition at a gallery on Rue Lafitte, a street known for its prestigious art galleries. At that time the 19-year-old Spaniard was unknown outside Barcelona, but he had already produced hundreds of paintings. His exhibition went well, and critics spoke favorably of him.

For 80 years Picasso was active, and few artists since have equaled his creative output. He was special because he became unusually famous in his own lifetime.

"Everyone wants to *understand* art," Picasso said. "Why don't we try to understand the song of a bird? Why do we love the night, the flowers, everything around us, without trying to understand them? People who try to explain pictures are usually barking up the wrong tree."

Several of Picasso's paintings rank among the most expensive in the world. *Garçon à la Pipe* sold for $104 million, which was a new record. *Dora Maar au Chat* sold for $95.2 million. Based his sales at auctions, Picasso is the top ranked artist of all time. Interestingly enough, more of his paintings have been stolen than those of any other artist.

Art is just one of God's gifts. God has given gifts to each of His children—a bright mind, music, and athletic ability—not to mention the gifts of time, influence, kindness, understanding, and friendship. Use your gift today to make the world a more beautiful place!

October 26

Wash Day

Purge me with hyssop, and I shall be clean;
wash me, and I shall be whiter than snow.
Psalm 51:7, NKJV.

On this day in history Hamilton Smith in Philadelphia, Pennsylvania, invented the first successful washing machine in 1858. I don't think we can even imagine what it must have been like to wash everything by hand. It was such a big job that in most homes all day Monday was set aside to do it. First, you set a big pot of water to heat on the wood burning stove. In it you shaved slivers of soap from a block that your mom had made with ashes, lard, and lye. Hot water was then carried from the kitchen and poured in a tub set out in the yard (in good weather).

All the clothes had to soak, and if they were really dirty they had to be boiled in a caldron of hot water and lye. Then came the hard part. You scrubbed out the stains and dirt on a wash board, a flat wooden frame that encased a corrugated sheet of fluted tin, sheet iron, copper or zinc on which each piece of clothing was vigorously rubbed up and down. Rinsing was a big job, made easier with two people working together. Think of rinsing and wringing your dad's overalls, or your bed sheets. At last you could hang them out to dry.

Try doing the washing for a family of nine or 10. Every week. Week in and week out. No washing machine, no laundromat, no break. And don't forget the ironing. Cotton dresses and blouses had to be ironed. So did the "good" tablecloths and pillowcases. You used the heavy black flatiron that you heated on the stove. You had more than one of them so when it cooled you didn't have to wait for it to reheat.

Today laundry isn't high on our list of worries. We come in at night and throw our sweaty, grass-stained, mud-globbed clothes in the laundry basket and never think to thank Mom or big sister for doing the laundry for us. We take so much for granted! We think so little of how the brains and energy of people in the past make our lives easy today.

We need to thank God, too, for the best washing machine in the history of the world. God's washing machine washes our hands, scrubs behind the ears, disinfects our mouth, and generally cleans us inside and out. It is, in fact, the blood of Jesus that makes us whiter than snow. When David hit rock bottom, he said it well for all of us. "Purge me with hyssop, and I shall be clean; wash me, and I shall be whiter than snow."

Quakers Hanged by Puritans

You will be handed over to be persecuted and put to death, and you will be hated by all nations because of me. Matthew 24:9, NIV.

America has always been considered the land of the free and the brave. A place where the Statue of Liberty beckons to everyone, inviting them to bring their "huddled masses yearning to breathe free." But it hasn't always been that way exactly.

The Puritans, like many others, came to Massachusetts to escape persecution by the State Church of England. And yet, shockingly enough, when others from other religions tried to settle among them, the Puritans persecuted them severely.

One October in 1656 two Quaker men were executed by the Puritans in the colony of Massachusetts. Why? Because the laws of Massachusetts at that time said Quakers were not allowed to live in the colony. They had all been banished for religious reasons, but some of them stayed anyway, and for that they were hanged in a public execution on the Boston Commons.

Later, in 1682, a man by the name of William Penn, a Quaker, came to live in America. He would become the most famous Quaker in American history. Penn befriended the Indians and, some say, almost singlehandedly brought peace and prosperity to the colony of Pennsylvania. He was persecuted too, but he stood firmly for the rights of everyone in his colony, whether they were Quakers or not.

Someday there will be great persecutions again in the United States. If religious people could be cruel and hateful in the days of the Puritans, we can expect it to happen again in the future. People who are under the influence of Satan are capable of just about anything—and human nature hasn't changed that much over the centuries.

The Bible is full of all kinds of stories about people who suffered under persecution because they stuck to their convictions and remained faithful to God. Noah was faithful in building the ark. Joseph was true to his loyalty to Potiphar, captain of the King's guard. Daniel was faithful in his prayers to God three times a day. Paul was faithful to Jesus in so many ways on his missionary journeys. What kept them going? "He who stands firm to the end will be saved. And this gospel of the kingdom will be preached in the whole world . . . and then the end will come" (Matt. 24:13, 14, NIV)—Jesus will come back to get us!

Statue of Liberty

*The Spirit of the Lord God is upon Me, because the Lord has
anointed Me to preach good tidings to the poor; He has sent Me
to heal the brokenhearted, to proclaim liberty to the captives,
and the opening of the prison to those who are bound.*
Isaiah 61:1, NKJV.

Imagine yourself an immigrant to the United States in 1887, steaming into
New York Harbor with thousands of others from the Austrian-Hungarian
Empire, from China, Russia, and many other lands. Seeking a refuge from
poverty or war. Looking for a home where there is space to spread out.
Wanting to start a small business. And then you see it. The giant copper-
plated statue you've heard so much about—the Statue of Liberty.

For more than a hundred years the Statue of Liberty has welcomed newcomers to the United States. How did Lady Liberty get into New York
Harbor? Where did she come from, and what does she represent?

The 151-foot woman with an outstretched arm holding a torch was the
creation of French sculptor Frederic-Auguste Bartholdi. Its framework of gigantic steel supports was designed by two men, one of them being
Alexandre-Gustave Eiffel, the architect of the Eiffel Tower. In May 1884, the
Statue of Liberty was completed in France, and in June 1885, the dismantled
statue arrived in the New York Harbor, inside more than 200 packing cases.
The statue's copper sheets were reassembled like a giant puzzle, and the last
rivet was pounded in during a dedication ceremony on October 28, 1886.

What a gift! What a testimony of friendship by the people of France. On
the Statue of Liberty's pedestal are inscribed the famous words, "Give me
your tired, your poor, your huddled masses yearning to breathe free, the
wretched refuse of your teeming shore. Send these, the homeless, tempest-
tossed to me. I lift my lamp beside the golden door."

Today America is still a marvelous nation to live in, not just because it
represents a land of opportunity, but because God's blessing still rests on this
land. He established the United States in the Western Hemisphere so we
could become a nation destined to take the gospel to the world. Our job
today is to help those who are lonely and discouraged. We need to bring the
good news that Jesus loves them. Our mission is to open Satan's prison doors
that hold people as prisoners of war in the battle with sin.

Floats Like a Butterfly, Stings Like a Bee

Fight the good fight of the faith. Take hold of the eternal life to which you were called.
1 Timothy 6:12, NIV.

Mohammed Ali is an old man now, but he was really something in his day. His parents named him Cassius Clay, but he picked up many nicknames throughout his life: The Thrilla in Manila and Louisville Lip are a couple.

On October 29, 1960, he fought his first professional boxing match. From that very first fight it was obvious that he was no ordinary boxer. His hands were huge, and his arms were about two inches longer than most other boxers which enabled him to dance around the ring, taking jabs at his opponent while avoiding the blows of the other fighter. You may even have heard a song on the radio that was written about him a long time ago: "Muhammad! Muhammad Ali! He floats like a butterfly and stings like a bee!"

Ali was known for taunting his opponents and the media with one-liners that some might call the earliest forms of rap.

Throughout his lifetime he received many honors. Four times he became the heavyweight champion of the world. He has also been a guest at the White House, and was proclaimed athlete of the century because he made such a big impact in professional sports.

It's a good thing that we don't have to fight for a living as Muhammad Ali did. It's nice to know that not everything in life is settled in a boxing ring.

However, Paul tells us in our Bible verse for today that there is some fighting we must do. We are fighting the good fight of faith against Satan and his angels. At times it appears that Satan will win because his temptations are so strong and he seems to have so many tricks up his sleeve. (After all, he is an experienced fighter.)

But none of that matters if you've given your heart to Jesus. He will step into the ring and help you become a champion. In fact, He'll do all the fighting for you.

Now, that's an offer you can't refuse.

War of the Worlds

For we do not wrestle against flesh and blood, but against principalities, against powers, against the rulers of the darkness of this age, against spiritual hosts of wickedness in the heavenly places.
Ephesians 6:12, NKJV.

In a way, most of us live in a fantasy world. We watch so much TV and so many movies that we hardly know what's right and wrong. Our ears are rarely without music. We've seen so many make-believe deaths that we're not touched when the daily news shows us the real thing.

Fantasy feeds our imaginations, because almost everything that entertains us is make-believe. Even so-called reality shows are not reality. Not in the slightest. Even in our everyday lives we're sheltered from the tragedy and crisis that once was common. But it wasn't always that way. In the 1920s and 1930s there was very little entertainment compared to today, and almost no outside entertainment entered the home, but families had radio, which brings us to our story.

On October 30, 1938, the Mercury Theater presented a radio special called War of the Worlds by H.G. Wells. As the story progressed, listeners thought the broadcast was a real report from a news station. Terror spread as people listened to the excited voice of the radio broadcaster supposedly reporting on a Martian landing. According to the radio report, America was being overrun by the little green men from Mars, carrying heat ray guns.

It's estimated that a million people along the east coast panicked and headed inland to escape the invaders. The broadcast was not planned as a radio hoax, but even after the whole thing was over, thousands refused to believe it wasn't true. Welles had no idea of the havoc it would cause. In some cases, "People begged police for gas masks to save them from the toxic gas and asked electric companies to turn off the power so that the Martians wouldn't see their lights. One woman ran into an Indianapolis church where evening services were being held and yelled, 'New York has been destroyed! It's the end of the world! Go home and prepare to die!' "

Today we face another kind of war of the worlds. We can't see it with our eyes, but it is raging all around us in the supernatural world. Paul tells us that we fight a very real battle with "mighty powers in this dark world, and against evil spirits in the heavenly places." But we don't have to worry because Jesus has already fought that battle. Satan is a defeated enemy and is on the run.

Houdini Dies

For the living know that they will die, but the dead know nothing.
Ecclesiastes 9:5, NKJV.

Houdini was one of the most famous escape artists of all time. Many of his stunts have never been successfully duplicated. He is best known for his ability to escape from any lock or handcuff people could put on him. As he became famous he performed more dangerous and dramatic acts to draw the crowds. One of Houdini's amazing tricks required him to escape from an iron-bound chest that had been thrown off a boat. In another feat he had to escape from a straight jacket while hanging from a skyscraper. And he often amazed crowds by escaping from a coffin that had been buried six feet underground.

But his greatest appeal seemed to come from his ability to play on the fear and anxieties of audiences. This was most obvious in stunts he pulled, such as his escape from a giant milk can filled with water, which all took place behind a closed curtain. Once chained inside a milk can full of water, Houdini would quickly escape then sit in a chair reading a book for several minutes beyond the time limit the crowds knew was safe. When the crowd was ready to pass out with fear for his safety, he'd finally emerge, still drenched with water and "gasping" for air.

Houdini didn't believe in what we call magic. Instead, he depended on his strength, agility, and concentration. He was interested in spiritualism, a belief in the idea that dead people can come back and talk with the living. Houdini made a deal with his wife and friends that whoever died first should contact the others from the dead.

On October 31, 1926, the great magician, Harry Houdini, did die. Some say his death was because of an accident that happened when a college boy was trying to test Houdini's physical strength. Others say it was because of an accident while practicing for one of his tricks as an escape artist. His wife waited for a message from him, as they had agreed, but it never came.

And that's no surprise, of course. Harry Houdini was dead. He couldn't communicate with the living because, like the Bible says, the dead know nothing. The saddest part about the whole thing was that this time around Houdini could not escape from his coffin—or from the sleep of death. Without God's gift of life, he was powerless. But Jesus has promised us that we don't need to be afraid of death. When Jesus comes again we can escape this world of sin and never again have to worry about being sick or dying. I can't wait!

Lisbon Earthquake

And out of the temple came a loud voice from the throne, saying, "It is done!" Then there came flashes of lightning, rumblings, peals of thunder and a severe earthquake. No earthquake like it has ever occurred since man has been on earth, so tremendous was the quake. The great city split into three parts, and the cities of the nations collapsed. Revelation 16:17-19, NIV.

On November 1, 1755, one of the worst earthquakes in European history hit the Continent. The epicenter of the earthquake hit Lisbon, Portugal, killing as many as 50,000 people. Portugal had never been more prosperous with the trade in diamonds and gold from their colony in Brazil. Lisbon was Portugal's capital and largest city, and a religious center of the Catholic Church. It was the biggest seaport on the Atlantic Ocean, and had a population of about 300,000 people.

Three shock waves within 10 minutes struck Lisbon, with the worst quake estimated at a magnitude of about 8.0 on the rector scale. Equipment for measuring quakes did not then exist, but the quakes were felt as far away as Morocco. It was the day after Halloween and celebrations for All Saints Day were in progress in churches all over the city.

Score of church buildings collapsed when a 20-foot tsunami rolled inland, killing thousands. Fires blazed all over the city and winds quickly spread the flames. Portugal's royal palace was destroyed, as were thousands of homes. Much of the country's cultural history, preserved in books, art and architecture, was wiped away in an instant. Many of the city's residents, including hundreds of escaped prisoners, fled Lisbon immediately. The death toll was estimated as high as 50,000.

For years some theologians viewed the Lisbon earthquake as one of the prophetic signs of Jesus coming, probably because it coincides well with the end of a great religious persecution that had gripped the dark ages for centuries. Of course, since it occurred more than 250 years ago it's hard to use it as a sign of Christ's soon return. The fact is that our world is growing old. If natural disasters don't destroy it, man-made pollution will do the job. Earthquakes, tsunamis, tornados and hurricanes . . . any and all of these disasters remind us that this world cannot last much longer. Jesus is coming again, and soon.

Traitor to His Country

*But Jesus said to him, "Judas, are you betraying
the Son of Man with a kiss?"
Luke 22:48, NKJV.*

Is there anything worse than betraying your country? Well, spying has always been a part of every war in American history, and so it was during the Revolutionary War. On the night of November 2, 1776, an American officer named William Demont deserted the Colonial Continental Army and defected to the British side. By his treachery he gave the British valuable information about where to find Fort Washington, the Continental Army's stronghold along the Hudson River in New York, and how best to capture it. Because of Demont's cowardly decision, the Colonial army was betrayed and thousands of American soldiers suffered.

How did he do it? It was simple: the American army trusted him. He entered the British camp south of Fort Washington and turned over top-secret information to Percy, the officer in charge. Fort Washington, built on top of a 230-foot-highhill, was a mile long. Vertical cliffs made it almost impossible to reach the fort from the Hudson River below. Three other nearby forts were loaded with cannon and should have been able to help protect Fort Washington from incoming enemies. Besides this, a line of sunken obstructions in the river were designed to keep British ships from coming up the Hudson.

However, the fort didn't have walls, and only long mounds of earthworks protected the soldiers entrenched there. This was exactly the kind of information that British General Howe needed in planning his attack. Fourteen days later General Howe captured the fort with his force of 8,900 men, seizing 43 cannon, 2,800 muskets, and nearly 3,000 POWs. William Demont was a traitor of the worst sort. He betrayed his country and his people.

But there's something worse: betraying God. Like Judas, do we sometimes dare to betray Jesus with a kiss? Do we sometimes profess loyalty and love for our Savior but secretly cherish sins that destroy us in the end?

Let's pray not. God is worthy of our trust—and He will never fail us!

The Order to Bomb Pearl Harbor

And war broke out in heaven: Michael and his angels fought with the dragon; and the dragon and his angels fought, but they did not prevail, nor was a place found for them in heaven any longer. Revelation 12:7, 8, NKJV.

A few years ago the movie *Pearl Harbor* became popular, and again we all heard the story about the World War II bombing of our naval station in Hawaii. Japanese Zero fighters zoomed down on an unsuspecting military base out in the middle of the Pacific, and nearly 3,000 soldiers and sailors lost their lives in the attack. Hundreds more became heroes in the aftermath, showing their courage and character.

It was a terrible day in American history, and some people wonder that the Japanese had such luck in hitting us where it hurt most. All eight battleships of the U.S. Pacific Fleet were sunk or badly damaged, plus 350 aircraft were trashed.

The attack was no accident. On November 3, 1941, the order to bomb Pearl Harbor was given—a whole month before the actual attack. Directed to the Japanese Fleet and titled "Top-secret Order, No. 1," it read: "In 34 days time Pearl Harbor is to be bombed, along with Mayala, the Dutch East Indies, and the Philippines."

Political relations between Japan and the United States had been going downhill for almost a year, and things weren't getting any better. Because of Japan's attacks in the Pacific, the United States seized all Japanese money in American banks and closed the Panama Canal to Japanese shipping. President Roosevelt threatened war on the Japanese if they attacked even one more target in Southeast Asia or the South Pacific.

Evidently the Japanese were tired of other nations telling them what to do, and the order came from Tokyo to strike the first blow on America: bomb Pearl Harbor. Japan had attacked China and the islands of the Pacific, and now they foolishly declared war on the West.

Like the attack on Pearl Harbor, the war between good and evil didn't just happen by accident—it was orchestrated by Satan, the dragon who had been in heaven. Who would have thought that the he who had been the covering cherub of God could come up with such a scheme? But praise God there was no place in heaven for the devil and his army. And his days on earth are numbered too. Aren't you glad?

King Tut's Tomb

For the living know that they will die; but the dead know nothing, and they have no more reward, for the memory of them is forgotten. Ecclesiastes 9:5, NKJV.

Egyptian pyramids look impressive on the outside, but inside is a maze of dank dark tunnels and passageways full of spider webs and snakes and . . . actually that's just stuff found in movies. The real pyramids are so old that nothing living would be found in them anyway. Not even a mummy, though the ancient Egyptians thought the pyramids provided a place for the pharaohs to live into the afterlife. Outrageous stories were told of riches buried with the pharaohs—rooms of gold furniture. Statues and art work. But no discovery had been made in modern times. Either it wasn't true, or else all the tombs of legend had been raided centuries ago.

The tombs *had* been raided. In fact, Egyptians stopped building pyramids because they were so easily broken into by grave robbers. Instead, they buried their royalty in rooms deep below the ground, reached only by complicated shafts and tunnels. And then on November 4, 1922, British archaeological Howard Carter found the entrance to King Tut's tomb in the Valley of the Kings. He contacted the man financing the exploration. And on November 26, Carter made a tiny breach in the top left hand corner of the doorway, and peered inside by the light of a candle. He didn't yet know if he'd found a tomb or merely a cache, but he did see a promising sealed doorway between two sentinel statues. When his sponsor asked if he saw anything, Carter replied, "Yes . . . wonderful things."

It was the tomb of the boy-king, King Tutankhamen, who had died at only 18, and what wonders they found! It seemed that everything inside the four-room burial chamber was made of gold. But the most amazing discovery was a stone sarcophagus containing nesting three coffins. Inside the final coffin of solid gold was the 3000-year-old mummy of King Tut.

But King Tut is not as famous as Moses, the favored prince of the Egyptian palace who was also destined to be Pharaoh. Moses gave it all up to lead God's people out of slavery and to the borders of the Promised Land. He died before going into the Promised Land, but then God resurrected him from the dead and took him to heaven. King Tut's mummy can't compare to that. With all Tut's preparation for the afterlife, he's still dead, mummified, and lying in a sarcophagus.

Monopoly Invented

The Lord gave, and the Lord has taken away;
blessed be the name of the Lord.
Job 1:21, NKJV.

Ever play Monopoly? Do families even play it any more? I hope yours did, for it puts you in good company. More than 500 million fans of the game around the world have bought the Parker Brother's board game. During the Depression an entrepreneur, Clarence Darrow, was trying to think of a way to make some money. Real money, not the kind you find in the Monopoly game. He invented the game of Monopoly, and on November 5, 1935, it was first marketed by Parker Brothers. Today it remains a classic, passed down from generation to generation, making it the world's most popular game.

Monopoly is designed around the idea of owning real estate, and charging other players rent for landing on your property. Houses or hotels can be built on most of the properties, making the rent you charge even higher. The purple-colored real estate on the beginning side of the board is the cheapest property to own, and it brings the lowest rent. Orange and red properties near the free parking space are mid-range in value and rent fees. The final group of properties near the finish line are dark blue and are reserved exclusively for the Rockefellers among us. Their titles, Park Place and Boardwalk, remind us of their importance in the game. Railroads and utility companies can be bought at modest prices, and there are other fines or bonuses that come your way when you land on specific Chance and Community Chest spaces.

The game of Monopoly is a little like everyday life, but not much. In Monopoly you're given $1,500 to start the game. Now you might be thinking that $1,500 is not a lot of money, but remember, the game was designed in 1935. If Parker Brothers was designing the game today, they'd have to give players about $60,000. That's a lot. But no one is going to give you $60,000 to get started in life. Not even your parents!

Playing Monopoly is fun, but it's not realistic. Life can be unfair, and nothing worth having is free. We need to remember that the best things in life come from God. Sometimes He blesses us because those blessings are good for us to have. Other times He takes away much of what we think is important. But the most important gift He can give you is always free. Eternal life. Now that's one thing Clarence Darrow could not put in his game of Monopoly.

Two Presidents— One Union

Choose for yourselves this day whom you will serve. . . .
As for me and my household, we will serve the Lord.
Joshua 24:15, NIV.

Have you ever run for an elected position in your class or school, such as student body president? You wanted the job, and were scared you wouldn't get it? What if when all the votes were in you found you'd been elected, but your opponent had rallied part of the student body and they'd elected her president too? Sound bizarre? Well it happened once in U.S. politics, and the result was deadly serious.

In 1860 the United States seemed on the verge of civil war. The Southern states wanted slavery. In fact, their whole economy was based on having enslaved people to work their plantations. But the Northern states were against it. The South said they should be able to make their own choices but the North, led by abolitionists, said that slavery was morally wrong. No one should own another human being, especially in the United States where all are supposed to be equal before God. And so the battle between the slave states and free states was heating up.

By the time the presidential election of 1860 rolled around, the biggest issue was states' rights, and it appeared that the North was going to prevail. Unfortunately, political rumors from the South said that if Lincoln was elected, they'd secede from the Union. Ridiculous! They couldn't do it! Just watch them—that's exactly what the Southern states did. On November 6, 1860, Abraham Lincoln was elected president—and 13 states in the South separated themselves from the Union. A year later, on November 6, 1861, Jefferson Davis was elected president of the Confederate States. Davis had been serving as the temporary president for almost a year, and the North and South had been fighting the Civil War for almost a year. It was an awful time for America. Depending upon where one lived, brother was literally pitted against brother and father against son. This time of open conflict split the country in half and eventually cost us the lives of half a million men.

Every day of our lives we have to make choices. And like the election of 1860, some decisions will set the course of our lives in ways that may be impossible to reverse. Like Joshua we need to make good choices that keep God in the picture.

Tacoma Bridge Collapses

And the rain descended, the floods came, and the winds blew and beat on that house; and it fell. And great was its fall. Matthew 7:27, 28, NKJV.

What's the longest bridge you've ever been on? While you were crossing did you think about what it would be like to have the bridge suddenly collapse under you? Well, that's exactly what happened to the Tacoma Narrows Bridge on the Puget Sound in Washington State on November 7, 1940. The bridge collapsed not from its own weight, but because of wind and resonance caused by vibrations in the metal girders. It was a mystery to the builders how a bridge that was designed to withstand winds up to 120 miles per hour could collapse so easily.

At 2,800 feet long and just 39 feet wide, the bridge was the third-longest suspension bridge in the world. But it was just too narrow. The engineers tried to cut costs by designing the bridge for only two lanes of traffic. When it opened it became a very popular ride because people liked the way it felt to ride across. When it was windy, the bridge would sway from side to side and move up and down. It was so dramatic, in fact, that drivers were reported that cars ahead of them would sometimes disappear and reappear several times as they crossed the bridge. These windy day rides became known as the cheapest roller-coaster ride in town, and the bridge earned the nickname Galloping Gertie. The designers tried to fix the problems but finally, after just four months of use the bridge collapsed spectacularly.

On November 7 a steady wind was blowing at 42 miles per hour, and the roadway began to twist back and forth violently. The last car on the bridge lost control partway across when the road tipped so sharply that the driver thought he was going to slide off the side of the bridge. He tried to get his daughter's cocker spaniel from the backseat of the car, but the dog snapped at him and refused to leave, and he had to leave without the dog. He crawled the last 500 feet to safety on his hands and knees before the bridge finally collapsed.

Jesus told the story about a house that was built on a weak foundation, and when the wind and rains came it finally collapsed. He invites us to build solidly on Him. Don't take shortcuts when it comes to your life decisions. Get a good education, treat your body right, choose your friends wisely, and Jesus will help you make your life a success.

Greedy for Gold

For the love of money is the root of all kinds of evil.
And some people, craving money, have wandered from
the true faith and pierced themselves with many sorrows.
1 Timothy 6:10, NLT.

Do you like money? I do. It's necessary. It buys things we have to have, and lots we have no use for! Money is a big part of our culture, and most of us believe that the more we have of it, the happier we'll be. But it just isn't so, and here's a story to prove it.

Hernando Cortez, a law school dropout from Spain, was in the hunt for gold. He had heard all kinds of fantastic stories about gold in the New World, and he was out to get as much of it as he could. In 1504 the conquistador arrived in the New World and conquered Santo Domingo. In 1511, it was Cuba. In 1518, he set sail west for the Mexican peninsula with 11 ships, 600 men, 16 horses, and some cannons. The nationals there could only stand in awe at the soldiers' armor and weapons, and especially the horses, which they'd never seen before.

Cortez had heard of the Aztecs, a fierce, warlike people that lived in what is now Western Mexico. It was said they had gold. Lots of it. Cortez was so crazy for gold that he decided in one brilliant move to burn his ships, so his soldiers couldn't abandon him and flee home. After trekking through steaming jungles and over the Sierra Madres Mountains, Cortez and his men were finally met by ambassadors from the Aztec ruler, Montezuma. They tried to bribe Cortez with expensive gifts in hopes that he'd leave them in peace and not enter the capital city of Tenochtitlán. But it's said that Cortez's eyes shone with greed at the sight of the golden gifts, and would have none of it. On November 8, 1519, Cortés and his men entered the Aztec capital. True to all the stories they had heard, the Aztecs had great wealth. Cortez took Montezuma hostage and forced the Aztecs to pay an enormous ransom—nearly eight tons in gold. A brutal war followed, and that was the beginning of the end of the Aztecs. Within two years their empire was in shambles. How it could be that one man with a group of soldiers and mercenaries could accomplish all that!

Cortez got his gold and his kingdom, but he died a bitter man. When he returned to Mexico after years at the royal court in Spain, he was ravaged with dysentery, and finally died of pleurisy at the age of 62. Paul was right. The love of money brings only evil and those who crave money bring trouble and unhappiness on themselves.

Night of Broken Glass

You who hate good and love evil; . . . they will cry to the Lord, but He will not hear them . . . because they have been evil in their deeds. Micah 3:2, 4, NKJV.

Munich, Germany. November 9, 1938.

Kristallnacht. "Night of broken glass."

It lasted two days. Shop windows were smashed and their owners beaten. The shops looted and burned. Merchandise destroyed. Gangs of Nazi youth stormed into Jewish homes, beat the young and the old and vandalized their possessions, including their sacred items of worship. Twenty thousand Jews were arrested, and 36 men, women, and children were murdered. This was only the beginning, for some historians say that the Holocaust started that night.

Sadly, most Germans did not oppose this treatment of their associates and neighbors. Maybe they felt helpless and afraid, or maybe they'd bought in to the anti-Jewish propaganda. Neither did Churches protest it. One by one, laws were passed, each one denying Jews another freedom. For example, Jews were required to turn over all precious metals to the government (jewelry, wedding rings, candle holders). Jews living in German towns had to live in ghettos. Their driver's licenses were taken away. Jews could not be outside after 9:00 p.m.

Then German leaders had a very important meeting. Concentration camps were already set up in Germany and other countries. Hitler sent out a letter saying that the Jewish question had to be solved one way or another. They called it The Final Solution—the killing of all Jews. Many years of suffering began for the Jewish people in Europe though much of the world was unaware until the end of World War II. In the years since many people have studied the Holocaust to try to understand how good, ordinary people can be so changed by hate that they will torture and kill.

Of course, hate doesn't always go to such extremes. It can take the form of small slights and hurts toward people who are "different." Kids who don't dress quite right, or act a little funny. Kids that just don't fit in. Be aware of this in your own school and church. Don't ever let yourself take even the first steps toward such evil.

Andersonville Warden Execution

*For the wages of sin is death, but the gift of God
is eternal life in Christ Jesus our Lord.
Romans 6:23, NKJV.*

The Civil War was the most tragic of all wars the United States has fought. We didn't send our troops to foreign soil to help win freedom for another country, and we weren't fighting because we'd been attacked. We were fighting each other. The "United" States were divided—politically and geographically. The South's insistence on owning slaves was only one reason. Another was whether states had to obey the federal government.

The number of people who died from battle and disease during the Civil War is appalling. But the atrocities committed in the POW camps are some of the most horrifying in American history. The conditions at the Andersonville, Georgia, camp were some of the worst. Quickly built in February, 1864, the pine stockade held thousands of men on just 27 acres. There were no barracks. Prisoners tried to build their own shacks and lean-tos out of wood scraps and blankets, but without shelter, the starving prisoners suffered terribly and many died of exposure as well as disease.

A stream flowed through the stockade but it soon turned into a huge swamp, polluted with human waste and disease. The stockade was built to hold 10,000 POWs, but at one time 32,000 men were crammed inside. There was no real medical treatment, and by late 1864 rations were down to a few tablespoons of mealy beans or rancid rice a day. When word of conditions at Andersonville leaked out, Northerners were horrified. One poet wrote about the camp: "There are deeds, crimes that may be forgiven, but this is not among them." When the war was over, prison commander Henry Wirz was arrested for murder, and the "conspiracy to injure the health and lives of Union soldiers." He showed little sympathy for the thousands who'd died, and this probably sealed his execution. Wirz insisted he was just following orders. However, the Bible says the wages of sin is death. It is never right to mistreat other human beings—no matter what their crimes. God Himself is merciful to all, and asks that we be compassionate too. No matter what.

The War to End All Wars

"Peace I leave with you, My peace I give to you; not as the world gives
do I give to you. Let not your heart be troubled, neither let it be afraid."
John 14:27, NKJV.

On this day in 1918, World War I—The War to end all Wars—finally ended and the world breathed one big sigh of relief. Never in earth's history had there been so many nations involved in warfare on such a large scale. So many countries were involved that it could hardly be considered anything but a world war. Many of them were not instigators, of course, but they got swept into it because of their alliances with countries that had joined the fight. Some historians list 32 countries and their empires, territories, and colonies as joining in the conflict, though not all were directly involved. Some say as many as 100. Surprisingly, many people in Europe celebrated when their country joined the war. Foolishly, they thought that in a few months their country would be the winner. Of course, that's not how it went at all.

It was called the Great War until 1939, when the second worldwide conflict began. Then it officially became World War I. Although WWI lasted only four years, it was 30 years in coming. The main instigators were Austria-Hungary, and Italy, and they were fighting against the Allies which included Great Britain, France, and Russia. The U.S. didn't join the conflict until the spring of 1917.

And then, in 1918, at the 11th hour, on the 11th day, of the 11th month, the Great War ended. Earlier that morning Germany had signed a peace agreement with the Allies in a railroad car north of Paris, France. The war left nine million soldiers dead and 21 million wounded. Another five million civilians died from disease, starvation, or exposure. Unfortunately, the peace treaty that ended the conflict didn't strengthen Europe. In fact, it was one of the causes of World War II.

Jesus told us that there would be wars until the end of the world, and that these would be signs of His second coming. Some of you reading this have lived through war or other serious trouble. If so, you know that God keeps His promise to be with us—no matter what. Today's scripture reminds us that the only kind of peace we can truly count on is the peace that Jesus personally gives.

First Meteor Shower on Record

"The stars of heaven will fall, and the powers in the heavens will be shaken."
Mark 13:25, NKJV.

Women cried. Men fell to their knees. Parents awoke their children and took them outside to watch the astounding beauty of the night sky filled with shooting stars—a thousand a minute seen from the Gulf of Mexico to Nova Scotia. And some remembered that Jesus said at the end of time "the stars of heaven" would fall—and believed it was the end of the world!

It was November 12, 1833, and people were stunned and afraid. Some meteors were no bigger than a drop of water while others rushed by so close they looked like a full moon. Surely everyone saw it. If they didn't wake up to the excited cries of neighbors, they were awakened by flashes of fireballs brightening their dark bedrooms.

The heavenly "fireworks" were caused by a repeating band of meteors called the Leonid meteor shower that appears every year in mid-November, but seems to be especially stunning every 33 or 34 years. It came again in 1833, more spectacular than ever during the early morning hours of eastern North America. The night sky was almost as bright as broad daylight.

From what is known, the 1833 shower was probably much like the peak Leonid years of 1966 and 1999, and included up to 150,000 meteors per hour. "It was the grandest and most beautiful scene my eyes have ever beheld," said one young boy.

Some people took it as a sign of the coming Judgment. In fact, the early believers in Christ's soon return pointed back to the falling of the stars as one of the signs of His soon coming. But others were fascinated by the scientific end of it, and the first organized study of meteor astronomy grew out of this interest.

In Matthew 24 Jesus tells some of the things that will happen near the end of time. Then He says, "Keep watch, because you do not know on what day your Lord will come" (Matt. 24:42, NIV). "The Son of Man will come . . . when you do not expect him" (verse 44). Let's be ready to meet Him.

Vietnam Vet Memorial

Greater love has no one than this, than to lay down one's life for his friends.
John 15:13, NKJV.

Maybe you've seen it. The long V-shaped black-granite wall adjacent to the National mall. It was dedicated on this date in 1982, toward the end of a weeklong national salute to Americans who served in the Vietnam War. Thousands of Vietnam veterans marched to its site for its dedication. The wall is inscribed with the names of the 57,939 Americans who died in the conflict, listed in order of death, not of rank, as is common in other memorials.

It was designed by an architecture student, Maya Lin. She is the daughter of Chinese immigrants and won a nationwide competition to create a design for the monument. At first, people didn't like it. It was too different. Where were the men in uniform? Where were the weapons. But the Memorial soon became one of the most visited in the U.S. capital. Visitors often make an etching of the name or leave a private offering—notes, flowers, dog tags, medals, photos, and even a pair of combat boots. No one ever imagined that so many personal items would be left there, and now more than 100,000 are stored in a museum resource center.

The list of names on the memorial seems to go on forever, names of the men and women who served in all branches of the military and who died in service. One is almost overwhelmed by the enormity of the sacrifice of these nearly 58,000 husbands and wives, and sons and daughters. The Vietnam war became very unpopular in the U.S. but somehow the Wall brought together both those who fought there and those who marched against the war.

Jesus was not always popular when He was on earth. Not everyone appreciated the things He said nor everything He did. Sometimes His own family was confused and distressed by His actions. He died pretty much alone, leaving even His disciples sick with sorrow and defeat. But Jesus did what He had to do in the war between good and evil, and now Christians around the whole world recognize Christ's death as the most selfless act of all time.

Children's Church

*Let the children come to me. Don't stop them! For the
Kingdom of God belongs to those who are like these children.
Mark 10:14, NLT.*

Have you ever taken part in a children's church program, leading out, or maybe helping in a children's camp meeting program? Well listen to this. On November 14, 1937, a one-of-a-kind church was dedicated to children in Milton, Massachusetts. It was, in fact, a miniature church built to scale at a cost of $5,000, and it was intended to be operated by children. It was 18' by 32', had a steeple, an organ, a church bell, and pews that were 2' 8" high. It even had its own pastor—Mrs. Dorothy Pomeroy.

Children's church programs are on the rise in America, and becoming more popular every year. More and more churches are offering children's church as apart of their ministry and regular worship program. Some offer it several times a year, some monthly, and others several times a week.

One mega church in St. Louis, Missouri, offers six children's worship services every Sunday. Children from the first through the sixth grade are welcome—but parents aren't allowed. Greeters meet every kid at the door to give them a name tag, and kid ushers seat them on the floor. (No chairs or pews—chairs seem to be a territorial issue for kids. With more than 200 kids in a typical service, seating arrangements can cause problems. Also, kids want to sit with the same friends each week, and that encourages undesirable clicks.) Kids aren't allowed to leave the Church during the program, and bathroom breaks are carefully monitored. And kids must be willing to participate by leading the praise service, reading Bible verses, and praying. They give personal testimonies, and join in drama with pantomime and puppets as part of the worship schedule. This is a real church with a real preacher and real Bible study. The children's church program requires five full-time adult employees and 15 volunteers and a full week of planning to pull off a program of this size.

If you would like to become a part of such a program, why not ask your local church or conference how you can help? You never know what great things God might do through you for children.

Armageddon Missile Match

"Nation will rise against nation, and kingdom against kingdom."
Luke 21:10, NKJV.

And they gathered them together to the place called in Hebrew, Armageddon
Revelation 16:16, NKJV.

In a long and rambling interview with an American reporter on November 15, 1957, Soviet leader, Nikita Khrushchev, claimed that the Soviet Union had missile superiority over the United States and challenged America to a missile shooting match to prove his claim. This news story fed the fears in the United States that America was falling farther and farther behind the Soviets in the arms race.

Krushchev said that both the Americans and Soviet people wanted peace but warned that although the Soviet Union would never start a war, some lunatics on our side might bring about a conflict. If there were war, he threatened, it "would be fought on the American continent, which can be reached by our rockets." He predicted that NATO forces in Europe would also be destroyed, and Europe would become a cemetery. While the Soviet Union would suffer immensely, the forces of communism would ultimately destroy capitalism.

The next day the United States flew in 88 German scientists to assist the nation in its production of rocket technology. Most of these men had served under the Nazi regime during World War II, and critics in the United States questioned the morality of placing them in the service of America. Nevertheless, the U.S. government, desperate to acquire scientific know-how and fearful that the Russians were also utilizing captured German scientists for the same end, welcomed the men with open arms. This situation pointed out one of the many ironies connected with the Cold War. The United States and the Soviet Union, once allies against Germany and the Nazi regime during World War II, were now in a fierce contest to acquire the best and brightest scientists—the very ones who had helped arm the German forces—to construct weapons systems with which to threaten each other.

Jesus said men's hearts would fail them for fear of what is happening on the earth. But we are not to worry. Shortly after these things, He promised, we "will see the Son of Man coming in a cloud with power and great glory" Luke 21:27, NKJV. Humans will not end the world—Jesus will!

Giant Bonfire Collapses

*But everyone who hears these sayings of Mine, and does not do
them, will be like a foolish man who built his house on the sand.
Matthew 7:26, NKJV.*

On November 16, 1999, work began on a giant bonfire on the campus of
Texas A&M University. Two days later it collapsed, killing 12 students
and injuring another 27. For nearly a century students in College Station,
Texas, had created a massive bonfire prior to their school's annual football
game against their archrival, the University of Texas. Part of the tradition was
the claim that it was the world's largest bonfire. The beloved pre-game tradition had been canceled only once, in 1963, following the assassination of
President John F. Kennedy. Over the years, the bonfire grew so big that its
construction became an elaborate project requiring days of work by teams of
student volunteers. On two previous occasions the bonfire had partially collapsed, but neither of the accidents had been disastrous.

The 1999 bonfire is reported to have required more than 7,000 logs and
the labor of as many as 70 workers at a time. Just after dawn on November
18, students were working near the top of the 59-foot-high pile (four feet
higher than had been authorized). Suddenly the base of the pile gave way,
and scores of students were caught in the huge log pile. Some of them, like
Caleb Hill who suffered only broken bones in his 50-foot fall, were lucky
enough to fall away from the pile. People ran around, calling out names and
crying. Other people seemed to be in shock. Cranes were immediately
brought in to remove the logs and free the students, but the process was
painstaking and slow, as any wrong movement could cause further collapse.
The last survivor was pulled from the pile about six hours later.

An investigation began into the causes of the collapse, and it was later
determined that the first stack of logs didn't have sufficient containment
strength. The wire used to tie the logs together wasn't strong enough for the
job. The steel cables that had been used in prior years weren't used this time.
In the words of one observer, "It was a complex and dangerous structure,
without adequate physical or engineering control."

If we don't have a good foundation, should we be surprised when our
lives fall apart? Only Jesus can guarantee success when it comes to such a
foundation. Ask Him to help you today.

Billion Dollar Bank

Give me neither poverty nor riches! Give me just enough to satisfy my needs. For if I grow rich, I may deny you and say, "Who is the Lord?" and if I am too poor, I may steal and thus insult God's holy name. Proverbs 30:8, 9, NLT.

On November 17, 1919, the National City Bank of New York City reported that it was worth $1 billion in assets (about $40 billion at today's rate of inflation). That was a long time ago, and many people since then have earned that much money all by themselves.

Bill Gates III is one of them. Best known as an American business tycoon, philanthropist, author, and chairman of Microsoft, a computer software company, Gates is one of the world's wealthiest people, being worth about $40 billion. (Before the stock market slump began in 2002 he was worth $85 billion.) One of the most successful billionaires of all time, he and his "geek" buddies at Microsoft and Apple almost singlehandedly launched the personal computer revolution.

Gates is worth billions, but even a billion dollars is a lot of money. *So how much is $1 billion dollars, exactly?*

Well, if you were counting out $10 bills—one per second, 24 hours a day, seven days a week—it would take you more than three years to count out $1 billion.

A stack of one billion dollar bills would reach more than 200 miles into the sky.

If you spent $100,000 a day it would take 27 years to spend $1 billion.

One thousand million dollars makes $1 billion.

So what would you do if you had a billion dollars? What could you do? At $20 an hour you could hire 1,000 construction workers for 25 years to build churches all over the world. That's what a billion dollars could do! You could pay for the sandwiches needed to feed 100,000 homeless people, 365 days a year, *for 30 years.* That's what a billion dollars could do! You could pay to have a Bible printed for every man, woman, and child in Brazil, Pakistan, Nigeria, Russia, Japan, Mexico, Egypt, and Argentina. That's what a billion dollars could do!

But too much money can be a bad thing if it is horded. Too much money can make us forget our need for God. Why not let Jesus take care of all your money problems today?

Jonestown Massacre

There is a way that seems right to a man, but its end is the way of death.
Proverbs 16:25, NKJV.

One of the largest mass suicides in history happened on this day in November 1978. The testimony of witnesses who escaped from the jungle compound minutes before everyone died tells quite another story. We can now safely call it a case of mass murder, not suicide; and Jim Jones, leader of the People's Temple, was the mastermind behind this tragedy. Leading his followers in a mass murder-suicide at their commune in Guyana, South America, Jones insisted that everyone drink the cyanide-laced fruit drink. The few cult members who refused were forced to drink it at gunpoint or were shot as they fled. The final death toll was 913, including 276 children.

Jim Jones, a very a charismatic leader, founded the People's Temple in Indianapolis, Indiana, in the 1950s. In 1965 he moved the group to northern California, settling first in Ukiah and, later, in San Francisco. In the 1970s his church was accused by the press of financial fraud, physical abuse of its members, and mistreatment of children. In response to the mounting criticism, Jones led several hundred of his followers to South America in 1977. It was there that he set up a settlement he named Jonestown in the jungles of Guyana.

A year later a group of former members convinced United States Congressman Leo Ryan to travel to Jonestown and investigate the commune. So on November 17, 1978, Ryan arrived with a group of journalists and other observers.

At first the visit went well, but the next day, as Ryan's group was about to leave, several People's Temple members approached them and asked for passage out of Guyana. Jones became distressed that his members would want to leave, and one of his lieutenants attacked Congressman Ryan with a knife. Ryan escaped unharmed, but Jones then ordered an ambush for him and his companions and had them killed at the airstrip as they attempted to board their charter planes. Jones immediately directed his followers in the mass suicide while he preached to them about "the beauty of dying" for the last time.

We may have to give our lives for Jesus some day, but He doesn't ask that we take it ourselves. He would rather that we become living sacrifices—witnesses—for Him each day.

Lincoln's Famous Speech

No man ever spoke like this Man.
John 7:46, NKJV.

Fourscore and seven years ago
our fathers brought forth on this continent a new nation,
conceived in liberty . . .

On this rainy day in November 1863, President Abraham Lincoln gave his famous Gettysburg Address on a battlefield in Pennsylvania to dedicate the battle zone where, only four months earlier, nearly 50,000 soldiers had been killed, wounded, or declared missing in action.

Lincoln spoke of the lives that had been given to preserve the United States of America. "We cannot dedicate—we cannot consecrate—we cannot hallow—this ground," he said. "The brave men, lying and dead, who have struggled here, have consecrated it." And then Lincoln added, "The world will little note, nor long remember, what we say here, but it can never forget what they did here."

Only 278 words.

Edward Everett, a famous orator and guest speaker at the ceremony, had already delivered a speech that lasted for two hours. Boring! If everybody hadn't been standing in the rain, they would have probably fallen asleep.

Lincoln's speech lasted only two minutes. He left the battlefield feeling as if the whole thing had been a flop. However, Everett later told Lincoln that the president's simple speech was beautiful, and that he had said more in two minutes than Everett had said in two hours. Today Lincoln's speech remains one of the most famous in American history. Its words still remind us of that day so long ago when simplicity trumped sophistication.

When Jesus was here He spoke simply, using words ordinary people could understand and remember, words that offered comfort and courage and hope. And people liked it. "No one ever spoke like this Man!" they said.

No fancy words.

No long sermons.

Just words that changed the world forever.

Whale Sinks Ship

There is the sea, vast and spacious, . . . and the leviathan,
which you formed to frolic there. These all look to you
to give them their food at the proper time.
Psalm 104:25-27, NIV.

What must it have been like to live before the flood when dinosaurs roamed the earth and giant creatures ruled the seas? Carcharodon Megalodon, for instance. It's estimated that this giant prehistoric shark was 40 to 50 feet long and weighed 48 tons (a large great white shark is about 20 feet long and weighs a little over two tons)—about as much as seven African elephants weighing in at seven tons each. That's bigger than T-Rex! In fact, next to the sperm whale, Megalodon was the largest predator the world has ever seen. Its fossilized teeth range in size from three to seven inches long, massive things that can be bigger than a man's hand. Providing nourishment for 48 tons of raw powered muscle was no small task. It probably dined on whales.

The really scary part is that today some of those creatures are still around. Some of them have attacked men at sea. In the days of Columbus sailors were afraid to sail too far into uncharted waters. They marked their maps, "Here there be dragons!" The legendry stories sailors told of sea serpents and giant squid that could attack and eat a boat may seem a bit far-fetched; nevertheless, the part about sea monsters taking ships down was true. On November 20, 1820, an American ship, 2,000 miles at sea, was sunk by an 80-ton sperm whale, similar to the whale in Melville's *Moby Dick*.

In the 1800s and 1900s the whaling industry, which was considered to be one of the most dangerous professions, was running full tilt. Men hunted down every whale they could find for whale oil, which was used for lamps and candles, and whale blubber, which was used for lubricating machine parts. As long as the men were on the bigger whaling ships used for processing the whales the adventure was pretty safe. However, there was always a chance that the whalers could die while they were in the small row boats that were used to chase down and harpoon angry whales.

God created all the creatures for us to enjoy. Unfortunately, in this sinful world people sometimes hunt down animals simply for sport. In the earth made new, though, these magnificent leviathan creatures will be able to cruise the deep blue seas in perfect freedom, just as God intended.

Who Shot JR?

Satan himself masquerades as an angel of light. It is not surprising,
then, if his servants masquerade as servants of righteousness.
2 Corinthians 11:14, 15, NIV.

Years ago there was a popular Prime Time television drama called *Dallas* whose characters wove a weekly web of deceit and blackmail and, sometimes, even murder. Company tycoons were ruthless in their business dealings, and characters were often drunk, or had problems with gambling, or were unfaithful to their spouses.

The oil tycoon, J. R. Ewing, developed into a backstabbing, double-dealing character everybody loved to hate. Of course the twists of plot for shows such as *Dallas* need to keep you guessing what's coming next so you'll come back for more. During the final moments of the season ending episode in March 1980, J. R. Ewing was shot. Not surprisingly, this inspired widespread media coverage and left everyone asking this fateful question for the next eight months: "Who shot J. R.?"

It all came to a head on November 21, 1980, when 350 million television viewers from around the globe tuned in to find out who shot J. R. Ewing, the company president of Ewing Oil. Now that's a lot of people! Eighty-three million people in the U.S. alone sat down to watch. Seventy-six percent of all U.S. televisions that were on that night were tuned in to *Dallas*. That's more people than watch the Super Bowl! Today that episode still stands as one of television's most famous cliffhangers. Not surprisingly, the show went on to run for another 12 seasons.

The producers of *Dallas* did their best to disguise the identity of J. R.'s killer—and that was just a TV show! Can you imagine what it will be like when attempts will be made to disguise things of real importance just before Jesus comes? Paul tells us that Satan, the murdering father of all lies, will attempt to deceive the world by disguising himself as an angel of light.

But the faithful followers of Jesus will know truth from error and will wait for the real coming of Jesus in the clouds of heaven. They will not be deceived by Satan in his robes of light or by his servants who masquerade as servants of righteousness.

Blackbeard the Pirate

Many sorrows come to the wicked, but unfailing love surrounds those who trust the Lord. So rejoice in the Lord and be glad . . . all you whose hearts are pure!"
Psalm 32:10, 11, NLT.

Who do you think was the most famous pirate in history? Captain Kidd from *Treasure Island?* Maybe Captain Hook from *Peter Pan?* Well, many historians would say Blackbeard the Pirate, because he was the most notorious villain of them all. No one really knows where he was born, but his career as a pirate began in 1713 when he joined the crew of pirate Benjamin Hornigold in the Caribbean. When Hornigold retired in 1717, Edward Teach, as Blackbeard was formally called, took over the command of a captured 26-gun French merchantman ship. He re-outfitted the ship with 40 cannon, renamed it *Queen Anne's Revenge,* and set out on a legendary spree of robbing and killing. *Queen Anne's Revenge* became the flagship of several pirate vessels with a crew of more than 200 sailors that ran the high seas. Blackbeard got his name from his long, dark beard which, some say, he lit on fire during battles to frighten his enemies. The infamous pirate and his crew were known for their cruelty as they terrorized the Caribbean islands. Before long, he was the most wanted criminal in the Western Hemisphere.

In May 1718 two of his vessels were shipwrecked, including the *Queen Anne's Revenge.* With only one vessel in his command, Blackbeard sailed to North Carolina and arranged a meeting with Governor Charles Eden, who secretly pardoned Blackbeard in exchange, of course, for a good share of his stolen booty. The well-to-do plantation owners in the colony of Virginia to the north heard about the arrangement and asked their governor, Alexander Spotswood, to send the British navy to capture Blackbeard. It was a real showdown, and in the bloody battle that followed Blackbeard's forces were defeated, and he was killed on the Outer Banks off North Carolina on November 22, 1718. Legend tells us that Blackbeard stood his ground until he died, pierced by five musket balls and cut to ribbons by 20 sword lacerations. His five-year career as the infamous looter of more than 30 ships was over.

The story of Blackbeard's adventures on the high seas sounds exciting—almost romantic—but that's just the stuff of trashy novels and movies. No one can really live a life like that and be happy. God has surrounded us with His promises of unfailing love. Why not choose to live for Him instead?

Wartime Rationing Ends

Behold, the days are coming," says the Lord God, "That I will send a famine on the land, not a famine of bread, nor a thirst for water, but of hearing the words of the Lord. They shall . . . run to and fro, seeking the word of the Lord, but shall not find it. Amos 8:11, 12, NKJV.

Have you ever been told that you could have only one piece of cake? Or one cookie? Or one can of soda? Can you imagine being told you could buy milk only on Tuesdays, gasoline on Thursdays, or oranges not at all? Well, during World War II, in the 1940s, that's exactly what went on. During the war every spare bit of food we could save was sent overseas to help feed millions of soldiers. Germany, Italy, and Japan had been desperately trying to take over the world, and rationing food was just one way of helping us win.

Rationing began in 1943 when every family was registered at their local schools. Each family was asked to send only one member for registration. Coupons were distributed based on family size, so rationing stamps became a kind of currency, or money. Red stamps bought all meats, butter, fat, and oil. Blue Stamps bought canned and dry vegetables, fruit, soups, baby food, and catsup. Shoes, coffee, gasoline, tires, and fuel oil were also rationed. Life during the war meant daily sacrifice, but few people complained because they knew the men and women on the battlefield were making the greater sacrifice. One rationing poster read: "Do with less so they'll have enough."

It all ended on November 23, 1945, when the war was finally over. The United States Government stopped wartime food rationing for some things, such as meat and butter. Everyone was so excited they probably ran out and bought something special so they could have a party and celebrate. Maybe they even bought some of whatever it was that had been rationed during the war—if they could find any. Chances are it took weeks to get the basics back on the store shelves, and months before the shelves got stocked again with everybody's favorites.

Some day there's going to be shortages again, but this time it won't be of food, shoes, or gasoline. It will be a shortage of the Word of God. People will run here and there, searching for words of comfort from God's people or the Bible, but earth's probation will have ended. The time for salvation will have passed. Don't let that happen to you! Begin storing up the Word of God in your heart today, and when the end comes, Jesus will give you all the strength you need.

Hijacker Jumps Into Storm

How you are fallen from heaven, O Lucifer, son of the morning!
How you are cut down to the ground, you who weakened the nations!
Isaiah 14:12, NKJV.

Most people have dreams they'd liked to realize before their life is over. Some want to deep-sea dive. Some want to parasail. Others want to write a book, be in a body-building contest, or go on a cruise around the world. And how about sky diving? That would be a real rush if you've never done it before. Maybe. But not if you had to do it the way D. B. Cooper did.

On November 24, 1971, a man calling himself Cooper parachuted from a 727 airliner over Washington State, at an altitude of 10,000 feet. It was terribly cold, well below zero at that altitude, and the flight happened to be going through a thunderstorm at the time. The wind was running at 100 miles per hour, and Cooper was wearing only a thin suit, a raincoat, and wraparound sunglasses. Why would he do such a thing? Was it some kind of a stunt for the *Guinness Book of World Records*? Was it a military exercise? No, actually Cooper was a hijacker, and he had on his person $200,000 in ransom money. He had shanghaied the jet shortly after takeoff by showing a flight attendant something that looked like a bomb. He asked the crew for $200,000, four parachutes, and "no funny stuff."

When the plane landed at the Seattle-Tacoma International Airport, authorities met Cooper's demands after he let the rest of the passengers go. And that was the last anyone ever heard of him. Rescue teams couldn't go in search of him at the time because of the storm in progress. Most authorities think he was killed during his suicide jump. Interestingly enough, 19 years later an 8-year-old boy uncovered nearly $6,000 of the ransom money in the sand along the north bank of the Columbia River, five miles from Vancouver, Washington. The fate of Cooper still remains a mystery.

Once upon a time, in the Garden of Eden, Lucifer hijacked our first parents, and he was jubilant, thinking he had won the battle between good and evil. But he failed to take into consideration one major point: he was dealing with the sovereign of the universe. God always has a contingency plan, and He had one then. From the beginning of time the Godhead had devised a plan that if sin should ever hijack the human race Jesus would pay the ransom and buy us back with *His* life. We are so blessed that He did. Can we ever thank Him enough?

November 25

We Can't Forget

He died for all, that those who live
should no longer live for themselves.
2 Corinthians 5:15, NIV.

A crowd estimated at 800,000 stood in silence as the flag-draped coffin, resting on a gun carriage drawn by six gray horses, passed by on its way to Arlington National Cemetery. The Marine band stepped out bravely, the Stars and Stripes fluttering slightly ahead of the caisson, the presidential flag behind. A riderless horse followed, prancing. The widow walked briskly behind the caisson, her brothers-in-law on either side, leading the most distinguished company of dignitaries ever assembled in the history of the United States. They had come in honor of her young husband. The representatives of the world followed, a phalanx arranged in the alphabetical order of their countries.

The president was buried to a 21-gun salute and three musket volleys. As a bugle sounded Taps, the remains of John F. Kennedy were lowered into the grave. It was the last formal act of the tragedy that had begun in Dallas, Texas, three days earlier, on November 22, 1963.

And after the prayers of the burial service there was nothing left to be said, only the echo of the challenge from his first inaugural address that is inscribed on his gravesite:

In the long history of the world only a few generations have been granted the role of defending freedom. In the hour of maximum danger I do not shrink from this responsibility—I welcome it. The energy, the faith, the devotion which we bring to this endeavor will light our country and all who serve it. And the glow from that fire can truly light the world.

A long time ago another Man was murdered not by a rifle bullet but by cruel nails driven into His outstretched hands. Three days later He came from his grave, shining, powerful, with everything yet to be said, His challenge echoing down through the centuries:

You will receive power when the Holy Spirit comes on you; and you will be my witnesses in Jerusalem, and in all Judea and Samaria, and to the ends of the earth (Acts 1:8, NIV).

"I will come back," He promised. "I will come back and take you to be with me!" (See John 14:3, NIV).

Diamond Hoax

We will no longer be immature like children. We won't be tossed and blown about by every wind of new teaching. We will not be influenced when people try to trick us with lies so clever they sound like the truth.
Ephesians 4:14, NLT.

Have you ever been tricked into believing something someone told you? Have you ever been cheated out of money that was rightfully yours, or ever had a friendship that you thought was for real only to find out later that it was no more sure than a puff of smoke?

Con artists pull off scams all the time, and many of them get away with it. It's not right, but it's the way things work out sometimes in this sinful old world. That's exactly what happened on this day in 1872. Philip Arnold and John Slack, two cousins from Kentucky, pulled off one of the biggest hoaxes in mining history. They convinced investors in San Francisco to buy stock in a worthless diamond mine in the northwestern corner of Colorado.

Inexperienced investors sometimes fell for this trick before the gag was discovered. Sometimes, though, if the hoax was good enough, even financial wizards could be fooled. And that's exactly what happened. Arnold and Slack played their con game perfectly. They came to San Francisco in 1872 and tried to deposit a bag of uncut diamonds at a bank. When questioned, the two men quickly disappeared, acting as if they were reluctant to talk about their discovery.

Intrigued, a bank director named William Ralston tracked down the men. Assuming he was dealing with unsophisticated country bumpkins, he set out to take control of the diamond mine. The two cousins agreed to take a blindfolded mining expert to the site, and the expert returned to report that the mine was indeed rich with diamonds and rubies. Ralston took the bait, formed his own mining company worth $10 million, and began selling stock. He paid Arnold and Slack $600,000, with promises of more to come. Now, today that would be small fry in our world of finance; however, we're talking about 1872 when $600,000 was equal to more than $70 million in today's money.

The book of Ephesians warns us about being spiritually naïve. We should be careful about new religious ideas that come along and not be easily influenced by tricksters who spin lies so cleverly that they sound like the truth. No one likes to be fooled, but wouldn't it be a tragedy if it cost us our salvation?

The Fat President

*Do you not know that your body is the temple of the Holy Spirit
who is in you, whom you have from God, and you are not your own?
For you were bought at a price; therefore glorify God in your
body and in your spirit, which are God's.
1 Corinthians 6:19, 20, NKJV.*

Many people are interested in stories about movie stars on television, radio, and that online bloggers share. The media digs up dirt on athletes and other famous celebrities—and even the president of the United States. It seems that gossip about what goes on at the White House "sells." Some newspapers and magazine make it their business to pry into the private lives of our president and his family, and comedians and late night television hosts have great fun poking fun at politicians.

This is nothing new. It's been going on for a very long time, even before television and radio were being used much to report the news. Evidently the press in the days of President Taft also enjoyed getting what info they could on the politicians of their day and were willing to pay for it. A White House housekeeper by the name of Elizabeth Jaffray knew a lot about the twenty-seventh President of the United States. According to the White House Historical Association, on November 27, 1911, she wrote in her diary that she thought President Taft was too fat. And though the President might not have wanted to admit it, at 355 pounds, she was probably right.

According to his biographers, President Taft had to have his shoes tied by his valet. And it usually took two (or more) men to help him get out of the bathtub. Once, when he was visiting the czar of Russia, his pants split while he was getting out of a carriage.

But Taft's weight didn't stop him from serving a full term as president. Nor did it keep him from becoming the chief justice of the Supreme Court after his term as president was over. (He was the first—and only—president to hold both offices.)

President Taft was a very successful man, but it still must have been hard to hear people make jokes about him. Even the president of the United States can get his feelings hurt. In today's verse Paul seems to have an answer for the president: "You are not your own, for you were bought with a price."

We are all worth more than we can possibly imagine, because Jesus gave His life for us.

Turkey Day

I will praise God's name in song and glorify him with thanksgiving.
Psalm 69:30, NIV.

Thanksgiving Day! Some people call it turkey day, and that's no surprise. Forty-five million turkeys are eaten every November. But there's so much more to be thankful for than just turkeys. Living in a free country, for instance. And being able to say what you think about our elected officials without fear of being thrown into prison. Or being able to travel from state to state without having to show special papers or identification.

Of course we should show our thankfulness, and Thanksgiving is the perfect holiday to do it. The day is so important to Americans, in fact, that several presidents have gotten into the spirit.

In 1863 President Lincoln announced that a national holiday would be observed the last Thursday of every November. And then in 1939 Franklin D. Roosevelt moved Thanksgiving back a week to stimulate Christmas shopping and the economy. However, in 1941 the United States Congress again declared that the fourth Thursday of November would indeed be the official day of celebration for Thanksgiving.

Thanksgiving Day usually has good memories for people because it's the day they spend with family. We celebrate by eating good food (mashed potatoes and gravy, cranberry sauce, turkey—or maybe veggie turkey—and pumpkin pie). We play a little football outside, and then watch more football on television after dinner. We play some board games while the old folks sit around and talk about boring stuff, and the little kids go outside after dark and play flashlight tag.

And we thank God for all His blessings during the previous year.

The Bible relates many stories about people who were blessed by God and thankful for it. Noah was grateful to God for bringing him and his family through the flood, and he offered up sacrifices under an arcing rainbow in the sky. Abraham was thankful to God for every blessing and gave his tithes to King Melchizedek. Jacob was thankful to God for sending him a dream of assurance, and promised to be faithful to his God. David was grateful to God for His watch care and wrote Psalm 23. Jesus thanked His Father for His disciples. Paul said he was content in whatever life situation he found himself.

What are you especially thankful for today?

C. S. Lewis Is Born

*I will open My mouth in parables; I will utter things
kept secret from the foundation of the world.
Matthew 13:35, NKJV.*

C. S. Lewis, one of the most famous authors of the twentieth century, was
born on this day in 1898. He's famous for many books and series of
books, including *The Screwtape Letters, Mere Christianity,* and *The Chronicles of
Narnia,* all of which became best sellers.

So who was C. S. Lewis? His family called him Jack, but he became famous as a writer, professor, medieval expert, and theologian. Lewis was a
good friend of Tolkien, who wrote *The Lord of the Rings.* Both men taught at
Oxford University in England, and it was Tolkien who convinced Lewis to become a born-again Christian.

Lewis's conversion had a big impact on his work, and when he began
speaking on the radio during World War II his views on God made him famous. He is well known for such one-liners as "a man can no more diminish
God's glory by refusing to worship Him, than a lunatic can put out the sun by
scribbling the word, 'darkness' on the walls of his cell."

When Lewis died suddenly of a heart attack, the news never made the
front page of newspapers because he died on the same day President
Kennedy in the United States was assassinated.

Lewis has been translated into more than 40 languages, and his books
are among some of the best-selling books of all time. The seven-book series,
The Chronicles of Narnia has been his most successful, selling more than 120
million, and has been made even more popular because of stage, radio, and
movie productions.

Lewis was best known for his ability to write appealing parables that provide spiritual lessons for young people. It seems that the best things can often
be said in a story, as Jesus well knew this when He captured everyone's attention with parables. No one could tell a story like Jesus did!

But then, we shouldn't be surprised—after all, He *is* God.

Mark Twain Born

Wisdom belongs to the aged, and understanding to the old. But true wisdom and power are found in God; counsel and understanding are his. Job 12:12, 13, NLT.

Samuel Clemens, one of the most famous writers of the 1800s, was born in Florida, Missouri, on this day in 1835. You might have read two of his best-known books—*Adventures of Huckleberry Finn* and *The Adventures of Tom Sawyer.* During his lifetime Twain became a friend to presidents, artists, industrialists, and European royalty. He enjoyed immense public popularity, and his keen wit and incisive satire earned him praise from both critics and peers.

Clemens began to work as a printer at the age of 13 then went on to write a series of travel comics. When he grew tired of that he became a steamboat captain for two years. It was during these years that he picked up his legendary nickname, Mark Twain, a term used by riverboat pilots to announce that the river has reached a depth of only two fathoms. The name stuck with him for the next 50 years.

Twain made a substantial amount of money through his writing, but he spent much of it in bad investments and had to claim bankruptcy. He then embarked on an around-the-world lecture tour to pay off his creditors in full, despite the fact that he was no longer under any legal obligation to do so because of the bankruptcy. Twain passed through a period of deep depression, which began in 1896 when his favorite daughter Susy died of meningitis. His wife, Olivia, died in 1904, and another daughter Jean died on Christmas Eve 1909. His gloom deepened with the sudden death of his close friend, Henry Rogers, five months later.

In spite of his setbacks in life, Mark Twain was well known for his ability to write with wit and humor. Some of his more memorable "sound bites" include: "If you tell the truth you don't have to remember anything." "A lie can travel halfway around the world, while the truth is putting on its shoes." "It is better to keep your mouth closed and let people think you are a fool, than to open it and remove all doubt."

Mark Twain had a way with words, but if we want to be truly wise we should look to God, where all wisdom and power are found. He knows everything, the beginning to the end. Why not try a dose of His wisdom today. If we pray, asking Him about the decisions we need to make in our lives, He'll be there for us.

Rosa Parks Arrested

*God shows no favoritism. In every nation he accepts
those who fear him and do what is right.
Acts 10:34, 35, NLT.*

Have you ever stood up for something you thought was right? What were the consequences? How did you feel? Sometimes it might seem as if the price is too great; but in the end standing up for yourself can be worth everything.

On December 1, 1955, Rosa Parks was sent to jail because she refused to give up her seat on a public bus to a White man. Would you be willing to do that? Remember, in those days there was very little sympathy or support for such a stand—but it was the right thing to do. Rosa Parks is remembered as the mother of the civil rights movement. In those days African-Americans were required to sit in the back of public buses and had to give up their seats to White riders if the front seats filled up.

Rosa was sitting in the first row of the Black section that day when the bus driver told her to give up her seat to a White man. Rosa refused, and with that one act she started a movement that would last well into the 1960s. She had heard talk by the civil rights leaders of Montgomery, Alabama, led by a young Baptist minister named Martin Luther King, Jr. This gave her courage to make her stand when she did. Dr. King then challenged African-Americans to boycott the public buses of Montgomery. "The great glory of American democracy is the right to protest for right," he said. But not everybody saw it that way, and at one point his home was bombed. Fortunately, he and his family escaped with their lives.

The boycott lasted for more than a year, and since African-Americans made up 70 percent of those who used the buses, the public busing system suffered financially. In November 1956 the United States Supreme Court finally outlawed segregation busing laws as a violation of the Fourteenth Amendment to the United States Constitution.

Rosa Parks had won, and she probably had done more for the civil rights movement than we can possibly imagine. When she died in 2005 she was celebrated as one of America's great pioneers in the civil right's movement.

God is fair. He doesn't discriminate. He has no favorites when it comes to race or age, country or religion. He loves everyone and wants us all to be saved in His kingdom.

Revolutionary Spy

By faith these people overthrew kingdoms, ruled with justice, and received what God had promised them. Hebrews 11:33, NLT.

Today we see all kinds of movies in which women do undercover work for the government. They drive, shoot, and skydive into enemy territory as well as any of the male agents. They work for the CIA, the FBI, and NSA. James Bond movies feature them. Mission Impossible movies include them. But there are also real examples in American history of women who have truly served their country and come away as true heroines. Lydia Darragh, a nurse in Philadelphia, is one such example. This is her story.

British General William Howe's headquarters were located across the street from the Darragh home. When his meeting room proved too small to hold meetings, without even asking, he moved right into a large upstairs room in the Darraghs' house. British military officers didn't ask permission in those days. They simply told the colonists what they would, and would not, do.

During the next weeks that followed Lydia fell into the habit of eavesdropping from an adjoining room whenever she could, taking notes on the British meetings. Then she hid the notes by sewing them into her coat, then passing them on to the American troops stationed outside the city.

Well, her vigilance paid off. On the night of December 2, 1777, she overheard especially the scary news that the British commanders were planning a surprise attack on Washington's army at Whitemarsh, Pennsylvania, on December 4 and 5. As usual, she sewed the message inside her clothes and waited for dawn. Saying that she needed to buy flour from a nearby mill just outside the British line, she made her way past the sentries and passed the information on to Washington and his army.

If she were living today the CIA just might make her an honorary member. They still talk about her deeds of heroism, and consider her as one of the first spies in American history. She was certainly a brave woman, and was willing to risk her life for her country. Her faith in the American cause must have helped her to be strong for her country and her God.

The Crazy President

The fear of the Lord is the beginning of knowledge,
but fools despise wisdom and discipline.
Proverbs 1:7, NIV.

If someone were to ask you to name the best president the United States ever had, you'd probably have a few favorites in mind. But if you were asked who you thought was the rowdiest president in the history of the United States you might have to think a bit. If you came up with the name of Andrew Jackson you'd probably be right.

On this December day in 1828 Andrew Jackson was elected the seventh President of the United States. He was elected as a popular favorite because his leadership in time of war had made him a national hero. He was definitely the people's president. However, by the time the inaugural ball came around in March, government leaders were beginning to wonder if they had made the right choice.

Jackson was the first president to invite the public to attend the White House ball in honor of his inauguration. The crowd of poor people, who came to the inaugural ball in their homemade clothes, became so large that Jackson's guards couldn't hold them out of the White House. In fact, the White House became so overcrowded with people that dishes and expensive decorations in the White House began to get broken. Some people even stood on good chairs in muddy boots just to get a look at the president. They were loud and outspoken, and White House attendants couldn't get them to quiet down. When the crowd became so wild and completely out of control, attendants poured punch in tubs and set them on the White House lawn in an effort to lure people out of the White House. There was no doubt that President Jackson was the people's favorite, and the inaugural ball proved it! From that day forward, though, he had a new nickname: King Mob.

President Jackson may not have been the most disciplined president, but he was a godly one, and he would have agreed with Solomon that "the fear of the Lord is the beginning of knowledge." If you want to be wise, become a disciplined person in as many areas of your life as you can—in your studies, in your daily exercise, in what you eat, and in your time with God. These kinds of discipline are the quickest ways to climb the ladder of success.

Smog Kills Thousands

Do not be afraid of the terrors of the night, . . .
Do not dread the disease that stalks in darkness...
Psalm 91:5, 6, NLT.

Fog has been used by poets and musicians and movie producers to portray a feeling of mystery and fear—and sometimes even romance. The foggy streets of London come to mind, or maybe the peat bogs of Scotland.

But when you add the effects of smoke and industrial pollution, you create an entirely new element: smog. Smog is a new concept of the modern era that seems to have arrived with the Industrial Revolution when factories began to dot the city landscapes of Europe and the eastern seaboard of the United States.

On this day in 1952 a blanket of smog that settled on the Thames River valley would eventually kill thousands in England. People couldn't see for more than five yards in front of their faces. It was during this four-day, man-made disaster that the word smog was first used.

A high-pressure air mass settled over the greater London area that day. When a front of cold air arrived from the west, the air over London became trapped in the city. Low temperatures didn't help much because people in the city had to burn extra coal in their furnaces to keep warm. The resulting smoke and soot, combined with sulfur dioxide from the factories and cars in London, created a heavy mantle of smog that began to smother the city.

By December 7 there was almost no sunlight, and eventually all travel and business in the metropolitan area of London came to a halt. By this time, however, the smog had caused several railway accidents, one of them near London Bridge. But the worst effect of the smog was the respiratory problems it brought to humans and animals. Thousands of new cases were reported to hospitals in the area, and it's estimated that as many as 8,000 people died in their sleep that weekend because of it.

When troubles come that can cause sickness, and even death, it can really be scary. Famous Bible heroes such as Moses, David, and Daniel knew what that was all about, but they had decided early in life that they were going to trust in God. Smog that can kill would be pretty scary, but not having God as your protector would be even worse.

Bicycle School

Then you shall delight yourself in the Lord;
And I will cause you to ride on the high hills of the earth.
Isaiah 58:14, NKJV.

When you tried to ride a bike for the first time, do you remember how hard it was to stay on, and how hard it was to keep your balance? Sometimes you'd lose all concentration and fall off, or even run into bushes and fences. Well, the first bicycles were even harder to ride. They were called bone shakers because of the way it felt when you rode over bumps in the road. Some were strangely shaped, with a huge wheel in the front and a tiny wheel in the back. In order to reach the high seat you had to climb up on a little step on the side of the frame, so riding was difficult at best, and always treacherous.

In spite of all this, riding became very stylish—and was very expensive. One popular bicycle during this time period was the Columbia Bicycle, a 60-inch-high wheeler that sold for $125 (compared to a sewing machine that could be bought for $13). In today's money a bike like that would cost more than $1,900! This might be the reason why some religious leaders at the time were saying that bicycles were a luxury, and were not a responsible way to spend one's money.

People who bought bicycles often would go riding in the park in the afternoon, all dressed up in their Sunday best. And that was a problem: How do you climb up there on that high seat while dressed in those nice clothes? (Especially women, who always wore dresses in those days.) And so the inevitable happened. Someone finally got smart and started a rider's ed program to teach people how to ride the Bone Shaker. And on December 5, 1868, the first American bicycle school opened in New York City.

Riding a bicycle today is a very common thing. Almost every child learns how to ride one by the time he's in school, and most people are pretty safe when they ride. The BMX trick bikes can be dangerous enough to satisfy the risk riders among us, but most of us aren't willing to take those kinds of chances on a bike.

Today Jesus offers you an opportunity to ride with Him on the high places of the earth. He offers you a chance for eternal safety and a life with Him that has no spiritual risks. Why not take Him up on the offer and find all your happiness in Him?

Jerry Rice, Sports Champion

Whatever your hand finds to do, do it with your might.
Ecclesiastes 9:10, NKJV.

On this day in history, December 6, 1992, Jerry Rice of the San Francisco 49ers became a legend in football when he caught his 101st touchdown pass. With that catch he broke Steve Largent's NFL record for most touchdowns by a wide receiver. Two years later he broke Jim Brown's all-time touchdown record (127). Not such a big deal? You're probably right. A bigger deal, though, is that he went on to make a total of 208 touchdowns before retiring from the league. The two current players that are the closest to Jerry's record, Ladanian Thomlinson and Terrell Owens, will have to play in the league another four or five years at their current pace to break Rice's standing record.

Rice also broke records in career receptions (1,328), touchdowns in a game (5), games with 100+ yards (67), consecutive 1,000 yard seasons (11), and Pro Bowl consecutive visits (10). Probably no one will ever break his string of records. Regarding his awesome career, popular posters list his stats and then add the comment, "Who's counting?"

One outstanding characteristic that set Rice apart from other players from the start was his habit of showing up at the locker room at least two hours before anyone else on his team. His clothes had to fit just right and look just right, and his mental game had to be in place.

Jerry graduated from Mississippi Valley State University and soon became a star wide receiver for the 49ers. As we all know, the San Francisco 49ers went on to dominate the professional football league throughout the late 1980s and early 1990s. He helped the 49ers win four Super Bowls beside NFL stars Joe Montana and Steve Young.

Today we're asked to be champions for God. Many who have gone before us have given their lives in service for God, expecting nothing in return but the approval of God. They didn't receive awards for athletic accomplishments, platinum record deals, or the most dollars at the movie box office. In fact, most of them didn't even win the record for most souls won or the most countries visited for God as a missionary. But they gave themselves willingly to carry the gospel to all the world, and they did it with all their energy and zeal. Now, those are champions for all of us to admire!

December 7

First U.S. State

And the chief captain answered, "With a great sum obtained I this freedom." And Paul said, "But I was free born." Acts 22:28.

The Revolutionary War was over. The Boston Tea Party was over. And so was Paul Revere's famous ride. The first shot heard 'round the world was fired at Lexington, Massachusetts. The signers of the Declaration of Independence had met and taken care of business. Nathan Hale had inspired everyone with his immortal words: "I regret that I have but one life to give my country." Washington had spent his famous winter at Valley Forge. General Cornwallis and his army had surrendered.

And now it really was over. Time to get down to some solid plans about the future of the United States of America. The original 13 colonies and 37 more states would eventually be accepted into the new nation; however, Delaware was the first to take the plunge. On December 7, 1787, the United States Constitution was ratified unanimously by the 30 delegates in attendance at the Delaware Constitutional Convention. And that act made Delaware the first official state of the future world power. Today Delaware is first in many respects:

The nation's first steam railroad line was located in New Castle, Delaware, in 1831; the first log cabin in America came to Delaware with the Finnish settlers in the 1600s; Betsy Ross's famous flag was first flown at the Battle of Cooch's Bridge, near Newark; the Blue Hen chicken is the official state bird (Blue Hen chicken? OK); the biggest frying pan in the United States was built in Delaware in 1950 to be used at the Delmarva Chicken Festival. Ten feet in diameter, it held 180 gallons of oil and could fry 800 chicken quarters.

Thomas Garrett, the greatest champion of the Underground Railroad, spent his fortune in the battle against slavery, helping more than 2,000 fugitive slaves move north through Delaware, an important stop on the Underground Railroad.

Like the Roman centurion in our verse today, many early Americans helped purchase the freedoms we hold dear. And like Paul, we should be so grateful if we were born in this nation, but regardless of national status, Jesus died so we could be free from sin. Amen!

Movie With a Scent

*Idols are merely things of silver and gold, shaped by
human hands. They have . . . eyes but cannot see. They
have ears but cannot hear, and noses but cannot smell.
Psalm 115:4-6, NLT.*

Movies are among some of the most exciting forms of entertainment today, designed to plug us into every sensory experience possible. As you watch James Bond skiing down a snow-covered slope you almost feel the snow spraying in your face. Or you can race along a crowded street in a high powered car with Matt Damon, but you won't really risk your life when the car crashes into a truck, cutting off the top half of the car. You even can be with that handsome actor in your mind's eye, without all the risks that might involve.

Movies can do this because of the fast-paced sensations a big screen can provide—the surround-sound of realistic theatre acoustics, and even the rush of air and movement of seats in some theatre productions (such as the family show at Disney World, Honey, I Shrunk the Kids, in which the movie producers spray water on the audience to simulate a dog sneezing.)

The movie industry is working to make the movies of the future even more alluring, and they've had a lot of practice. For instance, on December 8, 1959, *Behind the Great Wall,* one of the first successful movies with a built-in sensation of scent, was shown in theaters. The producers called the process AromaRama because it sent 100 different aromas into the air-conditioning system of the theater during the film—grass, exploding firecrackers, food, incense, burning torches, and horses.

But even more sensational ideas are being worked on right now that will completely revamp the movie industry. It's predicted that in the future anyone who attends a theater will be able to choose the character he wants to identify with. He'll then wear a special helmet with a built in eye scanner that lets him follow the plot of the movie and live out the part of the character he chooses. Now that's scary! When we turn ourselves over to such control by the movie industry it's time to get a reality check. The lifestyles of movie actors aren't usually worthy of our adoration and praise. Only God deserves such praise.

Livingstone Returns to England

Go therefore and make disciples of all the nations . . . ,
teaching them to observe all things that I have
commanded you; and lo, I am with you always.
Matthew 28:19, 20, NKJV.

On this day in 1856 Africa's most famous missionary returned home to England for his first visit. His name? David Livingstone. And what a celebrity he had become!

While he was only 10 years old David began working in the cotton mills of England, but spent his evenings in night school. He had his heart set on being a missionary doctor in China. Then he heard a missionary speak about "the smoke of a thousand villages where no one had yet heard the gospel story," and David decided to give his life for Africa.

When Livingstone arrived in Africa he was 25. He soon found that being a missionary to the interior of Africa in the usual sense was almost impossible. There were no maps of the area, and he had to fight enemies of every kind. From blood-sucking flies and mosquitoes to lions and slave traders, Livingstone's life was made miserable. The insects transmitted malaria and sleeping sickness, and he feared for his life with the wild lions. One day a wounded lion attacked Livingstone, ripping his arm open with one bite and breaking the bone. He almost died from infection.

But ignorance, superstition, and man's inhumanity to man were the worst of Africa's horrors, and it was these that Livingstone spent most of his time battling. His fight against the Dutch Boers, who were enslaving the Africans, became a nightmare. The Boers robbed him, destroyed his home, and threatened his life repeatedly. During one seven-month journey into the interior to help break the slave trade, he suffered 31 attacks of fever and dysentery, witnessed the horrors of polygamy and cannibalism and slavery, saw families broken up, and slave gangs chained together. He saw the bodies of unfortunate slaves who had died, their bodies lying by the wayside, hung in trees, or floating in the river.

David Livingstone's desire to be a missionary came from his love for God and his hope to one day see all of Africa freed from the grip of slavery. His work had helped ensure that the worst days of the slave trade were over. Jesus' challenge to go to all the world and preach the gospel was exactly what Livingstone wanted, and in the end he gladly gave his very life for it.

Human-powered Helicopter

For the Lord Himself will descend from heaven with a shout. . . . Then we who are alive and remain shall be caught up together with them in the clouds to meet the Lord in the air. And thus we shall always be with the Lord.
1 Thessalonians 4:16, 17, NKJV.

The helicopter is one of the coolest machines ever invented! A bit unpredictable at times, yes, but cool. On December 10, 1989, the first helicopter took flight, operating by human pedal power. The flight lasted approximately seven seconds, rising about 7 inches above a gymnasium floor. That doesn't sound like much, but it was a start. For a machine that many had envisioned since ancient times, it was a real breakthrough.

Students at the California Polytechnic State University in California developed the helicopter and named it the Da Vinci 3, based on a model designed by Leonardo da Vinci some 500 years before. Made of graphite-epoxy, wood, and mylar, the helicopter had a 140-foot-long rotor, driven by props at each end.

Helicopters have improved over the years in efficiency and in size. The largest helicopter ever built was the Mil V-12, a massive aircraft developed in the Soviet Union during the 1960s. The V-12 was a rather unusual helicopter that had two rotors mounted side by side at the ends of a large wing. Each rotor had a diameter of nearly 115 feet. The helicopter was so enormous that the distance from the edge of one rotor disk to the other was almost 220 feet, even wider than the wingspan of a Boeing 747.

Helicopters do lots of useful things. They check traffic, deliver emergency medical personnel, and carry soldiers on military missions. The helicopters we use today are much more efficient than anything Da Vinci came up with, but powered flight of any kind is still fairly antiquated compared to what angels can do. And some day we'll all be flying with them! Paul tries to explain it the best he can in the book of First Thessalonians. When Jesus comes, Paul says, He will descend from heaven with a shout and call everyone who is sleeping in the graves. Then He'll invite all of us who are still alive to meet Him in the air. That's incredible! We're going to fly! We'll be "caught up together with them in the clouds to meet the Lord in the air." When Paul puts it that way, it's hard to wait, isn't it?

December 11

Laughing Gas

A cheerful heart is good medicine,
but a broken spirit saps a person's strength.
Proverbs 17:22, NLT

What's the difference between a safe drug and a dangerous one? Or is there such a thing as a "safe" drug? Some drugs are natural remedies, such as golden seal or Echinacea. Others are over-the-counter drugs, such as Tylenol or Benadryl. Then there are the prescription drugs which require a doctor's prescription; and, of course, illegal drugs, such as cocaine, PCP, and crystal meth. These days we're more educated than ever before about the dangers of drugs. But it wasn't always so. In the old days doctors sometimes prescribed damaging drugs for people: tobacco for emphysema and morphine for toothaches. Actually, that's how laughing gas got its start.

Dr. Horace Wells, a dentist, first observed the painkilling properties of laughing gas when a friend from a traveling circus gave him some. So he decided to try it out on himself while having his dental partner pull out one of his teeth. December 11, 1844, is the first recorded use of the gas in a medical operation, and the sensation was bizarre. Dr. Wells thought it was great being able to laugh when he should have felt pain, instead of crying. When he tried it on his patients he thought he really was on to something, so he offered to give a demonstration to medical students at the Massachusetts General Hospital in Boston in 1845. Unfortunately, the gas wasn't administered properly and the patient cried out in pain. The audience jeered at Wells and left the lecture hall chanting, "Humbug! Humbug!"

Embarrassed, Dr. Wells gave up dentistry and became a traveling salesman, selling everything from canaries to shower curtains. And then he began selling an anesthetic drug called chloroform. He repeatedly used the drug on himself for demonstration purposes, and became addicted to the stuff. Finally he became so deranged from overdoses that he was committed to New York's infamous Tombs Prison, where he committed suicide.

The whole story is unfortunate. Wells was a doctor; he should have known better than to take drugs indiscriminately. The Bible gives us a good prescription for a heart free from worry: trust in God. A cheerful heart is good medicine, but being addicted to drugs or food or music or TV or pornography will destroy your heart and soul.

Priceless Artifact Sold

The kingdom of heaven is like something precious buried
in a field, which a man found and hid again; then in
his joy he goes and sells all he has and buys that field.
Matthew 13:44, Amplified Bible

On this day in history an American oil tycoon paid more than $5 million at an auction for one of Leonardo da Vinci's original manuscripts, which was in the form of a journal notebook. That was in 1980. That would be about $12 million in today's economy, not to mention the increase in value of a 500-year-old artifact. The manuscript, written around 1508, is one of 30 other notebooks that Da Vinci kept during his lifetime. He was in the habit of recording his thoughts and designs in these notebooks, and wrote on a variety of subjects. The $5 million notebook includes 72 pages with 300 different sets of notes and drawings, all relating to the science of water and its properties.

In 1690 a painter, Giuseppi Ghezzi, found the notebook in a chest of papers belonging to a sculptor who had studied Leonardo's work. In 1717 Thomas Coke, an English earl, bought the manuscript for his family's art collection. Two hundred and sixty-three years later the notebook showed up on an auction block in London where Lord Coke, a descendant of Thomas Coke, was forced to sell it to pay his taxes. In the days leading up to the sale art experts and the press figured the notebook would sell for $7- to $20 million. However, the bidding lasted less than two minutes, going for a mere $5.12 million. Even so, that was the highest amount ever paid for a manuscript up to that time. (A legendary Gutenberg Bible had sold for $2 million two years earlier.) The oil tycoon, Armand Hammer, was delighted to get it for that price and thought he had snagged a bargain. Lord Coke wasn't so happy, because the sale price didn't even cover his taxes.

How much is your relationship with God worth? And that personal copy of the Bible sitting on your shelf—is it worth as much as your favorite music? your favorite TV program? your time with friends? the spending money you earn? If we truly value God's Word we'll be willing not only to spend more time with it but sacrifice some of those other things in order to share His Word with others. Don't kid yourself: if Jesus mentioned it in several of His parables, it must be worth a lot!

Superman Rehab

The Lord is my shepherd; I shall not want. . . . Yea,
though I walk through the valley of the shadow of death,
I will fear no evil; for You are with me.
Psalm 23, NKJV.

Have you ever wished you could have the powers of Superman? How about even one of his super sonic skills? How about his strength? His ability to lift any object, no matter how heavy—cars in the street, Leer jets, railroad tank cars? How about his laser X-ray vision? That would be pretty cool. Just think—when you wanted to heat up a snack in a hurry, you could just turn on the old laser eyes. But flying? That would be the best! Going anywhere you wanted, anytime, and getting there so much faster. No more long commutes to school.

Well, all that's fine for the Man of Steel, but even Superman doesn't last forever. In the real life of the real-live character that played Superman for so many years, tragedy struck. And this time there was no returning to the ice castle at the North Pole. Superman was finished with his career of helping people and bringing criminals to justice.

Christopher Reeve, the actor who played Superman in the movie (and its three sequels) had a death-defying accident while horseback riding one day. He fell and landed on his head, breaking two vertebrae in his spine, and leaving him a quadriplegic. It was a catastrophe like nothing he had ever faced in real life or in his movies, and it changed his life forever. He was fortunate to have a wonderful wife, who was such a comfort to him during the long months of rehabilitation to help him get back as many life functions as possible.

It was a painful process, but finally, on December 13, Christopher Reeves was released from physical rehab and told he could go home. He was ready to get back to a regular life without the feeding tubes and special one-on-one sessions each day in the hospital ward. He and his wife, Dana, even found time for fund-raising that would help people with disabilities such as his. Unfortunately, Reeves died of heart failure in 2004 after being treated for an infection.

If you've been through anything remotely like Christopher Reeve you know how devastating the experience can be. It's so comforting to know that Jesus will walk through that valley of shadows with us. When He's with us, we don't ever need to be afraid.

The Birthday of Nostradamus

Beware of false prophets, who come to you in sheep's clothing. . . .
You will know them by their fruits.
Matthew 7:15, 16, NKJV.

Have you ever glanced at those magazines at the checkout stands in grocery stores, the ones that have all the photo shoots of has-been celebrities and stories about two-headed dogs that can talk in Russian and Japanese? *National Enquirer* magazine is usually full of prophecies about the future, such as Elvis Presley will come back in 2012 and give a full concert to benefit the diabetes foundation, or the pope will make a very important announcement that will change the world forever on New Year's Day of 2013, and Jesus will come again on Easter of that same year. Well, psychics and astrologers and prophets have been giving their predictions since Jesus went back to heaven; however, the question is which ones are genuine, and which ones are the fakes?

In 1503 a baby boy was born in Remi, France, who was destined to be one of the most famous predictors of all time. Michel de Nostradamus came from a Jewish family, but his parents had been forced to convert to Catholicism during the Inquisition, a time of great persecution for Christians everywhere.

A physician by trade, Nostradamus is best known today for being a seer, or prophet, who foretold the future. When he reached 50, he began writing predictions called "centuries," because each of his books contained 100 verses. In his lifetime he made more than 6,300 predictions and a collection of perpetual prophecies that ran until 3797 A.D. By the time he died in 1566, he was a very rich man. Supposedly, Nostrodame made predictions about Hitler, the two World Wars, the Kennedy assassinations, and the terrorist attacks in America. However, even his followers claim a "hit rate" of only about 10 percent in his predictions.

Jesus tells us to watch out for the fake prophets among us. Even though they have nothing that can really help you, they peddle it as if they were experts. These quacks aren't interested in you and your salvation; they want only your money. Jesus, on the other and, knows the future, and He's told us all about it in the Bible. Why not find out for yourself today?

Walt Disney Dies

Create in me a clean heart, O God; and renew a right spirit within me. Psalm 51:10.

What comes to mind when you hear the name Walt Disney? Disneyland? Disney Channel? Walt Disney, born on a farm in Missouri, was an exceptional artist who sold his first sketches to neighbors when he was only 7. He liked doing art in his spare time so much that he attended the Kansas City Art Institute at night while he was in high school. When he was 16 he went overseas with the Red Cross during World War I and drove an ambulance he had decorated with cartoon characters.

When the war was over Disney worked as a cartoonist for an advertising agency. Then he and his older brother Ray started a company called Laugh-O-Gram. Unfortunately, it went bankrupt, so they left for Hollywood with another plan in mind. With only $40 in their pocket and some art supplies, they built a studio in their uncle's garage and began creating animated cartoons.

In 1928 Disney created Mickey Mouse as the first synchronized sound cartoon ever made, doing the voiceovers for Mickey's squeaky voice himself. Other cartoon characters soon followed—the Three Little Pigs, Donald Duck, Daisy, Goofy, and Pluto. Then the movie, *Snow White and the Seven Dwarfs,* was incredibly successful during the Depression, bringing their little company $8 million. And the rest is history.

During his 43-year career Walt Disney earned nearly 1,000 honors from all over the world. He received seven Emmys and 48 Academy Awards. Harvard, Yale, UCLA, and the University of Southern California each conferred honorary degrees on him. Walt Disney died on December 15, 1966, but his legend lives on at Disneyland, Disney World, and EPCOT Center. Millions of children and adults over the generations have experienced joy and magic through his animated characters.

Disney was a great artist, creating much that is classic in American television. But the most important things in life have nothing to do with art—they have to do with the human heart. David knew what that was all about when he said, "Create in me a clean heart, O God; and renew a right spirit within me." Why not ask God to do that for you right now?

Earthquakes in the United States

And there will be great earthquakes in various places, and famines and pestilences; and there will be fearful sights and great signs from heaven. Luke 21:11, NKJV.

Our earth has been plagued with earthquakes since the days of Noah's flood. At that time forces from beneath our world's crusty mantle forced themselves upward, cracking the earth's surface into sections called plates. Anytime these plates shift up and down or slide back and forth, we have a quake. Really big shifts bring really big quakes—the bigger the shift, the bigger the shock. Every 500 or 600 years earthquakes of this magnitude hit the North American continent.

On this day in 1811 a series of earthquakes began that would turn out to be the worst in the history of the United States, centering on the state of Missouri.

In New Madrid, Missouri, a quake that registered 8.6 on the Richter scale slammed the Mississippi River Valley, starting a whole series of earthquakes that altered the landscape of the entire region. Fortunately, few people lived in the area at the time, so no one is known to have died. But it was a very peculiar earthquake, and changed the course of the Mississippi River by raising and lowering parts of the Mississippi Valley as much as 15 feet. For a while the river flowed back upstream, forming a new lake, called Reelfoot Lake, in Tennessee, that covered a huge area of 30,000 square miles.

The quake shocks were felt as far as the east coast of the United States, causing church bells to ring, and earthquakes and aftershocks continued to come and go during the winter and spring months. During that time, it's estimated that 2,000 seismic shocks were felt in the area, with five of them registering at least 8.0, or more, on the Richter scale. The quake fault runs through New Madrid and extends 120 miles south through five states: Missouri, Illinois, Kentucky, Tennessee, and Arkansas. Smaller quakes hit the area every 80 years or so, but thankfully, the catastrophic upheavals of 1811 and 1812 come only every few centuries.

Some day the earth will suffer the biggest quake of all time, probably as big as the ones experienced at the time of Noah's flood. Jesus was trying to warn us of these coming disasters and how hard it would seem to have to go through that time. But He also wanted to remind us that these are signs of His soon coming. Aren't you glad?

December 17

Debtor's Prison

And be kind to one another, tenderhearted, forgiving one another, even as God in Christ forgave you.
Ephesians 4:32, NKJV.

Today we think of prison as a place where we send our hardened criminals—people who are drug dealers, thieves, online scammers, child abusers, killers, and CEOs in big corporations who swindle people out of their hard earned pensions. However, prisons used to be for people who couldn't pay their debts. In a way that seems to make a little bit of sense. If a man isn't going to pay a debt he owes, it's as if he was stealing. Maybe he should have some time in jail to think about his priorities. Maybe he should have to pay a price for not paying the debt.

And yet, when you think about it, that kind of punishment doesn't really fit the crime. If he's a deadbeat, he's getting just what he wants. He gets to sit around and do nothing. As it is, prisoners earn very little while in the clink. In most prisons where there is a work program inmates can earn nowhere near minimum wage. For instance, in 2003 the minimum wage for a public worker was $5.15, but the average wage in prison was only 12 cents an hour.

Make no mistake! We need measures that will keep criminals from exploiting innocent victims and our society. We need a penalty for drug dealers who ruin people's lives and for corporate officials in high places who rob their clients of millions of dollars. Something must be done. But the general rule here is that you can't get your money from someone who doesn't have a job to earn the money and pay you back.

In the old days, of course, it was worse, much worse. People sometimes were kept in prison for 10 years, and even more if they tried to escape. The French movie, *Les Miserables,* is about a man in the mid-1800s who was out of work. He finally became so desperate that he stole a loaf of bread. He was put in prison for 10 years for this crime.

Well, in America we've tried to make things better. On this day in 1821 the state of Kentucky enacted a law that makes it illegal to send someone to debtors' prison. Wages can be garnished and property may be sold to pay the debt, but debtors' prison is out of the question.

Because we are all sinners we all deserve to pay a heavy price—eternal death. But Jesus has paid that price. He died for us so that we could be forever free from sin's debt.

Charles Wesley Is Born

A thousand may fall at your side, and ten thousand
at your right hand; but it shall not come near you.
Psalm 91:7, NKJV.

The Dark Ages was a frightening time to be alive. People had no education; they couldn't read or write, and knew very little about the world around them. Disease and poverty were a part of everyday life, and life expectancy was about 30 to 40 years. Times were hard, and most people had little hope that things would be better in the future. The nobility owned the land, and the peasants were so poor they could be sold along with the land on which they worked.

Because spiritual darkness was everywhere, the world was ripe for a religious awakening. So when the Protestant Reformation began in the 1500s, European society began to change. For the first time in ages people began to think for themselves. Superstitions of the Dark Ages began to give way to knowledge and enlightenment. And with this came great leaders, men and women who were not afraid to stand up to the Church of Rome.

Charles Wesley was just such a man. On this day in 1707 the famous reformer and cofounder of the Methodist church was born. Charles wrote more than 6,500 hymns, and some of his more famous hymns still used today include Hark the Herald Angels Sing, Love Divine, and Christ the Lord Is Risen Today.

Charles' brother, John, led the way in helping to raise up the Methodist church. They took many trips together, and in spite of the dangers they faced they were saved from death many times. Storms at sea, persecution by church leaders, and angry mobs were used by Satan to discourage the two Wesley brothers. Sometimes angels came in the form of men and protected them from demon-possessed crowds. Once a mobster threw a brick and hit John squarely between the eyes. The blood gushed out, but John said it felt as though only a piece of straw had hit him. What courage! These Christian reformers were poor men and didn't ask for things of this world to make them happy. They got their satisfaction from helping others and by spreading the gospel. A famous prayer the brothers often used went something like this: Lord, help me to do all the good I can, by all the means I can, in all the ways I can, in all the places I can, in all the times I can, to all the people I can, as long as ever I can.

The Christian church today owes much to Charles and John Wesley.

Personal Computer

But you, Daniel, shut up the words, and seal the book until the time of the end; many shall run to and fro, and knowledge shall increase.
Daniel 12:4, NKJV.

Bill Gates and Paul Allen of Microsoft fame got their start in the computer industry by working out of their home. Strangely enough, they delivered their first personal computer program to the manufacturer on something like an audio cassette.

The personal computer certainly did have humble beginnings, but in America that's the way it usually goes. Here are a few misguided quotes on what people thought of the personal computer when it first came out:

"Computers in the future may weigh no more than 1.5 tons"
    —*Popular Mechanics*, 1949.
"I think there is a world market for maybe five computers"
    —Chairman of IBM, 1943.
"The microchip? But what . . . is it good for?"
    —An engineer at IBM, 1968.
"There is no reason anyone would want a computer in their home"
    —Ken Olson, President, Chairman, and Founder of Digital
        Equipment Co. 1977.

Could any of these people have been further from the truth? Computers have evolved to become what they are today—society's greatest leap of knowledge since Gutenberg's printing press. From Commodore 64 versions with cassette tapes to floppy disc drives, and 3.5 diskette to flash drives e-mail transmissions, and digital inscriptions over the airways, computers totally dominate American society today—more than 180,000,000 strong. And they probably will until Jesus comes.

Today we even use computers to bring the Gospel of Jesus to others. Digitalized multimillion dollar printing presses, online Bible studies, and radio and satellite transmissions all speed the gospel on its way to the world. Knowledge has increased, just as Daniel prophesied it would, and the computer has been part of it.

However, inspiration tells us that the last great message of salvation to the world will be one-on-one, door-to-door evangelism. That means that as wonderful as personal computers have become, they will never have that personal touch.

Television Is Invented

But we all, with unveiled face, beholding as in a mirror the glory of the Lord, are being transformed into the same image from glory to glory. 2 Corinthians 3:18, NKJV.

If you were to ask scientists what they think is the one form of communication today that has changed our society the most, they might say television. As a way of communicating, computers are huge, and so is the Internet and, especially, cell phones. But the Internet wouldn't be possible without the computer. And the computer screen came about because of the invention of television. Even cell phones use technology first used by television. But that's not the point. Television has changed the way Americans see society and themselves. It has changed the way we are entertained and the way we entertain ourselves. It's become our favorite pastime.

In the earliest days of American history entertainment was often enjoyed with friends, but it usually involved work of some kind. People went to quilting bees, barn raisings, and husking bees. Before the invention of television a person played family games, such as I Spy or Charades, inside the house. If you wanted outdoor entertainment you went hunting or sledding, or played hide-and-seek. On Sunday afternoons you could opt for a ride in the buggy or the old Model-T. And if you wanted entertainment in public places you watched magicians in stage shows or listened to famous speakers who had traveled the world. People went to the circus and the county fair.

We still do some of those things, but it's not like it used to be. Nowadays if you are at the state fair you very well might be thinking, *I have to get home to watch my favorite program or sitcom on TV, or maybe a football game.* And that's why we can probably safely say that television has become the number one pastime in America.

Many people helped make the television a success down through the years, but it was a Russian-American electrical engineer named Vladimir Zworykin who really got the ball rolling. His patents for two cathode-ray tubes were revolutionary—one for sending messages, and one for receiving them. The basic concept has been used in most TVs and computers since that time.

When we watch television we become like the celebrities and performers we see there. If we spend more time with Jesus, we'll become more like Him. We'll behold His face and be changed by the glory of what He wants to accomplish in us.

Snow White

Whatever things are true, whatever things are noble, whatever things are just, whatever things are pure, whatever things are lovely, whatever things are of good report, if there is any virtue and if there is anything praiseworthy—meditate on these things. Philippians 4:8, NKJV.

In the early days of movies cartoon animations became popular as a form of entertainment. We tend to think of cartoons as something that has been designed for children, but of course that's not the case anymore. While all kinds of animated movies are marketed for children, many of the most popular ones have vocabulary and a plot line geared for adults. Movies such as *Aladdin, Lion King, the Mermaid, The Hunchback of Notre Dame, 101 Dalmatians,* and *Shrek* portray evilness in all its hideous forms, making their producers a lot of money. Buckets of it. Today animated movies compete with other regular box office hits, often edging them out for total sales. *Snow White and the Seven Dwarfs,* produced in 1937, was one of the first successful animated movies, and various versions of it have continued to be a favorite with families ever since. It was so successful, in fact, that on December 21, 1994, it became the first movie ever to earn $1 billion.

The movie industry has always tried to rate movies so that families can know which ones to watch without their children being negatively affected. But although the original *Snow White* had a PG rating, even in 1937 the movie was showing signs of evil, things such as magic mirrors, witches, and evil spells. Since then other movies, such as *Titanic,* have grossed as much, but *Titanic* did it in a much shorter period of time.

Much of entertainment for which we pay so much to see is ungodly, and that's sad. Why are we so fascinated by fairy tales and illusion (*Aladdin*)? Why all the hype for lovesick romances on TV (*Friends*)? Many family shows on television are steeped in superstition, hexes, and evil spells (*Beauty and the Beast*), satanic sorcery (*Lord of the Rings*), and the evil forces in our universe (*Star Trek* or *Star Wars*).

Will God be asking us someday to account for our time and money spent on such things? You can be sure of it! Will He forgive us for time wasted on frivolous movies that draw us away from Him instead of transforming us more and more into His image? Absolutely. With that in mind, why not start making those changes in your life today?

Dwight Moody Dies

You are My witnesses," says the Lord,
"and My servant whom I have chosen.
Isaiah 43:10, NKJV.

On December 22, 1899, one of the great Christian evangelists in American history died. Dwight Moody was an unusual man. When only 17 he went to work in his uncle's shoe store in Boston and surprised everyone with his unique ability to sell shoes. In fact, he was soon outselling all the other salespeople in the store combined. On slow days he would step out onto the sidewalk and convince customers to come into the store.

He was converted when he was 18 by a Sunday school teacher who came in the store one day and asked him if he would give his heart to Jesus. Simple as that! By the 1860s Moody had moved to Chicago and was preaching full time. Hundreds of thousands came to hear him in the big halls and stadiums of the day, and tens of thousands gave their hearts to Jesus while listening to him preach. He is perhaps most famous for starting the Moody Bible Institute.

Moody was known for his unusual methods of witnessing. At one point he made a vow that he would witness for God, no matter what the cost. In fact he determined that he would not rest at the end of each day unless he could say that he had spoken to someone about their salvation. One night Dwight was just getting into bed when he remembered that he hadn't personally witnessed to anyone that day about their salvation. Without hesitation, he jumped to his feet, pulled on his boots, and went out into the night to keep his promise. He immediately noticed a man standing under a street lamp. Without hesitation Mr. Moody walked right up and asked him that ever-important question: "Have you been saved by the blood of Jesus?" Only then did he look down and notice that he had failed to dress properly. He was standing under a street lamp at midnight, wearing little more than his long underwear. However, the incident changed the stranger's life. Years later this same man introduced himself to Dwight Moody at an evangelistic crusade and told him what a permanent impression that midnight visit had made on him. "If you would do that for me in your underwear, holding nothing back for Jesus, I felt I could do no less."

Such was the impact of Dwight Moody's life. He was an incredible witness for Jesus and, like the Apostle Paul, an unstoppable force for the cause of Christ.

A Prince Explores the West

How much better to get wisdom than gold! And to get understanding is to be chosen rather than silver.
Proverbs 16:16, NKJV.

Do you sometimes wish that you could head out and explore some uncharted land? Maybe an island someplace where no one has ever set foot . . . Or maybe it an ancient ruins deep in the silent jungles of the rain forest.

On this day in 1829 a royal prince of Germany did just that when he left St. Louis, Missouri, on an expedition up the Missouri River to study plant and animal life. His name was Prince Paul Wilhelm of Wurttemberg, and his story is quite the tale. He would one day become a duke, but for now he was just a prince out for fun.

He and his royal courtiers had taken a trip to America seven years before, arriving in New Orleans, then traveling up the Mississippi in a riverboat. When Prince Paul first met the famous William Clark (of Lewis and Clark fame), he could hardly believe it! Here was Clark, a tough woodsman, one of the original voyagers from President Jefferson's pioneer expedition up the Missouri River nearly two decades before! It was the small things on these trips that bothered Prince Paul the most. Bloodthirsty mosquitoes, for instance. They came in swarms and nearly drove him crazy. But Prince Paul was determined, and survived.

When it was time for him to return to Germany, Clark sent Jean Baptiste Charbonneau, his 16-year-old foster son, to travel with the Prince in Europe and Africa. (Charbonneau was the son of Sacagawea, the Indian woman who had helped lead the Lewis and Clarke expedition upriver in 1803.)

After his European-African trip, Prince Paul made the long voyage back to the United States. He could have chosen to live out his days in the lap of royal luxury, but he decided once again that he wanted to study nature, and experience the excitement of adventure that lay beyond his castle walls.

And that's what Prince Paul decided to do for the rest of his life. He gathered thousands of plants, minerals, and animal specimens, and he sketched them all. How much better to travel for the sake of learning than to go in search of gold or silver as so many have done. Learning can only bring wisdom, especially when it includes God.

Solar House

But for you who revere my name, the sun of righteousness will rise with healing in its wings"
Malachi 4:2, NIV.

The sun, which lies at the center of our solar system, is huge. It looks small in the sky, but that's because it's 93 million miles away. Think of driving that distance in your car. . . . If you could drive at a modest 60 miles per hour 24/7, 365 days a year, it would take you 176 years to get to the sun.

Compared to the Sun, the earth is tiny: If the sun were a basketball, the earth would be about the size of a pinhead—a mere speck! Proportionately speaking, the basketball and the pin would be about 100 feet apart, about a third the length of a football field. And if you were standing beside the basketball, you'd need a telescope to see the pinhead-sized earth.

The earth is approximately 8,000 miles in diameter, while the Sun is roughly 900,000 miles across. One hundred earths lined up, side-by-side, still wouldn't span the width of the sun. And it would take 1 million earths to fill the sun.

The sun is the single greatest source of energy in our solar system, and it's hot beyond imagination and will not be burning out for millions of years to come. It warms our earth and atmosphere, keeps our plants green, and helps us stay healthy.

One of the most innovative things it has been used for is to heat homes. On December 24, 1948, a house was completed that was heated entirely by solar power. A Dover, Massachusetts, family moved into the house on Christmas Eve. What a Christmas gift! The solar powered heater in this house was made of black sheet metal collector panels behind panes of glass. The panels pulled in the sun's heat, then stored it long term in a heat bin filled with a liquid sodium compound. As the heat rose from the bin, electric fans blew the heat through vents in the house.

The sun is vital to our life and health on this earth. We can't live without the sun, and we can't live without Jesus. His breath of life gives us energy to live, and His sacrifice on Calvary has bought us eternal life.

Look to Jesus today and let the healing in His wings revive you spiritually.

The Christmas Truce

For unto us a child is born, . . . and His name will be called Prince of Peace. Of the increase of his government and peace there will be no end. Isaiah 9:6, 7, NIV.

War had been raging for five months. Soldiers on both sides had been assured that they'd be home by Christmas. They couldn't know that the war would drag on for four long, bloody years. The previous June a Bosnian-Serb student had assassinated the heir to the Austro-Hungarian throne, a murder that triggered a fast paced series of events that ultimately led to World War I. On one side were France, the United Kingdom, and Russia; on the other, Germany and Austria-Hungary. By the end of August the countries were engaged in total war the likes of which had never been seen on earth—trench warfare. On the front lines, opposing men were separated at times by less than 100 feet, living in filthy trenches dug into the ground.

Then it happened—one of the most unusual events in military history: the Christmas Truce. Just after midnight on that Christmas Morning of 1914 the Germans stopped firing their guns, and the British began hearing a few German soldiers singing a Christmas carol that was soon picked up all along the German line as other soldiers joined in: Stille nacht, heilige nacht. British troops immediately recognized the melody as Silent Night and, one by one, British and German soldiers began laying down their weapons and climbing out of their trenches to venture into No Man's Land, a small patch of bombed-out earth between the two sides. Former enemy soldiers sat around a common campfire, exchanging small gifts from their meager belongings. Men who only hours earlier had been shooting to kill were now sharing Christmas festivities and showing each other family snapshots.

Then the truce ended at 8:30 a.m., December 26. After a truly silent night, Captain C. I. Stockwell of the Royal Welsh Fusiliers fired three shots into the air and stepped up onto the trench bank. A German officer, who had exchanged gifts with Captain Stockwell the previous night, appeared on his trench bank. They bowed, saluted, and climbed back into their trenches. A few minutes later, the German officer fired two shots into the air. The war was on again.

When Jesus came to earth that long-ago night the angels promised that He would bring peace to men. His life and death on the cross guaranteed that promise. Soon He will come again, and when he does there will be no more war. At last, and forever, there will be peace on earth.

Record Tsunami

God is our refuge and strength, a very present help in trouble.
Therefore we will not fear, . . . though the mountains be carried
into the midst of the sea; Though its waters roar and be troubled.
Psalm 46:1-3, NKJV.

What would you think if you were at the beach one day and suddenly saw the sea bed dry up as the waves rolled out to sea for thousands of yards, or maybe even miles? Would you be scared? That's what happened to Tilly Smith, a British girl who was on vacation in Thailand with her family on December 26, 2004. She remembered a class discussion about tsunamis from school and realized what was happening. She called to her parents excitedly, warning them that a gigantic tidal wave of sea water would soon come crashing back to the beach, destroying everything in its path.

And that's exactly what happened. But as a result of her quick thinking, Tilly and her parents managed to get themselves and 100 other people off the beach to safety. The tsunami was the result of a terrible earthquake (9.3 on the rector scale), the second largest earthquake in recorded history. It killed an estimated 230,000 people from Somalia on the east coast of Africa to Sumatra in Southeast Asia and left more than a million people homeless. Tragically, more than two-thirds of the victims were women and children.

Most earthquakes last for only a few seconds, but this one lasted almost 10 minutes, triggering more earthquakes as far away as Alaska. In fact, geologists said that the entire planet's surface probably moved at least a few centimeters. The quake caused the sea bed under the Indian Ocean to rise almost 10 feet, forcing seven cubic miles of water suddenly upward. This sent a growing tsunami wave, as high as 100 feet, crashing toward the shores of Somalia, Indonesia, Sumatra, Sri Lanka, southern India, and Thailand. Quakes in deep waters have less effect on the movement of ocean waters, but near the shorelines the continental shelves can't absorb the huge amounts of water being suddenly moved about. People from all over the world sent aid to the stricken countries that had been devastated by the tsunami. Even so, it will take decades before the economies of the region recover from the billions of dollars in damage.

God invites us to trust in Him during times of natural disaster. The ocean may be boiling and the mountains all around us may be moving out of place, but He is still our refuge and help.

Race for Space

I will not break my covenant. . . . It will be as eternal as the moon, My faithful witness in the sky!
Psalm 89:34-37, NLT.

When you were a kid you probably heard stories about the man in the moon. It probably sounds funny, now that you're more grown up. But did you know that people used to believe in that stuff? Books were written and movies were made about bizarre trips to the moon. Of course most people had no idea how really far away the moon was, how much energy it would take to get there, and what kind of life support systems would be needed to do it.

To be perfectly honest, in spite of all the research done, the calculations made, and stories written, most people probably never thought we'd ever actually visit the moon. It seemed too far-fetched an idea, too dangerous, and only remotely possible with the technology then available.

That all changed with the coming of the space age. Mission after mission was launched into the upper stratosphere to circle the globe, run scientific tests, and try to keep ahead of the Russians in the race for space.

We finally actually managed to send three astronauts in the first space capsule to the moon, to orbit 10 times around its bumpy, crater-covered surface. It was Christmas Eve when they began the first orbit. The astronauts, Frank Borman, James Lovell, Jr., and William Anders, never did see the man in the moon, but they did see the dark side of the moon, a side no one on earth had ever seen before. And they were the first humans to see the blue ball of our earth suspended in space.

Then NASA's Apollo 8 mission left its lunar orbit to begin the journey back to earth, landing safely in the Pacific Ocean on December 27, 1968. Their mission had been accomplished, and earth never looked better! There would be several lunar landing missions in the future, but for now the astronauts were just happy to be walking on earth's soil.

Getting to the moon was a really big deal for us earthlings, but it's no big deal for God. He made the moon. When God created the earth and the moon, He made a covenant with Adam that would last forever—as long as the moon was in the sky.

Pledge of Allegiance

Choose for yourselves this day whom you will serve. . . .
But as for me and my household, we will serve the Lord.
Joshua 24:15, NIV.

I pledge allegiance to the flag of the United States of America,
and to the Republic for which it stands:
one Nation under God, indivisible, with Liberty and Justice for all.

The Pledge of Allegiance is thought to have been written in 1892 by Francis Bellamy, a Baptist minister. Bellamy prepared a program for Columbus Day that year in celebration of the 400th anniversary of the discovery of America. In the program he included a flag raising ceremony and a flag salute, featuring his Pledge of Allegiance.

Bellamy's pledge was finally officially recognized by the United States Congress on December 28, 1945, after years of tinkering with the wording of phrases here and there. In 1954, when the words "under God" were added, the pledge became both a patriotic oath and a public prayer.

The United States is one of the most blessed nations ever. Food, money, cool inventions, and a high standard of living are part of our everyday life. U.S. citizens have more freedom to do what they want with their time, when they want, than almost any other country in the history of our planet.

And this country is compassionate—it has sent out more missionaries and more money overseas for disaster relief than any nation ever. We are truly blessed by God and proud to live in a country such as this. That's the reason people all across our land for centuries have been pledging their loyalty to the United States of America.

Some people would like to see the pledge of allegiance done away with because it mentions God's name, and they feel that this is offensive to those who don't believe in God.

But this is our chance to stand up for our God, and pledge our allegiance to Him. Why wouldn't we want to do that for Jesus who gave everything for us, and whose love and faithfulness never wavers? Like Joshua, "We too will serve the Lord, because He is our God." (Joshua 24:18, NIV).

The Lone Star State

*I will confirm my covenant with you and your descendants
after you, from generation to generation. This is the
everlasting covenant: I will always be your God.
Genesis 17:7, NLT.*

Texas has a long and colorful history. It's always been a place where wilderness and open skies are the biggest part of its horizon. In prehistoric times Texas was the home of many now-extinct mammals: wooly mammoths, saber tooth tigers, and giant beavers. Native Americans who lived in Texas before the Europeans arrived included the Mound Builders, Apache, Comanche, Cherokee, Choctaw, Kickapoo, Kiowa, and Wichita.

In 1820 Texas gained independence from Spain, and Mexico began welcoming American settlers to Texas. Stephen Austin led a large group of Americans into Texas, and before long they outnumbered the Mexicans. The Mexican government tried to control this groups of foreigners, but the settlers soon rebelled, and in 1836 Texas declared its independence from Mexico. Mexican General Santa Anna attacked the Alamo, and the Texas army of volunteers suffered defeat. However, just one month later Sam Houston captured Santa Anna, ending Mexico's plans to subdue Texas.

Texans elected Sam Houston as president, and 11 years later, on December 29, 1845, Texas entered the United States as the twenty-eighth state. The term, "six flags over Texas," came about because of the six countries that claimed and controlled the territory—Spain, France, Mexico, the Republic of Texas, the United States, and the Confederate States of America.

Texas, long been nicknamed the Lone Star State, is 268,820 square miles of *big*. The phrase, "everything's bigger in Texas," comes from the wide-open spaces of prairie and desert. It has always been seen as the heart of cattle country and home of the cowboy. The biggest state in the continental United States, Texas is the second largest state in both area and population.

When Texas entered the Union in 1845, it agreed to abide by the laws of the United States of America. Its new status gave it the lawful rights of every other state in the Union. God's covenant is much like that. We will always be part of Him because He has accepted us into the union of His family. We are His children and the offspring of His covenant with our spiritual fathers Adam, Noah, and Abraham.

U.S.S.R. is Born

*[Rehoboam] did evil, because he did not prepare his heart to seek the Lord.
2 Chron. 12:14, NKJV.*

When President Ronald Reagan was in the White House, he called the U.S.S.R. the Evil Empire, and in many ways it was. After all, communism says there is no God, and this puts them in direct conflict with Christianity.

On this day in 1922 Russia officially became the U.S.S.R. (Union Soviets Socialist Republic). Vladimir Lenin, the first premier, had some good ideas about how a socialist government should run. A job for everyone, and everyone for a job, was one of his slogans. Everyone should share the wealth, he said. The strong should help the weak. Unfortunately, it didn't quite work out that way. In a utopia somewhere it might have been ideal, but unless they have a real good reason, people just aren't going to be nice to each other.

Lenin had been in power only a few short years when he died mysteriously. Historians think it likely he was poisoned. Stalin, the next premier, was one of the most ruthless dictators and cut them off, allowing no grain to be shipped to them. It's estimated that Stalin killed more than 30 million of his own people before starving them into submission.

Khrushchev and Brezhnev followed Stalin, building the Soviet military machine to such proportions that the world trembled at their tread. Although the U.S.S.R. has since collapsed politically and has been greatly weakened economically, it is still thought the government can arm itself for a catastrophic war in any part of the world. Nuclear warheads on missiles are still installed in nuclear submarines that can stay under the surface of the sea for months—and even years—silently treading water. No one really knows for sure how many are still in operation.

Will the former U.S.S.R. end up destroying the world by nuclear war? Probably not. Could much of the earth be destroyed in this way? Maybe. The Bible doesn't rule that out completely. One thing is sure—the Soviet leaders are not believers in the God of heaven. Much like Rehoboam in ancient Israel, they have historically done evil because they haven't prepared their hearts to seek the Lord. Jesus will come whether the Soviets believe in Him or not. Let's not be like the Soviets, steadfastly resisting the power of God in their land.

Million Dollar Football Game

Do not love this world nor the things it offers you, . . . for the world offers only a craving for physical pleasure, a craving for everything we see, and pride in our achievements and possessions. These are not from the Father, but are from this world.
1 John 2:15, 16, NLT.

When people think about becoming rich they usually say they want to be a millionaire. So how much is a million dollars? Well, not that much anymore. The average annual wage in the United States today is just over $40,000. That means that if you make an average wage, in just 25 years you will have earned $1 million dollars. Of course you would have to save every penny you earned to actually be a millionaire, but the point is well made.

On December 31, 1961, a million-dollar football game took place between the Green Bay Packers and the New York Giants. It was the beginning of a new era for sports and football. The average salary of a professional football player in 1961 was $27,500, up from $9,500 in 1959. The average team had an annual budget of $332,000. (That 1961 salary today would be equivalent to about $240,000, and the team budget about $2.8 million.)

That's a far cry from today's salaries and team budgets. In 2007 the average professional football player was making $1.4 million, and the average team was worth $957 million. That would make the combined worth of the NFL's 32 teams more than $30 billion. The NFL is, by far, the richest sports league in the world. It generates more than $6 billion a year. A new six-year deal with NBC, CBS, Fox, and ESPN will pay the NFL more than $12.7 billion.

Will it never end? Ticket prices are up. Companies that want to air their commercials during the Super Bowl have to pay $3 million for 30 seconds—that computes to $100,000 per second. And that's just professional football. What about all the other major professional sports—basketball, baseball, hockey, and soccer? And what about college sports? Many college coaches now make as much as professional coaches. And television income from college games brings in amazing amounts of money.

Jesus asks us to avoid the things of this world that would steal us away from the Father—the love of money, obsession with sports, alcohol, drugs, ungodly friends, and movies and music that glorify Satan. Any of these can keep us out of heaven, if we let them. Let's pray that they won't. After all, none of these is worth the price of our heavenly crown.